Bombing to Provoke

Bombing to Provoke

Rockets, Missiles, and Drones as Instruments of Fear and Coercion

Jaganath Sankaran

OXFORD
UNIVERSITY PRESS

Oxford University Press is a department of the University of Oxford. It furthers
the University's objective of excellence in research, scholarship, and education
by publishing worldwide. Oxford is a registered trade mark of Oxford University
Press in the UK and certain other countries.

Published in the United States of America by Oxford University Press
198 Madison Avenue, New York, NY 10016, United States of America.

© Oxford University Press 2024

All rights reserved. No part of this publication may be reproduced, stored in
a retrieval system, or transmitted, in any form or by any means, without the
prior permission in writing of Oxford University Press, or as expressly permitted
by law, by license, or under terms agreed with the appropriate reproduction
rights organization. Inquiries concerning reproduction outside the scope of the
above should be sent to the Rights Department, Oxford University Press, at the
address above.

You must not circulate this work in any other form
and you must impose this same condition on any acquirer.

Library of Congress Cataloging-in-Publication Data
Names: Sankaran, Jaganath, author.
Title: Bombing to provoke : rockets, missiles, and drones as instruments
of fear and coercion / Jaganath Sankaran.
Description: New York, NY : Oxford university Press, [2024] |
Includes bibliographical references and index.
Identifiers: LCCN 2024028462 | ISBN 9780197792636 (paperback) |
ISBN 9780197792629 (hardback) | ISBN 9780197792643 (epub) |
ISBN 9780197792650 | ISBN 9780197792667
Subjects: LCSH: Bombings. | Bombing, Aerial. | Russian Invasion of Ukraine, 2022.
Classification: LCC HV6640.S36 2024 | DDC 363.325—dc23/eng/20240711
LC record available at https://lccn.loc.gov/2024028462

DOI: 10.1093/oso/9780197792629.001.0001

Paperback printed by Marquis Book Printing, Canada
Hardback printed by Bridgeport National Bindery, Inc., United States of America

This book is dedicated to the memory of my father and his unwavering commitment to my education.

Contents

Acknowledgments	ix
1. Introduction	1
2. Bombing to Provoke: The Coercive Logic of Aerospace Weapons	16
3. Hitler's Weapons of Vengeance	31
4. Missiles and the War of the Cities	47
5. Saddam's Scuds	62
6. Hezbollah's Katyusha Rockets and the Rules of Engagement	80
7. Houthis and the "Flying Lawnmowers"	97
8. Conclusion	113
Notes	125
Index	205

Acknowledgments

John Steinbruner, Nancy Gallagher, and Steve Fetter at the University of Maryland's School of Public Policy took a chance on me. They encouraged and supported me as I embarked on a unique trajectory of academic scholarship that employed the methods of physical sciences to generate insights and inform questions of political science and policymaking. This book and my other academic scholarship could not have materialized without them. I owe all my successes to their encouragement and support.

At the Lyndon B. Johnson School of Public Affairs, several faculty colleagues provided invaluable support and guidance. Jeremi Suri read and engaged with several of my drafts. He was indispensable in my efforts to identify avenues for further research. Jeremi Suri also played a pivotal role in helping me secure a contract with Oxford University Press. For all of this and many other gestures, I remain in his debt. Catherine Weaver, Joshua Busby, Alan Kuperman, and Sheena Greitens at the LBJ School read parts of the book and provided very helpful guidance. The Dean of the LBJ School, J. R. DeShazo, provided much-needed resources and time for me to navigate the complexities that COVID-19 introduced to the progression of my book project. I remain grateful for all their investments in my success.

Several scholars read and commented on parts of the book manuscript and other related material. Others provided invaluable feedback at presentations. Michael O'Hanlon at the Brookings Institution; Daniel Byman at Georgetown University; Charles Glaser, Professor Emeritus of Political Science and International Affairs at George Washington University; Sumit Ganguly at Indiana University; Aaron Karp at Old Dominion University; Dinshaw Mistry at the University of Cincinnati; Philip Haun at the US Naval War College; Daniel Sobelman at the Hebrew University of Jerusalem; Mauro Gilli at the Center for Security Studies, ETH Zurich; and Dan Altman at Georgia State University were extraordinarily generous with time and provided valuable suggestions to refine my arguments. Similarly, scholars in the School of Advanced Air and Space Studies at the US Air War College, scholars in the Air Command and Staff College at the US Air War College, scholars in the Program on Science and Global Security at Princeton University, and scholars in the Center for International Security and Cooperation at Stanford

x Acknowledgments

University offered very helpful feedback on my arguments. I remain extremely thankful for all their time and help.

The editorial team at Oxford University Press, particularly David McBride and Mary Funchion, were kind, patient, and encouraging. I am very grateful for their investment in my research.

Finally, my family endured my absence while I worked on my research and writing. I am deeply grateful for their support.

1

Introduction

How do aerospace weapons—rockets, missiles, and drones—work as instruments of provocation and coercion in war? The empirical record presents an interesting but complicated history. For instance, in the 2022 Russia–Ukraine War, Russia has unrelentingly bombarded Ukraine. In the first year of the war, Russia launched more than 5,000 missile and drone strikes into Ukrainian cities.[1] Between December 2003 and mid-January 2024, as many as 500 missiles and drones were fired at Ukraine.[2] In these campaigns, Russia has employed some of its most technologically advanced aerospace weapons—the Iskander ballistic missiles (5- to 10-meter accuracy), the Kalibr sea-launched cruise missiles (30-meter accuracy), the Kh-101 air-launched cruise missile (10-meter accuracy), the Kh-555 air-launched cruise missile (25-meter accuracy), the Kh-22/32 anti-ship cruise missile with radar-homing warheads, the Kh-47M2 Kinzhal hypersonic air-launched ballistic missile, the Zircon hypersonic cruise missile, the Lancet drone, and the Shahed drones.[3]

The Russian bombardment has provoked and forced Ukrainian decisionmakers to divert crucial air and missile defenses from the frontline to cities, making its troops vulnerable to Russian air strike.[4] However, Ukraine has so far managed to survive without having to make significant political concessions. The United States and other nations have surged air and missile defenses to Ukraine to blunt the effect of the Russian missile and drone campaign.[5] Ukraine withstood Russian aerospace bombardment without conceding or offering any political concessions.

On the other hand, the recent history of rocket warfare waged by Hamas against Israel presents a very different narrative. Despite possessing some of the most technologically advanced air and missile defense capabilities, Israel has remained vulnerable to provocation and coercion by rocket warfare.

As Israel's civil defense and missile defense capabilities have matured over the years, Israeli fatalities to rocket bombardment from Hamas have progressively declined. Between 2001 and 2010, Israel was bombarded with close to 5,000 rockets, but the total number of fatalities resulting from the rocket bombardment was 10—a fatality ratio of 500 rockets per Israeli death. In the

Bombing to Provoke. Jaganath Sankaran, Oxford University Press. © Oxford University Press 2024.
DOI: 10.1093/oso/9780197792629.003.0001

2 Bombing to Provoke

22 days of the 2008 war, Hamas launched a total of 660 rockets into Israel, killing three people—a ratio of 220:1. In the eight days of the 2012 war, Hamas launched approximately 1,500 rockets at Israel and killed five Israeli civilians—a fatality rate of 300:1. In the 50 days of the 2014 war, a total of slightly more than 4,500 rockets were fired at Israel, killing two persons—a fatality rate of approximately 2,225:1. Furthermore, the rockets fired by Hamas are terribly inaccurate.[6]

These limitations make the kinetic military effects of Hamas' rockets trivial. Yet Hamas has repeatedly managed to use its rockets to provoke Israel into attritional and diversionary conflicts and coerce Israel to renegotiate the terms of economic access to Gaza. For example, days before the 2014 war, Israeli Prime Minister Netanyahu announced that "Israel is not eager for war."[7] In a few days, however, Hamas' rocket bombardment had forced Israel into a war.[8] It did not matter that these rockets were inaccurate and had a low rate of fatalities. Israel's angst and the need to wage war were driven by the emotional response of Israelis, whose sense of well-being and security was being upended by the rocket bombardment. The problem for most Israelis "was not being hit, but the fear, uncertainty and stress."[9] These grievances and sense of vulnerability of Israeli citizens forced the Israeli government to take military action. Uzi Rubin argues that any Israeli government that did not demonstrate an effort to redress the fear and uncertainties of Israeli citizens would not have survived in political office for long.[10] However, once the war started, Israeli military casualties began increasing, and slowly, Israeli public support for the war weakened.[11] Israel had to renegotiate the terms of arrangement between Israel and Hamas and offer concessions to terminate the war. The rockets of Hamas proved to be strategically potent despite their low fatality rate.

While Russia's state-of-the-art missiles failed to coerce Ukraine, Hamas' technologically primitive rockets have succeeded in provoking and exacting limited concessions from Israel. How do we explain it? The 2014 Gaza War and the 2022 Russia–Ukraine conflict are recent examples of aerospace wars. Aerospace weapons, however, have been employed as instruments of fear, provocation, and coercion since World War II. However, the phenomenon has not received focused scholarly attention. The theorizing and empirical evaluation of the phenomenon is the goal of this book.

In the book, I offer a *bombing to provoke* theory to explain the provocative and coercive influence of rockets, missiles, and drones in warfare.[12] For the purposes of the book, provocation is defined as the use of aerospace weapons to strike fear among the target population and instigate the decisionmakers in the targeted state to engage in an attritional and diversionary military response. Coercion is defined as the threat or the use of force to extract political concessions from an adversary. The bombing to provoke theory posits that aerospace weapons—rockets, missiles, and drones—provoke and coerce by weaponizing fear and triggering a sense of vulnerability and defenselessness among the targeted population, including the decision makers. In some instances, these fears can lead to substantial unanticipated economic disruptions. Furthermore, these economic disruptions and fears amplify the political vulnerabilities of the decisionmakers in the target state and provoke them to overreact and commit militarily, often to an attritional and diversionary campaign, to redress the threat from the aerospace bombardment. I use the term diversionary to point out that the political need to suppress the aerospace threats may lead to the continued commitment of progressively more military resources even if early efforts at extinguishing the threat prove futile. Such diversionary military responses, in some instances, may also peel away vital resources from other efforts that could be more essential to the elimination of the root cause of the threat. I contend that the political overreactions and diversionary military responses are evidence of provocation. If the targeted state is unable to extinguish the aerospace threat, it may weaken its resolve and lead to political concessions. Such concessions, limited or otherwise, are evidence of coercion. I argue that coercion does not need to result in the complete defeat and capitulation of the target state.

The rest of the chapter is organized as follows. The next section reviews the history of aerospace weapons in warfare and highlights their provocative and coercive influence. The third section lays out the argument of the bombing to provoke theory and details the methodological approach used to test the theory and its predictions. The fourth and fifth sections describe the implications of the research for scholarship and policymaking, respectively. Finally, the sixth section lays out the organizational structure of the remainder of the book and describes how the following seven chapters serve to empirically illuminate the provocative and coercive influence of aerospace weapons.

A Historical Review of Aerospace Weapons in Warfare

During the 1991 Gulf War, Norman Schwarzkopf, the Commander-in-Chief of the Coalition forces, noted that "saying Scuds [ballistic missiles] are a danger to a nation is like saying that lightning is a danger to a nation. I frankly would be more afraid of standing out in a lightning storm in southern Georgia than I would standing out in the streets of Riyadh when the Scuds are coming down."[13] A few weeks later, Schwarzkopf complained to Wayne

4 Bombing to Provoke

Downing, Commander of the American Joint Special Operations Command (JSOC), that "the Scud is a pissant weapon that isn't doing a goddam thing. It's insignificant."[14]

On the other hand, American political leadership considered the Scud ballistic missiles a critical threat. American decisionmakers feared Scud missile attacks would catalyze the political collapse of the coalition of states arrayed against Saddam Hussein, stall the Coalition's military assault, and force a resolution on Saddam's terms.

Iraqi Foreign Minister and Deputy Prime Minister Tariq Aziz, a week before the war began, had declared that if Iraq was attacked, Baghdad would strike Israel using its arsenal of ballistic missiles.[15] In addition, the Iraqis had threatened a chemical weapons attack on Israel. In a speech on 1 April 1990, Saddam Hussein promised to "make fire eat up half of Israel."[16]

The American political leadership feared that any Israeli military response to Iraqi ballistic missile strikes might unravel the Coalition. President George H. W. Bush notes in his memoirs that the Coalition, which included several Arab states, could not be sustained if Israel entered the war.[17] The American political leadership desperately wanted to keep Israel out of the conflict. In a meeting with Israeli President Shamir on 11 December 1990, at the Oval Office, President Bush promised him that "if he [Saddam Hussein] attacks you, or if an attack becomes apparent, we have the capability to obliterate his military structure. We have a beautifully planned operation, calculated to demoralize him forever. If it must be followed by a ground campaign, we are ready."[18] He then asked for Israeli restraint.

President Bush promised Israel "the darndest search-and-destroy effort" to suppress the Scud missile bombardment.[19] Consequently, American decisionmakers, often overriding their military leaders' preferences, ordered a massive diversionary military operation to disrupt and disable Iraqi ballistic missile launch operations. Ultimately, by the end of the 1991 Gulf War, every type of strike and reconnaissance aircraft was diverted to the Coalition's counter-Scud operations without much success.[20] A permanent combat air patrol was established over western Iraq to hunt Scud missile launchers.[21] The counter-Scud strike operations surpassed the efforts undertaken to suppress enemy air defenses, disrupt Iraqi command and control, and destroy Iraq's military-industrial facilities.[22] The US-led Coalition generated approximately 2,500 anti-Scud sorties. In comparison, there were 2,990 sorties against airfields, 1,370 against surface-to-air missile batteries, 1,170 sorties against communication assets, and around 970 sorties against Iraqi nuclear-chemical-biological facilities.[23] As the Scuds kept falling, more and more military resources were diverted to the Scud-hunting mission. JSTARS radar planes, U-2 and TR-1 reconnaissance, and surveillance planes were reassigned to track Scud mobile launchers.[24]

The Iraqis had made their "pissant weapons" exceedingly effective tools. The Iraqi missile campaign provoked the American-led Coalition.[25] The missile campaign forced a diversionary military campaign by weaponizing fear and exploiting American and Israeli political vulnerabilities. It is anybody's guess what could have happened if the Iraqis had launched Scud missiles armed with chemical weapons into Israel.

On the other hand, the Iraqi air force proved to be absolutely useless against the American-led Coalition. Despite being armed with hundreds of fighter aircraft, the Iraqi air force was unable to attack the Coalition forces or defend Iraqi airspace.[26] Within 10 days of the Coalition's air campaign, nearly 75 of the Iraqi air force's state-of-the-art fighter aircraft fled to Iran.[27] The rest of the Iraqi air force fleet hunkered down in bunkers, ceding complete control of Iraqi airspace to American forces. As a result, despite the markers of a modern air power, the Iraqi air force became incapable of any offensive action against the Coalition or Israel.[28]

The story repeats itself in the four other cases studied in the book—the Germans against the British in World War II, Iraq against Iran in the Iran–Iraq War, the Hezbollah against Israel in the Second Lebanon War, and the Houthis against Saudi Arabia in the ongoing Yemeni War. In each case, a warring state or non-state actor, unable to use its air force meaningfully against its adversary, could employ rockets, missiles, and drones in a hybrid or stand-alone fashion to weaponize fear and provoke its adversary into an attritional and diversionary campaign of strategic significance. In three of the four cases, unable to extinguish the aerospace threat, the targeted state was coerced to offer concessions.

During World War II, Hitler's ballistic and cruise missile bombardment distracted, delayed, tormented, and provoked the Allied forces. In the months leading up to Operation Overlord—the war plan for landing Allied troops on the beaches of Normandy—British and American leaders constantly feared that the impending German missile bombardment would derail the crucial operation, despite the relative inaccuracies of the German V-1 and V-2 missiles.[29] Allied leaders worried that if the naval facilities at Southampton or other vital targets including London suffered repeated strikes, Operation Overlord would be derailed.[30] Hitler hoped his missile arsenal would derail the Normandy landings and provoke the Allies to execute a diversionary assault on the Cherbourg coast toward the missile launch sites.[31]

British political leaders also feared London would become the target of Hitler's vengeance.[32] These fears led to a diversionary military effort of

6 Bombing to Provoke

enormous magnitude.[33] Between 1 May 1943 and 31 March 1944, 40% of all Allied reconnaissance missions in the European theater were devoted to Operation Crossbow—the code name for Allied military operations against Hitler's missiles.[34] More than 1,250,000 aerial photographs and more than 4,000,000 prints were developed to identify German missile facilities and launch sites.[35] Eventually, the surveillance and reconnaissance mission undertaken as part of Crossbow operations became the most comprehensive of the entire war.[36] The reconnaissance and surveillance operations were followed by monumental missile defense and counterforce efforts. In the months before the Normandy landings, the British and American air forces delivered more than 100,000 bombs on presumed German missile-related targets. The Allied bombing efforts diverted a quarter of the total amount of bombs dropped by the Allies.[37] These diversionary bombing efforts were a relief to the Nazi forces because the Allies otherwise may have targeted German soldiers and front-line forces. By the end of the war, the Allied forces had undertaken 68,913 air sorties and dropped 122,133 tons of bombs on German missile-related targets.

In the 1980–1988 Iran–Iraq War, the accuracy and lethality of Iraqi Scud missile strikes was extremely limited. However, the strategic coercive impact of Iraq's ballistic missile strikes in the Iran–Iraq War was immense. The threat of chemically armed ballistic missile strikes on Tehran was one of the crucial factors necessary for Iranian capitulation in 1988.[38] The successful use of chemical warfare on the battlefield in early 1988 and Iraqi threats to launch chemically armed ballistic missiles targeting Tehran instilled fears in the minds of Iranians. Iranian leaders feared an Iraqi ballistic missile bombardment with chemical warheads on their cities was imminent. These fears were amplified by the failure of the international community to condemn Iraq's use of chemical weapons against civilians in the Kurdish town of Halabja.[39] Such fears played a major part in the Iranian decision to concede to a ceasefire with Iraq after resisting it for several years.[40]

In the 2006 Second Lebanon War, Hezbollah's continued Katyusha rocket bombardment enabled it to provoke and coerce the Israelis into withdrawing from the conflict without achieving any of its intended goals. Despite a tremendous attritional and diversionary effort, Israel's counterforce operations against Hezbollah's rocket forces proved futile. At the end of the war, a mutual deterrent was quickly reestablished between Israel and Hezbollah.

Finally, missiles and drones have played a pivotal role in the ongoing Yemeni War. As the war began in 2015, the Saudi-led Coalition expected a quick victory over the rag-tag Houthis in Yemen.[41] Saudi leaders believed that the superior airpower and military forces of the Coalition would defeat the Houthis in a matter of months.[42] Warning against such optimism, Hassan Nasrallah countered in a public address, "In the end, you will run out of targets, and the people will not have surrendered . . . ultimately you will be left with no other option except ground invasion . . . [which] is costly and the outcome is known in advance . . . defeat."[43] The statement, in hindsight, is exceeding prescient. After eight years of war, the Houthis have outmaneuvered the Saudi-led Coalition, denying it a path to military victory. The Houthis have forcefully demonstrated the ability to strike unimpeded at Saudi and Emirati oil and petroleum facilities, oil shipping routes, and other vital economic targets such as airports and major cities with missiles and drones. The continued strikes on oil facilities have heightened fears that future attacks may cause greater havoc and impose economic shocks.[44] The continued missile strikes on cities near the Saudi–Yemeni border and deep inside Saudi Arabia and the Emirates have become a source of political frustration. In 2019, the Emiratis withdrew their armed forces from the campaign, attributing their decision to the unsustainable military and political costs of the war.[45] It appears that the Houthis may have succeeded in coercing the Saudi-led Coalition into a negotiated settlement that accepts the status quo in Yemen.

Spread over almost 80 years of history, aerospace weapons have demonstrated a potent provocative and coercive capacity in warfare. How do we systematically explain the coercive influence of rockets, missiles, and drones? What are the implications for the future?

Argument and Method

On paper, aerospace weapons—rockets, missiles, and drones—appear very limited in their ability to provoke or coerce adversaries during war. In comparison to military aircraft and evaluated using the traditional measure of military effect—primarily the amount of ordnance delivered and the accuracy with which it is delivered—aerospace weapons manifest as poor tools of warfare. Janne Nolan, for instance, has noted that missiles are often "little more than symbolic augmentation."[46] While rockets, missiles, and drones have become increasingly accurate, salvos of aerospace weapons still cannot match the amount of ordnance that a dedicated air campaign can deliver to a target. Yet, as described above, these aerospace weapons have proved surprisingly effective in provoking the targeted states to engage in attritional and diversionary military campaigns, often significantly changing the course of wars. In some cases, the targeted state was further coerced into making concessions.

8 Bombing to Provoke

For the purposes of the research agenda of the book, I define provocation as the use of aerospace weapons to strike fear in the target population and instigate the decisionmakers in the targeted state to engage in an attritional and diversionary military response.[47] I define "coercion" as the threatened or limited use of force to extract political concessions from an adversary.[48] I argue that the mechanism by which states provoke and coerce using aerospace weapons is distinct. Rockets, missiles, and drones weaponize fear and intimidate and panic an adversary.[49] Aerospace weapons induce fear by threatening a chemical, biological, or nuclear strike or demonstrating the ability to bombard the target's economic and political core repeatedly, often despite the target state's military superiority.[50] These fears amplify the political vulnerabilities of the target state. Political vulnerabilities can include the need to limit and avoid civilian or military casualties, particularly if such casualties had not been anticipated in the planning stages of the war. It can also include the need to prevent strikes on critical economic, military, or civilian infrastructure targets. Political vulnerabilities can include the need to keep the conflict limited in geographic scope. It can include the need to avert a prolonged conflict. Political vulnerabilities can also include factors such as the need to keep alliance partners invested in the war effort. The fears and political vulnerabilities provoke the target state to divert substantial military resources to redress the threat from aerospace weapons. The diversion of resources may prolong the war, weaken the resolve of the targeted state and lead to concessions.

My argument leads to four predictions. First, states employing aerospace weapons in warfare should attempt to induce fear, provoke, and coerce their adversaries through operational tactics and communicated threats. Second, states targeted by aerospace weapons should actively respond to these fears and vulnerabilities in their internal and external political debates and by extensive military countermeasures. Third, states with the means to divert military resources to defend, suppress, and eventually extinguish the threat through defensive and offensive means will be able to overcome the provocation without offering concessions to end the war. Finally, states that are unable to effectively defend, suppress, and extinguish the bombardment may suffer a diminution of resolve and be coerced to offer concessions to end the war. I define "diminution of resolve" as the fading of political interest in continued fighting to attain the policy preferences decided upon at the beginning of hostilities.[51]

The book employs a structured, focused comparative case study methodology to test the argument and predictions. The book relies on five case studies that vary in time, geography, technology, type of government of the targeted state, and military capabilities of warring pairs. The five case study chapters seek to interrogate the weaponization of fear and the consequent political and military response of the targeted states. The case study chapters explore in depth the impact of fear induced by aerospace bombardment on the course and outcome of the war. The book employs a within-case process-tracing analysis methodology to observe and test the provocative and coercive effects of aerospace weapons. The book will also perform a cross-case comparative analysis to test the theoretical argument further. The case studies will employ a variety of source materials—archival documents, declassified intelligence documents, selected oral histories, and secondary written materials, including autobiographies of key personalities involved in the history of the five case studies—to perform the analyses.

Implications for Scholarship

The provocative and coercive logic of aerospace weapons—rockets, missiles, and drones—has not been studied rigorously in the security studies literature. Particularly, a theoretically structured empirical analysis of the wartime provocative and coercive role of rockets, missiles, and drones employed either as standalone weapons or used in a hybrid mode has not been performed. This book fills a critical knowledge gap and will be one of the few studies on the subject matter—exploring the role of rockets, missiles, and drones in warfare with theoretical rigor.

Aaron Karp provides an excellent chapter-length treatment on ballistic missiles in his book.[52] Karp's work anticipates many of my arguments and predictions. Dinshaw Mistry provides a book-length treatment of the proliferation risks of ballistic missiles and the efficacy of the Missile Technology Control Regime (MTCR).[53] Various other scholars have explored the subject matter of ballistic missiles in books and journal-length articles in a limited fashion and primarily from a policymaking perspective to understand the military capabilities of ballistic missiles in war.[54]

Recently Early et al. explored the factors that explain the proliferation of advanced cruise missile technologies.[55] Dennis Gormley offers a policy-oriented study on the effects of cruise missile proliferation on international security.[56] Scholarly research on drones has received much attention recently. Calcara et al. examines the effect of current and emerging drone technologies on the offense–defense balance, exploring the technological competition between drones and air defense systems.[57] Horowitz et al. study the broad strategic implications of drone proliferation for a variety of national security missions.[58] While they note that drones may have some value in interstate war, they do not explore it in detail. Amy Zegart theorizes that states that develop advanced lethal "drones of tomorrow" may possess coercive advantages against adversaries unable to acquire such technologically advanced drones.[59] The analysis performed in the book builds on these prior works but offers a detailed, empirically anchored treatment of the provocative and coercive influence of all three types of aerospace weapons.

Additionally, the book intervenes and informs crucial arguments in the field of international relations. While airpower theory has bifurcated the mechanisms of coercion into denial of military capability or punishment campaigns targeting civilians, the book suggests such a distinction may not be broadly applicable to all types of wartime provocation and coercion. The book advances the state of knowledge on wartime provocation and coercion using empirical data on rocket, missile, and drone warfare.[60] Aerospace weapons, irrespective of civilian or military targets, can provoke the target state to divert substantial military resources, thereby generating effects similar to a denial of military capability.

Furthermore, airpower coercion has tended to focus on the ability of relatively strong states to coerce because projecting airpower often requires air superiority. However, the book demonstrates that weaker states, or tactically weakened states unable to employ traditional airpower or retain air superiority, may be able to use aerospace weapons to provoke and coerce adversaries. This insight may explain the proliferation of ballistic missiles, cruise missiles, and drones.

Similarly, the book offers a valuable empirical contribution to scholars interrogating the role of emotions in international politics. The study of fear, and other emotions, has been a distinct subfield of international relations theory and has had an active research agenda for the past several decades.[61] It is generally understood that fear influences the behavior of states in war, and adversaries tend to find ways to capitalize on fear. However, the book offers empirical specificity. I argue and demonstrate that the provocative and coercive effect of aerospace weapons—rockets, missiles, and drones—directly depends on the ability to weaponize fear and induce panic in an adversary. In all five critical cases, the fear induced by aerospace weapons provoked the adversary into a significant diversionary military campaign, and in three cases, to offer other concessions. The analysis and results of the book should be much of interest to scholars researching emotions in international politics.

Implications for Policy

Understanding the nature of the threat posed by rockets, missiles, and drones to the United States and its allies is an urgent national security policy priority.

North Korea has amassed a large arsenal of rockets. In a regional war, North Korean rockets would pose a serious threat to Seoul and other nearby American military bases.[62] Rockets have also proliferated in the Middle East region. A 2019 US Department of Defense (DOD) report on Iran's military power, for instance, observes that Hezbollah possesses between 120,000 and 150,000 rockets arrayed against Israel.[63] In a future war between Hezbollah and Israel, these rockets would be highly destructive and may significantly complicate American efforts at diplomacy.

American forces have also directly encountered rocket bombardment. American military bases in Iraq have been repeatedly targeted with rockets by militia groups supported by Iran. In February 2021, a rocket attack killed a civilian contractor and wounded six others at the Ayn Al-Asad Airbase.[64] A month later, in March 2021, a barrage of BM-21 Grad rockets was fired again at the Ayn Al-Asad base. The March 2021 rocket strike came soon after American F-15E Strike Eagle aircrafts armed with "seven 500-pound satellite-guided bombs" were deployed on nine militia targets at the Syria–Iraq border.[65] The rocket attack led to one American fatality.[66] American troops in Syria have also faced rocket attacks.[67]

The proliferation of missiles poses another challenge for American policymakers. A 2020 report jointly published by the National Air and Space Intelligence Center (NASIC) and the Defense Intelligence Ballistic Missile Analysis Committee (DIBMAC) declared that ballistic and cruise missiles act as "instruments of coercion" and present a "significant threat to US and allied forces overseas, and to the United States homeland and territories."[68]

Three states—Iran, North Korea, and China—are seen as potential adversaries that would use their rocket and missile arsenals to complicate US efforts in a military contingency. Iran has the largest missile force "strategic deterrent" in the Middle East.[69] The 2019 Iran Military Power report published by the US Defense Intelligence Agency argues that "lacking a modern air force, Iran has embraced ballistic missiles as a long-range strike capability to dissuade its adversaries in the region—particularly the United States, Israel, and Saudi Arabia—from attacking Iran."[70] The report indicated that Iran would launch salvos of missiles targeting regional military bases, energy infrastructure targets, and population centers to inflict damage and weaken adversary operations in a militarized crisis.[71]

12 Bombing to Provoke

Iran has recently demonstrated the potency of its missiles. Two Iraqi military bases hosting American and Coalition troops, the Ayn al-Asad and Erbil Airbases, were struck by Iranian ballistic missile barrages on 8 January 2020.[72] The bombardment was retribution for an American drone strike that killed Qassim Suleimani, commander of Iran's Quds Forces.[73] Iran fired a total of 22 liquid-fueled ballistic missiles at the two bases.[74] Ayn al-Asad Airbase faced the brunt of the strikes, with as many as 16 ballistic missiles armed with 1,000-pound warheads targeting it.[75] Recollecting the traumatic experience, one Army officer stationed at the Ayn Al-Asad Airbase noted, "the fire was just rolling over the bunkers . . . like 70 feet in the air . . . we're going to burn to death."[76] Another Air Force Sergeant described the missile bombardment as akin to experiencing "old videos of Hiroshima . . . the bright light after it exploded, the cloud and the brightness."[77] Prior anticipation of the strikes enabled the dispersion of American troops and averted casualties. However, it still led to traumatic brain injuries in more than 100 American military personnel.[78] Similar traumatic brain injuries were reported in mid-October 2023 by American service members who experienced rocket and drones strikes at the Al Tanf garrison, Syria, and Al Asad air base, Iraq.[79]

North Korea, similar to Iran, possesses a modest air force. However, it has amassed a large arsenal of missiles. North Korean ballistic missiles can reach the United States and allied targets throughout the Asia-Pacific region. North Korean missile warfare doctrine calls for disrupting or delaying the arrival of US troops in a military contingency to ensure a fait accompli.[80] In the early stages of a conflict, major naval ports and air bases in South Korea and Japan would be critical targets and lie within the range of North Korean missiles.[81] North Korea has also indicated that it would be considering striking major cities and commercial ports in Japan with ballistic missiles to "intimidate the political leadership in Japan to stay out of a conflict."[82]

Additionally, as noted in the 2020 NASIC missile threat report, China has the "most active and diverse ballistic missile development program in the world" with the intent to diminish American and allied power projection capabilities in the Asia-Pacific theater.[83] The bulk of China's ballistic missiles is now targeted at "regional airbases, logistics and port facilities, communications, and other ground-based infrastructure" that would play an important in a regional military contingency.[84] The 2019 US Missile Defense Review (MDR) arrives at a similar conclusion, noting that China's missile arsenal is intended to generate "coercive political and military advantages in a regional crisis or conflict."[85] The MDR report also highlights the emerging cruise missile threats from Russia and China.[86]

Finally, the prolific employment of drones in the ongoing Yemeni War, the ongoing Russian–Ukraine War, and the 2022 Armenia–Azerbaijan conflict has highlighted the need to understand their use—both as a separate class of weapons and when used in a hybrid fashion with missiles and rockets as instruments of provocation and coercion in warfare.[87]

How should American policymakers prepare and respond to these aerospace threats? The insights emerging from the book offer two policy recommendations. First, the strategic political effect of an aerospace bombardment campaign far exceeds the tactical, physical impacts of the campaign.[88] American decisionmakers will need to become conscious of and sensitive to the fact that a rocket, missile, and drone campaign would have a larger political effect and provoke a diversionary response. In a future contingency, American allies facing the brunt of aerospace strikes may demand significant diversionary military efforts, even if traditional military-tactical considerations argue against such diversions. Accordingly, American decisionmakers should be ready to thread the needle in attaining a balance between such diversionary efforts while making sure such efforts do not derail the goals of a war.

Second, if the past is any clue, air and missile defenses may not suffice to defeat aerospace bombardment. American decisionmakers and allied leaders need to be educated on the practical limitations of air and missile defenses. The Yemeni War, for instance, suggests that even with technological advances, air and missile defenses may not be enough to completely defeat a large arsenal of aerospace weapons. Therefore, in addition to air and missile defenses, diversionary military efforts may also require significant offensive counterforce operations on the adversary. Such offensive operations, however, carry escalatory risk if the war is intended to be of a limited nature. American decisionmakers will need to anticipate and mitigate these escalatory pressures.

Plan of the Book

The book contains seven more chapters. The second chapter develops in more detail the theoretical argument that aerospace weapons act as instruments of provocation and coercion by effectively weaponizing fear. The chapter lays out the logic of how fear provokes the target state to divert scarce military resources to defend and defeat the missile threat, and in some cases, coerces the target state to offer other political concessions. Finally, the chapter describes the methodological approach used to assess the argument and test the predictions.

14 Bombing to Provoke

The following five chapters test the theory using a structured, focused comparative case study methodology. The five case study chapters seek to interrogate the real and perceived weaponization of fear and the consequent political and military response of the target states to aerospace bombardment. The case studies will employ a variety of source materials—archival documents, declassified intelligence documents, selected oral histories, and secondary written materials, including autobiographies of key personalities involved in the history of the four case studies—to perform the analyses.

The third chapter is a detailed case study on the impact of German V-1 cruise missiles and V-2 ballistic missiles on the Allied forces and their war plans. Dwight Eisenhower, the Supreme Commander of the Allied Expeditionary Force in Europe during World War II, writes that if the German missile attacks had occurred six months earlier, Operation Overlord "might have been written off."[89] The chapter explores why and how close the German missile campaign came to paralyzing the most critical Allied operation in World War II—the Normandy landing. Finally, the third chapter will detail the political and military effects of the provocation caused by the German V-weapons throughout the war.[90]

The fourth chapter is a detailed case study of the Iran—Iraq War, focusing on the 1988 War of the Cities missile campaign. Iraq's persistent missile strikes and the threat of an impending escalation to chemical warfare on Tehran provoked and coerced Iran to accept a cease-fire on terms that were seen as unfavorable.[91] Iraq's ballistic missiles were seen as an effective coup de grace weapon that led to Iranian capitulation.[92] The case study will delve deeper to understand the mechanisms that coerced Iran to accept the ceasefire.

The fifth chapter is a detailed case study on Saddam Hussein's Scud missile campaign and the political and military reactions it provoked from the Israeli and American leadership during the 1991 Gulf War. The chapter analyzes how Saddam Hussein weaponized fear by using his ballistic missile arsenal to threaten an impending escalation to chemical warfare convincingly. The chapter details the political constraints imposed on American decisionmaking by Israeli fears over Saddam's missile campaign. Finally, the chapter examines the large diversionary military efforts undertaken by the US-led Coalition to defeat and suppress the missile threat.

The sixth chapter is a detailed case study on Hezbollah's Katyusha rockets. Since 1996, Hezbollah has used the rockets in a number of conflicts to provoke and coerce the Israelis into accepting negotiated rules of engagement. The chapter conducts an in-depth study on the provocative and coercive role of rockets in the 2006 Second Lebanon War. During the war, Hezbollah fired nearly 4,000 rockets into Israel.[93] The Israeli political leadership was forced to commit more and more airpower and then ground troops to eradicate the bombardment. By the end, however, Israel was unsuccessful in eliminating the rocket threat. Israel was coerced to retreat and accept a negotiated settlement. At the end of the war, a mutual deterrence between Israel and Hezbollah was re-established.

The seventh chapter is a detailed case study of the political and military impact of ballistic missiles, cruise missiles, and drones in the Yemeni conflict between the Houthi rebels and the Saudi Arabia-led Coalition forces. The continued missile and drone strikes by the Houthis on cities near the Saudi–Yemeni border and deep inside Saudi Arabia and the Emirates have become a source of economic vulnerability and political frustration. The Houthis have tormented and provoked the Saudi-led Coalition with hundreds of aerospace strikes and have, arguably, coerced the Coalition to come to terms with its agenda. The chapter investigates the provocative and coercive effect of the Houthi aerospace campaign over the past eight years.

The concluding chapter reiterates the scholarly contributions of the book. Additionally, the concluding chapter details the implications of the insights emerging from the book for American national security policymakers facing a proliferation of rockets, missiles, and drones among adversarial states. Finally, the concluding chapter highlights the insights gained in the case studies, the limitations of the analysis, and potential avenues for future research.

2
Bombing to Provoke
The Coercive Logic of Aerospace Weapons

R. V. Jones, the British head of scientific intelligence during World War II, characterizes Hitler's missile bombardment on London as one of the biggest scares in history.[1] The "biggest scare in history" provoked large-scale evacuations and massive diversionary military countermeasures.

By August 1944, close to 1,450,000 people had left London, a much larger number than during the Blitz.[2] The British political leadership, fearing Hitler's missile campaign, considered enacting *Black Plan*, a contingency designed for the evacuation of the Cabinet, members of the Parliament, and 16,000 other essential officials from London.[3] Furthermore, British and American military commanders in World War II, fearing the potential impact of the German missile campaign, considered revising war plans for landing troops on the Normandy beach.[4]

The fears induced by Hitler's missiles provoked the Allied forces to engage in a massive diversionary military countermeasure campaign. Between August 1943 and March 1945, the Allied forces undertook 68,913 air strike sorties and expended close to 122,000 tons of bombs to suppress the missile launches.[5] Hitler's V-1 and V-2 missiles did not lead to a German victory but had an immense strategic impact on the character of World War II.

Similar effects occurred in the 1980–1988 Iran-Iraq War, the 1991 Gulf War, the 2006 Second Lebanon War, and the ongoing Yemeni War. In all these four wars, bombardment campaigns executed with aerospace weapons— rockets, missiles, and drones—induced fears in the adversary. These fears had a strategic impact on the targeted adversary's decisionmaking. The fears provoked significant attritional and diversionary military countermeasures and, in some instances, altered the outcome of these wars. For example, at the end of the Iran–Iraq War the Iranian leaders, fearing the effects of missile strikes armed with chemical warheads, were coerced to accept a ceasefire they had previously rejected. In the 1991 Gulf War, similar fears of missile strikes armed with chemical weapons animated the American and Israeli political decisionmaking. Israeli civilians were told to carry their gas masks constantly. Director-General of Israel's Ministry of Defense, Major General

Bombing to Provoke. Jaganath Sankaran, Oxford University Press. © Oxford University Press 2024.
DOI: 10.1093/oso/9780197792629.003.0002

(Res.) David Ivri argued that Israel's "morale or psychology" would be forever altered even if a "few [such] missiles" fell on Tel Aviv.[6] These fears provoked a tremendous diversionary military countermeasures by the US-led Coalition against Saddam Hussein's Scud missiles. However, the US-led Coalition was able to afford these diversionary countermeasures, maintain its political resolve, and defeat Iraq without making political concessions. In the 2006 Second Lebanon War, Hezbollah's Katyusha rocket bombardment provoked and coerced the Israelis into retreating without being able to achieve its stated war goals. Furthermore, Hezbollah has now managed to institute a deterrent relationship of sorts against Israel.[7] Finally, in the ongoing Yemeni War, the hundreds of Houthi ballistic missiles, cruise missiles, and drone strikes have coerced the Saudis into accepting a truce.

What explains the provocative and coercive effects of aerospace weapons? I argue that the mechanism by which states provoke and coerce using aerospace weapons is distinct. Rockets, missiles, and drones weaponize fear and provoke a visceral overreaction, particularly a large diversion of military effort and resources despite the relative inefficiencies of these weapons to cause fatalities. For instance, in the 1991 Gulf War, there were two Israeli casualties from the Iraqi missile strikes.[8] Yet, as discussed below in the chapter on the 1991 Gulf War, the fears over what these weapons could do triggered a disproportionate diversionary campaign. The appropriate response would have been to augment civil defense measures such as the construction of blast shelters and focus all military efforts at more quickly defeating Saddam Hussein.

Aerospace weapons induce fear in the adversary by threatening a chemical, biological, or nuclear strike or by demonstrating the ability to strike repeatedly at the economic and political core of the target. The fears amplify the target state's political vulnerabilities. Decisionmakers in the target state face political pressure to take military action to redress the threat to the economy and the people. The fears and political vulnerabilities provoke the target state to divert substantial military resources to redress the aerospace threats. The diversion of military resources may prolong the war effort and increase the cost of prosecuting the war. States with the ability to extinguish the threat through air and missile defense operations and counterforce operations should be able to remain resolute and weather the aerospace bombardment without offering any political concessions. On the other hand, states that do not have the military means to extinguish the aerospace threat may suffer a diminution of resolve and be forced to make concessions to end the war. The targeted state should not be defeated on the battlefield and possess the means to continue prosecuting the war; however, it should decide to offer political concessions to end the war of its own volition.

To conceptually develop the argument further, the rest of this chapter is organized as follows. In the next section, I begin by exploring the emotion of fear and its role in the decisionmaking processes of leaders engaged in war. I postulate a theoretical basis to connect fear to wartime decisionmaking, provocation, and coercion. In the second section, I define coercion and discuss its application to aerospace weapons. I lay out the metrics that should be used to measure the provocative and coercive effect of aerospace weapons in wartime. In the third section, I reiterate and expand on the predictions of the argument. In the fourth section, I detail the methodology adopted to assess the argument. Finally, in the fifth section of the chapter, I outline the scope and limits of the bombing to provoke theory.

Weaponizing Fear

Emotions—fear, trust, empathy—have implicitly been at the center of the study of international politics. International politics scholars have studied the politics of dictators who have weaponized fear.[9] Scholars have analyzed the politics of democracies that have responded disproportionately when subject to fear.[10] The strategic use of emotions, primarily fear, is at the core of several theories of political realism.[11] However, significant challenges remain in developing a general theory of emotions in international politics. The logic of the transition from individual emotions to collective choices is complex. At the root of the complexity is the question: If states are not biological entities capable of experiencing emotions, how do emotions influence their behavior?[12] Despite the challenges, scholars have offered ways to directly address the role of emotions in international politics and war in recent years.[13]

Fear, for the purposes of the research agenda of this book, is defined as an "aversive, activated" emotional state brought on by the "dread of impending disaster and an intense urge to defend oneself."[14] I argue that fear is the core emotion that induces the political and military response to bombardment by rockets, missiles, and drones. The emotion of fear modifies the decisionmaking calculus of leaders. Fear affects decisionmakers' appraisal tendencies and action tendencies.[15]

Appraisal tendencies refer to both what and how decisionmakers think under fear. Fear can make decisionmakers "hypervigilant" and lead them to singularly focus their attention on the threat while ignoring other factors.[16] One possible explanation for such hypervigilance is the argument that the psychological and neural mechanisms activated by fear cause "a feeling something is wrong" to be taken as evidence for "something really is wrong" and lead individuals to spend more attention and resources on the threat.[17] Additionally, fear can inhibit cognitive functioning, slow down reasoning, and tend to bias logic in favor of pessimistic risk analysis.[18] Experimental and observational studies in psychology, economics, and reasoning have repeatedly suggested that fear induces a biased attitude to the collection of information, with individuals favoring information that reinforces the remote possibility of the threat while neglecting probabilistic information that says otherwise.[19] In war, rationality and emotions often exert countervailing pressures on leaders deciding on matters of operational tactics and strategy.[20]

These fear-induced appraisal tendencies provoke overreactive action tendencies.[21] *Action tendencies* refer to what we choose to do in the face of appraisal tendencies skewed by fear.[22] One overwhelming action tendency is to fight back against the perceived threat when decisionmakers believe they have the means to overcome and eventually extinguish the threat.[23] The response of nation-states to terrorism offers ample validation for such tendencies to fight perceived threats with a disproportionate commitment of resources. It has been long recognized that terrorism employs violence for dramatic effect to coerce the targeted state into a costly and detrimental fight.[24] For example, one study of terrorist hijacking of airplanes observes that more important than the loss of life in such acts is the loss of perspective in the policy response to the threat.[25] The study suggests that states, in responding to such events, often overreact and inadvertently impose a much greater political and economic cost on their societies than the event itself can accomplish.

The American response to the 9/11 terrorist attack offers another illustration.[26] Detailing the logic of Al Qaeda in the immediate aftermath of the 9/11 terrorist attack, John Steinbruner argued that the goal of Al Qaeda was to "provoke dysfunctional reaction" from American policymakers.[27] Steinbruner argued that "terrorism is an auto-immune disease—it is designed to get the political system attacked and do a lot of damage to itself. The US government will struggle with overreaction and go to extreme measures . . . the problem will be to finding judicious balance between security measures that will be sensible and those that will do more harm than good."[28] In hindsight, it can now be argued that the American response was characterized by several misguided policies and overreactions to the threat.[29] The 9/11 attacks maximized the psychological effects of fear in the minds of American decisionmakers, provoked a disproportionate sense of vulnerability, and coerced it into fighting back with a costly war.

Similarly, I postulate that states subjected to bombardment with rockets, missiles, and drones experience fear and a disproportionate sense of vulnerability and defenselessness. Such fears alter the appraisal and action tendencies of decisionmakers. These fears provoke the states and their decisionmakers to fight back against aerospace threats even if the direct destructive effect of the bombardments may be limited.[30] I argue that the fear-induced action tendency to fight back is the trigger for target states to overreact politically and respond militarily against the aerospace bombardment with diversionary efforts. I contend that these political reactions and diversionary military responses are evidence of successful provocation. If the targeted state is unable to extinguish the aerospace threat and is compelled to negotiate and offer political concessions, limited or otherwise, to end the war, it is evidence of coercion.

Aerospace Weapons, Fear, and Coercion

Coercion, for the purposes of the research agenda of the book, is defined as the threatened or limited use of force to extract political concessions from an adversary.[31] In the case of rockets, missiles, and drones, coercion requires the ability to use these weapons to persuade the adversary to change its political goals and accept a negotiated settlement.[32] The use of the weapon reinforces the adversary's fear of further escalation and continued vulnerability.[33] Furthermore, the coercive effect of the weapon should not be easily diluted by the adversary's military capabilities.[34]

Aerospace weapons—rockets, missiles, and drones—perform excellently on these parameters. Rockets, missiles, and drones possess a variety of tactical advantages. They can be launched without air superiority at an adversary's homeland or military targets to demonstrate force. They can strike at the enemy's most vital targets without invading or putting oneself in harm's way.[35] Often, defensive and offensive countermeasures have a limited ability to neutralize the bombardment. Extinguishing aerospace threats is hard and requires occupying the enemy's territory or a complete defeat and surrender of the enemy.

These characteristics enable even weaker actors to attempt to use aerospace weapons to provoke and coerce stronger adversaries. Previous analysis of wartime airpower coercion has tended to focus on the ability of relatively strong states to coerce because, traditionally, projecting airpower with fighters and bombers often required air superiority.[36] However, this book demonstrates that relatively weaker states can use aerospace weapons to provoke, and in some cases, coerce their adversaries. A weak state (or a tactically weakened state) can coerce its adversary using aerospace weapons if it can employ them to create strategic threats in the minds of the adversary.[37]

The Mechanics of Aerospace Provocation and Coercion

Airpower theory, broadly speaking, has bifurcated the mechanisms of wartime coercion into two main categories: denial of military capabilities and punishment campaigns targeting civilians. Pape for instance, writes "there are two fundamental types of coercion: coercion by punishment and coercion by denial. Coercion by punishment operates by raising the cost or risks to civilians. . . . It may take the form of killing military personnel in large numbers to exploit casualty sensitivity of opponents. Coercion by denial operates by using military means . . . to destroy enough of the opponent's military power to thwart its territorial ambitions."[38] Pape argues that punishment campaigns are ineffective.[39] However, a crucial aspect of his analysis is an emphasis on cases where the geopolitical stakes between the belligerents are perceived at the core of their national interests. Pape acknowledges this limitation noting that "punishment strategies will work only when core values are not at stake."[40]

Such a clear distinction between denial and punishment campaigns may not be applicable to all types of wartime provocation or coercion efforts. Aerospace bombardment targeting cities and critical infrastructure, while appearing as punishment campaigns, can in some instances produce the effects of a denial campaign by provoking the adversary to divert substantial military resources to defend against the strikes or to retaliate in kind.[41] The British political-military responses to aerial bombardments during World War I illustrates the phenomenon.

During World War I, beginning in late 1914 and continuing until May 1918, the Germans bombarded London using Zeppelins and aircraft.[42] The bombardment campaign was a very minor threat to London.[43] The casualties from the aerial bombardment represented less than one-tenth of one percent of the total British war casualties, and the cost of damages caused amounted to an even smaller fraction of one percent of the damages the British suffered during the war.[44]

However, the novelty of aerial bombardment and the fear it created profoundly affected the psychology of London's citizens and the British political leadership. David Lloyd George, the British Prime Minister during World War I, writes that the bombings "led to a fierce demand for reprisals."[45] At a secret session of the British Parliament, Prime Minister Lloyd George noted that the Germans were trying to force the British "to withdraw" their military aircraft from the frontlines in France "in order to protect our towns."[46] A clear articulation of the diversionary effect of bombardment campaigns. While Prime Minister Lloyd George could resist the immediate diversion of a large

22 Bombing to Provoke

volume of military resources away from the frontlines, the aerial bombardment necessitated several other diversions of crucial military assets.

Reacting to the pressure to respond to the bombings, Prime Minister Lloyd George and his War Cabinet proposed redirecting squadrons of the Royal Flying Corps engaged in the frontlines to conduct reprisal strikes on Mannheim and to provide air defense of the homeland.[47] On objections from General Douglas Haig, the Cabinet held back on the proposal to engage in reprisal strikes. However, over the objections of Haig, a squadron of aircraft was reallocated from battlefield operations to the defense of London.[48]

Furthermore, by June 1917, the War Cabinet had to almost double the size of the Royal Flying Corps from 108 to 200 squadrons to establish homeland air defenses against the German aerial bombardment.[49] As the German aerial bombardment continued over the next several months, as many as 300,000 Londoners were sheltered in the underground network of tunnels.[50] Even though the physical effects of the aerial bombardment were limited, the random nature of it was a deep source of psychological fear for the inhabitants of London. It was equally unsettling for the military personnel attempting to defend London. For instance, on 29 September 1917, the anti-aircraft batteries defending London had expended 12,700 shells trying to shoot down roughly seven German aircraft.[51] The next day 14,000 shells were expended without a single hit.[52] In a matter of days, the stock of ammunition for air defense had been depleted to very low levels, and several anti-aircraft guns had been fired into uselessness.[53] The War Cabinet had to divert a large portion of Britain's monthly production inventory of 3-inch guns for October, initially earmarked for merchant ships, to the defense of London.[54]

Similarly, the Japanese response to the Doolittle raids in World War II offers another illustration of a campaign that, while exhibiting the characteristics of a punishment strike, provoked the diversion of significant military resources, altered war plans, and arguably, contributed in some measure to Japan's defeat. The April 1942 Doolittle raids to hit Japanese "sacred home soil" were conceived by US forces as a limited retribution in the immediate aftermath of the Pearl Harbor attack.[55] The raids by themselves were a "pinprick" to the Japanese military forces.[56]

But their second- and third-order effects had a clear denial of military capabilities outcome.[57] The overflight of the imperial palace by American planes shocked Japanese military leaders. The raids embarrassed and surprised them. The raids shocked and induced fears in the minds of the Japanese citizens and decisionmakers who until then believed that their homeland would never be subject to bombardment.[58] These emotions provoked a series of attritional and diversionary military countermeasures that undermined Japanese war efforts. The Doolittle raids triggered a diversion of Japanese Army forces to conduct punitive operations.[59] The raids also triggered a diversion of four Japanese fighter groups for homeland defense.[60] These fighter groups remained in Japan and away from the battlefront during 1942 and 1943, even though no further American bombing raids occurred during this period.[61] Finally, provoked by the Doolittle raids, the Japanese navy spread itself thin in two major.[62] The Japanese launched operations in the Fiji/New Caledonia theater and in quick succession proceeded with the Battle of Midway. These operations led to strategic reverses for the Japanese Navy, including the loss of four fleet carriers, and forced it into a defensive posture for the first time after the outbreak of war.[63] After the Battle of Midway, the Japanese were unable to regain their naval dominance in the Pacific theater.

The Psychology of Aerospace Coercion and Weapons of Mass Destruction

A crucial aspect of coercing an adversary is demonstrating resolve while underscoring and capitalizing on the adversary's casualty sensitivity.[64] In the 1940s, battling French colonialists, Ho Chi Minh warned, "You can kill ten of my men for every one I kill of yours, but even at those odds, you will lose and I will win."[65] The warning is an apt example of demonstrating resolve and tolerance for pain.

In another example, Deputy Chief of PLA General Staff, Lieutenant General Xiong Guangkai attempted to demonstrate Chinese resolve during the 1995–1996 Third Taiwan Straits Crisis. In a conversation with US Assistant Secretary of Defense Chas. Freeman, Xiong Guangkai argued that America did not have the willpower to fight painful wars of attrition over the sovereignty of Taiwan. He states, "We've watched you in Somalia, Haiti, and Bosnia, and you don't have the will."[66] He then threateningly warns, "in the end, you care a lot more about Los Angeles than Taipei."[67] Demonstrating resolve, a tolerance for pain, and a willingness to suffer can, in principle, alter the adversary's cost–benefit calculus and decisionmaking.[68]

The other part of coercion is the manipulation of the adversary's fears of high future costs through tactics and threats.[69] The threat of weapons of mass destruction (WMD) delivered using aerospace weapons—particularly ballistic missiles—can, in principle, be a potent way of manipulating such fears and coercing concession.

In theory, the threat of nuclear weapons bombardment heightens the targeted state's casualty sensitivity, induces fear in its decisionmakers, and triggers a desire to end the conflict, especially if the geopolitical stakes are unequal.[70] Against a multistate military coalition, threatening nuclear strikes on any one entity of the coalition or even other neutral states could, in theory, unravel the coalition.[71] If significant troops commitments have not been made or if the general population were previously insulated from the effects of the war, the coercer could use the threat of nuclear weapons to induce fear among the adversary's decisionmakers by threatening to expand the war in ways not anticipated at the beginning of hostilities. In essence, if core interests are not at stake for the targeted state, threatening an escalation to nuclear warfare may cause a diminution in its resolve and hasten a favorable resolution.[72]

However, the massive destructive potential of nuclear weapons imposes a significant credibility cost for the coercer. The use of nuclear weapons may instantaneously shift the stakes.[73] The use of nuclear weapons that leads to a very large number of deaths can motivate the targeted state to reinvest in the conflict by responding massively, including retaliating with nuclear weapons. The use of nuclear weapons by a regional adversary against the United States, for instance, may immediately galvanize American public and elite consensus to act strongly and punish the perpetrator.[74]

These constraints may not exist in the use of chemical weapons. While nuclear weapons are extremely destructive, chemical weapons do not fall in the same category.[75] It is very complicated to efficiently weaponize and distribute chemical weapons.[76] Additionally, chemical agents are quickly dissipated by wind conditions and sunlight.[77] Furthermore, military personnel wearing protective gear can negate the effects of chemical warfare. During World War I, among those hospitalized by exposure to mustard agents, only 2–3 succumbed to it.[78] Similarly, civilians wearing gas masks and taking appropriate protective measures can efficiently evade the effects of chemical weapons.[79] In such instances, conventional high explosives can cause much more significant casualties than chemical weapons.[80]

Yet the threat of chemical warfare triggers imageries of a ghastly and horrendous death, provokes fear, and leads to an overreaction often disproportionate to the threat. Biological weapons, while more potent, produce a similar emotional overreaction. The 2001 anthrax scare in the United States is an example. The confirmed incidents were few, and there were four casualties.[81] But the entire nation was gripped with anxiety. The anxiety of the threat drove people and decisionmakers to focus on the effects of the outcome "rather than the extremely low probability of the harm" faced.[82] These anxieties, fears, and overreactions are crucial to understanding the coercive leverages of chemical or biological weapons in aerospace warfare.

The mechanisms of fear and overreaction also explain why conventional aerospace bombardment provokes adversaries into diverting military resources against the threat. Decisionmakers can face political pressure to retaliate if the aerospace bombardment campaign imposes unanticipated economic costs, evokes a sense of vulnerability and defenselessness, or threatens fatalities that were not expected initially. Decisionmakers may also undertake diversionary efforts to avert popular demands for early withdrawal.[83] Finally, dictators and oppressive leaders constantly fear internal threats to their regimes. They may believe that prolonged aerospace bombardment campaigns could empower domestic opponents (or disillusion supportive elite power groups) and weaken their political control in the near future. These fears can convince decisionmakers in autocratic states to divert military resources. If they find themselves unable to divert sufficient military resources, decisionmakers may be forced to offer concessions to end the bombardment.[84]

Is Coercion a Binary Measure?

A military campaign of coercion can span a period of time in a conflict where each side responds to the other and the changing geopolitical security environment.[85] Moreover, coercion often acts alongside other instruments of military and diplomatic power, reinforcing each other and affecting the net calculus of the adversary. The instrument of coercion seen in isolation may have limited direct effects. However, combined with other military instruments and geopolitical factors, it may generate multiplicative effects and force a concession or a significant rethinking of goals that may not have occurred without the catalyzing effect of the coercive bombardment. The evaluation of a wartime coercion campaign should, therefore, measure the marginal changes in the adversary's political and military preferences over time in response to the efforts undertaken by the coercer rather than a binary success or failure metric measured at the end of a conflict.[86]

Coercion does not need to result in complete defeat and capitulation of the adversary. Wartime coercion is analytically distinct from victory in war. Coercion can threaten the adversary and force limited concessions while not leading to the adversary's capitulation. For example, coercion can entail a renegotiated rules of engagement on what type of force can be used in the future and against which targets it is permitted.[87] Hezbollah, for instance, has repeatedly managed to coerce, negotiate, and enforce rules of engagement that tied Israeli hands from fully exploiting its military superiority, including constraints on its air force and limits to the geographic scope of the conflict.

26 Bombing to Provoke

Despite the bitterness of these rules of engagement, Israel accepted them because they ensured the safety of Israeli citizens at an acceptable geopolitical cost.[88]

Predictions

My arguments lead to four predictions. First, states employing rockets, missiles, and drones in provocative and coercive warfare should attempt to induce fear in the adversary through their operational tactics and communicated threats.[89] In particular, the state or non-state actor employing these aerospace weapons should attempt to induce fear by threatening bombardment with chemical, biological, or nuclear warheads or threatening to repeatedly bombard the adversary's vital economic and political targets.

The second prediction of my argument is that states targeted by rocket, missile, and drone bombardment should fear these aerospace weapons disproportionately and actively react to these fears in their internal and external political debates and by employing extensive military countermeasures against the threat. Internal and external political debates can manifest in military threat assessments, evacuation plans, communication with military allies, publicly disseminated warnings to citizens, etc. Military countermeasures against aerospace weapons include both defensive and offensive efforts to suppress the strikes.

The third prediction of my argument is that states with the means to divert military resources to defend, suppress, and eventually extinguish the aerospace threats will be able to overcome the coercion without offering major concessions to end the war. Missile defenses and military counterforce strikes may provide limited protection. However, military countermeasures alone will not suffice. The broader military capability to wage a comprehensive war to defeat the adversary is often essential to overcome the aerospace coercion.

For instance, in the case of World War II, the Allied forces remained resolute in their goal to depose the Nazi regime and liberate territory held by Nazi forces. The Allied forces also committed several thousands of heavy and light anti-aircraft guns, squadrons of fighter planes, two hundred of the most advanced radar systems, and more than a quarter of a million military personnel to shoot down incoming German missiles.[90] Yet these defensive efforts had to be supplemented with a monumental military counterforce offensive operation to suppress the missile strikes.[91] But these counterforce operations did not extinguish the German missile strikes. Eliminating the missile threat required the military occupation of the launch sites.

Similarly, in the 1991 Gulf War, the US-led Coalition was persistent in its resolve to eject Saddam Hussein from Kuwait. It rejected a Soviet Union-brokered ceasefire. American forces deployed the Patriot missile defense systems. However, these missile defenses were not effective.[92] The US-led Coalition also embarked on a massive counterforce military operation to destroy Iraqi Scud missile launchers. Yet the very significant counterforce effort was without much success.[93] Throughout the war, the Iraqis would prove adept at employing shoot-and-scoot and other techniques to evade detection and attacks on their mobile Scud launchers.[94] Extinguishing the missile threat required the US-led Coalition to defeat Saddam Hussein's army.

The fourth prediction of my argument is that states that are unable to effectively defend, suppress, and extinguish the aerospace bombardment may suffer a diminution of resolve and be coerced to offer concessions to end the war.

These predictions will be thoroughly evaluated in the five empirical chapters.

Assessment of the Argument

This book employs a structured, focused comparative case study methodology to test the argument and predictions. I explore whether there is general congruence between attempts to weaponize fear, generate provocative effects (manifesting in fear and diversionary military countermeasures) and attempts to coerce the targeted state to offer concessions. I process trace through events in each case study to document and assess the observable implications of my theory. I employ a variety of source materials—archival documents, declassified intelligence documents, selected oral histories, and secondary written materials, including autobiographies of key personalities involved in the history of the five case studies—to perform the analyses.

I employ a within-case process-tracing analysis methodology to observe and test the provocative and coercive effects of aerospace weapons in each of the five case studies. In each empirical chapter, I begin by laying out the historical and political context of the conflict. I then measure the military balance of power between the warring states using quantitative and qualitative indicators. The evaluation of the military balance of power helps in identifying confounding factors, if any, that may have acted along with the aerospace weapons to provoke and coerce the target state. In cases where the state employing aerospace weapons does not possess any other alternate means to strike the target, the effect is linear. In cases where the state employing aerospace weapons also possessed other weaponry, I pay attention to how the state was able to employ other weapons to reinforce the effect of aerospace weapons. I document the military balance of power at the beginning of the war and its evolution throughout the conflict.

After discussing the military balance of power, I study the weaponization of fear—the ability of a state to induce fear in its target. Fear, as a variable, presents measurement challenges.[95] I use second- and third-order metrics to capture the observable implication of weaponizing fear. For instance, I capture the coercive threats issued by the state or non-state actor employing aerospace weapons aiming to induce fear in the adversary. I detail the military operations and tactics used by these actors that reinforce these threats. I capture the threat assessments and other statements issued by the targeted state in the throes of fear. These assessments and statements offer a peek into the mindset of the population and key decisionmakers. These threat assessments are documented using declassified official military estimates, archival documents detailing conversations between key decisionmakers, and the recollection of key decisionmakers as captured in secondary sources.

The provocative effect of aerospace weapons is observed in the political overreaction and military response by the target state to the fear of bombardment. I extensively document the political and military response or lack thereof. I process trace the decisionmaking of leaders as they react and respond politically and militarily to the aerospace bombardment. I also detail the ability or lack thereof of the targeted state to overcome the bombardment and terminate the war without offering concessions. I conclude each empirical chapter by summarizing the congruence between attempts to weaponize fear, provoke, and coerce the target state. The book also performs a cross-case comparative analysis in the concluding chapter to test the theoretical argument further. The cross-case comparative analysis seeks to evaluate the generalizability of the five case studies. The cross-case comparative analysis will reiterate that aerospace weapons manipulate fear, provoke, and coerce adversaries, albeit with differing capacities in different situations.

Case Selection and Scope

The provocative and coercive logic of rockets, missiles, and drones, used separately or in a hybrid fashion, has not been studied rigorously in the security studies literature. Furthermore, real-world cases of extensive use of aerospace weapons in warfare are relatively few. Several of the instances are recent and have not been extensively studied in a theoretically grounded framework.[96]

Therefore, this book should be seen as an early attempt to establish hypotheses that explain the observed effect of these aerospace weapons in warfare and to generalize these hypotheses to enable a predictive analysis of future threats.

Five case studies have been chosen to illuminate the mechanisms that enable aerospace weapons to manipulate fear, provoke, and coerce the target states. These case studies were chosen because of the representative variation of the effects of aerospace provocation and coercion on the course and outcome of the war in these cases.

I examine five cases: Germany in World War II against the Allied forces, Iraq in the Iran–Iraq War against Iran, Iraq in the 1991 Gulf War against the US-led Coalition, Hezbollah in the 2006 Second Lebanon War against Israel, and Houthis in the ongoing Yemeni War against the Saudi-led Coalition. These five cases provide many types of leverage for testing my theoretical argument and predictions. In all five cases, one state or non-state actor relied extensively on aerospace weapons to provoke and coerce its adversary. In three cases— Iraq in the 1991 Gulf War, Hezbollah in the 2006 Second Lebanon War, and Houthis in the Yemeni War—aerospace weapons were the only means for the actors to strike deep inside adversary territory. In the other two cases—Iraq in the Iran–Iraq War and Germany in World War II—while, in theory, other means such as military aircraft existed, they were either militarily unable to breach the adversary's air defenses or not able to generate the same provocative and coercive effects of aerospace weapons. While all five case studies demonstrate the provocative effect of aerospace weapons and the resulting diversionary military countermeasures, in two of the cases, the coercer did not secure any concessions.

These five cases, therefore, provide vital leverage for theory-building and causal process observations. The five case studies vary in time, geography, technology, type of government of the targeted state, and military capabilities of warring pairs. Between World War II and the conflict in Yemen, the technological capabilities of aerospace weapons and defenses against them vary substantially. In each case study, I detail the state of technology and its impact on the argument. The warring pairs in the five cases vary in military culture. For instance, Germany in World War II is seen as an innovator. Iraqi armed forces under Saddam Hussein are generally considered poor military innovators. Similar variations in the capability to innovate are present on the targeted states' side. Despite these variations in capacity for innovation, I can observe the provocative effects of missile warfare.

Intuition would suggest that democracies would be more susceptible to political vulnerabilities and hence provoked to overreact when rockets, missiles, and drones are raining down on their populace. Three of the case studies, Allied forces in World War II, Israel and the United States in the 1991 Gulf War, and Israel in the 2006 Second Lebanon War, involved democracies facing aerospace bombardment. But in the other two cases, the targeted states, Iran and Saudi Arabia, are non-democracies. Yet I can observe the provocative effect of aerospace strike campaigns in these two cases as well. These findings lend credence to the generalizability of my argument.

However, the selection of these five cases limits the scope of the theoretical argument in five ways. First, all case studies involve rockets and missiles that are relatively inaccurate. But it should be noted that the case studies have representative variations in the accuracies of the aerospace weapons under consideration. These variations in weapons accuracy in each of the case studies do not alter the validity of the theory. Furthermore, preliminary evidence from the ongoing Russia–Ukraine War, where modern, accurate missiles have been employed, does not seem to limit the theory put forward in this book. Second, the drones discussed in the book are variants of loitering munitions that perform a functional role similar to missiles. It is worthwhile to note that the drones employed by Russia in the war against Ukraine perform a similar role. However, further empirical testing is needed to determine if the theoretical argument forwarded in this book applies to unmanned combat aerial vehicles (UCAVs) that perform similar to aircraft. Third, in the two cases involving WMDs, Iraq was the state attempting to provoke and coerce and, in both cases, chemical weapons were at play. More empirical datapoints on the combination of aerospace weapons and WMDs would further validate the assertions of their coercive influence. It is conceivable that the use of aerospace weapons with WMDs could generate greater coercive effects. Fourth, all the case studies deal with non-nuclear states using short-range missiles and rockets. While short-range missiles may be used for nuclear or conventional attacks, long-range missiles (with intercontinental range) are exclusively designed and structured for nuclear delivery. Therefore, the theory as it stands cannot directly speak to the provocative and coercive effect of using intercontinental-range missiles by nuclear powers. Finally, the theory is focused on wartime provocation and coercion. As a result, it does not provide a directly translatable framework to study the use of aerospace weapons in coercive diplomacy during nonmilitarized crises.[97]

3
Hitler's Weapons of Vengeance

Hitler's V-1 "flying bomb" cruise missiles and V-2 ballistic missiles profoundly affected the character of World War II.[1] The missiles single-handedly provoked the Allied forces into a massive diversion of military resources in the effort to hunt and destroy the missiles.[2]

Hitler had declared that the missile attacks would be synchronized with the Allied invasion of France, hoping to derail the Normandy landings and force the Allies to execute a diversionary assault on the Cherbourg coast toward the missile launch sites.[3] Any changes or delays to the plans to land Allied troops on the beaches of Normandy would have eliminated the crucial element of surprise vital to the successful Allied invasion of Europe.[4] As a result, in the months leading up to Operation Overlord—the war plan for landing Allied troops on the beaches of Normandy—British and American leaders constantly feared that the impending German missile bombardment would derail the operation.[5]

The fear prevailed despite the technological limitations of Hitler's missile arsenal.[6] The British and American military planners were well aware of the accuracy limitations of the German missiles.[7] However, British and American military analysts remained extremely worried about German strikes on the crucial ports of Portsmouth and Southampton. An American military estimate suggested that if the Germans withheld their attacks on the ports to just before Operation Overlord, the missile strikes could create maximum confusion at a critical time and completely disrupt it.[8] On the other hand, British political leaders feared London was the target of Hitler's vengeance.[9]

At the end of an 18 July 1944 Crossbow Committee meeting, British Prime Minister Winston Churchill argued that if Hitler's missile attacks continued, he was willing to engage in gas warfare on German cities in retaliation.[10] When the Chiefs of Staff advocated against the use of gas on both moral and practical grounds, Churchill responded: "I am not at all convinced by this negative report. But clearly, I cannot make head against the parsons and the warriors at the same time. The matter should be kept under review and brought up again when *things get worse* [emphasis added]."[11] In a memorandum, Churchill, distressed by the German missile bombardment, had argued that if the missile

Bombing to Provoke. Jaganath Sankaran, Oxford University Press. © Oxford University Press 2024.
DOI: 10.1093/oso/9780197792629.003.0003

32   Bombing to Provoke

attacks continued, he was ready to do anything that would hit the enemy.[12] He expressed willingness to "drench the cities of the Ruhr and many other cities in Germany" in poisonous gas.[13]

Hitler's missiles weaponized fear. The fear of German missile bombardment provoked a plethora of political and military responses from the British and American forces. Churchill's demands for chemical warfare may have been a step too far. However, the German missile attacks provoked an enormous effort to suppress the missiles. A continuous reconnaissance of the northern French coast was undertaken to surveil suspected missile launch sites. Additionally, extensive surveillance of research facilities and factories suspected of involvement in the manufacture of the missiles was performed. Between 1 May 1943 and 31 March 1944, 40% of all Allied reconnaissance missions in the European theater were devoted to Operation Crossbow—the code name for Allied military operations against German missiles.[14] These surveillance and reconnaissance missions undertaken for Crossbow operations were the largest effort of the entire war.[15]

The reconnaissance and surveillance operations were followed by monumental missile defense and counterforce efforts. In an attempt to defend against the missiles, the Allied forces committed several thousands of heavy and light anti-aircraft guns, several squadrons of fighter planes to shoot down incoming missiles, 200 of the most advanced radar systems, and more than a quarter of a million military personnel.[16] As part of the counterforce efforts, during July and August 1944, 40% of the Royal Air Force (RAF) Bomber Command strikes were redirected to Crossbow targets at the expense of other critical targets.[17] By the time the Allied troops had captured the missile launch sites in northern France, 7,469 tons of bombs had been used just on the four large sites at Wizernes, Watten, Mimoyecques, and Siracourt, with little effect on the missile launch rate.[18]

Adolf Galland, the Commander of Hitler's Luftwaffe fighter forces, writes that Allied bombing progressively increased between June and August, adding up to 100,000 bombs targeted at German V-weapons facilities.[19] He observes that these bombing efforts diverted a quarter of the total Allied bombing effort that otherwise may have targeted German frontline forces.[20] Hitler reportedly made similar claims. At a German war conference meeting, Hitler declared that the missile strikes were diverting hundreds of Allied aircraft and bombs from the Fatherland and the battlefield, providing substantial relief.[21] In essence, the Germans had created a diversionary problem of immense magnitude for the Allied forces.[22]

The counterforce strikes against the missile-related targets continued until the end of the war. Between August 1943 and March 1945, the attempts

Table 3.1 Total allied crossbow bombing efforts, August 1943 to March 1945

	Sorties	Bomb tonnage
Eighth Air Force (US)	17,211	30,350
RAF Bomber Command	19,584	72,141
RAF Fighter Command	4,627	988
Ninth (Tactical) Air Force (US) and Second Tactical Air Force (RAF)	27,491	18,654
Totals	68,913	122,133

Reproduced from David Irving, *The Mare's Nest* (Boston, MA: Little. Brown and Company, 1965), 308 n. Used with permission of David Irving—Focal Point International LLC.

to suppress the missile launches cost the Allies 68,913 air strike sorties and close to 122,000 tons of bombs (see Table 3.1). In the early stages of the Crossbow counterforce missions, the US Eighth Air Force (USAAF) lost 462 men and 49 heavy bombers, the US Ninth Air Force lost 148 men and 30 medium bombers, and other USAAF and RAF units lost 161 men and 75 aircraft.[23]

Hitler's missiles did not lead to a German victory, but they did have an immense strategic impact on the character of World War II. In his excellent study of the German missile campaign, Aaron Karp argues that the V-1 and V-2 missiles were not a frivolity but an opportunity that failed to materialize at the right time and in the right amount.[24] This chapter explores how close the weapon came to success before it failed and why it failed.

The rest of the chapter proceeds as follows. The next section provides a brief historical background to Hitler's decision to acquire missiles. The third section outlines the military balance of power and its relevance to the German missile campaign. The fourth section examines the fears instilled in the minds of British and American leaders by the missile threat. The fifth section details the many political and military measures enacted by the Allies in response to the missile threat. Finally, the sixth section summarizes the impact of Hitler's missile warfare on Allied military plans and operations during World War II.

The History and Politics of the Dispute

Hitler's decisions before and during World War II were motivated by a desire to exact revenge. In June 1940, the French Government under Marshal Pétain sought an armistice from the invading German army.[25] Hitler insisted on one particularly symbolic act—that the armistice agreement be signed in the same railway carriage in which defeated Germany signed the 1918 armistice.[26] The railway carriage was towed to Compiegne for signing the 1940 armistice and then blown up.[27] The symbolic blowing up of the railway carriage best showcases Hitler's intense desire to seek revenge for the perceived injustices of the Versailles Treaty that ended World War I.

At the end of World War I, Germany's Ebert government—the Weimar Republic—under the terms of the Treaty of Versailles had to immediately surrender the plurality of its heavy weaponry and reduce its army to 100,000 men.[28] The German army was barred from developing or possessing battle tanks and was limited to relying upon light artillery.[29] The postwar Weimar Republic was also forced to relinquish its air force of 1,700 aircraft and was forbidden from maintaining one in the future.[30] The German navy, the third largest before World War I, was reduced to a coastal defense force with obsolete ships.[31] The region of Alsace Lorraine was returned to France. Roy Irons notes that, as a consequence of the Treaty of Versailles, Germany's arable land was reduced by 15%; its iron deposits reduced by 75%; and its steel, pig iron, and coal resources significantly reduced.[32] Finally, Germany had to accept to pay the victorious states 132 billion gold marks as war reparations.[33]

The Versailles Treaty rendered the German army impotent. After World War I, it was tasked with defending a nation surrounded by states with which it had troubled relations. In the west was the long-standing enemy, the French. In the southeast was Czechoslovakia, a French ally.[34] In the east was Poland, a nation recently carved partially from German territory.[35] However, the German army was denied the military means to deter or defend against these states. The German army's irrelevance was amply demonstrated in 1922, when France and Belgium quickly invaded and seized Germany's industrialized Ruhr Valley.[36]

Hitler believed that German defeat in World War I did not occur on the battlefield.[37] Instead, in his mind, it was a defeat caused by the failure of German will and morale. He blamed the Allied powers, the socialist Weimar government that signed the Versailles Treaty, and the Jews and Marxists who spread revolutionary ideas to weaken Germany.[38] Hitler slowly rearmed Germany, promising restoration of its former glory and seeking revenge on those he perceived wronged Germany during and after World War I.

In Germany's quest for rearmament, missiles proved to be an ideal weapon. Researching, experimenting, and developing the V-1 and V-2 missiles circumvented the constraints on the development of heavy artillery imposed by the Versailles Treaty.[39] In 1929, Colonel Karl Emil Becker of the German army's Heeeres Waffenampt (Army weapons board) at the Ballistiche und

Munitions-abteilung (ballistic and munitions department) began exploring military uses for rocket weapons.[40] In 1930, Captain Walter Dornberger was charged with the responsibility of developing solid-propellant and liquid-propellant missiles.[41] Dornberger recruited Wernher von Braun and employed him in missile research at the German army's Versuchsstelle (experimental station) at Kummersdorf-West.[42] From 1933 to 1937, the German missile program progressed steadily.

The Military Balance of Power

As World War II unfolded, Hitler repeatedly sought ways to bomb England. In a radio broadcast on 4 September 1940, Hitler was incensed at the British bombing of Berlin. He proclaimed,

> for three months I have been holding back the order to retaliate, but Churchill mistook that for a sign of weakness. We are going to give them their answer night after night from now on. When the British Air Force drops two or three or four thousand kilograms of bombs, then we will in one night drop 150-, 230-, 300- or 400,000 kilograms. When they declare they will increase their attacks on our cities, then we will raze their cities to the ground. We will stop the handiwork of those night air pirates, so help us God![43]

Again, on 28 March 1942, following a British raid on the historic German city of Lübeck, Hitler furiously demanded that the German armed forces immediately retaliate.[44] Beginning in March 1943, under Sir Arthur Harris, the British air force launched a series of bombing attacks on industrial cities in the German Ruhr. On 24 July 1943, the British air force began bombing Hamburg, Germany's second-largest city, forcing the evacuation of more than 1,000,000 citizens and causing 40,000 deaths within the next nine days.[45]

On the morning of 25 July 1943, Hitler, disappointed with the retaliatory options provided to him by his air force experts, angrily declared, "You can only smash terror with counter-terror!"[46] He announced to his military advisors that coercing the British to stop the bombing of German cities required systematic targeting of Britain's cities.[47]

While Hitler repeatedly promised and demanded that British cities be bombed, the Luftwaffe had limited options to enact his demands. The Luftwaffe did not possess the bomber planes needed to exact revenge on Britain. Herman Goering, Commander-in-Chief of the Luftwaffe, canceled Germany's heavy bomber program in 1938.[48] By 1942, the Luftwaffe's medium bombers were being destroyed quickly on the Russian front and in the Mediterranean conflict. The decision to cancel the heavy bomber became painfully obvious but was too late to correct.[49] Any attempts to restart a modern long-range bomber development program would have been futile. The Allies had established significant air superiority over the European continent by then. The British and American air forces would have persistently bombed the industries and the large airfields needed to develop and deploy a heavy bomber force.[50]

Furthermore, the Luftwaffe's fighter aircraft strength was drastically diminished by 1942. Luftwaffe's aircraft inventory fell from 3,692 in 1940 to 2,872 in early 1942.[51] The Luftwaffe was rushed from one combat theater to another, beginning with the operations over Poland and France, followed by the Battle of Britain, and then successively in the Balkans, North Africa, and the Russian theater.[52] Compounding its losses after the Battle of Britain, the German high command significantly underestimated British capacity to produce aircraft and overestimated the quantum of British losses.[53] As a result, in 1942, Germany produced only 1,460 fighter aircraft, several of which were downed in the Russian theater and the Mediterranean.[54] The British produced nearly 8,118 aircraft in the same year and received 671 from North America. Along with the growing deficit in the inventory of fighter aircraft, the Luftwaffe suffered very high pilot attrition rates.[55] Soon the Luftwaffe had to rely on insufficiently trained novice pilots, further accelerating pilot attrition.[56] By late 1943, the Luftwaffe's problems had as much to do with the supply of trained pilots and aviation fuel as the supply of fighter aircraft.[57]

By early 1944, the Luftwaffe was rendered inefficient.[58] As the Allied invasion of occupied France commenced, the Luftwaffe faced insurmountable obstacles in satisfying the Fuhrer's demand to strike the British homeland. The Luftwaffe had to produce many more fighter aircraft and train pilots faster just to maintain a static defensive posture over the German homeland.[59] Furthermore, the German aircraft factories and other related facilities were constantly hit by Allied bombers.[60]

Hitler desperately wanted to strike back at Britain. The V-1 and V-2 missiles provided a way for Hitler to bombard Britain's cities. The missile program may have drained resources from the German aircraft production efforts, but, given the shortages of aviation fuel and trained aircrew, it was, in many ways, a substitute for them.[61] Hitler hoped that if vast quantities of German missiles became ready on time, it could "blow London off the map."[62] Hitler believed repeated missile barrages on London would force the Allies to alter their invasion plans in ways favorable to the Germans.

Weaponizing Fear

Fear animated the British thinking as they prepared for Hitler's missile strikes. The Allies, fearing German missile strikes, executed massive bombing campaigns to destroy German missile launch facilities and other related infrastructure.[63] Additionally, fearing the missile strikes, plans were drawn by British political leaders for a mass evacuation of London.[64]

R. V. Jones, the British head of scientific intelligence during World War II, offers an illustration of the fear-induced provocative influence of Hitler's missiles. Jones observes that British politicians "seemed far more frightened by one ton of explosive delivered by rocket than by five tons delivered by aircraft."[65] Jones, describing the effects on British decisionmakers' psyche, writes

> Here is a 13 ton missile which traces out a flaming ascent to heights hitherto beyond the reach of man, and hurls itself 200 miles across the stratosphere at unparalleled speed to descend—with luck—on a defenceless target ... to raise one of the *biggest scares in history* [emphasis added].[66]

By June 1943, the British War Cabinet believed that the German long-range missile program had reached an advanced stage. A British joint parliamentary report pointedly noted that Hitler would use long-range missiles to retaliate against England for the bombing of the Ruhr as soon as possible.[67] In early missile threat assessments, most British policymakers believed the V-2 ballistic missile would contain a 10-ton high-explosive warhead.[68] British and American experts also worried that the V-weapons might be armed with chemical or radiological warheads.[69] In June 1943, an investigation of the German Long-Range Rocket Development headed by Sir Findlater Stewart, the Chairman of the Home Defence Executive, iterated three characteristics of the anticipated German V-2 ballistic missile bombardment: (1) the missile would contain as much as 10 tons of high explosives, (2) the missiles could have a range of 150 miles or so, and (3) the Germans would be able to fire one rocket every hour daily for four weeks.[70]

The Findlater Stewart Committee estimated the destructive effect of each missile under the assumption of two types of warheads.[71] The Type A warhead was assumed to be armed with an instantaneous fuse, and damages were primarily caused by the blast wave. The Type B warhead was assumed to be armed with a delay fuse, and damage was caused by earth shock and flying debris. The Committee findings noted that one missile armed with a Type A warhead would cause complete or partial demolition of property over a radius of 850 feet, and significant blast impact would extend further.[72] The Committee findings noted that one missile armed with a Type B warhead would form a crater of 160 feet in diameter and 45 feet deep with a much larger demolition radius, and underground infrastructure such as buried shelters and tube railways would be damaged.[73] After its analysis, the Findlater Stewart Committee estimated that each missile would kill 600, seriously injure 1,200, and slightly injure 2,400.[74] The Committee, in its final estimation, calculated that if one missile struck every hour for four weeks, it would cause the complete destruction of London.[75] The Committee estimated the casualties in just 24 hours could exceed 10,000 killed and 20,000 seriously injured if the missiles were dispersed over the four-mile radius.[76]

Based on its estimation, the Committee suggested that it may be impossible to continue the British Government from London. The Committee noted that the *Black Plan*—a detailed plan for the evacuation of the Cabinet, members of the Parliament, and 16,000 other essential officials—might have to be revived if Hitler's missile threat materialized.[77] In response to the Committee's findings, the British Chiefs of Staff asked for an investigation into the possibility of producing an additional 100,000 Morrison shelters.[78] However, fearing that these additional Morrison shelters may not suffice, the committee warned that a "panic refugee movement may start" once the missiles started falling on London and suggested that military personnel would have to be deployed to "enforce 'stand firm' orders."[79]

On the other hand, British and American military leaders feared that an extensive German missile campaign on London and other targets might derail Operation Overlord. British and American military analysts estimated that the German missile strikes would be capable of delivering the 2,000-ton equivalent of high explosives on the Southampton and Portsmouth ports every 24 hours and could progressively increase the ordnance delivered until the beginning of Operation Overlord.[80] British and American military planners evaluated the possibility of radical revisions to Operation Overlord, including the possibility of executing the Normandy landing from naval bases beyond the reach of German missiles.[81] On 8 January 1944, the Chief of Staff to Supreme Allied Commander (COSSAC) outlined contingency plans for the dispersion of American and British naval forces and alternate arrangements for Operation Overlord in the event the German missile assault materialized.[82]

The Political and Military Response to Hitler's Missiles

Even before the first German missiles had left their launching pad, the fear of their destructive potential was impacting Allied conduct of warfare against Nazi Germany. The neutralization of Hitler's missiles became an urgent political and military priority for the Allied forces. The anticipated threat of missile bombardment provoked a massive diversion of Allied reconnaissance efforts and bombing campaigns to avert these feared attacks.

Phase 1: Will the Missiles Kill Overlord?

The British received a variety of intelligence on the German V-1 and V-2 missiles as early as 1939. As information accumulated, worries grew about what these missiles could achieve. In April 1943, Duncan Sandys was authorized to study the scope of the threats from the missiles. The study concluded that the threat was real, but very few other details were known.[83] Consequently, a major aerial reconnaissance effort was instituted that, with time, became the "most comprehensive such operation undertaken during the entire war."[84] Between 1 May 1943 and 31 March 1944, 40% of all Allied reconnaissance missions in the European theater were devoted to Crossbow efforts. More than 1,250,000 aerial photographs and more than 4,000,000 prints were developed during Crossbow reconnaissance efforts.[85]

In May 1943, for the first time, Allied photographic intelligence discerned at Peenemünde, located on the Isle of Usedom on the Baltic Sea coast, an elevated ramp and the tiny T-shaped structure above the ramp as an airplane without a cockpit.[86] As a result, the German missile research effort at Peenemünde near the Baltic Sea coast received focused attention. Simultaneously, Allied intelligence was also able to observe the construction of a "large and unorthodox military installation of inexplicable purpose" at Watten on the Channel coast of France.[87] In the next few months, aerial reconnaissance discovered similar large sites at Lottinghem, Wizernes, Mimoyyecques, Siracourt, Martinvast, and Sottevast.[88]

On 17 August 1943, a large fleet of US Eighth Air Force and RAF heavy bombers bombed Peenemünde. The mission was codenamed Operation Hydra.[89] A total of 596 RAF bombers flew on the highly classified mission to hit targets at Peenemünde. The bombing raid employed some of the most advanced bombing capabilities and techniques available at the time. Five hundred ninety-six bombers of mixed type—including Short Stirlings,

40 Bombing to Provoke

Avro Lancasters, Handley-Page Halifaxes, and de Havilland Mosquitos—conducted a coordinated strike in waves of bombing assaults.[90] Five hundred seventeen of the 596 bombers dropped nearly 2,000 tons of high explosives at the Peenemünde installation and facilities.[91] In Operation Hydra, the British RAF Group No. 5 and Group No. 6 lost 14.5% and 19.5% of their forces, respectively, including several senior officers.[92] The Peenemünde strike initially appeared to be very successful.[93] The British were so confident that the Peenemünde strike had destroyed the facilities that they turned down an offer from the US Air Force to carry out a daytime precision attack again.[94] However, questions about the success of the Peenemünde strikes later emerged. Colonel Walter Dornberger argued that damage to vital installations was negligible.[95] Furthermore, while the strikes had killed 732 people, a large majority were laborers, not scientists, involved in the missile program.[96]

Ten days later, on 27 August 1943, the US Eighth Air Force undertook its first Crossbow operation, employing 187 B-17s to destroy the constructions at Watten.[97] Watten was again bombed on 7 September 1943.[98] Watten and the other large sites were subject to continued bombardment attacks throughout the Fall and Winter of 1943.

In October 1943, Allied intelligence discovered a second type of concrete structure that resembled "gigantic skis laid on edge" in the Pas-de-Calais region and other sites on the tip of the French Cherbourg peninsula.[99] Over the next month, large-scale reconnaissance efforts revealed that all the "ski sites" at the Pas-de-Calais were pointed in the direction of London, and the ski sites at the Cherbourg peninsula were pointed in the direction of Bristol.[100] Joseph Angell, who served with the US Army Air Forces during the war, notes that it was clear these sites were directionally vectored to launch the missiles against London and the British ports, which served as the staging area for the forthcoming Allied invasion of Europe.[101]

In an effort to disable these ski sites, the Eight Air Force undertook Mission No. 164 on 24 December 1943, the largest of its bombing operations to date, and sent more than 1,300 US aircraft to bomb and destroy the ski sites.[102] A total of 722 heavy bombers dropped 1,700 tons of bombs on 23 ski sites as part of the bombing operation.[103] A *New York Times* editorial on 24 December 1943 noted

> Hitler had now created a diversion . . . [and] have at least won a breathing spell for themselves and temporarily at least diverted part of Anglo-American air power from battered German cities . . . the threat alone has succeeded in lightening the weight of attack upon Germany to the extent that planes, which cannot be in two places at once, have had to be employed to deal with it.[104]

As preparations for Operation Overlord drew close, British and American leaders were forced to execute an all-out assault on the missile launch sites. The British Chiefs of Staff had insisted that the German missile threat be neutralized immediately to preclude the need to divert forces during Operation Overlord.[105] On 18 April 1944, Sir Hastings Ismay, the British War Cabinet Secretary, requested Dwight Eisenhower, the Supreme Commander of the Allied Expeditionary Force in Europe, to sanction air strike attacks against all the suspected V-missile sites.[106]

US Army Air Forces Commander General Henry H. "Hap" Arnold and US Strategic Air Force in Europe (USSTAF) Commander General Carl Spaatz opposed any diversion of air strikes, instead arguing that the focus should be on bombarding German cities and industries as part of Operation Pointblank—the Combined Bomber Offensive war plan designed to cripple German military capabilities before the beginning of the Normandy landings.[107] Eisenhower overruled them. On 19 April 1944, Eisenhower declared that attacking the ski sites would take priority over all Allied air operations.[108] By the end of the month, the Operation Crossbow campaign targeting German missile facilities and launch sites had grown by 50%, with 7,500 tons of bombs delivered to the missile launch sites in 4,150 sorties.[109]

The much-feared threat to Operation Overlord did not manifest. On 6 June 1944, the Allied forces launched Operation Overlord. On 12 June 1944, six days after the Allied troops had reached the Normandy coast, the first salvo of V-1 "flying bomb" cruise missile strikes occurred.[110] It was a bust. The British were expecting 400 tons of explosives in the first 10 hours.[111] However, a mere 10 V-1 cruise missiles were launched before operational difficulties made the Germans abandon their plans momentarily. Four of the 10 V-1 cruise missiles had crashed on take-off, and one had failed to explode.[112] Four missiles struck London, and one exploded on a railroad bridge in London city.[113]

Lord Cherwell, a skeptic of the effectiveness of the German missiles, exuberantly said to R. V. Jones, "the mountain hath groaned and given forth a mouse!"[114] Jones pleaded against dismissing the threat. He pointed out that the Germans had launched more missiles during the trials at Peenemünde and must be capable of launching more than 10 missiles.[115]

Phase II: Hitler Decrees London Is the Target

In the aftermath of the Normandy landings, Hitler demanded that London immediately become the target of the V-1 missile bombardment.[116] On 15 June 1944, the Germans reinitiated their strikes on London and managed to launch 244 V-1 missiles.[117] On 16 June 1944, the British war cabinet decided that London would have to withstand the bombardment.[118]

An extensive defensive shield was activated to defeat the V-1 missile strikes. A three-layered defensive structure composed of a thick balloon belt in the center of Greater London, a 20-mile belt of 400 heavy anti-aircraft (HAA) guns immediately outside the balloon belt, and finally, a layer of fighter aircraft outside the HAA belt was erected.[119] In this defensive structure, an incoming V-1 missile would first be shot down or otherwise neutralized by the fighter planes. The fighter planes employed in the missile defense operations were stripped of their heavy armor and paint. Their engines were modified to use 150 octane fuel, thus increasing their speed to chase and shoot the incoming missiles.[120]

If the fighter aircraft were unable to shoot down a missile, the HAA belt would engage it. Finally, the balloon belt would attempt to snag missiles that passed through the fighter aircraft and the HAA belt.[121] While potent, the defensive architecture had substantial limitations. On 23 June 1944, Duncan Sandys reported that approximately 370 missiles of an estimated 1,000 launched by the Germans had reached London.[122]

The aerial bombing of the missile launch sites received renewed urgency from the British. On the night of 16 June 1944, after the German missile raids, British heavy bombers flew 315 sorties and delivered 1,500 tons of high explosives on missile launch sites and supply depots.[123] The Chiefs of Staff sent an urgent request to Eisenhower asking him to undertake every possible measure to neutralize the threat, with the proviso that these efforts do not interfere with the unfolding war on the Continent.[124] On 18 June 1944, Eisenhower ordered the Allied bomber forces to concentrate on Crossbow targets with immediate priority.[125]

Throughout July and August 1944, the Germans fired nearly 100 V-1 cruise missiles every 24 hours.[126] In a 2 August 1944 speech to the House of Commons, Prime Minister Churchill announced that 5,735 missiles had been fired at Britain in July, killing 4,735 people.[127] Churchill reported that 17,000 houses had been destroyed, and a million had been evacuated from London.[128] Churchill captures the fear and emotional trauma inflicted on Londoners and British political leaders by the missile campaign in his postwar memoirs. He writes that Hitler's missile campaign imposed a much greater burden on Londoners than the Blitz of 1940–1941. Churchill writes that the combination of the "blind impersonal nature" of the missile bombardment alongside the fact "no human enemy" could be shot down severely strained the willingness of London's residents to withstand the missile attacks.[129] By August 1944, close to 1,450,000 people had left London, a much larger number than during the Blitz.[130] Industrial productivity in London decreased by 25%.[131] Roy Irons notes that more than 700,000 person-months were lost during the missile campaign on London.[132]

On 3 August 1944, the Combined Chiefs of Staff again requested Eisenhower to eliminate the threats by diverting military resources as needed.[133] In an attempt to suppress the German missile bombardment, the British RAF delivered 24,300 tons of explosives in July and 25,300 tons of explosives in August on Crossbow targets.[134] In addition, RAF bombers used 12,000-pound bombs called Tallboys to destroy the larger sites in northern France.[135] The US Eighth Air Force dropped 10,900 tons of explosives.[136] The Allied Air Forces expended one-fourth of their combat sorties and around one-fifth of their tonnage of bombs on Crossbow targets in July and August 1944.[137]

Despite these military counterforce strikes, the rate of missile launches barely diminished.[138] The Germans had established modified ski sites that could be quickly built and effectively camouflaged.[139] The Germans were launching most of their missiles from these modified ski sites, which proved extremely difficult to target and bomb.[140] Air Marshal Roderic Hill, the Commander of the Air Defense of Great Britain, describes the counterforce attack as "locking the stable door after the horse had been stolen."[141] Hill observes that there was no meaningful effect on the rate of missile firing from the counterforce bombings.[142]

The Allied troops soon captured the missile launch sites on the French coast. On 1 September 1944, the last missile launched from France was fired.[143] A majority of the decisionmakers believed the German missile campaign was over. With the War Cabinet's approval, Herbert Morrison, the Home Secretary, suspended the evacuation of London.[144] At a press conference, Duncan Sandys announced that "except for a few last shots . . . the Battle of London is over."[145]

Phase III: The Missile War on the Port of Antwerp

The next day, on the evening of 8 September 1944, the Germans for the first time launched their V-2 ballistic missiles at London.[146] The first V-2 missile fell at Chiswick, and the second one at Epping.[147]

These two missile strikes, and the fear that more would follow, provoked a military response that profoundly affected the course of World War II. On 9 September 1944, the Vice Chief of the Imperial Staff sent an urgent message to Field Marshall Montgomery, demanding the redirection of Allied troops to

44 Bombing to Provoke

capture the Antwerp-Utrecht-Rotterdam area, the locations from which the V-2 missiles were launched.[148]

The message prompted Field Marshall Montgomery to institute a major change to the direction of the Allied thrust into the Nazi heartland. Originally, the invasion plan had involved a paratrooper assault to seize a bridge across the Rhine River at Wesel, followed by an armored thrust to capture the northern parts of Germany and the Ruhr.[149] Instead, the message from the Vice Chief of the Imperial Staff provoked a decision to undertake the paratrooper operation (Operation Market Garden) across the Rhine and the Meuse River toward Arnhem.[150]

On 17 September 1944, Operation Market Garden began with the air-dropping of three airborne paratrooper divisions to capture bridges along the Meuse and the Rhine. However, Operation Market Garden stalled.[151] Furthermore, Field Marshall Montgomery's failed thrust came at the cost of General Patton's advance into Germany's heartland. Logistical difficulties meant that there was not enough fuel to enable both Patton's and Montgomery's advances into Germany.[152] The fear of what might happen when more rockets exploded in the streets of London led Eisenhower to privilege Field Marshall Montgomery's assault on Arnhem.[153]

Logistical difficulties compounded as the Allied forces moved further into Europe. General Eisenhower, writing to General Marshall, identified the Antwerp port as indispensable to Allied operations.[154] Realizing the importance of the Antwerp port to the Allied offensive into Germany, the Germans mounted a sustained missile campaign on the port.[155]

Similar to the defense of London, the missile attacks on Antwerp forced the Allies to expend a vast cache of defensive weaponry to thwart the German missile attacks. At its peak, the Allied defense of Antwerp required 22,000 men, 208 US 90 mm guns, 128 British 3.7-inch guns, and 188 37 mm and 40 mm guns.[156] Additionally, the radars in England were transferred to Belgium at Eisenhower's direct request.[157] In one week, the air defense forces deployed to Antwerp were able to destroy 94% of the incoming missiles. However, in the process, 532,000 rounds of ammunition were expended.[158] Despite these Allied efforts, German missile forces could still maintain a continuous bombardment for a six-month period over the city and port of Antwerp, except for a single day. The missile impacting the Antwerp port damaged or destroyed two warehouses, twenty berths, one canal lock, one 150-ton floating crane, and one hundred-fifty ships.[159] The German missile bombardment forced the war material discharge rate at the Antwerp port to be reduced to less than a third of what was initially planned.[160] The German missile campaign continued until Allied forces could physically occupy launching sites and directly threaten the troops involved in the launching operations.

Conclusion

The German missile campaign did not win the war for Hitler's army. However, very few weapons are directly responsible for winning a war. The exalted Sherman tank was not valued because it was the ultimate weapon that won World War II. Instead, it was valued because it made the campaign relatively effective for the Allied forces. Similarly, if one examines the German missile campaign's impact on the conduct of the conflict, it turns out to be highly effective.

The missile campaign had a tremendous impact on World War II's operational and strategic decisions. The German missile attacks distracted, delayed, tormented, and provoked the Allied forces. The German missile campaign terrorized Londoners and the citizens of Antwerp, inducing fear and catalyzing diversionary political and military responses.[161] Throughout its course, the missile campaign imposed substantial military and political costs on the Allies, forcing significant changes to the Allied war planning.

The British Air Ministry, in a secret report circulated on 4 November 1944, observed that the German missile campaign had managed to force the Allies to expend their resources at four times the net cost of the price Germany paid to obtain their V-1 and V-2 missile capabilities.[162] The V-1 missile campaign cost the Allies £47,635,190.[163] In comparison, the Germans had expended an estimated £12,600,670 on the manufacture and launching of V-1 cruise missiles and the erection and defense of the launching-site systems.[164]

The German missile campaign was effective but not enough to coerce significant political concessions. The Allied powers were able to commit many resources to the diversionary countermeasure campaign to sustain their war efforts. The Allied powers were also persistent in their resolve to remove the Nazi regime from power. The campaign's impact may have been much more potent if the German war machine had brought the V-weapons into action before the landing of Allied troops on the beaches of Normandy. Eisenhower writes that Operation Overlord might have been impossible if the missiles had been used on the Portsmouth-Southampton region six months earlier.[165]

General Curtis LeMay, Commander of the Third Air Division in the European theater during World War II, makes a similar argument. In his biography, he writes, "It's impossible to estimate what trouble, what actual suffering and lives and wealth were saved to us by the delay. If Hitler had been

46 Bombing to Provoke

able to get his buzz-bomb program working in the field—Get the V-1's flying, and the V-2's a little earlier than they did, there might have been an entirely different story to tell."[166] The impact of the V-1 and V-2 missiles was stupendous. If a larger number of the missiles had been ready before Operation Overlord, it could have changed the course of the war. Unfortunately for the Germans and fortunately for the Allied forces, the missiles were too little too late to thwart Operation Overlord.[167]

Several factors stood in the way of the early deployment of the missiles. Germans internal politics inhibited diligent planning for the production and use of V-missiles.[168] These difficulties were compounded by Hitler's vacillations on the utility of the V-missiles.[169] Hitler was particularly skeptical about the V-weapons in the early 1940s, then changed his mind in the spring of 1942, and again grew skeptical in the early spring of 1943, before finally embracing them.[170] Air Chief Marshall Sir Philip Joubert de la Ferté, who served as a senior commander in the British RAF during World War II, writes that "Hitler had been unconvinced of the value of the weapon when he visited the experimental station in March 1939, and in 1940 he had reduced its claims to a low level of priority, an act for which we in Britain should be deeply grateful."[171]

4

Missiles and the War of the Cities

On 22 September 1980, Iraq invaded Iran. Saddam Hussein had hoped for a short war and an easy victory. The reality turned out to be very different. Over the course of the next eight years, 367,000 were killed and more than 700,000 were wounded.[1] The war ended on 20 August 1988, after Iran begrudgingly accepted United Nations Resolution 598, which called for an immediate ceasefire and the withdrawal of all troops from foreign soil, restoring the ante-bellum status quo.[2]

Iran's military collapse in 1988 was surprisingly quick. In 1987, Iran had the upper hand over Iraq. It had captured strategic territory in the Al-Faw penin-sula and was at the doorsteps of Basra. Before 1988, Iran repeatedly rejected ceasefire proposals. However, within a year or so, Iran was desperate to end the war. A multitude of factors worked against Iran. Iraq had begun to manu-facture and effectively use large quantities of chemical weapons on the battle-field to defeat entrenched Iranian forces.[3] The crucial tipping point, however, was Iraq's newfound ability in 1988 to threaten Tehran with chemically armed ballistic missile strikes. Iraq's repeated missile strikes on Tehran and threats of escalation to chemical warfare catalyzed fear among its residents and signifi-cantly contributed to Ayatollah Ruhollah Khomeini's decision to end the war.[4]

Missiles had been used since the beginning of hostilities in the Iran–Iraq War. Iran and Iraq had been engaged in missile strikes on cities from the be-ginning of the war. Saddam Hussein had very little compunction in striking targets that would put Iranian civilians in gross danger. As detailed below, in a 6 October 1980 conversation with his military leaders, Saddam Hussein demanded striking the Karnak Dam, hoping to flood Tehran and, failing that, destroy a vital power plant even though his military advisors seemed doubtful of the utility of such a strike.[5]

SADDAM HUSSEIN: This dam has a power plant as well.

PLANNING DIRECTOR: Yes, Sir, an electrical power plant. . . . The technicians from the Ministry of Irrigation were with us and they will draw up a work plan for both dams and what will be submerged by these dams? . . . The two dams that Your Excellency pointed out are located northeast and northwest of Tehran, one of them is located

---

Bombing to Provoke. Jaganath Sankaran, Oxford University Press. © Oxford University Press 2024.
DOI: 10.1093/oso/9780197792629.003.0004

48   Bombing to Provoke

near Karag and I think it is used to provide water to the city of Tehran, also to provide limited amounts of water to the district of Tehran

SADDAM HUSSEIN: And the dam would flood Tehran.

PLANNING DIRECTOR: Sir, according to our information and the information provided by the
Ministry of Irrigation, it is not of the magnitude that Your Excellency is suggesting.

SADDAM HUSSEIN: It would not flood it?

PLANNING DIRECTOR: No, Sir.

SADDAM HUSSEIN: Are there any power plants on it?

PLANNING DIRECTOR: Yes, there is one power plant on it, Sir.

SADDAM HUSSEIN: Then let us strike it. We are not losing anything whether or not Tehran is
flooded. The damage would be in the power plant.

Saddam Hussein repeatedly struck Iranian cities with missiles aiming to
coerce its leaders into capitulation. The Iranians reciprocated with limited
missile strikes and aerial bombardment of Iraqi cities. However, a combination of very low launch rates and poor targeting accuracies ensured that the
effect of Iraqi missile strikes was limited.[6] Soon civilians in targeted Iranian
cities found ways to survive the Iraqi missile attacks.[7]

However, missile warfare quickly obtained surprising potency in 1988.
Iranians could no longer ignore Iraqi missile strikes. The successful use of
chemical warfare on the battlefield in 1988 instilled fear of further Iraqi
escalation in the minds of Iranians. Iranians feared an imminent Iraqi ballistic missile bombardment with chemical warheads on their cities.[8] These
fears were amplified by the failure of the international community to condemn Iraq's use of chemical weapons against civilians in the Kurdish town
of Halabja.[9] Such fears played a major part in the Iranian decision to accept the ceasefire with Iraq.[10] Several other factors were necessary for the
Iranian capitulation.[11] However, the threat of chemically armed ballistic
missile strikes was one of the crucial factors in coercing the Iranians to
concede.

The strategic and psychological impact of potential chemically armed ballistic missile strikes on Tehran and other cities was immense. By threatening
an escalation to chemical warfare, the Iraqi missile strikes had a clear and decisive coercive impact on Iranian willpower.[12] The rest of the chapter develops
these arguments in detail. The following section provides a brief historical
background to the Iran–Iraq War. The third section outlines the military balance of power at the beginning of the war. Next, it discusses how the balance of
power evolved between the belligerents as the war progressed. The fourth section examines how the Iraqis weaponized the fear of chemically weapons and
ballistic missiles. The fifth section details how the lack of military responses

diminished Iranian political resolve and forced its decisionmakers to capitulate. Finally, the sixth section summarizes the influence of ballistic missiles on the outcome of the Iran–Iraq War.

The History and Politics of the Dispute

At the core of the territorial dispute between Iran and Iraq was the Shatt al-Arab waterway, a water body connecting the Persian Gulf to Basra in Iraq and Khorramshahr and Abadan in Iran.[13] At the beginning of the 20th century, the newly independent states of Iran and Iraq were demarcating their boundaries, which had a long and contested history.[14] Iraq demanded sovereignty over the entire Shatt al-Arab waterway. On the other hand, Iran demanded that it be divided along the deepest location (i.e., the midpoint) of the waterway—the *thalweg* principle. Additionally, Iran argued that both states should have freedom of navigation in the waterway and the right to station warships.[15] A 1936 coup led to a weak Iraqi government. As a result, Iraq was forced to sign the 1937 Iran–Iraq Frontier Treaty and, arguably, conceded to the *thalweg* principle.[16] The Treaty gave Iran control of the island of Abadan and the Shatt al-Arab, up to the midpoint of the waterway for 5 miles around Khorramshahr.[17] However, the agreement gave Iraq complete control over the rest of the Shatt al-Arab waterway and the right to collect tolls from transitioning ships.[18]

Iran and Iraq managed to keep their dispute in stasis for the next 20 years. However, beginning in 1958, Iraq suffered a series of military coups. As a way to relieve internal political pressures, the new Iraqi government espoused an aggressive posture toward Iran and made several territorial demands from the Iranians.[19] In response, Iran's ruler, Mohammad Reza Shah Pahlavi, revived demands that the *thalweg* principle be extended to the entire Shatt al-Arab waterway.[20] In 1969, Iran's Shah regime abrogated the 1937 Treaty.

By late 1971, as the British were disengaging from their imperial control of the Gulf region, they coordinated with the United States to strengthen the regime of Iran's Shah.[21] Iran's Shah, supported by the United States, the United Kingdom, and Israel, started to support the Kurdish guerillas in an attempt to destabilize Iraq.[22] As tensions escalated significantly, Iran and Iraq attempted to reconcile. The Algiers Agreement (formally called the Iran–Iraq Treaty on International Borders and Good Neighborly Relations) was signed in 1975 by the Shah of Iran and Saddam Hussein, then vice-president of Iraq, to delimit their boundaries in accordance with the *thalweg* principle and to desist from supporting subversive activities in each other's territories.[23] Iraqis, and Saddam Hussein, saw the Algiers Agreement as a victory for Iran. "Baghdad swallowed the bitter pill" after being "harassed and exhausted by the Iranian-backed Kurdish insurgency to the point where it was left with only three bombs for its air force."[24]

Ayatollah Khomeini came to power in the 1979 Iranian Revolution, after the overthrow of the Shah. The ascension of Khomeini led to a combination of misperceptions and inflated expectations by both sides that started and then prolonged the Iran–Iraq War. Saddam Hussein feared that Iran's Shiite revolution would spread to Iraq and destabilize his regime. On this point, Saddam Hussein may have been right. Khomeini attempted to destabilize the secular Baathist regime, hoping the Shia majority in Iraq would revolt against Saddam Hussein.[25] After early attempts at reconciliation failed, Saddam Hussein felt that there was no modus vivendi to be found with the radical Khomeini, whose ideology demanded the overthrow of the Baathist Iraqi regime and the establishment of a Shiite order in Iraq.[26]

Saddam Hussein also hoped that taking on Iran would give him regional supremacy in the Arab world.[27] In starting the war, he misperceived the impact war would have on revolutionary Iran. Saddam Hussein hoped for a quick disintegration of Khomeini's regime or a rush by the Ayatollah to sue for peace and accept limited territorial losses. Saddam Hussein and his Baathist compatriots presumed the Arab majorities in the Iranian province of Khuzestan would join the Iraqi army in liberating the region.[28] He hoped for quick territorial gains in the oil-rich Khuzestan province.[29] He was gravely wrong. The war (*jang-i tahmili*) galvanized Iranian society.[30] The war morphed into a central feature of the revolution unfolding in Iran.[31] The Iranian clergy embraced the war as an opportunity to eliminate Iraq's blasphemous Baathist regime.[32] However, having embraced the absolute goal of overthrowing Saddam Hussein, Ayatollah Khomeini continued the war long after it had stopped serving Iranian interests. Despite severe casualties and losses, Khomeini refused to accept several ceasefire proposals and insisted on a total victory in the war between Islam and the blasphemous regime of Saddam Hussein.[33]

Once drawn into the war, the Iranian leadership discounted their military weaknesses and assumed they could substitute religious zeal for military acumen. Ayatollah Khomeini, in one of his speeches, declares, "the cause of God can never be defeated, nor is there any turning back from it."[34] Similarly, Akbar Hashemi Rafsanjani, the Speaker of the Iranian Parliament, declared that the faith of the Iranian troops was superior to Iraq's firepower.[35] As the war dragged on, the zeal of Iranian youth diminished, leaving Iran at a disadvantage against a better-armed foe.

The Military Balance of Power

In 1980, at the beginning of the Iran–Iraq War, Iran and Iraq had significant quantities of modern weaponry (see Table 4.1). Revolutionary Iran was in possession of weaponry acquired from the United States under the Shah regime, while Iraq had well-developed arms-supply arrangements with the Soviet Union and France. However, both sides quickly used up their weapons cache and became dependent on foreign replenishment. During the remaining years of war, all major Western powers and the Soviet Union provided advanced weapons to Iraq while denying such assistance to Iran. Iraq managed to import a much larger quantity and variety of weapons during the war.[36] As Table 4.1 shows, the balance of

Table 4.1 Iraqi & Iranian military order of battle

	Iraq		Iran	
	1980	1988	1980	1988
Armed forces strength and ratio				
Total armed forces	242,250	1,000,000	246,000	644,800
Armed force personnel/1000 inhabitants	18.9	63.3	6.3	13.2
Ground forces				
Active army force personnel	200,000	955,000	150,000	305,000
Reserve army force personnel	250,000	–	400,000	350,000
Active para-military personnel	250,000	250,000	–	600,000
Reserve para-military personnel	–	400,000	–	3,050,000
Battle tanks	2,500	4,500	1740	1575
Armored fighting vehicles	2,000	3,200	1075	1800
Artillery equipment	1,000	2,800	1000	1750
Air forces				
Active air force personnel	38,000	40,000	70,000	39,800
Aircraft	335	484	445	90
Helicopters	250	372	750	423
Naval forces				
Active naval personnel	4,250	5,000	26,000	50,000
Destroyers and frigates	1	1	7	8
Mine warfare vessels	8	8	–	5
Missile craft	12	8	9	10

Adapted from Dilip Hiro, *The Longest War: The Iran–Iraq Military Conflict* (New York: Routledge Chapman & Hall, Inc., 1991), 297, 299.

military power had shifted significantly toward Iraq by 1988, when the war ended.

During the Shah regime, Iran was the recipient of high-technology exports from Western states, while Iraq was denied such weaponry.[37] But, after the Islamic revolution, weapons export and support to Iran dried up very quickly. The United States decided that revolutionary Iran had to be contained. The siege of the American embassy in 1979 and the unfolding hostage crisis further cemented American concerns about the radical nature of the new regime in Iran.[38] The American government started to view Saddam Hussein as a potential ally against Iran. In a 14 December 1983 State Department memo, William Eagleton, the head of US interest in Baghdad, equated "any major reversals of Iraq's fortunes as a strategic defeat for the West."[39] The memo was written for Ambassador Donald Rumsfeld, who was scheduled to meet with Tariq Aziz and Saddam Hussein to explore cooperation and restore diplomatic relations. Similarly, Secretary of State George Shultz writes in his autobiography that, by early 1984, Iran's forces "were pushing the Iraqi army back inside Iraq, and soon they could threaten Kuwait and Saudi Arabia. . . . Iraq's retreat as the numerically far greater Iranian forces swept forward was all too apparent. If Iraq collapsed, that could not only intimidate but inundate our friends in the Gulf and be a strategic disaster for the United States."[40] Opinion was coalescing within the US government to provide Iraq access to weapons and other support.[41]

In a 1994 National Security Decision Directive (NSSD 139), fearing an Iraqi military defeat, the Reagan administration decided on three immediate steps to support the Iraqi regime.[42] First, the NSSD advocated for indirect security assistance and improved intelligence sharing to strengthen Iraq's defense against Iran.[43] Second, the NSSD advocated arranging overt and covert assistance to Iraq from friendly states such as France and Jordan.[44] Third, the NSSD advocated condemning the use of chemical weapons while simultaneously emphasizing Iran's ruthless and inhuman combat tactics and its unwillingness to accept ceasefire proposals designed to end the war.

The Soviet Union started with a neutral disposition at the beginning of the Iran–Iraq War but quickly shifted to supporting Iraq with a massive influx of weapons and arms.[45] The Soviet Union was strictly neutral until 1982, denying Iraq weaponry.[46] In 1983, the Soviet Union signed an agreement with Iraq valued at $230 million to expedite the supply of weapons and the establishment of rocket and aircraft repair facilities in Iraq.[47] By 1986, the Soviets offered Iraq an arms deal package that included more than 2,000 tanks (including 800 T-72s), 300 fighter aircraft, 300 surface-to-surface missiles, and other heavy artillery weapons and armored personnel carriers.[48]

Iraq, financed by other Arab states, was soon the recipient of a comprehensive arsenal of weapons throughout the Iran–Iraq War.[49] Iran, however, was denied all access to Western and Soviet arms. Iran's source of weaponry was limited to China, North Korea, Syria, and Libya. After 1986, the United States rigorously implemented Operation Staunch, further cutting off Iran's access to essential spares, maintenance equipment, and new weapons.[50] As the war intensified, Iran had to cannibalize parts and pay heftily to maintain its military equipment.[51]

Further limiting Iran's war-waging ability was the loss of trained and experienced military personnel.[52] Ayatollah Khomeini believed the Iranian army inherited from the Shah regime was disloyal and counterrevolutionary. Therefore, Khomeini and the new rulers of Iran systematically purged the Iranian armed forces with executions or forcible retirements, while several others fled, fearing persecution.[53] The *Pasdaran*, otherwise known as the Iranian Revolutionary Guards, was established by the new Iranian regime. The Iranians also instituted the *Basij* or *Basij e-mustazafin*, the voluntary militia. However, neither the *Pasdaran* nor the *Basij* had the military acumen of a professional army.

Weaponizing Fear: Chemical Weapons and Ballistic Missiles

Since the beginning of the Iran–Iraq War, Saddam Hussein had searched for ways to use chemical weapons to his advantage. In 1981, Saddam Hussein had indicated a desire to weaponize his missiles with chemical and biological warheads to strike fear among Iranians by striking military and civilian targets.[54] In a conversation with his military advisors, he suggests immediately exploring such programs.[55]

Saddam Hussein and his military leaders constantly threatened Iran with chemical warfare, hoping to coerce the Iranian decisionmakers to end the war on preferential terms. The Iraqi military high command issued a statement in September 1983 warning that chemical weapons "will be used for the first time in war . . . were not used in previous attacks for humanitarian and ethical reasons. . . . If you execute the orders of Khomeini's warmongering regime and go to the fronts, your death will be certain because this time we will use a weapon that will destroy any moving creature on the fronts."[56]

In a 1984 *Time* magazine article, Iraqi Major General Sabah al Fakhri declared an intent to expand the use of chemical weapons against the Iranian armed forces. He stated, "If a superpower threatened the US, what would it

54 Bombing to Provoke

do? We too have our dignity and honor. We are not going to meet the invader with flowers and perfume. We are going to use all available means at our disposal to defend the nation."[57] In the same article, the commander of the Iraqi Third Corps, Major General Maher Abed al Rashid, stated that "If you gave me some insecticide that I could squirt at this swarm of mosquitos, I would use it so that they would be exterminated, thus benefiting humanity by saving the world from these pests."[58]

By 1982, the Iraqis had used chemical weapons on the battlefield, albeit inefficiently.[59] In December 1983, Iraqis used chemical bombs during the Ramadan Operation.[60] During the 1984 Khaybar and 1985 Badr Operations, Iraqis used chemical bombs and shells against Iranian forces.[61] However, the Iraqi operations were executed ineptly.[62] Iranian regular military, the *Pasdaran*, and the volunteer *Basij* forces managed to survive and succeed in these battles despite Iraqi use of chemical weapons. During the 1986 Val Fajr-8 Operation, Iraqis again used chemical weapons on Iranian forces without any significant effect. Iranian forces also managed to strike an Iraqi chemical weapons depot in the Al-Faw peninsula during the Val Fajr-8 Operation, exposing several Iraqi troops to these chemical weapons.[63]

At the end of the Val Fajr-8 Operation, the Iranians captured significant Iraqi territory in the Al-Faw peninsula, south of Basra.[64] The occupation of the Al-Faw peninsula threatened to deny Iraq its only outlet to the Gulf and, therefore, its ability to export oil. The occupation also threatened Basra, a large Iraqi city, and placed Iranian troops close to Kuwait and Saudi Arabia, states that were financially supporting the Iraqi campaign against Iran.[65] In early 1988, Iranian troops and anti-Baath Iraqi Kurds launched the Val Fajr-10 Operation and threatened to seize the Dharbandikhan Dam, a vital source of electricity to Baghdad.

Iraq responded vigorously. Iraqi battlefield use of chemical weapons took on a renewed scope, scale, and efficacy in March 1988.[66] On 17 and 18 March 1988, Saddam Hussein executed a massive and brutal chemical campaign against Iranian troops and their Kurdish collaborators, gassing the town of Halabja.[67] Lieutenant General Ra'ad Majid Rashid al-Hamdani, who commanded and served as a staff officer in various armored and reconnaissance units during the Iran–Iraq War, recounts that the Iraqi Republican Guard launched 720 chemical missiles. He also notes that the Iraqi artillery battalions launched nearly 200 artillery shells.[68] In addition, the Iraqi air force carried out 20 bombing missions to deliver chemical agents into Halabja.[69] Lieutenant General al-Hamdani describes the Halabja chemical attack as a highly effective campaign that obliterated Iran's 84th division.[70] The chemical attack also decimated the Kurdish civilian population in Halabja.

The Halabja campaign was exceedingly brutal.[71] It was also militarily successful. Iranian forces abandoned their positions and retreated. The chemical attacks also succeeded in dislodging a decades-long insurgency that had until very recently been able to control, much to Saddam Hussein's chagrin, large swaths of territory in Iraq's north.[72]

After Halabja, Saddam Hussein and his military leadership pressed forward to retain their momentum against Iran. The Iraqi military trained extensively in employing chemical weapons. Using satellite imagery obtained from the United States, the Iraqi armed forces recreated the details of the Iranian military field positions in training camps. They practiced maneuvers to strike Iranian troops in the upcoming Al-Faw campaign.[73] As a result, Iraqi chemical warfare became increasingly potent on the battlefield in the last year of the war. Additionally, by 1988, Saddam Hussein was willing to suspend his distrust of the Iraqi military. He supported military professionalism and promoted capable officers over political, regional, or tribal loyalties.[74] He was also willing to loosen command and control prerogatives on the use of chemical weapons to facilitate military efficiency. A declassified CIA document asserts that the delegation of chemical weapons release authority to military commanders permitted better integration of chemical weapons into Iraqi battlefield planning.[75]

On 17 and 18 April 1988, Iraqi forces used more than 100 tons of chemical weapons against occupying Iranian troops in the Al-Faw peninsula.[76] Lieutenant General al-Hamdani indicates that when the reports from the battlefield came in, the Iraqi commanders were surprised at how quickly they had managed to liberate Al-Faw.[77] A CIA estimate makes a similar claim, noting that "the suddenness and severity of this attack disrupted Iranian command and control, decimated key units, and threw the Iranian defenders into disarray. The resulting victory took only 30 hours, which surprised even the Iraqi military planners."[78] The Al-Faw campaign terrified Iranian troops.[79]

The defeat at Al-Faw was a major military and psychological setback for the Iranian troops and their leaders. A succession of military routs followed the Iranian collapse at Al-Faw. At the end of April 1988, Saddam Hussein ordered a second offensive on Iranian troops stationed near Basra. The Iraqi army was able to regain its lost territories in 10 hours.[80] At the end of the Basra offensive, Iraqis captured 100 Iranian tanks and more than 100 artillery pieces.[81] The Iranian forces were thoroughly defeated, and any chance of overwhelming Saddam Hussein's forces disappeared.[82] After Al-Faw, the Iraqis quickly followed up with massed chemical attacks in successful battles at Fish Lake and Majnoon Islands.[83]

56　Bombing to Provoke

Iraq's battlefield victories began to diminish the Iranian resolve. During the early stages of the Iran–Iraq war, Iran initially benefitted from a population willing to die for the sake of the Islamic revolution.[84] In the early years of the war, volunteer *Basij* forces provided more troops than the *Pasdaran* could train and arm.[85] Ayatollah Khomeini and Iran's other revolutionary leaders manipulated the concept of martyrdom to push human waves of poorly trained but highly motivated *Basij* forces against the Iraqi army.[86] At the beginning of the war, schoolboys were recruited into the *Basij* hastily with "Passports to Paradise" application forms, offered rudimentary training, and pushed into the battlefield against fortified Iraqi positions.[87] However, as the war dragged on, the enthusiasm of the Iranian armed forces and its population waned and dissipated. By 1988, Iranian leaders could not recruit soldiers to sustain the war with Iraq.

Iraq's battlefield victories were followed by Iraqi threats to target Tehran with Scud missiles armed with chemical warheads if Iran did not accept a ceasefire agreement to end the war.[88] In March 1988, Iraqi officials leaked to the international press that they would target several Iranian cities with chemical weapons to punish the Iraqi leadership.[89] Documents retrieved from the Saddam Hussein regime offer evidence that the Iraqis were seriously debating such measures. In a 24 March 1988 conversation among senior members of the Iraqi leadership, Brigadier General Hussein Kamil, the head of Iraqi Military Industries, declares

> my personal point of view is that the war will stop when Iraq becomes capable of deeply harming the Iranians at the front lines—and not only at the front lines. . . . Harming the enemy in locations deep inside Iran and its cities [is a way to] reach the [Mullahs] in Tehran, who do not see, do not hear, who are secluded in rooms, and do not care about the thousands who die there. . . . The ability to harm Iran deep inside, in their main cities, as well as on the battlefield, is what is required of us.[90]

Similarly, in a 6 March 1987 conversation with his advisors, Saddam Hussein seemed to support striking Iranian cities with chemical weapons.[91] The conversation unfolds as follows:

ABDUL-GHANI ABDUL-GHAFUR: Sir, I support the opinion to strike cities because cities have residents and economic facilities. Striking cities has a psychological effect that frustrates the Persian enemy and reveal's Khomeini's deception . . . and leads the Iranians themselves to hate him. It is true that [striking the] economic facilities slows down the Persian economy, but at the same time, striking the cities has economic and psychological effects that we need. The type of cities to strike must be, certainly, important cities with a deeper impact, if possible, but at the same time this is an issue to be left to the General Command and to Your Excellency. . . . On March 21, the situation escalates inside Iran on a large scale and I believe if there is a possibility to strike them at that time inside the cities, any city, it could have a psychological effect as far as defeating the Persian enemy, and a higher positive psychological effect for the Iraqis . . .

SA'DOUN HAMMADI: Is the chemical weapon as effective as we think? I mean the way we think of it as civilians?

SADDAM HUSSEIN: Yes, it's effective against those who do not use masks momentarily, just like the way we as civilians think of it.

SA'DOUN HAMMADI: You mean it exterminates by the thousands?

SADDAM HUSSEIN: Yes, it exterminates by the thousands. It exterminates by the thousands and make them restrain from drinking or eating the available food and makes them leave the city for a period of time until it is fully decontaminated [inaudible background comments]. They can do nothing, they cannot sleep on a mattress, eat, drink or anything; they will leave [inaudible] naked.

Iraq had already begun targeting Tehran and other Iranian cities with its Scud missile arsenal.[92] The threat of chemical attacks on cities further amplified the potency of these missile strikes. The Iraqi leadership threatened to destroy Iranian cities using "all available weapons" until Iran agreed to end the war.[93] Staff Colonel Abd al-Wahhab al-Saeidy, an Iraqi military officer, suggests that the Iraqis had also signaled to Khomeini that if he did not halt the war, Iraq would launch chemically armed ballistic missiles at Iranian cities.[94]

Iranian political leaders and citizens grew increasingly fearful of an Iraqi chemical weapons strike on Iranian cities. Almost one-fourth of the 10 million Tehran residents fled the city, living with family outside the city or in evacuation camps provided by the Iranian government.[95] Iranian leaders were unable to reassure citizens or prevent the exodus out of Tehran. Iranian Parliamentary Speaker Ali Akbar Hashemi Rafsanjani stated in an Iranian news conference, "we didn't request the people to leave their houses . . . but we encourage them to be far away from danger; we are very anxious about our people."[96] A Tehran radio program demonstrated a warning signal for a chemical weapons attack with "three beeps" and offered steps for civilians to protect themselves after an attack.[97] The Tehran radio commentator gloomily observed, "God willing, we hope such a thing will never happen . . . [but] the enemy is so mean, it could do anything."[98] Iranian popular support and resolve had faded. Iranians were gripped by fear.

Iraq had successfully weaponized fear, and its Scud ballistic missiles were an essential variable in the factors that catalyzed fear in the minds of Iranians.

The Political and Military Response

Iran did not have a political or a military riposte to Iraq's missile warfare in 1988. Iran and Iraq had been engaged in protracted air and missile campaigns throughout the eight years of war. These air and missile campaigns—the War of the Cities—had become routine. At least four iterations of the War of the Cities had transpired by the beginning of 1988. The first War of the Cities occurred in February 1984. In the first iteration, Iraq targeted 11 Iranian cities with ballistic missiles.[99] The second iteration of the War of the Cities occurred between 22 March and 8 April 1985. Until early 1985, only Iraq possessed missiles. However, in March 1985, Iran obtained Scud-B missiles from Libya and promptly launched them against Iraq.[100] The third iteration of the War of the Cities occurred 17–25 January 1987. The fourth iteration of the War of the Cities occurred February–April 1987.[101]

The fifth iteration of the War of the Cities in 1988 was different. Iraq now had three distinct advantages. First, Iraq had acquired a vast arsenal of Soviet missiles.[102] Second, by 1988, Iraq had indigenously developed a mechanism to extend the range of its Scud missiles. The longer-range Scud derivative, the Al-Hussein ballistic missile, could now reach cities deep inside Iran. For the first time in eight years, Iraq could now target Tehran with ballistic missiles.[103] Finally, Iraq demonstrated the capability and willingness to deploy its chemical weapons with impunity. In the eyes of Iranian decisionmakers, Iraq now seemed to have the geopolitical sanction and the technological capability to fire chemically armed ballistic missiles at Iranian cities.

As the fifth War of the Cities unfolded, Iraq managed to continuously fire three or four ballistic missiles at Tehran daily for 52 days, striking fear among its residents.[104] The fear of chemical attacks caused a quarter of Tehran residents to flee the city, disrupting and weakening the Iranian economy.[105] The regularity of the ballistic missile strikes shocked the Iranian leadership.[106] Iran had no military response to the Iraqi ballistic missile bombardment of Tehran. Iran did not have any missile defense capability. Iran's Army and Air Force did not have the military capability to dissuade the Iraqis from targeting Tehran.

Iran, similarly, had no political or military response to the Iraqi use of chemical weapons. It was utterly vulnerable to the internal political disagreements provoked by the fear of chemical attacks. The Iranian leadership was ideologically ill-prepared to react to Iraqi chemical warfare. At the beginning of the war, Iran's initial reaction to Iraqi chemical warfare was moralistic and diplomatic. Ayatollah Khomeini insisted that the use of chemical weapons was not permitted by Islamic law.[107] Iran sought to highlight Iraqi excesses by providing foreign journalists and diplomats firsthand evidence of Iraq's chemical weapons use. Iran had the United Nations investigate the chemical warfare attacks and dispatched victims to European and Asian capitals hoping to stimulate actions against the Iraqis.[108] However, these measures did not provoke a significant international outcry or attempts to restrain and alter Iraqi behavior. As the war unfolded, Iran found itself without stockpiles of chemical weapons to retaliate against Iraq.[109] Furthermore, Iran's battlefield defensive preparations against chemical warfare were abysmal.[110]

After the excesses of the Halabja and Al-Faw campaigns, Iranians again hoped for a global outcry against Iraq. Iranians broadcasted the horrors of Halabja as evidence of Saddam Hussein's brutality to the world.[111] However, by early 1988, the major powers were leaning heavily toward Iraq, supporting Iraq's demand for a ceasefire and an end to the war. In a 24 April 1988 news article, Elaine Sciolino of the *New York Times* observed that "the Reagan administration's gradual tilt towards Iraq is beginning to look like a full-fledged embrace."[112] US diplomatic efforts shielded Iraq. American efforts delivered a UN Security Council resolution that was the "minimum necessary morally, the maximum possible politically" without unanimously chastising Iraq.[113] American diplomats worked to ensure both Iran and Iraq were criticized for using chemical weaponry.[114] Iran's attempts to galvanize international sanctions against Iraq failed. Iranian Parliament Speaker, Hashemi Rafsanjani, noted in frustration that it was "clear that the moral teachings of the world are not very effective when war reaches a serious stage; the world does not respect its own resolutions, and closes its eyes to the violations and all the aggressions which are committed on the battlefield."[115]

Iran had exhausted all its means. Residents of Tehran feared barrages of Iraqi missiles armed with chemical warheads and were starting to question the utility of continuing to wage war. Iranian soldiers were demoralized and were no longer willing to fight after witnessing the brutality of Iraq's battlefield use of chemical weapons. Furthermore, Iran's propaganda efforts meant to incite young recruits by showing films of Halabja victims at military training schools backfired. Instead, it instilled more fear and weakened support for the war.[116] Iranian soldiers refused to fight a losing battle.[117] Iranian decisionmakers' resolve evaporated. Iranian decisionmakers conceded to the UN resolution and ended the war.

Conclusion

At the beginning of 1987, Iran appeared to be winning the war. Iran had won several battles and seized vital Iraqi territory. Iranians celebrated Iran's battlefield victories publicly and anticipated an end to the war on favorable terms. Khomeini had gone so far as to prematurely issue a *fatwa* declaring the end of the war was to occur in March 1987.[118]

Iranian authorities had constructed an artificial lake in Tehran to recreate a model of the Shatt al-Arab waterway and the Al-Faw peninsula.[119] On the artificial lake, Iranian authorities recreated scenes from the Val Fajr-8 Operation to celebrate the capture of the Al-Faw peninsula from Iraq. The Al-Faw battle was "replayed daily for audiences of up to one hundred thousand, using audiotapes of the actual communications . . . [Iranian troops] surrounding the town of Fao by landing troops in the rear by helicopter, capturing the rocket-launcher sites, and reaching the local salt factory. Then, at the right moment, when the proper offensive got going, sound effects were used to simulate air strikes and artillery and machine-gun fire. The effect was quite electrifying— for the victors and their spectators."[120] Iranian citizens were being told total victory was over the horizon.

The outlook changed drastically for Iran in 1988. Iranian battlefield losses accumulated rapidly in the last year of the war. After the Halabja and Al-Faw reversals, Iranian soldiers were unwilling to fight and die. After the Al-Faw defeat, Iranian troops' commitment to the war disappeared.[121] Iranian forces suffered a string of defeats. Iranian zeal against Saddam Hussein's Baathist regime had dissolved, and its leaders could not reconstitute it.[122] Early in the war, Iranian citizens were willing to suffer through economic hardships, fuel rations, and electricity cuts as long as victory was possible. After the Halabja, Al-Faw, and other defeats, the enthusiasm of the Iranian population could not be sustained.[123] The Iranian population had grown tired of the war. It was now clear Iran was losing. In a bold show of political opposition, Mehdi Bazargan, the head of the only opposition party allowed by Iran, made a scathing public rebuke of the policy of continuing the losing war.[124]

The internal disillusion over the war was compounded by several external factors. Iran was finding itself increasingly at odds with the US Navy in the Persian Gulf. On 14 April 1988, the USS *Samuel B. Roberts* (FFG-58) struck an Iranian mine in the Gulf while escorting Kuwaiti oil tankers.[125] In response, the US Navy launched Operation Praying Mantis, destroying two Iranian naval observation posts, three Iranian warships, and six Iranian naval speedboats[126] On 4 July 1988, USS *Vincennes* (CG 49) mistakenly shot down an Iran Air commercial airliner, killing 290 passengers. Iranian leadership believed the act was intentional and a message meant to highlight Iranian geopolitical isolation.[127]

It was increasingly clear that all the major powers were supporting Iraq. The lack of international outcry over Iraq's massive use of chemical weapons was profoundly discouraging for Iranian decisionmakers. Saddam Hussein and his military leaders astutely exploited the fears of Iran's urban population by threatening barrages of Iraqi missile strikes tipped with chemical warheads.[128] In the end, despite the small scale of the missile campaign, the Iraqi missile campaign achieved its intended effect. The resolve of Iranian leaders and its citizens to continue fighting was lost. Iranian decisionmakers choose to accept a ceasefire they had previously dismissed. Several factors may have led to the Ayatollah's decision to concede and accept the ceasefire resolution, but the fear of ballistic missiles striking Tehran with chemical weapons was a vital factor.

5
Saddam's Scuds

The Scud missiles fired by Saddam Hussein into Israel during the 1991 Gulf War were inaccurate weapons.[1] They did not have the guidance and control subsystems to enable the missile warheads to aim for a target accurately. As a result, the Scud missiles, at first look, appear as an anachronism in a war celebrated for sophisticated weaponry and precision strikes.[2]

The Commander-in-Chief of the Coalition Forces, Norman Schwarzkopf, believed the Scud missiles were ineffective and insignificant to the outcome of the war.[3] Schwarzkopf declared that the Scud "is a pissant weapon that isn't doing a goddam thing. It's insignificant."[4] While Schwarzkopf's characterizations may have been too cavalier, he was not incorrect to question the utility of a Scud missile, or a volley of conventionally armed Scud missiles fired at a target. The Scud missiles did not and could not have mattered from a traditional military perspective that solely measures efficacy in terms of bombardment and damage.[5]

Yet these missiles effectively weaponized fear of impending chemical warfare. The Scud missile strikes provoked the United States and Israel to expend enormous political capital and military resources. Saddam Hussein hoped these provocations would compel the US-led Coalition to hasten its ground assault, leading to American casualties and weakening the resolve of the US-led Coalition. Saddam Hussein hoped that weakening the resolve of the Coalition would enable him to coerce concessions. While Saddam Hussein's attempt at coercing political concessions failed, the Scud missiles proved highly effective at provoking a massive attritional and diversionary military campaign. By the end of the war, the US-led Coalition's Scud-hunting operations required the daily diversion of almost a fighter wing.[6] The US-led Coalition generated approximately 2,500 anti-Scud sorties. In comparison, there were 2,990 sorties against airfields, 1,370 against surface-to-air missiles batteries, 1,170 sorties communication assets, and around 970 sorties against Iraqi nuclear-chemical-biological facilities.[7] Additionally, the United States deployed a force of 400 Delta Commandos to enhance the Scud-hunting operations.[8] Simply put, the Iraqis had made their "pissant weapons" exceedingly

Bombing to Provoke. Jaganath Sankaran, Oxford University Press. © Oxford University Press 2024.
DOI: 10.1093/oso/9780197792629.003.0005

effective tools in provoking the American-led Coalition into a diversionary Scud-hunting military campaign.[9]

The American political leadership mandated the Scud-hunting efforts, often overriding the preferences of military planners.[10] After the first series of Scud had been fired by Iraq into Israel on the night of 19 January 1991, there was a tremendous American political effort to restrain the Israelis from retaliating. The next day Secretary of Defense Dick Cheney erupted in anger after seeing the Air Tasking Order, which indicated a reduction in Scud-hunting missions. Michael Gordon and General Bernard Trainor write, "the defense secretary rarely got angry in public; he was too self-contained and composed for that. Cheney's anger was a cool, icy, disciplined anger, not a hot, shouting rage. But after the briefer ticked off the moderate number of Scud sorties, Cheney erupted."[11] At the meeting that included Colin Powell and other members of the armed forces, Cheney shouted: "Goddamn it, I want some coverage out there. If I have to talk to Schwarzkopf, I'll do it. . . . As long as I am secretary of defense, the Defense Department will do as I tell them. The number one priority is to keep Israel out of the war."[12] The American political leadership continuously demanded a significant military effort be diverted and dedicated solely to the Scud-hunting mission throughout the war.

American political leaders considered the Scud missiles a crucial threat to the goals of the campaign to eject Saddam Hussein's troops from Kuwait. President Bush understood that the principal purpose of Saddam Hussein's Scud attacks was to draw Israel into the war and break up the Coalition.[13] In a 23 January 1991 letter to Israeli Prime Minister Shamir after the first wave of Scud strikes, President Bush implored him to show restraint despite Saddam Hussein's attack on Israel.[14] President Bush wrote

He [Saddam Hussein] is hoping you will respond. Saddam more than anyone knows just how great a price for his ambition and how much the Coalition arrayed against him is accomplishing. We ought not do anything that would risk relieving the pressure he faces. I fear that an Israeli military reprisal, no matter how justified, would do just that.[15]

The George H. W. Bush administration worked tirelessly to keep Israel from retaliating militarily to Iraqi missile strikes. Israel's restraint was purchased by promises of a swift and overwhelming American military response against the Scud menace, even if traditional military threat assessments did not require it. President George H. W. Bush promised Israel "the darndest search-and-destroy effort that's even been undertaken" to suppress the Scud missile campaign.[16]

Bombing to Provoke

The rest of the chapter examines in detail how Saddam Hussein provoked the United States to alter tactics and expend crucial resources on the missile threat. The following section begins by providing a brief historical background to the war. The third section outlines the military balance of power between the belligerents. The fourth section explores the reasons that enabled the Scud missiles to weaponize fear and capitalize on the political vulnerabilities of the United States and Israel. The fifth and sixth sections detail the political and military responses to the fear induced by the Scud missile attacks. Finally, the seventh section concludes with some lessons learned.

The History and Politics of the Dispute

Saddam Hussein grew increasingly paranoid between the end of the Iran–Iraq War in August 1988 and the Iraqi invasion of Kuwait on 2 August 1990. His paranoia was motivated by two fears. First, Saddam Hussein feared that Israel, with American and British assistance, was attempting to impede the progress of Iraq's military-industrial development.[17] Second, he feared that his neighboring Arab states had been co-opted into a Western-Zionist plot to undermine Iraq. Saddam Hussein claimed that Kuwait and other Arab states were driving a "poisoned dagger" into Iraq's back and engaging in economic warfare against it at the behest of Western powers.[18] I examine each of these fears in more detail below.

The Western-Zionist Plot

On 6 October 1989, US Secretary of State James Baker had a tense meeting with Iraq's Foreign Minister, Tariq Aziz. Foreign Minister Aziz accused the US government of interference in Iraq's internal affairs and subverting the legitimate activities of the Iraqi state.[19] Secretary Baker was surprised by these allegations.[20] The conversation prompted Secretary Baker to send a written message later that month to Foreign Minister Aziz, reassuring him that there were no American efforts to weaken or destabilize Iraq.[21]

A few days before the meeting with Foreign Minister Aziz, the George H. W. Bush administration, in its review of Middle East Policy had argued that normal relations between the United States and Iraq was in America's longer-term interests and would also increase political stability in the Middle East.[22] The policy review, National Security Directive 26, further recommended that the United States offer economic and political incentives for Iraq to increase

American influence with the country.[23] The policy review also argued that economic and political engagement with Iraq would serve to moderate Iraqi behavior. The desire to induce moderation in Iraqi behavior was partly driven by the increasing hostility of Iraq toward Israel after the end of the Iran–Iraq War.

In June 1989, for instance, Saddam Hussein sanctioned the construction of several ballistic missile bases, including the H-2 and H-3 bases in western Iraq, that could be used to target Israeli cities with the Al-Hussein and Al-Abbas missiles.[24] The H-2 and H-3 missile bases were conceived as part of an Iraqi deterrent strategy that aimed to threaten massive strikes on Israeli cities using long-range ballistic missiles.[25] In July 1989, Iraqi Mirage F-15E aircraft stationed in Jordan began performing reconnaissance flights along the Israeli–Jordanian border. These flights, in principle, could have provided targeting information, including information on Israel's Dimona nuclear reactor, which was situated 35–40 kilometers from the border.[26] Finally, Iraqi military personnel were suspected of surveying the Israeli–Jordanian border region to identify invasion routes into Israel.[27] All these Iraqi actions were driven by Saddam Hussein's desire to establish a deterrent against Israel. He obsessively worried that Israel was planning to strike Iraqi military facilities in an operation similar to the 1981 strike on the Osirak reactor.[28]

A series of incidents beginning in August 1989 further stoked Saddam Hussein's paranoia. An explosion in mid-August 1989 destroyed an Iraqi military plant associated with Iraq's Condor-2 solid-fuel missile program.[29] Saddam Hussein attributed the explosion at the plant to Israeli sabotage.[30] Immediately after this incident, Iraq arrested Farzad Rabati Bazoft, a 32-year-old Iranian Kurd and a British resident.[31] Iraq charged that Bazoft was spying for Israel. He accused Bazoft of providing targeting information on Iraqi military installations to Israel.[32] Bazoft was sentenced to death.[33] In a speech on 5 January 1990, Saddam Hussein declared, "we want to assert and warn that any attempt by the Zionist entity to strike against our scientific and military installations will be confronted with a precise reaction, using the means available to us according to the legitimate right to self-defense."[34]

Two incidents further cemented Saddam Hussein's belief that Israel, the United States, and Britain were conspiring against Iraq. First, on 22 March 1990, Gerald Bull, a Canadian expert involved in Iraq's experimental long-range artillery research, was assassinated.[35] Saddam Hussein immediately construed the murder as part of an Israeli covert operation to undermine Iraqi military capabilities. Second, on 28 March 1990, American and British officials arrested five individuals for attempting to smuggle high-speed electronic capacitors, known as krytrons, from the United States into Iraq.[36] American and British official alleged that the krytrons were intended for

66   Bombing to Provoke

Iraq's nuclear weapons program. Saddam Hussein characterized the seizure of the krytrons as a "Western-Zionist plot" to deny Iraq its legitimate need for advanced technology.[37] He suggested that these incidents were part of a campaign to recreate the geopolitical conditions to attack Iraq, similar to the Israeli strike on the Osirak reactor.[38]

On 1 April 1990, Saddam Hussein made his infamous speech threatening that the United States was deluded in providing Israel a cover to strike Iraqi industrial facilities. Saddam Hussein announced that he would use chemical weapons and "burn half of Israel" if it tried to attack Iraq.[39] Saddam Hussein's speech was seen as exceedingly incendiary by the United States. US Secretary of State James Baker writes that the speech irrevocably changed the George H. W. Bush administration's strategic views on Iraq.[40] However, there were still attempts to reassure Saddam Hussein.[41] At a 12 April 1990 meeting, Senator Dole conveyed to Saddam Hussein that the American government wanted better relations with Iraq.[42] Following the meeting, Senator Dole advised the Bush administration to engage with him and reduce tensions.[43] Brent Scowcroft responding to Senator Dole, reiterated that the Bush administration believed the United States was better off doing business with Iraq rather than isolating it.[44]

Saddam Hussein was not only spewing vitriol against Israel but also against his Arab neighbors, particularly Kuwait and the United Arab Emirates (UAE). In July 1990, he claimed that both states' were part of the "Imperialist-Zionist plot" against Iraq.[45] The Iraqi Army, meanwhile, was assembling at the Iraqi–Kuwaiti border. The George H. W. Bush administration continued to engage with Saddam Hussein, hoping to dissuade him from any military adventures. A few days before the Iraqi invasion of Kuwait, American ambassador April Glaspie met directly with him to attempt to pacify him.[46] Ambassador Glaspie then sent a cable to Washington urging the Bush administration to temper its criticism of Saddam Hussein's decision to amass troops near the Kuwaiti border.[47] A week later, Saddam Hussein's army invaded Kuwait.

The Poisoned Dagger of the Arab States

Iraq's invasion of Kuwait was a surprise. Neither the Arab states nor the United States had expected it. During the eight-year Iran–Iraq War, Iraq had borrowed and spent $50.5 billion on the purchase of military hardware in addition to approximately between $45 and $55 billion in loans and grants from other Arab states.[48] As a result of the military spending, Iraq's economy was in deep trouble. By late 1989, Iraq was expanding the austerity programs started during the Iran–Iraq War.[49] Additionally, in an attempt to reduce net public expenditure, Iraq demobilized 200,000 soldiers after the war.[50] Saddam Hussein needed urgent financial assistance to rebuild Iraq and restore economic prosperity.

The prevailing belief was Saddam Hussein would secure such assistance by pursuing friendly relations with his Arab neighbors and the West, not through territorial aggression and annexation.[51] Several Arab leaders believed Saddam Hussein was posturing to bargain for financial relief.[52] For example, on 25 July 1990, Egyptian President Hosni Mubarak communicated to the American leadership that he believed Saddam Hussein had no intention of attacking Kuwait.[53] Similarly, five days before the Iraqi invasion of Kuwait, on 29 July 1990, in a phone call to President Bush, King Hussein of Jordan argued that nothing would happen in the region.[54]

The hopes of these Arab leaders were not entirely unjustified. Iraq had built a stable and positive relationship with its Arab neighbors during the Iran–Iraq War. The war brought Iraq, Kuwait, Saudi Arabia, and Jordan together against a common revolutionary foe.[55] During the Iran–Iraq War, Saudi Arabia and Kuwait provided significant financial, diplomatic, and logistical support to Iraq.[56] Kuwait had loaned $2 billion to Iraq interest-free to support its war with Iran.[57] Kuwait supplemented that loan with another $4 billion later.[58] Kuwait was also logistically crucial to Iraq's war efforts against Iran. Kuwait served as a point of disembarkation and a safe transport corridor of vital goods for the Iraqi economy, with 500 to 1,000 heavy trucks moving between Kuwait and Iraq daily.[59] Given all these interactions with Kuwait, it would have been reasonable to presume Iraq's dealing with its Arab neighbor would be congenial.

However, Saddam Hussein believed that Iraq had emerged as the preeminent state in the Arab world. Saddam Hussein began to see himself as the preeminent leader of the Arab nations in the aftermath of the Iran–Iraq War. In a speech at the Arab summit held in May 1990, Saddam Hussein proudly pointed out that Iraq had shed rivers of blood (*anhar al-damm*) and blocked the Eastern Gateway (*al-bawwabah al-shariqiyyah*) to the Arab world against Iranian hordes.[60] In his view, Iraq's brave actions rescued Arab nations from the Iranian revolutionary army.[61] Saddam further argued that Iraq was singularly capable of deterring future Iranian or Israeli aggression. Saddam Hussein then demanded its war debts be canceled. He asked the Arab states—whose very survival was owed to him—to pay for revitalizing the Iraqi economy and its military-industrial infrastructure.[62]

68 Bombing to Provoke

Table 5.1 Armed forces of Iraq and the United States in 1990

Country	Iraq	United States
Total regular armed forces		
Active	1,000,000	2,117,900
Reserves		1,819,300
Ground forces		
Regular army		
Active	955,000	761,100
Reserves	–	1,043,000
Para-military		
Active	250,000	–
Reserves	600,000	
In-service equipment		
Battle tanks	5,500	15,440
Armored combat vehicles	7,500	31,435
Major artillery	3,500	5,725
Combat helicopters	159	1,612
Aircraft		696
Air forces		
Regular air force	40,000	571,000
In-service equipment	689	3,921
Combat aircraft		
Naval forces		
Regular navy	5,000	590,500
In-service equipment		
Surface combatants	5 (frigates)	220
Patrol and coastal combatants	38	30
Mine warfare vessels	8	29
Marine forces		
Regular marine corps	–	195,300
In-service equipment		
Battle tanks	–	716
Armored combat vehicles	–	2,025
Major artillery	–	1,054

Adapted from Dilip Hiro, *Desert Shield to Desert Storm: The Second Gulf War* (London: Harper Collins, 1992), 525.

During the Arab summit speech, Saddam Hussein proceeded to accuse other Gulf countries of exceeding the oil-production quotas set by the Organization of Petroleum Exporting Countries (OPEC). He argued that the action of these Gulf countries had caused oil prices to plummet to $7 per barrel even though OPEC had set production limits to support a price of $18 per barrel.[63] Saddam called the overproduction an "act of war" against Iraq.

He declared, "I must frankly tell you that we have reached a stage where we can no longer take any more pressure."[64] Saddam Hussein demanded that the Gulf states set higher oil prices immediately.[65]

Tariq Aziz, Iraqi Foreign Minister, reiterated President Saddam Hussein's demands in a 15 July 1990 memorandum to the Secretary-General of the Arab League. Foreign Minister Aziz called for the cancelation of Iraqi debts accrued during the Iran–Iraq War.[66] Foreign Minister Aziz outlined a litany of complaints against Kuwait in the memorandum. He named Kuwait as one of the two "culprits" engaged in the overproduction of oil as part of "an imperialist-Zionist plot" against Iraq.[67] Aziz accused Kuwait of cross-drilling into Iraqi territory from 1980 to 1990 and stealing oil from the Rumaila oil field worth $2.4 billion.[68] He claimed Kuwait owed $2.4 billion to Iraq. Finally, re-upping historical grievances, Foreign Minister Aziz claimed that Iraqi–Kuwaiti border delineation remained unsolved due to Kuwaiti intransigence.[69]

Two days later, on 17 July 1990, Saddam accused his Arab neighbors of thrusting a "poisoned dagger" into Iraq's back at the behest of Western imperialist states.[70] Saddam's speech, in hindsight, contained all the elements of a pretext for the military invasion of Kuwait. On 24 July 1990, two Iraqi armored divisions were positioned on the Iraqi–Kuwaiti border and poised to attack.[71] The next day, in a conversation with US Ambassador April Glaspie, Saddam declared that Kuwait was depriving Iraqi people of economic well-being.[72] He then ominously stated: "We don't want war because we know what war means. But do not push us to consider war as the only solution to live proudly and to provide our people with a good living."[73]

Within days, convinced of an Arab-Western-Zionist conspiracy to destroy Iraq, Saddam ordered his troops to invade Kuwait, believing that war was the solution to relieve Iraq's economic pains.

The Military Balance of Power

The Iraqi military was seen as a formidable military power in the prelude to Operation Desert Shield and Desert Storm. While proponents and antagonists debated ferociously on the political merits of the impending conflict, both sides conceded that the Iraqi military was a formidable force, and any conflict would be protracted and bloody. See Table 5.1 for the balance of military forces between the United States and Iraq in 1990.

In a presentation to President Bush immediately after the Iraqi invasion of Kuwait, Schwarzkopf laid out Iraq's military strength.[74] Schwarzkopf began by arguing that Iraq was a formidable foe.[75] He noted that, among the world's standing armies, Saddam Hussein's army was one of the largest.[76] He described Saddam's arsenal of weaponry as some of the best in the region.[77] The Iraqi armed forces possessed Soviet T-72 tanks, South African 155-mm heavy artillery, advanced multiple rocket launchers, a robust arsenal of advanced anti-ship missiles, Soviet MiG-29 fighters and Su-24 long-range fighter-bombers, French M-1 Mirage fighters, etc.[78]

Schwarzkopf, however, noted that centralized command and control, lack of offensive experience against a technically advanced military adversary, and dependence on foreign supplies for spare parts were significant weaknesses of the Iraqi army.[79] As it later turned out, the actual Iraqi military fighting capacity lagged far behind the potential of its weapons inventory. In particular, the Iraqi air force, despite its potential on paper as a modern air force was incapable of any offensive action against the Coalition or Israel.[80] Within 10 days of the Coalition's air campaign, nearly 75 of the Iraqi air force's state-of-the-art fighter aircraft fled to Iran. The rest of the Iraqi air force fleet hunkered down in bunkers ceding complete control of Iraqi airspace to American forces.

A very detailed Order of Battle handbook published by the US Army Intelligence and Threat Analysis Center (USAITAC) and distributed widely to military personnel deployed to Iraq reiterated Schwarzkopf's preliminary evaluation. The handbook warned that the Iraqi Army, the eighth largest at the time of the hostilities, is "one of the best equipped and most combat-experienced in the world."[81] Stressing the potential of the Iraqi army to fight the Coalition forces, the handbook suggested that the Iraqi Army could conduct multi-corps combined-arms operations with air support.[82]

Even days before the start of armed hostilities, American military leaders did not anticipate the overwhelming victory that awaited the Coalition troops. Schwarzkopf, describing his expectation a week before the war, writes: "we knew we would win, but we had no idea what our casualties would be, how the American public would react, or even whether the coalition would hold together."[83]

Saddam Hussein vigorously attempted to exploit these doubts, fears, and other perceived political vulnerabilities. He firmly believed that the balance of resolve favored him while presuming that American casualty aversion weakened President Bush's resolve. In a conversation with the American ambassador, April Glaspie, before the invasion of Kuwait, Saddam declared to her: "yours is a society which cannot accept 10,000 dead in one battle . . . everyone can cause harm according to their ability and their size . . . we would not care if you fired one hundred missiles for each missile we fired."[84] On 18 January 1991—a day before the start of the war—Saddam Hussein, repeated his warning that rivers of American blood would be shed.[85]

Saddam Hussein's strategy was simple: use the Scud missiles to provoke the Israelis and force the Coalition forces to attempt a premature ground assault.[86] Saddam Hussein believed such a premature assault would have led to heavy casualties, popular domestic disillusionment among the states in the Coalition, and, eventually, withdrawal from the war.[87] Saddam's war-winning strategy was not very complex. He hoped the Americans would retreat if he could inflict 10,000 casualties with his army of almost a million armed with advanced weapon systems.[88]

Weaponizing Fear: Scuds and Weapons of Mass Destruction

Iraq possessed a well-equipped arsenal of missiles and weapons of mass destruction (WMD). Iraq—aided by German, Austrian, and Italian technology infusion and expertise—had established an advanced industrial capability to manufacture ballistic missiles.[89] By 1990, Iraq had the means to produce the Al-Hussein and Al-Abbas ballistic missiles.[90] The Al-Hussein missile had been employed against Iran in the War of the Cities military campaign. It had a range of approximately 650 kilometers and an accuracy of 500 meters.[91] The Al-Abbas missile was tested in April 1988.[92] Both missiles had poor targeting accuracies, making them useful only as terror weapons against large cities.[93] In addition, Iraq had another solid-fuel missile, the Tamuz I (or Fahd), under development.[94] US Intelligence agencies also suspected that the Soviet Union had supplied SS-21 and SS-12 missiles to Iraq at the end of the Iran–Iraq War.[95] In addition, Iraq had also started production of chemical and biological warheads to amplify the coercive powers of its ballistic missile arsenal.[96] In 1990, Iraq was presumed to have produced over a thousand tons of chemical weapons including mustard gas blister agents and the nerve agents sarin and tabun.[97] Iraq was also believed to possess a viable biological weapons arsenal.[98] Iraq was suspected of stockpiling botulin toxin.[99]

While Iraq's conventional capabilities had given pause to American military planners, Saddam's arsenal of missiles and chemical and biological weapons were feared to be a significant impediment to any military action against the Iraqi forces.[100] A CIA estimate warned, "the Iraqis have at least a limited number of chemical warheads for their Scud and modified-Scud missiles . . . the nonpersistent nerve agent sarin and the semipersistent nerve agent GF would be the most likely fills for such warheads. The Iraqis might even have some warheads filled with the persistent nerve agent VX."[101]

A postwar estimation by UN inspectors suggested that Iraq had 70 warheads armed with sarin gas for its Scud missiles.[102]

American and Israeli leaders were constantly worried about the possibility of a chemical or biological weapons attack by Saddam Hussein. Saddam Hussein actively manipulated such worries. In December 1990, Iraqi Parliament Speaker Sadi Mehdi publicly announced Iraq would use chemical weapons to defend itself on and off the battlefield.[103] After a 9 January 1991 meeting with US Secretary of State James Baker, Iraqi Foreign Minister Tariq Aziz declared, "if Iraq was attacked by American and other forces . . . Baghdad would 'absolutely' respond by attacking Israel."[104] Saddam Hussein, similarly, had declared that "Tel Aviv would receive the first blow" if Iraq was attacked irrespective of whether or not Israel joins any multinational Coalition.[105]

American and Israeli leaders made several preparations in anticipation of Iraqi chemical weapons warfare. A comprehensive effort was undertaken to procure vaccines, antibiotics, and military gear that could enable US forces to operate in a contaminated environment.[106] Schwarzkopf notes in his autobiography that he expected extensive use of such weapons once the offensive operations began.[107] He writes

> my nightmare was that our units would reach the barriers in the very first hours of the attack, be unable to get through, and then be hit with a chemical barrage . . . they'd end up milling around in confusion—or worse, they'd panic. The United States has not fought in a gas attack since World War I. The possibility of mass casualties from chemical weapons was the main reason we had sixty-three hospitals, two hospital ships, and eighteen thousand beds ready in the war zone.[108]

Similarly, the Israeli leadership was worried about Scuds armed with chemical warheads striking cities. Moshe Arens, the Israeli defense minister, writes that Israel's "primary concern was the danger of chemical weapons . . . [Israelis] were told to carry their gas masks with them wherever they went."[109]

The Political Response to the Fear of Scud Attacks

Saddam Hussein's incessant threats worried the Israelis. Israeli leaders, hoping to deter him, repeatedly signaled that any attack would provoke swift retaliation. In April 1990, the Director-General of Israel's Ministry of Defense, Major General (Res.) David Ivri argued that Israel's "morale or psychology" would be forever altered even if a "few missiles" fell on Tel Aviv.[110] He suggested that the Israeli population would not accept it and would demand military action.[111]

On 9 August 1990, Israeli Prime Minister Yitzhak Shamir warned that any attack on Israel would lead to a "great disaster" for the aggressor.[112] A week later, Israeli Defense Minister Moshe Arens warned Saddam Hussein that he would encounter "a forceful Israeli response" if Israel were attacked.[113] On 26 September 1990, Israel's Foreign Minister David Levy warned that "whoever attacks Israel won't live to remember it."[114] Levy followed up on his warning in a speech to the UN General Assembly declaring Israel's retribution would be severe if Saddam Hussein launched his missiles against Israel.[115]

Saddam Hussein's threats to attack Israel and Israeli promises of retaliation led to serious concerns in the George H. W. Bush administration. President Bush notes in memoirs that "Israel remained very carefully placed outside the coalition" to obtain Arab participation in the efforts to restore Kuwait's sovereignty.[116] He writes that the Coalition would not survive if Israel was involved in the military effort to eject Saddam Hussein's forces from Kuwait.[117] Colin Powell, the chairman of the Joint Chiefs of Staff, similarly writes about "the supersensitive need to keep Israel out of the fight."[118] He writes that Arab states would not tolerate fighting alongside Israel against a fellow Arab state.[119]

Saddam Hussein well understood these political constraints animating the Bush administration's decisionmaking. The threat to attack Israel was a strategic ploy by Saddam Hussein. Popular opinion in the Arab world might have required other Arab members of the Coalition to break away if Israel had launched an offensive against Iraq. Conceivably, even Iran may have had to side with Iraq.[120] For all these reasons, Saddam Hussein wanted to provoke the Israelis into retaliating. His goal was to engineer a split in the Coalition.[121]

As the possibility of military hostilities became increasingly apparent, President Bush's worries increased. Bush recounts the severe political challenges he faced in defeating Saddam Hussein's ploy to break up the Coalition.[122] In a meeting with Israeli President Shamir on 11 December 1990, at the Oval Office, President Bush promised to vigorously strike at Saddam Hussein's forces if Israel was attacked.[123] He then asked for Israeli restraint, noting, "I know your position about responding to an attack and I respect it. But if we could consult first, our preference would be for Israel not to respond until you have seen our reply. We have common objectives, and I would like to fulfil them."[124]

The Israelis understood the American political imperative to keep Israel out of the Coalition.[125] President Shamir, however, countered that the Israeli government was obliged to defend its people. He responded that Israel would initiate military actions against Iraq if its national interest demanded such an action.[126] Israeli leaders continued to threaten a forceful response to any missile strikes by Saddam Hussein on Israel. On 9 January 1991, a week before the

74 Bombing to Provoke

beginning of the war, Foreign Minister Levy, in a conversation with a visiting US Congressional delegation, announced that Israel would retaliate if the protection of its citizens required such an action.[127] The next day, Israeli Defense Minister Moshe Arens publicly stated Israel's willingness to retaliate without any hesitation.[128]

American and Israeli fears were put to the test on the evening of 19 January 1991—which later came to be called *Scud Thursday*.[129] Brent Scowcroft, writing about the events of that evening, recalls the moment when the principals in President Bush's cabinet learned Saddam Hussein had launched the first wave of Scud missiles. As the initial reports of the Scud attack came in around 7 PM, Richard Hass, James Baker, Larry Eagleburger, John Sununu, and a few other senior Bush administration officials rushed to Scowcroft's office. At the same time, Cheney joined via phone from the National Military Command Center. Cheney reported that Israeli Defense Minister Arens had requested American assistance to deconflict the airspace and facilitate an Israeli counterstrike.[130] Scowcroft recalls that Cheney "doubted we could stop them, and we could make a bad situation worse by trying" to stop the Israelis.[131] Instead, Cheney suggested that the United States let the Israelis "go, go fast, and get it over with."[132] Scowcroft and Hass countered that any such action, even if justified, would unravel the Coalition.[133]

As these conversations occurred, information that some of the missiles carried nerve gas reached them.[134] The news of a missile attack armed with chemical warheads altered the dynamics of the discussion. Eagleburger reportedly remarked, "if Cheney was not right before, he almost certainly was now."[135] Scowcroft, Cheney, and others were exploring options to persuade the Israelis to hold off and buy time.[136] Secretary of State Baker reached out to the ambassadors of the Arab states involved in the Coalition to gauge their reaction to an Israeli retaliatory strike.[137] The Saudi ambassador, Prince Bandar bin Sultan, remained adamant that Israel should not be permitted to overfly Saudi airspace and strike Iraq.[138]

However, a few hours later, new reports clarified that the Scuds had not carried nerve gas.[139] An Israeli civil defense team had gotten a false reading from a Scud missile fuel tank.[140] The American leadership got a respite, and, for the moment, the Israelis agreed to restrain themselves.[141] The US-led Coalition remained intact.

Such dramatic scenes were a constant feature for the duration of the conflict. American political efforts to dissuade Israel from initiating military actions continued throughout the war. A few days after the events of Scud Thursday, the United States rushed Patriot missile defense units to Israel. In a telephone conversation, President Bush pleaded with President Shamir to leave it to the Coalition to act against Iraq.[142] The message was to stay out of the conflict and let US forces do the job for Israel.[143] President Bush conveyed to the Israeli President that it took immense effort to assemble the Coalition against Saddam Hussein and that he did not want it jeopardized.[144]

President Shamir, however, continued to insist that Israel had to do something to preserve its carefully cultivated deterrent posture.[145] Over the years, the Israelis had meticulously built a reputation for swift and overwhelming retribution against any attacks. The Israeli leadership was now worried that by not responding to Saddam Hussein's missile bombardment, other Arab state and non-state actors might conclude that Israel was no longer able to act independently and retaliate.[146]

As more Scuds kept falling on Israel, the domestic political pressure on President Shamir to respond militarily grew.[147] The Israeli leadership repeatedly demanded that the US deconflict airspace and facilitate an Israeli strike. A memorandum of conversation between Israeli and American leaders offers a stark portrayal of the political pressure Israel was applying on the Bush administration. In the 11 February 1991 meeting, Defense Minister Arens states, "there's a feeling in Israel that we are at war. Some 31 SCUDS have been launched at Israel; some killed, hundreds injured, thousands of homes destroyed. SCUDS have a large blast effect, resulting in scenes not seen in the West since World War II."[148] He then asks for "a chance to contribute" to the Scud-hunting operations.[149] President Bush, in frustration, asks, "What can you do better than what we're doing?"[150] Defense Minister Arens replies, "I don't want to be presumptuous. We might do it differently; we would add other dimensions: [redaction] We feel this could be an important addition to finding and destroying them. It would also give the Prime Minister a chance to contribute."[151]

President Bush, again challenging Defense Minister Arens, asks

> But how could you do it? Tell us how to do it and we'll do it. I need to know why you believe you can do something we can't. I have a lot of considerations to balance. You mentioned [redaction]. We've tried to help, and we have. . . . I am trying to get rid of one of your greatest enemies, Saddam Hussein. This is the big picture, the biggest picture. This should appeal to Israel.[152]

Recalling the meeting, President Bush writes in his memoirs that Defense Minister Arens was not appeased by the American Scud-hunting efforts.[153]

On 19 February 1991, after a missile salvo, Israel again readied its air forces to strike Iraq. The Israelis were apparently preparing to send 100 fighter planes across Saudi Arabia airspace and into Iraq.[154] President Bush writes that the Saudis raised hell and declared that any such major breach would not be tolerated.[155] The same went for the Jordanians. If the Saudis or the Jordanians intercepted Israeli planes, a secondary conflict could break out, and the Coalition might not hold.[156] President Bush, in a phone conversation with President Shamir, again pleaded for patience, arguing: "you were hit by missiles, and while I am not telling you what to do . . . I just want to make one last appeal, recognizing how hard for you it is to wait. We are hitting those same targets that you would be going after."[157]

President Shamir, while sympathetic to the concerns of President Bush over holding the Coalition together, responded that Israel could not endure the Iraqi missile strikes much longer.[158] He argued that the Israeli people could not understand why Israel's armed forces were not doing anything.[159] He asked that a way for Israel to participate in the war be found.[160] Lawrence Eagleburger and Paul Wolfowitz were immediately dispatched to appease Israeli leaders and demonstrate American commitment to Israel's security.[161] A renewed redirection of military efforts was undertaken to suppress Iraqi Scud missile attacks. Additionally, as an alternative to direct Israeli participation, they were asked to supply a list of targets that American and coalition forces should target.[162]

The Military Response to the Fear of Scud Attacks

The political need to suppress the Iraqi Scud missile threat permeated American war plans. At the beginning of the Coalition's air campaign, Scud missile fixed launch sites (at the H-2 and H-3 airfields), missile storage facilities, and missile production sites were placed on a target list and vigorously attacked. As early as 2 September 1990, Lieutenant General Charles Horner, the commander of the US and allied Air Forces, had tasked Major General Buster C. Glosson to target the Iraqi H-2 airfield at the beginning of the air strikes to prevent Saddam Hussein from retaliating with the Scud missiles.[163]

The Israelis had conveyed to President Bush that they would restrain themselves on the condition the H-2 airfield was destroyed.[164] On the first night of the air campaign, strikes against the H-2 airfield were timed to coincide with the strikes on Baghdad to forestall Scud launches as bombs struck Baghdad.[165] At the beginning of the air strikes, 19 F-15E Strike Eagles outfitted with LANTIRN targeting pods hit the H-2 airfield with MK-20 Rockeyes free fall and unguided cluster munitions to destroy the airfield.[166] Additionally, four F-15Es were separately maintained in alert status to quickly neutralize any mobile Scud launchers that might attempt to fire their missiles at Israel.[167]

Thirty minutes into the air campaign, 20 TLAMs struck the Scud facility at Taji.[168] The BQM-74 drones targeted Scud storage facilities across Iraq.[169] Finally, two separate air raids targeted the Scud C2 fiber optic communication networks.[170] The following day, Navy E-2C Hawkeye airborne early warning aircraft and F-14s patrolled the skies near the H-2 and H-3 airfields to reassure the Israelis that all efforts were being taken to neutralize the Scud threat.[171]

However, the early strikes against Scud targets did not neutralize the mobile Scud launchers.[172] Once the ground war started, Iraqi missile bombardment began promptly. Immediately enormous political pressure was directed at Schwarzkopf to divert more military resources to the Scud hunting mission.[173] General Schwarzkopf and other leaders of the US armed forces resented the political intrusion into operational planning. Lieutenant General Horner, complaining to Schwarzkopf, argued: "Sir, this is insane. We can't have a bunch of Israelis who have no idea of our overall campaign plan telling us where to put bombs. We're throwing bombs into dunes. We're starting to endanger pilots' lives."[174] Yet the campaign to strike these targets continued throughout Operation Desert Storm.

As the Scuds kept falling, more and more military resources were diverted to the Scud-hunting mission. JSTARS radar planes, and U-2 and TR-1 reconnaissance and surveillance planes were reassigned to track Scud mobile launchers.[175] Pioneer drones were deployed to look out for Scud launchers.[176] At its peak, one-third of the missions scheduled each day was repurposed and diverted toward the Scud-hunt mandate to respond to the political pressure to do something.[177] At one point, the fighter pilots were instructed to "drop a bomb every half hour" on suspected Scud missile site to intimidate Iraqi missile crews[178] American F-15 and F-16 aircraft risked exposure to anti-aircraft weapons to strike Scud storage and launch sites.[179] A-10 Warthogs jets were also pressed into action against Scud mobile launch vehicles. A permanent combat air patrol was established over western Iraq.[180] While these efforts diminished the missile firing rate, they did not eliminate the threat.[181]

The Gulf War Air Power Survey notes, "by war's end, nearly every type of strike and reconnaissance aircraft employed in the war participated in the attempt to bring this [Scud] threat under control" but without much success.[182] Over the course of the war, the Iraqis would prove adept at employing shoot-and-scoot and other techniques to evade detection and attacks on their mobile Scud launchers.[183] A Defense Intelligence Agency (DIA) postmortem of the Scud-hunting effort notes that throughout the war Iraq was able to initiate launches from new launch areas and to retarget short-range ballistic missiles to new targets.[184] Patriot missile defenses were proving unable to engage and destroy the Scuds.[185]

Conclusion

Saddam Hussein's Scud missiles greatly influenced the conduct of the 1991 Gulf War.[186] The Scud missiles had accomplished something that nothing else in Iraq's armed forces could do, almost collapsing the Coalition and fundamentally altering the course of the battle.[187] The Scud ballistic missiles were crucial to generating this effect. In principle, Saddam Hussein's air force could have also delivered chemical weapons. But defeating American and Israeli air defenses was beyond the ability of the Iraqi air force. On the other hand, Iraq's ballistic missiles could not be effectively defended against by the American forces or the Israelis. The invulnerability of Scuds enabled Iraq to weaponize fear and capitalize on American and Israeli political vulnerabilities.

Saddam Hussein wanted to provoke Israel to attack Iraq. He almost succeeded. In one instance, Israeli Defense Minister Moshe Arens had told the US Secretary of State, James Baker: "We don't have a choice. We have to go. They've hit us. We have to hit them back. Israel can't sit here and be hit with missiles and do nothing."[188] Any Israeli involvement would have rendered the Coalition asunder and jeopardized its ability to remove Saddam Hussein's forces from Kuwait.

American decisionmakers wanted to avert Israeli involvement in the war by any means necessary. The American leadership was also committed to removing Saddam Hussein's army from Kuwaiti territory. President Bush had rejected a Soviet Union-brokered ceasefire that would have ended the conflict but given Saddam Hussein an "unspecified time" to evacuate Kuwait.[189] American decisionmakers were persistent that any negotiated settlement and ceasefire would have to include an immediate and unconditional Iraqi withdrawal.[190] As a result, the American leadership was willing to divert a vast array of weapons to conduct a countermeasure campaign against the Scud missiles. The American and allied militaries also possessed the capacity to conduct these diversionary military countermeasure efforts without taxing the war effort.

The American political leadership greatly exerted itself to provide Israeli President Shamir an excuse not to act against Iraqi missile strafing. A massive American diplomatic effort was undertaken to allow the Israeli leadership to posture in their public reactions while blaming the Americans for restraining them.[191] Similarly, a massive diversionary military effort was taken to hunt Scuds to reassure the Israelis.

The American diplomatic and military efforts worked. Israel stayed out of the conflict, the Coalition held together, and Saddam Hussein's forces were ejected from Kuwait. We also know that chemically armed ballistic missiles were not used in the 1991 Gulf War.[192] It is anybody's guess what would have occurred if the counterfactual had transpired.[193] In explaining his restraint, Israel's President Yitzhak Shamir writes, "I can think of nothing that went more against my grain as a Jew and a Zionist, nothing more opposed to the ideology on which my life has been based, more than the decision I took in the crisis preceding the Gulf War—and implemented throughout the war—to ask the people of Israel to accept the burden of restraint in the face of attack."[194] President Shamir might not have been able to observe restraint if chemical weapons had been launched at the Israeli populace, irrespective of their military effect. The war, possibly its outcome, may have been very different if Saddam Hussein had lobbed Scuds with chemical warheads into Israel.

6

Hezbollah's Katyusha Rockets and the Rules of Engagement

Hezbollah's Katyusha rockets emerged as potent tools of provocation and coercion soon after their introduction into the Middle Eastern theater. In July 1993, at the end of Operation Accountability, Israel begrudgingly acceded to negotiated rules of engagement between Israel and Hezbollah. The new rules accepted periodic surges in localized violence between Israeli forces and Hezbollah but forbade the targeting of civilians.[1] The rules of engagement required Israel not to engage in military operations that harmed Lebanese civilians in exchange for the cessation of Katyusha rocket attacks by Hezbollah into the settlements of northern Israel.[2] By 1993, Hezbollah had coerced Israel into accepting these new rules of engagement using the threat of rocket bombardment. These rules were reinforced in the 1996 "April Understanding" at the end of Operation Grapes of Wrath.[3] The rules of engagement, however, permitted the targeting of military personnel.

On the morning of 12 July 2006, Hezbollah forces targeted a small Israeli Defense Forces (IDF) patrol close to the border, assaulting and killing three Israeli soldiers and kidnapping two soldiers, Eldad Regev and Ehud Goldwasser. In an attempt to impede detection of the kidnappings, Hezbollah fighters unleashed rocket and sniper fire on multiple IDF posts. A couple of hours later, Israeli armored vehicles attempting to aid the ambushed soldiers crossed into Lebanon. However, an improvised explosive device (IED) destroyed one of the Merkava 4 tanks, killing its crew of four.[4]

Hezbollah may have believed its attack on the IDF was not an escalation. Immediately after the kidnappings, a Hezbollah leader responding to queries from Geir Pedersen, the UN representative in Lebanon, stating, "we only acted according to the general rules of the game between us and Israel."[5] But the Israeli government was angered by the kidnappings and unwilling to tolerate any further provocations by Hezbollah. Israel's political leadership also believed that it could exact revenge, secure the kidnapped soldiers, and teach Hezbollah a lesson using only air power.[6] The Israeli Air Force (IAF) had unchallenged air superiority and fire power, which it believed would deliver a

Bombing to Provoke. Jaganath Sankaran, Oxford University Press. © Oxford University Press 2024.
DOI: 10.1093/oso/9780197792629.003.0006

quick victory in a few days. By noon, Israeli military command had activated a standing order, codenamed Fourth Dimension, executing air strikes on 69 bridges in southern Lebanon to impede the escape of the kidnappers deeper into Lebanon.[7] Subsequently, the IAF began a targeted aerial campaign against Hezbollah's rockets and other infrastructure on 13 July 2006.

In a press conference, Hassan Nasrallah announced, "we do not want to escalate things in the south . . . we do not want to push the region into war."[8] However, he also argued that no military operation would return the Israeli captured soldiers, and a prisoner swap was the only way for Israel to recover the kidnapped soldiers.[9] Hassan Nasrallah accused Israel of "changing the rules of the game." He continued, "you wanted an open war, an open war is what you will get. It will be a full-scale war. To Haifa and—believe me—beyond Haifa and beyond beyond Haifa."[10]

Hezbollah promptly began its rocket bombardment and continued doing so throughout the war, despite the IAF's massive efforts to suppress rocket launches. Realizing the crucial role of the Katyusha rockets in coercing Israel to offer limited concessions in the past, Hezbollah went to great lengths to ensure its ability to launch as many rockets for as long as the fighting continued. Hezbollah built underground bunkers to protect its rocket launchers and used camouflaging techniques to avoid detection.[11]

In the 34 days of the Second Lebanon War, Hezbollah fired nearly 4,000 rockets into Israel.[12] Uzi Rubin, evaluating Israeli counterforce strikes against Hezbollah's rockets, notes that "Israel's efforts to block the attack, or even to lessen the severity of the damage incurred, proved, on the whole, almost as futile as in the 1980s and 1990s . . . terminating only when a general ceasefire brought the fighting to a halt."[13]

During the month-long bombardment of Israel's civilian population, 300,000 residents left their homes and sought refuge in the southern parts of Israel.[14] More than a million Israelis were forced to live in bomb shelters.[15] The towns that suffered the most hits—Kiryat Shmona, Naharia, and Safed—became "ghost towns" in which all economic and civic life ceased.[16] A variety of vital industrial and economic nodes in northern Israel were shut down.[17]

As the rockets kept falling on Israel, Prime Minister Olmert and his cabinet came under increasing pressure to commit more airpower and then ground troops to eradicate the rocket bombardment. By the end of the war, Israel's political resolve had faded. It had to withdraw, unable to accomplish the missions it had embarked upon, including the retrieval of the two kidnapped soldiers. While Hezbollah was initially weakened militarily, it was able to quickly replenish its arsenal and reestablish its military posture.

Bombing to Provoke

The rest of this chapter examines in detail how Hezbollah's rocket bombardment provoked and coerced the Israeli leadership during the Second Lebanon War. The following section begins by providing a brief historical background. The third section outlines the military balance of power between the belligerents. The third section details the tactics employed by Hezbollah to fight against a militarily superior Israel. The fourth section details how Hezbollah had used its rockets before the 2006 Second Lebanon War to weaponize fear, provoke Israel, and coerce limited concessions. The fifth section details the political and military responses to the Katyusha rockets strikes and their impact on Israel's resolve during the 2006 Second Lebanon war. Finally, the sixth section concludes with a detailed review of changes that have occurred since the war .

The History and Politics of the Dispute

In the immediate aftermath of its independence in 1946, Lebanon suffered several structural and geopolitical weaknesses. While Shiites composed almost 40% of the Lebanese population, their influence in the politics and economy of the country was curtailed. Lebanon's Maronite Christian and Sunni Muslim communities dominated its national politics.[18] Lebanon's Shiites in the southern region remained marginalized and disillusioned. Furthermore, the Lebanese national army was militarily weak and unable to defend Lebanese territories against other regional actors.

The political paralysis and military weakness enabled the establishment of the Palestine Liberation Organization (PLO) in the Shiite majority southern Lebanon, turning the region into a battleground between PLO forces and the IDF.[19] The role of PLO forces was further strengthened by the Cairo Agreement, signed in 1969. The Cairo Agreement formalized and permitted PLO forces to conduct attacks against Israel from Lebanese soil while reaffirming, in principle, Lebanese sovereignty in the region.[20] However, in the early 1970s, southern Lebanon witnessed periodic battles between PLO forces and the Lebanese army.[21] Lebanon descended into a civil war in 1975, further weakening political stability.

In 1982, Israel, responding to repeated PLO's cross-border attacks, launched the First Lebanon War (or the Peace of Galilee war), and invaded southern Lebanon. Israel hoped to destroy the political and military infrastructure of the PLO in southern Lebanon.[22] While the first Lebanon war eliminated the PLO threat to Israel, it did not lead to political stability or the restoration of Lebanese central authority in southern Lebanon. Iran quickly exploited the political vacuum in the aftermath of the First Lebanon War to establish Hezbollah.[23]

In 1985, facing stiff armed resistance from Hezbollah and other actors, Israel withdrew partially and established a security zone inside southern Lebanon on the Israeli–Lebanese border.[24] Within the security zone, the IDF and the Southern Lebanon Army (SLA) built several fortified outposts to conduct military operations intended to prevent and dissuade cross-border strikes by Hezbollah.[25]

In its formative years, Hezbollah had to compete for influence with other militant organizations, such as Amal. Amal, like Hezbollah, was resisting the Israeli occupation of southern Lebanon. However, with Iranian and Syrian support, Hezbollah gained prominence.[26] In the early 1990s, Hezbollah began targeting Israeli settlements in northern Israel with Katyusha rockets supplied by Iran and Syria. By 1996, an uneasy understanding—the new rules of engagement—was established between Israel and Hezbollah. Hezbollah agreed to desist from rocket attacks on Israeli settlements if the IDF did not cause Lebanese civilian casualties in its military operations. Neither side committed to a cessation of military activities.

In 2000, Israel unilaterally withdrew completely from southern Lebanon.[27] The withdrawal of Israeli forces from Lebanon raised questions about the continued need for Hezbollah's continued existence as an armed militia.[28] However, Hezbollah and the government of Lebanon claiming Israel has continued to occupy Lebanese territory in the Shebaa Farms region, justified the continuation of Hezbollah's struggle against Israel.[29] On 16 May 2000, Hassan Nasrallah declared at a rally, "we shall fight until [we have] liberated the last inch of our land and for as long as the state of Lebanon says that the Sha'aba Farms are Lebanese, we don't care what the international community says."[30]

Since 2000, Hezbollah had prepared militarily to resist and counter an Israeli invasion.[31] Hezbollah had also engaged in several minor skirmishes with the IDF and kidnapped IDF personnel to bargain for the release of prisoners held in Israel. The kidnapping of Israeli Defense Forces reservists Regev and Goldwasser, on 12 July 2006, was the fifth attempt by Hezbollah to kidnap IDF soldiers.[32] Two months before the kidnappings that led to the Second Lebanon War, Hezbollah had attempted and failed to carry out a similar operation.[33] Israel had immediately alerted American and French diplomats, warning that any kidnappings would provoke a large-scale Israeli military retaliation.[34] Israel had hoped that the Americans and the French would convey the warning to Hezbollah. It is not clear if the warning was conveyed.

The Military Balance of Power

In 2006, Israel had military superiority over all its regional adversaries, including Hezbollah and other Arab states.[35] Furthermore, Hezbollah was well aware of its military inferiority. As the 2006 Second Lebanon war unfolded, Hassan Nasrallah in a televised address declared, "we are not a regular army, and we will not fight like a regular army."[36] Hassan Nasrallah's address points to a clear understanding of the disparities in the balance of power. More importantly, it suggests a commitment to offset Israel's superior capabilities with unconventional weapons and tactics.

In the years preceding the Second Lebanon War, Hezbollah undertook a targeted arms acquisition strategy to dilute the efficiency of Israel's military advantages and to amplify its ability to wage an asymmetric nontraditional war. Hezbollah diligently built a network of underground bunkers and established a disaggregated command and control process to enable small units of Hezbollah fighters to effectively engage IDF forces.[37] Hezbollah's underground bunkers were capable of independently sustaining fighter units for several weeks without resupply.[38] After the war, Israeli soldiers were surprised to discover bunkers almost 40 meters deep in solid rock and extending half a mile or more.[39] These bunkers had running water, lighting, ventilation, and significant medical facilities, including operating rooms.[40] Nearly 600 bunkers with ammunition and weapons were strategically placed in southern Lebanon to enable Hezbollah fighter units to engage and slow down invading Israeli forces.[41] On the first day of ground battle, the Israeli forces were surprised by the firepower, perseverance, and tactics of Hezbollah fighters. An Israeli soldier recounting the experience notes, "we didn't know what hit us." He continued, "evidently, they had never heard that an Arab solider is supposed to run away after a short engagement with the Israelis. We expected a tent and three Kalashnikovs—that was the intelligence we were given. Instead, we found a hydraulic steel door leading to a well-equipped network of tunnels."[42]

Hezbollah had also amassed a large arsenal of rockets and missiles before the war. At the beginning of the 2006 Second Lebanon War, Hezbollah's arsenal included approximately 13,000 107 mm and 122 mm short-range Katyusha rockets and nearly 1,000 medium- and long-range rockets and missiles, including the Fajr-3, Fajr-5, and Zelzal (see Table 6.1).[43]

The short-range Katyusha rockets proved particularly effective. Despite Israel's extended counterforce campaign against the rockets, Hezbollah was able to maintain a continuous bombardment of Israeli cities and settlements. The IAF had significant difficulties identifying and eradicating these rockets

Table 6.1 Hezbollah rocket and missile arsenal during the Second Lebanon War

	Name	Caliber (millimeters)/ warhead weight (kilograms)	Maximum range (kilometers)	Comments
Short-range systems	Katyusha	122/30	20	
	Katyusha extended range	122	35	
Medium-range systems	Fajr-3	240/44	43	12 barrels, truck-mounted launcher
	Uragan	220	70	Syrian-made
	Fajr-5	333/90	75	4 barrels, truck-mounted launcher
Long-range systems	Khalibar-1	302/100	75–100	
	Zelzal-2	610/600	210	
	C-701 (shore-to-ship missile)		15	
	C-802 Noor (shore-to-ship missile)		210	

Adapted from Andrew Exum, "Hizballah at War: A Military Assessment" (Washington, DC: Washington Institute for Near East Policy, December 2006), 4, https://www.washingtoninstitute.org/policy-analysis/hizballah-war-military-assessment © 2006 The Washington Institute for Near East Policy.[a]

[a] Makovsky and White, "Lessons and Implications of the Israel–Hizballah War," 40.

because of their very low signatures and active measures taken by the Hezbollah to prevent the targeting of the short-range Katyusha rockets.[44]

Hezbollah planned to wage an asymmetric war of attrition. Hezbollah believed it had more political resolve than the Israelis, who were burdened with a strong sense of casualty sensitivity. In a 2003 interview, Hassan Nasrallah noted that Hezbollah would strike at Israel's point of weakness, the inability to bear extensive human losses.[45] Hezbollah's leadership believed that as long as it was able to inflict casualties on the IDF, sending back Israeli soldiers in body bags, it could emerge victorious by merely surviving the onslaught of the Israeli campaign.[46] In Hezbollah's conception, while Israel needed a clear victory in any war, Hezbollah needed to just "survive and demonstrate its survivability."[47]

Hezbollah's logic was not new. Since the early 1990s, Hezbollah had espoused an asymmetric doctrine of warfare stressing the value of avoiding direct force-on-force confrontations with the militarily superior Israeli forces. Instead, Hezbollah employed surprise hit-and-run campaigns. For example, a 1996 Hezbollah Concept of Operations document entitled "Hizballah: 13 Principles of Warfare" was intercepted and translated by the IDF.[48] The essence of the Concept of Operations document was a commitment to wage limited battles with the IDF to impose military and civilian casualties while minimizing Hezbollah's casualties. An elaboration of some of these concepts and their perceived successes was offered by Hezbollah's Deputy Secretary-General, Sheik Naim Qassem in 2004.[49] Qassem writes that Hezbollah would not wage a classic war with obvious frontlines and rear. He instead talks about hit-and-run campaigns leaving Israel with no target to strike back.[50]

The strategic principle that guided Hezbollah in the 2006 Second Lebanon War was a logical extension of these concepts. In the Second Lebanon War, Hezbollah relied on a "victory by not losing concept" that entailed a greater tolerance for pain and a willingness to suffer in order to coerce limited concessions and (re)establish a deterrent against Israel.[51] As Hassan Nasrallah argued during the war in a televised interview to Al-Jazeera, "the victory we are talking about is when the resistance survives. When its will is not broken, then this is victory. . . . When we are not defeated militarily, then this is victory."[52]

Hezbollah employed a two-pronged tactic in the 2006 Second Lebanon War. First, rockets and missiles deployed across Lebanon were used to continuously strike at cities and settlements in northern Israel, causing civilian casualties and economic distress. Second, Hezbollah mounted a surprisingly robust forward defense in southern Lebanon using its underground bunkers to enable its fighting units to engage, slow down, and impose casualties on

Israeli military forces. Hezbollah believed if the forward defense on the ground held back Israeli forces long enough, growing political pressure on Israel's leaders could coerce them into offering concessions to terminate the war. Additionally, Hezbollah had purposefully collocated its infrastructure with Lebanese civilian infrastructure to ensure that any retaliatory Israeli air strikes would invariably cause collateral damages and civilian deaths.[53] Such Lebanese civilian casualties were expected to stoke international pressure on Israel to end the conflict.[54] In essence, Hezbollah had hoped that the combination of Israeli military deaths and Israeli and Lebanese civilian casualties would weaken Israel's resolve and accelerate a withdrawal from the conflict.

Weaponizing Fear: Katyushas and the Rules of Engagement

Rockets have repeatedly played a prominent role in the conflicts between Hezbollah and Israel. Long before the 2006 Second Lebanon War, Hezbollah had successfully used its rockets to coerce Israel into accepting a mutual deterrent. The deterrent, institutionalized in the form of rules of engagement, tolerated the continuation of Hezbollah's armed resistance against Israeli occupation but forbade the launching of rockets into Israeli territory. In exchange, Israeli forces agreed to avoid military operations against Hezbollah that might also cause Lebanese civilian casualties.

In its early years as an armed resistance, Hezbollah had used its Katyusha rockets to strike Israeli and South Lebanon Army forces inside the Israeli occupation zones but refrained from launching cross-border strikes into Israel. The first cross-border rocket strikes on Israeli population centers occurred in 1992, in response to the Israeli assassination of Sayyed Abbas Mussawi, the secretary general of Hezbollah. For the first time a barrage of two dozen 122 mm Katyusha rockets was launched into Israel. At the end of three days of fighting that followed, close to 100 rockets were launched and a third of the rockets struck Kiryat Shemona in northern Galilee, in Israel.[55] After the 1992 incident, Hassan Nasrallah warned in his message to Israel, "if you attack us, we will use our Katyushas; if you do not attack us, we will not use our Katyushas."[56] A clear message of aerospace coercion.

Over the next few years, a tit-for-tat reciprocity emerged. Immediately after any Israeli military operation that caused Lebanese civilian casualties, Hezbollah would fire its Katyusha rockets into Israel. Soon Israel found itself in an untenable position. Israel had occupied southern Lebanon to prevent terrorist attacks and rocket strikes on residents of northern Israel. However, every time Israel responded to Hezbollah assaults on Israeli forces in the occupied zones, it led to collateral Lebanese civilian casualties or material damages. Hezbollah immediately responded with cross-border rocket strikes. Israeli forces could not find a way to effectively challenge Hezbollah without provoking Katyusha rocket salvos into Israeli territory.[57] Hezbollah had established a balance of terror against the occupying Israeli forces through its ability to strike northern Israel with the Katyusha rockets. Eventually Hezbollah's retaliatory rocket strikes defeated the purpose of Israeli military presence in southern Lebanon.

In July 1993, Prime Minister Yitzhak Rabin launched Operation Accountability hoping to eradicate the rocket threat once and for all.[58] But at the end of the seven-day Operation Accountability campaign, new tacit rules of engagement had emerged between the State of Israel and the Hezbollah. These new rules of engagement were articulated in a 1993 oral agreement between Israel and Hezbollah.[59] The rules accepted periodic surges in localized violence and the targeting of armed combatants by both parties but codified the existence of a mutual deterrence against the targeting of civilians.[60] Israel agreed it would not engage in military operations that harmed Lebanese civilians in exchange for cessation of rocket attacks by Hezbollah into northern Israel.[61] Hezbollah had coerced Israel to accept a bargained peace. Hassan Nasrallah, in an interview after the 1993 Operation, confidently declared that the Katyusha rocket bombardment had "led to a new formula based on mutual forced displacement, mutual destruction, and equal terror."[62]

The rules of engagement held on and off for the next few years.[63] Hezbollah constantly endeavored to firmly reinforce the coercive effects of its rocket campaigns. After a March 1995 rocket strike, for instance, Hassan Nasrallah declared, "there is no safety for anyone if our people are not safe. . . . Zionist settlers in northern Israel should know that their racist and aggressive government, their settlements and the residents inside, will not be in a better condition than our towns and their residents."[64]

In 1996, Israel launched Operation Grapes of Wrath, again hoping to permanently end Hezbollah's cross-border rocket strikes. Days before the military operation, Israeli Minister of Public Security Moshe Shalal said, "Israel must not restrain itself, and it has to teach Hezbollah a lesson that the lives of our citizens are not fair game."[65] During the 1996 operation, the IAF had complete air superiority. The IAF also had overwhelming technological superiority. Israeli drones were pressed into service to identify rocket launches quickly. Immediately after the launches were identified, F-16s fitted with precision-guided munitions attempted to strike and destroy the rocket launchers.[66] The IAF launched 2,350 aerial sorties including 600 raids.[67]

Furthermore, radar-directed artillery units fired close to 25,000 shells into Lebanese territory.[68] Yet Hezbollah forces managed to fire 746 Katyusha rockets during the conflict with close to 80% striking northern Israel.[69] An article in the *Jerusalem Post* noted that "despite all its bravado and state-of-the-art weapons systems, the IDF's attempts to stop Hezbollah from firing Katyushas into northern Israel is like a tiger trying to catch a mosquito in his teeth."[70]

At the end of the 16-day 1996 operation, the tacit rules of engagement were further cemented and more formally codified in a memorandum. The arrangement came to be known as the "April Understanding" that reaffirmed the commitment to safeguard civilians on both sides of the border but permitted Hezbollah to continue its armed resistance of the Israeli occupation of southern Lebanon.[71] A monitoring group with delegates from Lebanon, Syria, France, Israel, and the United States was established as part of the April Understanding to observe and report violations.[72]

It is worthwhile to stress that the provocative and coercive value of the Katyusha rockets did not emerge from their destructive potential. Instead, the rockets weaponized fear, exploited Israeli political vulnerabilities, and exhausted the resolve of Israeli decisionmakers. A resident of Kiryat Shmona, recalling the distressing experience of the 1996 conflict, states

> the point of the Katyushas is simply to destroy the morale of the people here . . . my six-year-old daughter is afraid of every noise she hears. Lots of kids here have severe problems in school—they can't concentrate, they have nightmares. Living in Kiryat Shmona you wake up every morning and check to see that you're still alive. That's the point of the rockets.[73]

In a conflict with Hezbollah, any expectation of sustained rocket bombardment requires the immediate relocation of the Israeli population or their sequestration in bunkers for extended periods of time, disrupting the normal life and economic activities. For instance, when fighting flared up in February 2000, the mere anticipation of rocket bombardment paralyzed northern Israel.[74] Fearing rocket strikes, Israel ordered residents to either seek protection in bunkers or leave for southern Israel promptly.[75] Almost 80% of the residents in Kiryat Shemona left.[76] At the end of the fighting, local economic losses were determined to be $2.4 million per day, yet not a single Katyusha rocket was fired.[77] Hezbollah did not fire its rockets—just the fear of such rocket strikes did the damage.

Such fear of rockets cast a long shadow on Israeli strategy as the 2006 Second Lebanon War unfolded.

The Political and Military Response

At midnight on 12 July, Lieutenant General Dan Halutz, the Israeli Chief of Staff, authorized Israeli air strikes on Hezbollah long-range missile arsenal. The operation codenamed Specific Weight successfully destroyed 59 long-range rocket launchers in 34 minutes.[78] Halutz called Israeli Prime Minister Ehud Olmert and reported, "all the long-range rockets have been destroyed. We've won the war."[79] Brigadier General Yossi Beidetz, Israel's head of the Military Intelligence's research division, declared Operation Specific Weight a singular achievement. He informed the political leadership that Hezbollah was surprised by Israel's swiftness.[80] However, he suggested that Hezbollah still retained the ability to use its large arsenal of short-range Katyusha rockets.[81]

On the morning of 13 July, Hezbollah responded to the initial Israeli air strikes with a heavy bombardment of Katyusha rockets.[82] In retaliation to the rocket bombardment, Israeli planes began striking Hezbollah strongholds in the Dahiya neighborhood of Beirut in the early evening of 14 July. As Israel began its aerial campaign against Hezbollah targets, the Israeli political leadership was highly resolved and believed the offensive would end very quickly and Hezbollah would soon sue for peace, unable to bear the withering air strikes.[83] Dan Halutz, Israeli Chief of Staff, proclaimed that the IDF would "turn back the clock in Lebanon by 20 years" with its aerial campaign if Hezbollah did not concede immediately.[84] Similarly, Israeli Prime Minister Olmert claimed the war in Lebanon offered "an almost unique opportunity" to change the rules of engagement.[85] Israeli Foreign Minister Tzipi Livni proclaimed that the war could catalyze "a process that will bring about a long-term and fundamental change in the political reality" in Lebanon.[86] These beliefs were reinforced by the belief that Israel would be able to defeat Hezbollah with air power alone.[87]

An Israeli air strikes on 14 July leveled the multistory Hezbollah headquarters and al-Manar TV station building.[88] A few hours later, Hassan Nasrallah declared,

> This is total war that Israel is waging, revenge for the past. You will soon discover how much your new government is stupid and inexperienced. . . . You wanted war? Alright then, we've been preparing for such a war. Believe me, the response will reach much further than Haifa. The equation "Beirut-Haifa" is no longer valid. It is you who have violated it and you who will pay the price. You wanted a change in the game rules—you will get it.[89]

Hezbollah began its rocket bombardment again. The IAF launched a massive aerial campaign to find and destroy the short-range Katyusha rocket launchers and storage bunkers. The IAF, however, was not able to suppress the short-range rocket bombardment. Hezbollah forces had anticipated the aerial campaign and had implemented procedures to thwart Israeli efforts to disarm Hezbollah rockets. For instance, in several cases, the Katyusha launchers were mounted on pneumatic platforms that were connected to timers and could be raised and lower from bunkers remotely and quickly fire in preprogrammed directions to hit specific targets inside Israel.[90] Additionally, once the rockets had been launched, Hezbollah units covered the launchers in fire retardant blankets to prevent Israeli drones from picking up the heat signatures of the rocket launchers.[91] In other cases, the rocket launchers were emplaced in bunkers that could withstand Israeli strikes.[92] A week after the war began, Hezbollah units still managed to fire their rockets at Israeli settlements, often from territory under the control of Israeli forces.[93]

As the rockets kept falling, Israeli leaders were forced to commit more resources and ramp up the aerial strikes. In frustration over the inability to stop the bombardment, the IAF expanded the list of targets to include Hezbollah-linked civilian targets "to exact punishment" on the Lebanese government and supporters of Hezbollah.[94] The expanded list of targets included Beirut airport, the Dahiya neighborhood of Beirut, and a plethora of transportation infrastructure in southern Lebanon.[95] While the air strikes had little to no impact on Hezbollah's rocket campaign, the collateral damages caused by the air strikes stoked international criticism on Israel's conduct of the war.

On July 30, an IAF strike collapsed a building in Kafr Qana causing the death of 28 civilians.[96] Israel, while apologetic for the casualties, argued that the target was a rocket launch site situated next to the building.[97] However, horrific images of death and injuries to civilians galvanized global condemnation on the perceived disproportionality of Israel's attacks.[98] European powers and Arab states that initially criticized Hezbollah for instigating the war had to alter their position and call on Israel to cease its military operations.[99] Hezbollah further exploited the incident by tightly controlling the media, ensuring journalists "took the right photo."[100] Hezbollah, however, stopped journalists from reporting on Hezbollah's military activities or from independently questioning Lebanese residents in southern Lebanon.[101]

92　Bombing to Provoke

Despite the IAF's diligent efforts, there was no reduction in the rocket bombardment. Israeli Prime Minister Olmert, on the other hand, remained resolute and promised to forever eliminate the rocket threats from Hezbollah. In a 1 August 2006 address to the Israeli National Defense College, Olmert proclaimed, "no one will ever threaten this nation again by firing on missiles on it because this nation will deal with the missiles and triumph over them. The truth is—we will never bend again."[102] The next morning Hezbollah launched 250 Katyushas.

On 6 August, a Katyusha rocket struck an IDF vehicle in Kfar Giladi and killed 12 soldiers.[103] Harel and Issacharoff write it was the "day the prime minister lost the war."[104] Popular support for the war evaporated, and a sense of weariness grew in Israel. At a 7 August cabinet meeting, there was strong emphasis on putting a stop to the rocket bombardment.[105] The meeting led to the approval of a major ground offensive in Lebanon, a decision that the Prime Minister and others had hoped to avoid when the war began.[106]

Israeli expectations of a quick victory executed exclusively with air power were dashed. The IAF carried out an unprecedented number of aerial sorties during the Second Lebanon War to prevent Hezbollah's rocket bombardment. The IAF flew close to 10,000 aircraft combat sorties and bombed about 7,000 targets, using about 19,000 bombs and about 2,000 missiles, including precision-guided munitions.[107] These strikes led to the deaths of approximately 1,200 Lebanese civilians and wounded close to 4,400.[108] Yet, despite Israel's substantial efforts and the initial success against long-range missiles, Hezbollah's short-range rocket bombardment persisted throughout the war (see Table 6.2 and Figure 6.1). Israel was unable to extinguish the aerospace bombardment.

Table 6.2 Effects of Hezbollah's rocket campaign

Rockets landing in northern Israel	3,790
Rockets hitting communities	901
Civilians killed	42
Civilians wounded	4,262
Civilians treated for shock and anxiety	2,773
Civilians killed per rocket	0.01

Reproduced from David Makovsky and Jeffrey White, "Lessons and Implications of the Israel–Hizballah War: A Preliminary Assessment" (Washington, DC: The Washington Institute for Near East Policy, October 2006), 43, https://www.washingtoninstitute.org/policy-analysis/lessons-and-implications-israel-hizballah-war-preliminary-assessment © 2006 The Washington Institute for Near East Policy.[a]

[a] Cordesman, Sullivan, and Sullivan, *Lessons of the 2006 Israeli-Hezbollah War*, 103.

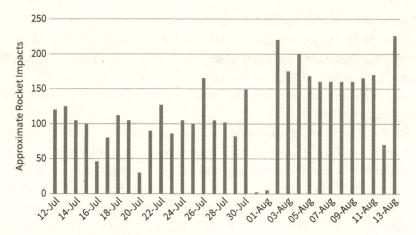

Figure 6.1 Distribution of rocket impacts.
Adapted from "Second Lebanon War: Hezbollah Rocket Attacks (July–August 2006)," Jewish Virtual Library, accessed October 29, 2022, https://www.jewishvirtuallibrary.org/hezbollah-rocket-attacks-during-second-lebanon-war

The Winograd Commission, established to investigate Israeli shortfalls in the conflict, describing the impact of the Hezbollah rocket campaign notes in its report.

> A semi-military organization of a few thousand men resisted, for a few weeks, the strongest army in the Middle East, which enjoyed full air superiority and size and technology advantages. The barrage of rockets aimed at Israel's civilian population lasted throughout the war, and the IDF did not provide an effective response to it. The fabric of life under fire was seriously disrupted, and many civilians either left their home temporarily or spent their time in shelters.[109]

The initial Israeli aerial campaign that was launched on the night of 12 July spiraled into a larger operation and eventually lead to a substantial commitment of ground forces.[110] Hezbollah's rocket campaign had provoked Israel into committing its ground forces into an attritional war. Israeli leaders were exceedingly sensitive to casualties.[111] Furthermore, Israeli ground forces were woefully underprepared to fight, whereas Hezbollah units had prepared six years for such a battle, with the goal of inflicting casualties.[112] The terrain of southern Lebanon forced Israeli ground forces and armored units into predictable advances along narrow wadis (valleys), where Hezbollah fighter units held the high ground and were well-armed to ambush. In one of the final battles of the war—the Battle of Wadi Saluki—Hezbollah fighters ambushed Israeli troops hitting 11 of 24 Merkava tanks with anti-tank missiles and killing

94 Bombing to Provoke

12 Israeli soldiers without suffering any casualties.[113] In the last two days of the war, 34 Israeli soldiers died.[114] The resolve of Israeli decisionmakers was completed expended. Having planned for a quick and decisive victory, the prolonged conflict and the increasing casualties led them to concede. While Israel had the military means to continue prosecuting the war, its leader withdrew from the fight.

On 14 August, Israel, the Lebanese government, and Hezbollah accepted UN Security Council Resolution 1701 and ceased hostilities. Israel agreed to withdraw from southern Lebanon, and the Lebanese government agreed to the deployment of United Nations Interim Force in Lebanon (UNIFIL) troops throughout southern Lebanon. At the end of the 34-day war, Israel was unable to achieve its stated goals.[115] In the days following the war, there was some expectations that Hezbollah would be weakened. However, as detailed below, those expectations did not materialize.

Conclusion

Two years after the Second Lebanon War, Major General Gadi Eisen, IDF Northern Command Chief, in an October 2008 interview outlined a new Israeli doctrine. Addressing Hezbollah's threats of rocket warfare, he warned, "what happened in the Dahiya quarter of Beirut in 2006 will happen in every village from which Israel is fired on."[116] He continued, "we will apply disproportionate force on it (village) and cause great damage and destruction there. From our standpoint, these are not civilian villages, they are military bases. This is not a recommendation. This is a plan. And it has been approved."[117]

Predictably, Hezbollah has challenged the new doctrine. Hassan Nasrallah, in a 3 August 2010 speech warned,

> if you destroy a building in the Dahiyah we will destroy buildings in Tel Aviv. . . . I am not saying that if you attack the Dahiyah we will attack Tel Aviv. Rather, I am saying that if you attack the Rafik al-Hariri International Airport in Beirut, we will attack Ben Gurion Airport in Tel Aviv. If you bomb our ports—we will bomb your ports. If you attack our refineries, we will bomb your refineries. If you bomb our factories, we will bomb your factories. And if you bomb our power plants—we will bomb your power plants![118]

Hassan Nasrallah was attempting to reestablish the rules of engagement as they existed between the IDF and Hezbollah before the 2006 Second Lebanon War. He may have been successful. The Israelis seem to have acknowledged the role of rockets and missiles in providing Hezbollah with a degree of deterrence against Israel. In 2010, General Gadi Eisenkot noted in a lecture, "some may argue that mutual deterrence has taken shape. They, too, have established a very impressive capability; we wield very impressive capabilities, and both parties do not want a confrontation."[119] A few years later, in 2014, General Yair Golan remarked that "a sort of mutual balance of deterrence" has emerged between Hezbollah and Israel.[120]

Hezbollah now has the means to execute massive and sustained rocket bombardment across Israeli territory. Hezbollah is now feared to possess 150,000 rockets and missiles.[121] A vast majority of these—close to 100,000—are short-range rockets, consisting of 107 mm standard rockets with a range of up to 8 kilometers and 122 mm rockets with ranges of 20–40 kilometers.[122] Hezbollah has also acquired several medium- and long-range missiles, such as the Fajr-3, Fajr-5, 220 mm rockets, and 302 mm Syrian-made rockets, and the Zelzal missiles.[123] Finally, in 2010, Israel and the United States suggested that Syria may have transferred Scud missiles to Hezbollah forces.[124]

Israeli experts speculate that, in a future war, Hezbollah forces could fire 1,000–3,000 rockets and missiles every day for a week.[125] Such a huge number of rockets fired into Israel in a future war would be an immense challenge to Israeli defenses. For comparison, Hezbollah's fired an average of about 22 rockets per day during Operation Accountability in 1993, approximately 40 rockets per day during Operation Grapes of Wrath in 1996, and approximately 115 rockets per day in the Second Lebanon War of 2006.[126] In October 2021, Israel ran a military exercise simulating a war with Hezbollah that involves "massive rocket and missile barrages at Israel . . . including chemical weapons attacks, direct hits on toxic chemical storage facilities within Israel," producing nationwide power outages and overwhelming the country's hospitals while simultaneously facing domestic riots in Arab-Jewish neighborhoods across the country.[127] The exercises revealed that massive rocket and missile bombardments in a future war could overwhelm the capacity of Israeli emergency responses and civil defenses.

The IAF has diligently developed the capability to strike thousands of targets in a future contingency.[128] The IAF is presumed to be able to immediately generate close to 620 short-range fighter combat sorties per day with its inventory of F-15, F-16, and F-35 squadrons. With its reserve forces mobilized, the IAF may be able to generate 1,600–1,800 short-range combat sorties per day.[129] The IAF should, in principle, be able to suppress the rocket bombardment to some extent. However, as seen in past conflicts described above, every counterforce effort has limitations.

96   Bombing to Provoke

Hezbollah has been actively preparing to deny the IAF to ability to execute a large-scale first strike on its rocket and missile arsenal. Hezbollah has acquired a range of air defense weaponry, including Igla and Igla-S (SA-18 and SA-24), Buk-2 (SA-17), and Pantsir (SA-22) surface-to-air systems.[130] These air defense weapons will constraint the IAF's ability to operate freely against Hezbollah. Additionally, the longer-range precise missiles could be employed by Hezbollah to target Israeli airfields, thus impacting the IAF's ability to operate at a desired tempo.[131]

Israel's missile defenses offer a degree of protection against Hezbollah's rockets and missiles. Israel has developed the Arrow, David Sling, and Iron Dome systems.[132] However, these systems suffer relative cost disadvantages.[133] In a future contingency, these missile defenses may need to be used to primarily protect key military and industrial facilities, leaving cities and settlements vulnerable.[134] If so, Israel's missile defenses do not eliminate the strategic vulnerabilities facing its society. Given Hezbollah's ability to fire a very large number of rockets, even if a fraction gets through, it would pose monumental challenges.[135]

Since the 2006 Second Lebanon War, both Hezbollah and the IDF have acquired weapons to offset each other's vulnerabilities. While it is unclear if these weapons would offer one side a decisive win, it seems that the next war, if there is one, will be extremely violent and brutal.

7

Houthis and the "Flying Lawnmowers"

On the morning of 26 March 2015, Saudi Arabia—supported by a coalition consisting of the United Arab Emirates (UAE), Bahrain, Qatar, Egypt, Jordan, Kuwait, Morocco, Sudan, Djibouti, Eritrea, and Somalia—launched Operation Decisive Storm, the military campaign to oust the Houthi rebels and restore the government of Abdrabuh Mansour Hadi in Yemen.

The Saudis, one of the most potent military powers in the region, believed victory would be swift and decisive. John Brennan, who served as the director of the American Central Intelligence Agency (CIA) in 2015, recalls Saudi Prince Mohammed Bin Salman, the intellectual architect of Operation Decisive Storm, as being exceedingly presumptuous on the prospects for a successful campaign. In his autobiography, Brennan recalls his conversation with Prince Salman.

> As CIA director, I had several meetings with MBS [aka Mohammed Bin Salman]. He came across as well read, intelligent, energetic, cunning, and politically savvy, but also extremely unrealistic when it came to Saudi Arabia's ability to influence events in the region. I met with MBS shortly after he was appointed minister of defense in early 2015. He was organizing the start of a Saudi-led military coalition to fight against Houthi rebel forces that had ousted the Saudi-supported government in Yemen. "We'll finish off the Houthis in a couple of months," he said confidently. "And then we'll turn our attention to cleaning up the situation in the north," an apparent reference to Syria and Iraq. I looked at him with a rather blank stare and wondered to myself what he had been smoking.[1]

After eight years, Brennan's reactions seem apt. Operation Decisive Storm has been profoundly indecisive. The air campaign waged by the Saudi-led Coalition, while devastating to Yemeni infrastructure and its people, has not altered the political will of the Houthis to resist the Saudi-led Coalition.[2]

The Saudi-led Coalition's air and ground campaigns have pummeled the Houthi forces. The Coalition has carried out 24,800 air raids since 2015.[3] By early 2018, within three years of the war, the Saudi-led Coalition had also carried out more than 100,000 military combat missions over Yemen,

Bombing to Provoke. Jaganath Sankaran, Oxford University Press. © Oxford University Press 2024.
DOI: 10.1093/oso/9780197792629.003.0007

98 Bombing to Provoke

sometimes as many as 300 missions a day.[4] These operations have often targeted several of Yemen's critical civilian infrastructures. The Saudi-led Coalition, for instance, has conducted repeated air strikes and enforced naval blockades on the Hodeidah and Saleef ports and other disembarkation points on the Red Sea coast controlled by Houthi forces.[5] The Saudis argue that their bombing and blockade of these ports are intended to prevent the ingress of weapons into Yemen. However, these military measures have, in effect, decimated Yemen's food production capacities and distribution networks.[6] As many as 16.2 million Yemeni people out of 30 million are expected to face acute food insecurity.[7]

Despite these aerial strikes and blockades, the Houthis remain a potent force in Yemen. At the beginning of hostilities in 2015, the Houthis quickly managed to survive the Coalition airstrikes and have since managed to challenge the Saudi-led Coalition militarily.[8] By 2017, the Houthis had gained control over most of Northern Yemen and "outright military victory" by any one side was highly improbable.[9] By 2018, another report by the United Nations Panel of Experts observed that "Yemen, as a State, has all but ceased to exist . . . no one side has either the political support or the military strength to reunite the country or to achieve victory on the battlefield."[10]

By 2019, the Houthis had emerged as a powerful political-military force in Yemen capable of resisting and retaliating against the Saudi-led Coalition. In September 2019, the Houthis claimed to have successfully carried out a cross-border raid into Saudi Arabian territory abutting northern Yemen and killed 500 soldiers, captured 2,000 soldiers, and seized several Saudi Arabian military vehicles.[11] A Houthi spokesperson, Mohammed Abdul Salam, issued a statement proclaiming "Operation Victory from God is the largest military one since the brutal aggression began. The enemy suffered losses . . . and wide swathes of territory were liberated in only a few days."[12] The Houthis have continued to consolidate their control in northern Yemen.[13] In October 2021, Houthis launched a major military campaign to take control of the well-fortified Marib province, a vital access point to Yemen's oil and gas infrastructure and the last remaining province under the control of the Hadi government in northern Yemen.[14] A precarious truce, arranged by the United Nations on 2 April 2022, has temporarily halted the fighting in Marib.[15] However, if fighting reignited, the Houthis could still take control of Marib.[16]

The Houthis have also taken the war to the Saudi and Emirati homeland. Robert Karem, the US Assistant Secretary of Defense for Policy, noted in his 2018 Senate testimony that the Houthis have been able to strike "at major population centers, international airports, and military installations, including bases where US forces are present [with missiles and drones]. They have also fired countless rockets into southern Saudi Arabia."[17] He further noted that "for Saudis and Emiratis, whose citizens are under attack or threat of attack . . . the conflict in Yemen is a core national security interest."[18] The Houthis have launched approximately 430 missiles and 851 drones as of December 2021.[19]

The Houthis have repeatedly attacked vital targets inside Saudi Arabia and the United Arab Emirates with missiles and drones, imposing painful economic and political costs. Houthi missile strikes may have killed and wounded hundreds of Saudi civilians and displaced thousands from southern Saudi Arabian cities in the region bordering Yemen.[20] After each of these strikes, the Houthis employed coercive propaganda, threatening further strikes unless the Saudis ceased their military campaigns in Yemen. Take, for example, the strike on Aramco facilities in Abqaiq and Khurais on 16 September 2019.[21] Immediately after the attack, Yahya Saree, the Houthi spokesperson, stated that the attacks were "in retaliation to the air strikes and the targeting of our civilians" and warned that "targets will keep expanding" unless Saudi air strikes ceased.[22] Saudi Arabia's Defense Ministry spokesperson, Lieutenant Colonel Turki al-Maliki, when asked why Saudi Arabia, despite massive efforts on missile and air defenses, could not avert the attack on Abqaiq and Khurais, responded that "there is no country in the world being attacked with such amount of ballistic missiles."[23]

The provocative and coercive effect of missiles and drones constitutes an essential explanatory variable in understanding how the Houthis have prosecuted—and arguably won—the war against the Saudi-led Coalition. The Houthis have forcefully demonstrated the ability to strike unimpeded at Saudi and Emirati oil and petroleum facilities, oil shipping routes, and other vital economic targets such as airports and major cities using missiles and drones. The continued strikes on oil facilities have heightened fears of the potential for future attacks to cause much greater havoc and impose economic shocks.[24] The continued strikes on cities, not just near the Saudi–Yemeni border but also deep inside Saudi Arabia and the Emirates, has become a source of political embarrassment for the leadership in these countries.[25] Simultaneously, the Houthis have denied the Saudi-led Coalition any prospects of a quick victory in the land war. In essence, the Houthis have denied rewards and imposed costs on the Saudi-led Coalition. It appears that the Houthis have succeeded in diminishing the resolve of the Saudi-led Coalition and coercing it into a negotiated settlement that accepts the status quo in Yemen. Even if that is reversed, the role of missiles and drones in enabling the Houthis to prolong and coerce the Saudis into settlement talks demands careful study.

The rest of this chapter explores the provocative and coercive influence of the Houthis' missile and drone warfare. The following section offers a short historical primer on the Houthi movement. The third section discusses the military balance of power between the Houthis and the Saudi-led Coalition. The fourth section details the coercive logic and bargaining rhetoric that the Houthis employ in combination with their missile and drone campaigns. The fifth details how persistent missile and drone strikes have induced fears of lasting economic damage, heightened political vulnerabilities, diluted resolve, and coerced the Saudis and the Emiratis to negotiate with the Houthis and disengage from the Yemeni conflict. Finally, the sixth section concludes with some lessons learned from the Houthi missile and drone campaigns.

The History and Politics of the Dispute

In 1990, North Yemen (Yemen Arab Republic) and South Yemen (Republic of Yemen) unified to establish the Republic of Yemen. Ali Abdallah Saleh became President of unified Yemen. However, the several tribal, cultural, and North–South divisions persisted. These divisions were compounded as the unified Yemini government largely ignored the region of Sa'dah in the northern part of Yemen. Development projects were diverted away from the Sa'dah region.[26] Furthermore, the Houthis, a Zaydi Shiite faction native to the Sa'dah region, which for centuries had been at the top of the country's social pyramid, now faced religious and political marginalization by the Yemeni government.[27]

In 1992, the Houthis, led by Hussein Badr al-Din al-Houthi, organized as a political entity and attempted to reclaim their influence in Yemen.[28] Initially, the Houthis existed as part of the Yemeni political establishment, with its representative serving in the Yemeni Parliament from 1993 to 1997.[29] However, the inability of the Ali Abdallah Saleh government to provide social services, basic welfare, and security to the Sa'dah region and an attitude of indifference led to the rise of anti-regime sentiments within the Houthi movement and eventually led to an armed insurgency against the Yemeni government.[30]

Over six years, between 2004 and 2010, six wars of insurgency occurred between the Houthis and the Ali Abdallah Saleh government.[31] The first war of insurgency lasted from 22 June to 10 September 2004, and was effectively won by the Saleh regime, whose military troops faced a small group of poorly organized dissidents.[32] In the early years, the Houthis relied exclusively on limited ambushes and hit-and-run tactics against the Yemeni army. The Saleh government was dismissive of the Houthi insurgency, portraying the movement as a proxy of Iran and Lebanese Hezbollah. The Saleh government dismissed the Houthi movement as a political nuisance.[33] In September 2004, President Saleh's forces killed Hussein Badr al-Din al-Houthi, the leader of the Houthi movement. The insurgency, however, continued to grow.[34] The second war of insurgency lasted from 19 March to 11 April 2005. In the second war, the Houthis attracted support from a broader range of tribal factions.[35] The third war of insurgency expanded the influence of the Houthis further and lasted from 30 November 2005 to 23 February 2006.[36] The fourth war of insurgency lasted four months (from 16 February to 17 June 2007). At this stage of the insurgency, the Saleh government was engaging in persistent air strikes and indiscriminate shelling against the Houthis.[37] The fourth iteration ended after the Qatari Emirate intervened and arranged for a cessation of hostilities.[38] The fifth war of insurgency lasted from 2 May to 17 July 2008, with fighting occurring as far as Sana'a in the southern part of Yemen.[39] In the fifth iteration, several previously pro-Saleh tribes were now aligned with the Houthis against the government.[40] The sixth war of insurgency lasted from 11 August 2009 to 11 February 2010. By 2010, the Houthis had managed to seize and hold strategic towns and coerce well-armed Yemeni military forces into surrender.[41] In a short six-year period, the Houthis morphed to pose an existential threat to the Saleh regime.

The 2011 Arab Spring further aggravated the political opposition to the Saleh regime in Yemen.

The Arab Spring led to large-scale nationwide protests against the government's poor economic performance and widespread corruption.[42] The Houthis coopted these protests. In November 2011, in a power transfer deal mediated by the Gulf Cooperation Council (GCC), President Ali Abdallah Saleh was pushed out of power and replaced by his Vice President, Abdrabuh Mansour Hadi, with the backing of Saudi Arabia.[43]

In early 2014, the political order in Yemen imploded completely. Different factions—former President Saleh, the new President Abdrabuh Mansour Hadi, and General Ali Mohsen al-Ahmar—worked against each other to capture power.[44] While the chaos in Sana'a was unfolding, the Houthis consolidated their power and control over the territories they controlled. In July 2014, the Houthis moved out of Sa'dah, capturing a military base in Amran.[45] The Houthis gained momentum and, on 21 September 2014, walked into the Yemeni capital city, Sana'a, almost entirely unopposed. Former President Ali Abdallah Saleh gave tacit support to the Houthis and convinced some Yemeni troops to stand down.[46] The Houthis rapidly took control of the Yemeni state apparatus. General Ali Mohsen al-Ahmar's military base fell to the Houthis, and he was forced to seek protection in the Saudi Arabian embassy.[47] The

Houthis forced President Abdrabuh Mansour Hadi to resign and placed him under house arrest.[48]

President Hadi later fled to Saudi Arabia. On 24 March 2015, President Hadi, citing Article 51 of the UN Charter and the Arab League Charter, formally requested Saudi Arabian military intervention to restore his government.[49] Two days later, on 26 March 2015, the Saudi Arabia-led Coalition launched Operation Decisive Storm to drive the Houthis out of Sana'a.[50] Saudi Arabian and the UAE air forces began a bombing campaign followed by a ground intervention to restore the Hadi government.[51] Other members of the Coalition—Bahrain, Qatar, Egypt, Jordan, Kuwait, Morocco, Sudan, Djibouti, Eritrea, and Somalia—offered varying degrees of basing support and other assistance.[52]

The Military Balance of Power

The intervention of the Saudi-led Coalition in 2015 pitted the Houthis against a military power it could not match. Saudi Arabia and other member states of the Coalition possessed far superior armies, navies, and air forces than the Houthis. However, the Houthis have become a highly capable guerilla force, combining their knowledge of local terrain with small unit tactics.[53] The Houthis receive arms and military support from Iran.[54] The Houthis also armed themselves with military equipment and weapons captured from the Coalition and its allied militias operating inside Yemen. In April 2015, for instance, Houthis seized RPG-26s airdropped by the Coalition. The RPG-26 variants were accidentally airdropped into Houthi territory. Houthis publicly posted a picture of the shipment "holding a thank-you note addressed to King Salman."[55] In other instances, corruption has led to siphoning of arms meant for Yemeni government forces to the Houthi forces.[56] The Houthis were also politically astute. They have honed the skills to negotiate and offer incentives to coopt various Yemeni political factions into allying with them.[57] Alternatively, the Houthis threaten compliance out of these various political factions if inducements fail.[58] While the Houthis often are unable to hold on to the territory they capture or suffer massive aerial attacks in retribution, the fact that they are able to mount these operations is by itself impressive.

Like most guerilla forces, the Houthis aimed to win the war by dragging it out and averting complete defeat while continuing to impose a political and military cost on the superior foe. Ballistic missiles, often used along with drones, offer a highly effective way to impose such political and military costs. The Saudi-led Coalition went to great lengths to deny the Houthis access to Yemen's ballistic missile arsenal. In April 2015, the Coalition mounted a month-long aerial strike campaign as part of Operation Decisive Storm to neutralize the Yemeni ballistic missile arsenal. Saudi Arabia received extensive American assistance to destroy Yemen's missile arsenal.[59] A joint Saudi-US cell to share real-time surveillance and targeting information was established in Riyadh.[60] By the end of the month-long campaign, the Saudis had completed more than 2,140 sorties and had expended at least 1,000 precision weapons on destroying the ammunition depots believed to contain missiles and rockets.[61] Saudi forces declared the campaign a success and touted the destruction of the Yemeni missile arsenal and launchers.[62] A spokesperson for the Coalition declared that Saudi-led forces had succeeded in destroying 80% of the Houthi weapons depots.[63] He further asserted that the Saudi-led military operation had destroyed the Houthi ballistic missile arsenal, and these would not pose any future threat to Saudi Arabia or neighboring countries.[64]

Such confidence was misplaced. The Houthis salvaged Yemen's missile arsenal. Major General Sharaf Lakman, a spokesperson for the Houthis, has suggested that the Houthis were able to repair and repurpose the missiles damaged in the Saudi airstrikes.[65] The Houthis also coopted the Yemeni government's missile forces.[66] The Houthis established three missile brigades commanded by the former Hadi regime commander, Major-General Muhammad Nasser Ahmed al-Atifi.[67] In June 2015, the Houthis launched their first missile salvo at Khamis Mushayt, a Saudi Arabian city 60 miles from the Yemeni border. The missile barrages have persisted since then. By 2016, the Houthis had come into possession of hundreds of ballistic missiles and rockets, including Scuds, shorter-range OTR-21 Tochka, 9K52 Luna-M (FROG-7) missiles, anti-ship missiles, Katyusha rockets, and Grad unguided missiles.[68]

The Houthis have shown an incredible capacity to innovate and operationalize their missile and drone arsenal, possibly aided by Iran and Hezbollah.[69] They have repurposed their arsenals of S-75 (SA-2 Guideline) surface-to-air missiles (SAMs) into missiles—the Qaher-1.[70] The Houthis have repurposed the Yemeni Missile Research and Development Center to design and assemble the Burqan missiles.[71] The Houthis quickly developed the indigenous capacity to assemble short-range ballistic missiles.[72]

Weaponizing Fear

The Houthis have used their missiles, rockets, and drones to bombard, provoke and coerce the Saudi-led Coalition. As the land campaign stalemated, the Houthis employed persistent missile strikes to induce fears of lasting economic damage and amplify political vulnerabilities, in turn provoking and coercing the Saudis and the Emiratis to alter their political and military preferences.

Houthi missile strikes on Saudi and Emirati cities impose "strategic pressure" by exposing the vulnerability of civilians.[73] Missile strikes on vital economic assets, or even threatening to do so, impose a disproportionately higher cost on the Saudis and their allies attempting to defend these assets.[74] The Saudis rely on Patriot missile defenses to defend against Houthi missiles. However, each Patriot missile defense interceptor costs approximately $1 million per piece, whereas the "flying lawn mowers" launched by the Houthis cost less than $10,000 each.[75] Even for a wealthy state such as Saudi Arabia, missile defenses offer short-term protection, not a long-term solution to missile strikes.

The Houthis employ their missiles and drones in combination with propaganda campaigns "issuing numerous threats" against the Saudis or Emiratis and "releasing video footage of past attacks" to generate domestic political pressures and coerce concessions.[76] The Houthis envision the media rhetoric that often goes along with their missile and drone strikes as a way to coerce the Saudi-led Coalition to moderate their military operations and, over the long term, force the Saudis and the United Arab Emirates to recognize the Houthis as a legitimate political power in Yemen.[77]

In 2019, for instance, Abdul Ghani al-Zubeidi, editor-in-chief for a Houthi-affiliated magazine, publicly declared that Houthi forces are "adopting a strategy of crippling movement in Jizan and Abha airports, which are take-off points of most of the aggressors' [Saudi and UAE] aircraft."[78] He then warned, "if strikes in Yemen persist, we will move to the next stage, which is targeting more distant airports in Riyadh and Jeddah."[79] The coercive message was clear: we escalate if you escalate, and we scale back if you scale back.

The Houthis may be learning these coercive bargaining tactics from Hezbollah. al-Zubeidi's warning shows strong rhetorical similarities to speeches made by Hassan Nasrallah, Secretary-General of Lebanese Hezbollah. In his 3 August 2010 "Speech of Deterrence" (*Khitaab al radaa*), Nasrallah had warned, "If you attack the Rafik al-Hariri International Airport in Beirut, we will attack Ben Gurion Airport in Tel Aviv. If you bomb our ports—we will bomb your ports. If you attack our refineries, we will bomb your refineries.[80]

While Hezbollah was deterring Israeli aggression, the Houthis aim to coerce the Saudis to halt their aggression. The Houthis have repeatedly used these tactics. More recently, after a 26 March 2022 drone and missile attack targeting Aramco oil facilities in Jeddah, the Houthis adopted a coercive logic to bargain with the Saudis.[81] Mahdi al-Mashat, a Houthi leader, declared a unilateral ceasefire immediately after the strikes and offered to make it "a final and permanent commitment in the event that Saudi Arabia commits to ending the siege and stopping its raids on Yemen once and for all."[82] Implicit in the offer was the threat of renewed strikes if the Saudis did not reciprocate. Three days later, the Saudi-led Coalition responded with a separate ceasefire announcement.[83] The Houthis have adopted a similar logic of fear and coercion against the United Arab Emirates, promising to strike "strategic, vital, sensitive and influential targets . . . [and] strongly shake the Emirati economy" if its interests are undermined by the Emiratis.[84]

The Political and Military Response to the Houthi Missile War

In 2015, when the Yemeni war began, the UAE leadership was determined to stay and finish the fight with the Houthis. In early September 2015, a Houthi missile strike hit an ammunition depot in Marib, killing 60 Emirati, Saudi, and Bahrani soldiers, including senior Saudi and Emirati personnel.[85] The UAE troops suffered the most, with 45 casualties.[86] Anwar Gargash, the UAE Minister of State for Foreign Affairs, proclaimed, "Let it be known to the enemy that the United Arab Emirates' determination is strengthened by the sacrifices of its people and the bravery of its armed forces."[87] He promised UAE's determination to accomplish the Coalitions' mission.[88]

The UAE air force responded with a massive aerial strike on Houthi hideouts.[89] Yet, within four years, the Houthis have successfully worn down Emirati resolve. Missile and drone strikes are a big part of the Houthi strategy. Conventional guerilla warfare tactics have made it possible for the Houthis to fend off military advances by forces supported by the United Arab Emirates.[90] In addition, missile and drone strikes provide the Houthis with an effective way to impose a cost on the Emiratis. For example, a 2017 Burqan-1 ballistic missile strike on a Saudi-UAE military base on Zuqar Island caused the death of around 80 soldiers.[91] Another missile strike on the al-Jala military base in Aden killed a high-ranking commander of the UAE-supported Security Belt Forces, Brigadier General Munir Mahmoud Ahmad al-Mashali, and more than 30 soldiers.[92]

The United Arab Emirates had grown weary of the grinding and costly war.[93] In 2019, the Emiratis withdrew their armed forces from the campaign as the political and military costs became too high to pay for a campaign that was not at the core of UAE national survival and security.[94] Anwar Gargash, the UAE Minister of State for Foreign Affairs, was now advocating for a peace process that takes "account of the legitimate aspirations of all parts of Yemeni society. That includes the Houthis. Houthi militias have wreaked havoc on the country, but they are a part of Yemeni society and they will have a role in its future."[95] The United Arab Emirates has withdrawn its armed forces from the battlefield but has continued to support and train certain militia groups fighting the Houthis to maintain leverage over the future of Yemen.[96] The United Arab Emirates has also established air bases on strategic islands overlooking the Bab Al-Mandab straits.[97]

As the United Arab Emirates was beginning to pull back its troops in Yemen, Houthi spokesman al-Zubeidi delivered a coercive warning, "there is an understanding with Abu Dhabi not to escalate the situation in western Yemen through their [local Yemeni] allies. Otherwise, Houthis will have a strong response and will come after Abu Dhabi's ports and airports."[98] Again, on 26 September 2019, Houthi-affiliated Lieutenant General Abed Al-Thour repeated the coercive warning in an Al-Masirah television program, proclaiming that "with its aerial strikes and missile force, Yemen will send the UAE back to a time before its foundation" if it reengaged militarily.[99] It can be reasonably argued that the Houthis coerced the Emiratis to partially concede and withdraw. The Houthi missile and drone strikes were essential to that outcome. Since 2019, the Houthis have in a few instances engaged in missile and drone strikes on targets inside United Arab Emirates.[100]

The Missile War at Sea

In late 2016, the Houthis began attempting a sea denial strategy against the United Arab Emirates and the Saudis using anti-ship cruise missiles and improvised explosive devices.[101] In the first attempt, on 1 October 2016, the Houthis fired an anti-ship missile (probably a radar-guided Chinese-made C-801 or a C-802) targeting the UAE's HSV-2 Swift traversing the narrow Bab Al-Mandab straits.[102] The Bab Al-Mandab strait is a key transit route for ships passing from the Mediterranean through the Suez Canal into the Indian Ocean, carrying a large proportion of the world's oil supply. Some estimates suggest that between 500,000 and 700,000 barrels per day (bpd) of crude oil exports transit through the Bab Al-Mandab.[103] The Houthi forces put out a statement that "rockets targeted an Emirati warship as it approached the coast of Mokha. It was completely destroyed."[104] The United Arab Emirates, however, did not confirm any details except to note that one of its vessels was involved in an incident.[105]

The United States quickly dispatched two guided missile destroyers—the *USS Nitze* (DDG-94) and the *USS Mason* (DDG-87)—to positions off the Yemeni coast to prevent further escalation.[106] The two destroyers were supported by a third afloat forward staging base ship, the *USS Ponce* (AFSB(I)-15).[107] The American destroyer *USS Mason* came under missile attack on 9 October 2016. The destroyer had to deploy decoys and missile defense interceptors to avert a strike.[108] A US Department of Defense spokesperson noted, "Anybody who puts US Navy ships at risk does so at their own peril."[109] A second attempted missile attack on *USS Mason* occurred on 12 October 2016.[110] On 15 October 2016, the *USS Mason* was fired on again. The United States responded with "limited self-defense" Tomahawk cruise missile strikes against coastal radar facilities in Yemen.[111] After the American strike on Yemeni coastal radar installations, the Pentagon press secretary stated that the United States will continue to respond as appropriate to maintain freedom of navigation in the Red Sea and the Bab al-Mandeb.[112]

The Houthis, however, have continued to threaten and target military and civilian ships in the Bab Al-Mandab straits. In June 2017, the Houthis struck a UAE naval vessel.[113] In January 2018, Saleh al-Samad, the chief of the Houthi political council, warned, "if the aggressors keep pushing toward Hodeidah and if the political solution hits a wall, there are some strategic choices that will be taken as a no return point, including blocking the international navigation in the Red Sea."[114] In May 2018, the Houthis attacked and damaged a Turkish freighter.[115] On 25 July 2018, the Houthis attempted to strike two Saudi oil tankers and may have possibly damaged one of those tankers, forcing Saudi Arabia to halt temporarily all shipments through the Bab Al-Mandab straits.[116] Khalid al-Falih, Saudi Arabia's Energy Minister, declared that he was "halting all oil shipments" temporarily "until the situation becomes clearer and the maritime transit through Bab al-Mandab is safe."[117] Since 2018, while the Saudis, with American support, have managed to keep the Bab Al-Mandab straits open, there is a constant fear that the Houthis might shut down navigation in the Red Sea.[118] The Houthis are still able to harass and impede the transit of ships in the Bab Al-Mandab straits.[119]

The Houthi Missile and Drone War Against Saudi Arabia

The missile and drone attacks on the Saudis far outnumbered the assault on the United Arab Emirates. The Houthis have fired several ballistic missiles, cruise missiles, and drones at economic targets in Saudi Arabia, with a particular emphasis on oil and petroleum processing facilities. After they target these Saudi Arabian economic targets, the Houthis' propaganda apparatus promptly delivers coercive messages. The messages invariably characterize the attacks as retribution for Saudi air strikes and contain an implicit bargain of mutual de-escalation. For instance, on 16 September 2019, the Houthis attacked Saudi Arabia's Aramco petroleum processing facilities in Abqaiq and Khurais using a combination of drones and cruise missiles.[120] The facility in Abqaiq is seen as "the mother lode" for an adversarial attack on Saudi Arabia's oil infrastructure.[121] The Abqaiq facility is a vital node processing crude from several Saudi oil fields. It is the world's largest processing facility, with a capacity to produce 7 million barrels per day.[122] Similarly, the Khurais facility produces 1.5 million barrels per day.[123] The missile and drone attack reportedly disrupted almost half the Kingdom's oil production and caused prices to rise to a six-month high momentarily.[124] Yahya Saree, the Houthi spokesperson, in a statement read out on Houthis' Al Masirah TV, said that "these attacks are our right, and we warn the Saudis that our targets will keep expanding. We have a right to strike back in retaliation to the air strikes and the targeting of our civilians for the last five years."[125]

On 20 March 2022, the Houthis executed a coordinated barrage of missile and drone strikes on several critical infrastructure targets, including a liquified natural gas plant in the Saudi port city of Yanbu, an oil facility in the Saudi port city of Jeddah, a water desalination plant in Al-Shaqeeq on the Red Sea coast, a power station in southwestern Saudi Arabia, an Aramco terminal in Jizan, and a target in Khamis Mushayt.[126] The Yanbu Aramco Sinopec Refining Company, a $10 billion joint venture between China and Aramco, usually has an output of 400,000 barrels per day. It suffered damage causing a temporary reduction in its production.[127] A Houthi spokesman declared the missile and drone strikes were a response to the "continued aggression and unjust siege of our people" by the Saudi-led Coalition."[128] Again, within a week, on 26 March 2022, Houthis targeted an Aramco oil depot in Jeddah.[129] The targeted oil depot accounted for more than a quarter of Saudi Arabia's supply.[130] Immediately after, the Houthis in a coercive bargaining attempt offered to end these strikes if "Saudi Arabia commits to ending the siege and stopping its raids on Yemen once and for all."[131]

While the attacks on oil and petroleum facilities seek to impose economic pressures, the Houthis have repeatedly struck cities and military bases to impose political pressure on the Saudis and its allies. On 14 December 2015, a short-range OTR-21 Tochka ballistic missile struck a Coalition military base near Bab al-Mandeb's straits, killing 152 soldiers, including the commander of Saudi Special Forces, Colonel Abdullah Al- Sahyan.[132] On 11 April 2018, Houthis fired several missiles targeting the defense ministry in Riyadh and other sites. The Houthis claimed the missile attacks were "in retaliation for air raids on Yemen by the Western-backed coalition."[133] On 21 January 2020, Houthi ballistic missiles struck a mosque in the al-Estiqbal military camp of the Yemeni government, killing more than 116 soldiers.[134] On 23 June 2020, the Houthis targeted the Saudi Ministry of Defense and the King Salman Air Base in Riyadh, along with targets in Jizan and Najran. The strikes were undertaken with a combination of Zulfiqar ballistic missiles, Quds cruise missiles, and Samad-3 drones.[135] Yahya Saree, a spokesperson for the Houthis, claimed in a television interview that a large number of ballistic missiles and drones bombarded the Saudi military headquarters and King Salman Air Base as a response to Saudi aggression.[136]

On 13 July 2020, the Houthis announced a successful "military operation" with ballistic missiles and drones targeting several military bases in the Southern Saudi Arabian border regions of Jizan, Najran, and Assir.[137] The Houthis claimed the attack had "killed and injured dozens of ranking [Saudi] military officers."[138] Again, on 12 July 2022, Houthis claimed that a coordinated missile-drone strike struck and disabled "military aircraft, pilot accommodation and Patriot systems in Khamis Mushait" and other military targets at airports in Abha, Jizan, and Najran as retribution for Coalition air strikes on Houthi-controlled territory.[139]

Interspersed among the strikes on military bases, the Houthis have periodically bombarded Riyadh and other major cities to augment the political pressure on the Saudis. In September 2016, the Houthi regime launched their 800-kilometer Burqan ballistic missile at Ta'if, Saudi Arabia's summer capital city, and at Jeddah, the kingdom's largest port city.[140] On 28 October 2016, the Houthis allegedly targeted Mecca with a Burqan missile.[141] The Houthis launched a Burqan-2H on 4 November 2017, targeting the Riyadh international airport in retaliation for a Saudi-led Coalition air strike.[142] A message put out by the Houthi-controlled Yemeni news channel Al-Masirah declared, "we repeatedly affirmed that capitals of aggression states won't be spared from our ballistic missiles in retaliation for the constant targeting of civilians."[143] Saudi Arabia accused Iran of orchestrating the missile strike.[144]

On 19 December 2017, the Houthis fired a missile at Riyadh. The Saudis claimed that the missile targeted residential areas. However, the Houthis said the target was King Salman's Palace.[145] The missile attack was designed to spread fear among the political elite.[146] On 25 August 2019, the Houthis reportedly fired 10 Badr-1 short-range ballistic missiles targeting the Jizan airport, killing and wounding dozens.[147] On 20 February 2020, the Houthis attempted to strike several cities simultaneously, including possibly Riyadh, a few days before a scheduled G20 meeting.[148] On 16 June 2020, the Houthis launched a ballistic missile targeting Najran in Southern Saudi Arabia.[149] On 23 June 2020, the Houthis targeted Riyadh with the coordinated launch of three ballistic missiles and eight bomb-laden drones.[150] On 20 November 2021, the Houthis launched a barrage of ballistic missiles and unmanned aerial vehicles (UAVs) targeting Jeddah, Abha, Jizan, and Najran.[151] A Houthi military spokesperson said the attacks were a response to the Saudi-led Coalition's "continuation of its crime and siege" of Yemen.[152]

These strikes on vital economic infrastructure, military bases, and major cities have imposed unanticipated severe costs on the Saudis and diminished their resolve. A United Nations Panel of Experts report points out that the missile strikes have forced Saudi Arabia "to deploy disproportionately costly counter-measures to protect itself from such attacks."[153] The Saudi-led Coalition forces may be spending approximately $5–6 billion monthly on various military countermeasures.[154] The Patriot missile defenses are at the center of these countermeasures. As pointed out earlier in the chapter, each Patriot missile defense interceptor the Saudis employ costs $1 million. In contrast, the Houthis' missiles cost less than $10,000 each.[155] The constant barrage of missile attacks by the Houthis has forced the Saudis to deplete their Patriot missile defense interceptors, requiring desperate efforts to replenish its inventory.[156] Furthermore, the Houthis have found ingenious ways to defeat Patriot missile defenses. The Houthis used drones to strike and damage Patriot missile defenses and then launched missiles before the missile defense system could be fixed.[157] The Houthis employed similar tactics to defeat the missile defenses of the United Arab Emirates. Using open-source GPS coordinates of the Patriot systems, the Houthis programmed their Qasef-1 drone to attack UAE Patriot missile defense systems radars. Once the radars were disabled, the Houthis targeted other sites with missiles unhindered.[158]

The Saudis have received extensive American support in their missile-hunting mission. In 2018, American Green Beret Army special forces were secretly deployed to aid the Saudi-led Coalitions missile-hunting operations.[159] The special forces were involved in locating and destroying ballistic missiles and the launch sites used by the Houthis to attack Riyadh and other Saudi Arabian cities.[160] The Saudi-led Coalition has also undertaken resource-intensive interdiction operations in weapons smuggling routes.[161] Finally, the Saudis have responded to missile strikes with disproportionately heavy barrages of airstrikes to punish and dissuade the Houthis.[162]

None of these military measures has worked. By December 2021, the Houthis were firing almost a dozen ballistic missiles along with repeated drone strikes every week.[163] When the conflict began the Saudi leadership anticipated victory against the Houthis within months. Yet eight years later, the war has dragged on, and the Houthis have imposed severe costs on the Saudis and the Emiratis using their missiles and drones. As costs mounted, Saudi (and Emirati) resolve has faded away. The Saudis and other members of the Coalition had broad geopolitical stake in the Yemeni conflict, but their national survival is not dependent on the conflict. As a result, the Saudis have come to begrudgingly accept that the Houthis will have to be a part of an eventual political settlement in Yemen.

Conclusion

In 2015, the Saudis and Emiratis expected a quick victory over the Houthis in Yemen. However, eight years later, there is no apparent path to military victory for the Saudi-led Coalition. The Houthis have denied any meaningful territorial gains to the Saudi-led Coalition. The Houthis have also imposed economic and political costs on the Saudis and Emiratis by bombarding them with missile and drone strikes. The missile and drone strikes have stoked fears of economic shocks and political embarrassment. Despite massive investment in missile-hunting and defense operations, Houthi bombardments have not decreased. A large-scale Saudi ground invasion is improbable and possibly infeasible. The Saudis and the Emiratis are now looking for an exit ramp to extricate themselves from Yemen while securing their borders and homeland.[164]

On 1 April 2022, the UN Special Envoy for Yemen, Hans Grundberg, announced a two-month truce between the Houthis and the Saudi-led Coalition. Grundberg noted that both parties "accepted to halt all offensive" operations and facilitate the transit of ships carrying essential goods into the Hudaydah port and commercial flights to operate from Sana'a airport.[165] Bruce Riedel credits chief UN negotiator Grundberg with crafting a framework for the ceasefire agreement that "effectively ignores the existing UN Security Council resolutions which call for Houthi disarmament and territorial surrender" and avoids zero-sum negotiations.[166] The Saudi-led Coalition has agreed to the exile of President Hadi as part of the truce agreement.[167] Instead, a Presidential Leadership Council consisting of several factions was established under the leadership of Rashad al-Alimi.[168] In June 2022, the Houthis and the Saudis directly held talks on border security.[169] The Houthis have signaled a commitment to the process.[170] However, the Houthis have resisted lifting the siege on Taiz, a city controlled by Yemeni government forces.[171] The truce, while extended for two months, is precariously resting.

It remains to be seen if the truce will lead to permanent peace and political reconciliation.

Recent developments suggest a negotiated peace could take hold. In March 2023, Saudi Arabia and Iran, in a Chinese-brokered deal, agreed to restore diplomatic ties. As part of the deal, Iran has momentarily agreed to stop arming the Houthis.[172] In September 2023, a delegation of Houthi negotiators met with their Saudi counterparts in Riyadh for five days in an attempt to arrive at a potential agreement.[173] However, during the truce, the Houthis have also considerably augmented their arsenal of ballistic missiles, cruise missiles, and loitering drones and may be using it to pressure the Saudis at the negotiating table.[174] Speaking at a military parade on 21 September 2023, immediately after the meeting in Riyadh, Houthi Defense Minister Mohammed al-Atifi said, "we repeat our warnings to foreign forces . . . that we will not accept their presence on our lands."[175] A statement from the Houthi military further noted, "peace will be achieved only by imposing a deterrent military equation that forces the enemy to submit" to the legitimate demands of the Houthis.[176]

Irrespective of how the truce between the Houthis and the Saudis pans out, the ability of the Houthis to gain a seat at the bargaining table cannot be explained without accounting for the missile and drone campaigns the Houthis waged against the Saudi-led Coalition.

8

Conclusion

In a 1962 conversation with Shimon Peres, Israel's then Deputy Defense Minister, President John F. Kennedy asked, "on this subject of missiles, the danger is that there's no point in having missiles unless you placed nonconventional warheads on them. Don't you agree that the warheads are more dangerous than the missiles?"[1] Shimon Peres replies to President Kennedy, "let me say that a missile with a conventional warhead is very different from a bomb released from a plane . . . it sows terror and enhances the sense of power of those who employ it."[2]

More than 60 years later, the argument made by Shimon Peres remains valid. The world is still facing increasingly dangerous threats from rockets, missiles, and drones. This book offers a theory to understand and systematically explore these threats. In the bombing to provoke theory, I argue that rockets, missiles, and drones remain potent at inducing fear and panicking an adversary. Rockets, missiles, and drones give weak states and non-state actors the means to attempt what a bullfighter does with a red cape: force an emotionally charged response from an adversary. Aerospace weapons induce fear in an adversary by threatening a chemical, biological, or nuclear strike or by demonstrating the ability to bombard the target's economic and political core repeatedly. These fears amplify the political vulnerabilities of the target state. The fears and political vulnerabilities provoke the target state to divert substantial military resources to redress the aerospace threat. If the targeted state is unable to extinguish the aerospace threat, it may weaken its resolve and lead to political concessions. Such concessions, limited or otherwise, are evidence of coercion.

This book examined the empirical validity of the argument using five critical case studies and employed four predictions to examine the theoretical argument. First, states employing aerospace weapons in warfare should attempt to induce fear in the adversary through their operational tactics and communicated threats. Second, the decisionmakers of the states targeted by aerospace weapons should actively respond to these fears in their debates. As a result of these fears, states subject to aerospace bombardment will respond with diversionary military countermeasures. Third, states with the means to

---

Bombing to Provoke. Jaganath Sankaran, Oxford University Press. © Oxford University Press 2024.
DOI: 10.1093/oso/9780197792629.003.0008

divert military resources to defend, suppress, and eventually extinguish the threat through defensive and offensive means will be able to overcome the coercion without offering other major concessions to end the war. Finally, states that are unable to effectively defend, suppress, and eventually extinguish the bombardment may suffer a diminution of resolve and be forced to offer concessions to end the war.

In all five case studies, as detailed in the first prediction, the analysis demonstrates that states employing aerospace weapons actively sought to induce fear in their quarry through tactics and threats. In the case of World War II, the repeated use of the V-1 and V-2 missiles on vital economic and political targets induced fear in the Allied forces. The V-1 and V-2 bombardment distracted, delayed, tormented, and provoked the Allied forces until the very end of the war. In the case of the 1981–1988 Iran–Iraq War, the threat of an impending chemically armed ballistic missile bombardment was weaponized to strike fear in the minds of Iranian decisionmakers and citizens. For example, the Iraqis were publicly threatening to "'level' Iranian cities using 'all available weapons' until Iran agrees to a settlement."[3] The Iraqis had also privately signaled to Khomeini that if he did not halt the war, Iraq would launch chemically armed ballistic missiles at Iranian cities.[4] The threat of chemical weapons delivered by ballistic missiles was vital to Iranian capitulation in the Iran–Iraq War. In the case of the 1991 Gulf War, Saddam Hussein and his Foreign Minister Tariq Aziz had explicitly declared before the war that Israel could be hit with missiles if Iraq was attacked.[5] As the war unfolded, the missile bombardment and the possibility of a chemical weapons strike were used to induce fear and provoke the American forces into a diversionary military campaign. In the cases of the 2006 Second Lebanon War and the ongoing Yemeni War, a robust campaign of coercive threats and the repeated bombardment of vital targets stoked fears and political disillusionment in the target. These findings validate the first prediction that states employing ballistic missiles in warfare should attempt to induce fear in the adversary through their operational tactics and communicated threats.

The second prediction argues that states subjected to aerospace bombardment should actively respond to the fears in their internal and external political debates. In four of the five cases—World War II, the 1981–1988 Iran–Iraq War, the 1991 Gulf War, and the 2006 Second Lebanon War—I can process trace and observe the political debates and vulnerabilities generated by the fear of rockets, missiles, and drones. I employ a variety of source materials— archival documents, declassified intelligence documents, selected oral histories, and secondary written materials, including autobiographies of key personalities involved in the history of the four case studies—to capture the internal and external political debates and military threat assessments made by the target state in the throes of fear. These internal and external political debates and military threat assessments show that fear was a causal factor in provoking the target states to respond with diversionary military efforts.

In the case of World War II, the 1991 Gulf War, and the 2006 Second Lebanon War, I have been able to extensively document the internal and external political debates and military threat assessments. In these three case studies, the targets involved democratic states—the United States, Britain, and Israel—as targets. In the case of the Iran—Iraq War, Iranian autocratic leaders exhibited fear and political vulnerability in their internal and external political debates. For instance, after more than a million residents had left Tehran fearing chemically armed missile strikes, Iranian Parliamentary Speaker Ali Akbar Hashemi Rafsanjani stated in a news conference, "we didn't request the people to leave their houses . . . but we encourage them to be far away from danger; we are very anxious about our people."[6]

In the fifth case study, the ongoing Yemeni War, I was not able to access evidence that would detail internal political debates in Saudi Arabia or its Coalition allies. However, other public statements lend some credence to the prediction that aerospace bombardment heightens the political vulnerability of the target state. In the future, if and when evidence from the Saudi internal deliberations becomes available, it will provide vital verification on the ability of ballistic missiles to induce fear in an adversary.

The other aspect of the second prediction argues that states targeted by aerospace weapons should react to the fears by diverting military assets to counter the threat. In four of the five case studies—World War II, the 1991 Gulf War, the 2006 Second Lebanon War, and the ongoing Yemeni War—I am able to observe extensive diversionary military countermeasures, both defensive and offensive, undertaken to defeat and suppress the missile threat. In World War II, the Allied Forces undertook a massive missile defense and counterforce effort. The Allied forces committed thousands of heavy and light anti-aircraft guns, squadrons of fighter planes to shoot down incoming missiles, 200 of the most advanced radar systems, and more than a quarter of a million military personnel to defend against incoming missiles.[7] Additionally, as part of its counterforce efforts, between August 1943 and March 1945, the Allied air forces undertook 68,913 air strike sorties and dropped close to 122,000 tons of bombs on missile-related targets.

In the 1991 Gulf War, Patriot missile defenses were rushed to the theater but proved ineffective.[8] The US-led forces undertook an enormous counterforce operation to suppress Saddam Hussein's missiles. Norman Schwarzkopf, the commander of the US-led Coalition, notes that, at its peak, "one-third of the more than two thousand combat and support missions scheduled each day for the strategic air campaign" were repurposed and diverted toward hunting Scud missiles to respond to the political pressure to do something.[9] Atkinson writes that, at one point, the fighter pilots were instructed to "drop a bomb every half hour on any suspected Scud site" to dissuade Iraqi missile launch crews.[10]

In the 2006 Second Lebanon War, Hezbollah fired nearly 4,000 rockets into Israel.[11] As the rockets kept falling, Israeli leaders were forced to commit more resources and ramp up the aerial strikes. In frustration over the inability to stop the bombardment, the Israeli Air Force (IAF) expanded the list of targets "to exact punishment."[12] The IAF flew nearly 10,000 aircraft combat sorties and bombed about 7,000 targets, using about 19,000 bombs and about 2,000 missiles, including precision-guided munitions.[13] Yet, despite Israel's substantial efforts, Hezbollah's short-range rocket bombardment persisted throughout the war.

Finally, in the ongoing Yemeni War, the Saudis have procured a large arsenal of Patriot missile defense interceptors to defend against Houthi missiles.[14] However, the Houthis have managed to subvert these defensive systems.[15] Saudi Arabia's Defense Ministry spokesperson, Lieutenant Colonel Turki al Maliki, when asked why Saudi Arabia, despite massive efforts on missile defenses, could not avert the 2019 attack on Abqaiq and Khurais, responded that "there is no country in the world being attacked with such amount of ballistic missiles."[16] The Saudis have also carried out 24,800 air raids on various Houthi targets, including missile launch and preparation sites to eliminate the threat.[17] These diversionary military countermeasures observed across the four cases demonstrate the provocative effect of aerospace weapons.

The third prediction of the argument claims that states with the means to divert military resources to defend, suppress, and eventually extinguish the missile threat through defensive and offensive means will be able to overcome the coercion without offering other major concessions to end the war. The third prediction is validated in the cases of World War II and the 1991 Gulf War. In both cases, the political resolve to defeat the adversary was persistent throughout the war. In the case of the 1991 Gulf War, an alternative political resolution brokered by the Soviet Union was rejected by the United States because it was persistent in its resolve to eject Saddam Hussein's forces from Kuwait. In the case of World War II, there is no indication that the decisionmakers wavered from their commitment to depose the Nazi regime. In both cases, the targeted states were able to divert significant military resources to suppress and extinguish the aerospace threat.

As a corollary, the fourth prediction argues that states that are unable to effectively defend, suppress, and eventually extinguish the missile campaign may suffer a diminution of resolve and be forced to offer concessions to end the war. This prediction plays out in the 1981–1988 Iran–Iraq War, the 2006 Second Lebanon War, and the ongoing Yemeni War. In the case of the Iran–Iraq War, the Iranians had no means to defend against Iraqi missiles or to mount a robust counterforce campaign to suppress the missile strikes. Ultimately, the Iranians, while not losing the war on the battlefield, accepted a ceasefire agreement coerced by the threat of missile strikes armed with chemical weapons on major Iranian cities. In the case of the 2006 Second Lebanon War, Hezbollah employed a two-pronged tactic to stall Israeli forces and deny them victory. Hezbollah mounted a surprisingly robust forward defense to impose casualties on Israeli troops. Additionally, rocket bombardment was used to continuously strike at cities and settlements in northern Israel, causing civilian casualties and economic distress. Hezbollah believed if the forward defense on the ground imposed casualties and held back Israeli forces long enough, the political pressure on Israel's leaders could coerce them into offering concessions. Hezbollah's strategy worked. While Israel had the military capability to continue waging the war, its resolve had diminished. After 34 days of intense combat, Israel withdrew, unable to achieve its stated goals.[18] Finally, in the ongoing Yemeni War, the Saudis have been able to afford the costly diversionary military efforts to suppress the missile threats until now.[19] However, after eight years of war and without an end in sight, their political resolve has diminished. The Saudis have begun negotiating with the Houthis to extricate themselves from the war.

Directions for Future Research

My argument and the four predictions made in this book were tested on the five case studies discussed above. There remain several directions for future research on the subject. One obvious direction is to test the predictions on similar cases to refine the scope conditions further. The 1979–1989 Soviet–Afghan War is a prime example. In the Soviet–Afghan War, as many as 2,000 Scud missiles were fired at Afghani rebel targets.[20] Future research can determine if the Soviet bombardment produced provocative effects as predicted by the theory. The Soviet–Afghan War did not end with a favorable result for the Soviets. It could be valuable to understand why, despite general military superiority and a sustained aerospace bombardment, the Soviets lost the war. Another viable case study is the naval war between the British Fleet and Argentine forces during the 1982 Falklands War. In the 1982 Falklands War, the Exocet anti-ship cruise missiles used by the Argentine forces became the British Fleet's "most feared threat."[21] The use of these cruise missiles struck fear in the minds of the British and forced several diversionary military measures.[22] A case study testing the congruence between the Falklands War and the arguments described in this book would also sharpen its scope.

Three other recent conflicts—the 2020 Nagorno-Karabakh War, the 2022 Russia–Ukraine War, and the 2023 Israel–Hamas War—also offer case studies to refine the theory further. In the 44-day war between Armenia and Azerbaijan, the Azeris employed rockets, missiles, and drones to successfully wrest control of the Nagorno-Karbakh region from Armenia. Azerbaijan used its drones to exploit gaps and vulnerabilities in Armenia's air defenses, eventually rendering the air defenses inert and gaining air superiority.[23] The air superiority enabled Azeri infantry units to take over Armenian-held territories. A case study based on the Nagorno-Karabakh conflict would be vital to exploring the coercive effects of drones and their role in combined arms warfare.

In the ongoing Russia–Ukraine War, ballistic missiles, cruise missiles, and drones have been employed extensively. Russian bombardment aims to exhaust Ukraine's defenses, wear down Ukrainian resolve, and coerce it into a settlement. Russia has adopted various tactics to degrade and deplete Ukrainian air defenses. Russia has employed hybrid aerospace strikes, using salvos of cruise missiles, ballistic missiles, and drones launched from several location across a range of azimuths to overload air defenses and maximize the probability of penetration.[24] It has also used drones as a probing tool to ferret out air defense systems and then target its missiles to engage them.[25] Russia has also used missiles with concrete ballast payloads to exhaust Ukrainian air defense interceptors.[26] The Russian aerospace bombardment has provoked a diversion of air and missile defense resources away from the frontline to the interior of Ukraine.[27] The diversion has rendered Ukrainian troops vulnerable to Russian tactical air strikes. As more details emerge, a case study on the Russia–Ukraine War could offer crucial leverage in testing the theory detailed in this book and determining the limits of the coercive effects of aerospace weapons.

Hamas has repeatedly used rockets to provoke and coerce Israel into conflicts and negotiated settlements. Rockets played a significant role in the gambit to the 2023 Israel–Hamas War. On 7 October 2023, using a massive rocket barrage as cover, Hamas militants stormed into Israeli towns, killing and abducing several Israelis.[28] Hamas has claimed that it launched 5,000 rockets on 7 October, whereas Israeli Defense Forces suggest that 2,200 rockets were fired.[29] By 31 October 2023, more than 8,500 rockets had been fired at Israel.[30] Most of these Hamas rockets were inaccurate and are indigenously built in Gaza with Iranian assistance.[31] But given the very large volume of rocket barrages, the Iron Dome defense system has come under duress and has been unable to intercept all the rockets striking populated areas and other critical facilities.[32] However, preliminary evidence suggests that the Iron Dome defense system has performed to the satisfaction of Israel's Ministry of Defense.[33] A few days after the 7 October attack, the Houthis targeted Israel with missiles and drones, prompting rare activation of Israel's Arrow missile defense system.[34] Israel's air and missile defense would be brought under immense strain if Hamas, Hezbollah, and the Houthis coordinated their rocket and missile strikes. A case study on the coercive effect of rockets in the wars between Hamas and Israel would inform and clarify the scope of the bombing to provoke theory.

Another possible direction for future research may be to explore the effects of aerospace campaigns that precede and accompany a broader air campaign. Example case studies include, among others, the American cruise missile campaign in the 1991 Gulf War, the cruise missile campaign that supported NATO's operations in Bosnia, and the 2011 allied cruise missile assault in the Libyan War. The 2020 Iranian ballistic missiles strike on the Ayn al Asad military base in retaliation for the killing of Iranian General Qassem Soleimani may be another interesting case study.[35] These case studies can provide empirical leverage to further test and refine the arguments and predictions made in this book.

Implications for Policy

The findings that emerge in this book have immediate policy relevance. Understanding the character of the threat posed by aerospace weapons to the United States and its allies is an urgent policy priority. A 2020 report jointly published by the National Air and Space Intelligence Center (NASIC) and the Defense Intelligence Ballistic Missile Analysis Committee (DIBMAC) declared that cruise and ballistic missiles would be used as "instruments of coercion" by adversaries seeking to end a crisis or a conflict with the United States or its allies on preferential terms.[36] The 2020 NASIC-DIBMAC report observed that missiles are an effective weapon for states facing adversaries with air superiority and formidable air defense systems.[37] In particular, three nation-states—Iran, North Korea, and China—are seen as potential adversaries that would use their ballistic missile arsenals to complicate US efforts in a contingency and coerce concessions.

Iran has the largest rocket, missile, and drone arsenal in the Middle East.[38] A 2019 US Defense Intelligence Agency (DIA) report argues that Iran developed its aerospace weapons to dissuade its regional adversaries and the United States.[39] Iran's aerospace weapons serve as its strategic deterrent.[40] Iran has also shared technology and transferred aerospace weapons to several regional actors that challenge the United States and its allies, despite UN resolutions that prohibit such weapons transfer.[41] The DIA report indicated that Iran would target regional military bases, energy infrastructure targets, and population centers to coerce its adversaries.[42] Fears over Iran's missiles have galvanized concerns among US allies in the Middle East. In June 2022, top military officials from Israel, Saudi Arabia, Qatar, Egypt, and Jordan met with US military commanders secretly to discuss ways to "coordinate against Iran's growing missile and drone capabilities."[43] While any coordination may be limited, even the possibility of such exploratory talks demonstrates the potency of Iran's missile force.

North Korea has amassed a large arsenal of rockets and missiles targeting US regional and allied targets throughout the Asia-Pacific region. North Korea's rockets and close-range ballistic missiles are aimed at Seoul and nearby military installations. These rockets can "inflict severe damage and heavy casualties" on South Koreans and deployed American personnel.[44] North Korean regional missiles can hit targets throughout the Korean peninsula, Japan, and other longer-range American bases.[45] In a congressional hearing in 2017, a North Korean defector who formerly served as deputy chief of mission at the London embassy claimed that as soon as American and allied preparations for a military action commenced, North Korea would immediately initiate "artillery and short-range missile fire" on a range of targets.[46] North Korean doctrine still maintains these goals of disrupting or delaying the arrival of US troops in a military contingency using its aerospace weapons.[47] In the early stages of a conflict, major naval ports and air bases in South Korea and Japan would be critical targets and lie within the range of North Korean missiles.[48] North Korea has also indicated that it would consider striking major cities and commercial ports in Japan with ballistic missiles to instill fear and coerce Japan to stay out of any conflict.[49]

Finally, the 2019 US Missile Defense Review (MDR) notes that China's large missile arsenal is intended to generate "coercive political and military advantages in a regional crisis or conflict."[50] The bulk of China's missile arsenal is now targeted at regional airbases, logistics, communications, and port facilities that would play an important role in a regional military contingency involving the United States and its allies.[51] American policymakers have noted that China, as a non-signatory to the Intermediate-Range Nuclear Forces (INF) Treaty, has been able to assemble an extensive array of regional ballistic and cruise missiles, "titling the conventional military balance of power in East Asia in its favor" and has seriously eroded the American conventional deterrent.[52] The threat of the Chinese missile arsenal was a significant factor in the US decision to withdraw from the INF Treaty in 2019. Then National Security Advisor John Bolton, referencing China's missile program, noted a "new strategic reality," and the INF Treaty did not account for it.[53] He complained that the INF Treaty was a "bilateral treaty in a multipolar ballistic missile world."[54]

The Iranian, North Korean, and Chinese missile arsenals pose significant challenges for American policymakers. The insights emerging from this book offer important policy lessons for American policymakers. First, the strategic effect of a ballistic missile campaign far exceeds the purely physical impacts of the bombardment campaign. Allies facing the brunt of a ballistic missile campaign will demand significant diversionary military efforts even if traditional military-tactical considerations may argue against such diversions.

Air and missile defenses provide one mechanism to partially dilute the strategic effects of an adversary's missile bombardment. Air and missile defenses may reassure US allies. However, such defenses will not suffice, as demonstrated in the ongoing Yemeni War and Russia–Ukraine War. Air and missile defenses are often too costly, vulnerable to defeat, and have limited operational effectiveness. As the Yemeni War case study in the book suggests, even with recent technological advances, air and missile defenses may not be the perfect shield that can fully defend against an aerospace bombardment campaign. Therefore, in addition to air and missile defenses, diversionary military efforts will require significant offensive counterforce operations on the adversary. The practical demands of such offensive operations may lead to tensions between the United States and its allies and between political leaders and military officers.

For instance, in World War II, while American commanders often protested against orders to engage in diversionary counterforce strikes on missile-related targets, they were consistently overruled by the military and political high command. US Army Air Forces Commander General Henry H. "Hap" Arnold and US Strategic Air Force in Europe (USSTAF) Commander General Carl Spaatz strongly argued against any diversion of air strikes to V-1 and V-2 targets, instead arguing that the focus should be on bombarding German cities and industries designed to cripple German military capabilities before the beginning of the Normandy landings.[55] General Spaatz, protesting against the diversion of air strikes to missile-related targets, argued that if "things kept up this way, he would not have enough aircraft to support Operation Overlord much less Operation Pointblank."[56] American air force experts also believed the British approach to bombing German missile sites was flawed. American military leaders, after extensive field testing at Eglin Air Base in Florida, believed minimum-altitude bombing conducted by fighter aircraft, rather than bombers, was the ideal approach to hit Crossbow targets. However, British Air Chief Marshal Leigh-Mallory insisted on using heavy bombers at high altitudes to avoid German anti-aircraft defenses. General Arnold was angered at "British obstinacy" and disregard for hard evidence.[57] However, Eisenhower overruled his American deputies. Eisenhower, threading the delicate balance of coalition management in wartime, conceded to Leigh-Mallory and approved the continued use of heavy bombers despite the evidence emerging from the Eglin field tests.[58] Eisenhower declared that attacking the large and ski sites would take priority over all Allied air operations.[59]

Similarly, in the 1991 Gulf War, field commanders protested against the diversion of military assets to the Scud-hunting mission, arguing instead for striking Saddam Hussein's military assets and industrial facilities. The American military and political high command overruled the field commanders. At a meeting that included Colin Powell and other members of the armed forces, Secretary of Defense Richard Cheney shouted: "Goddamn it, I want some coverage out there. If I have to talk to Schwarzkopf, I'll do it. . . . As long as I am secretary of defense, the Defense Department will do as I tell them. The number one priority is to keep Israel out of the war."[60] On another occasion, Colin Powell had snapped at Schwarzkopf in a phone call, yelling, "Goddam it, I want some fucking airplanes out there."[61] President George H. W. Bush had promised Israel "the darndest search-and-destroy effort that's even been undertaken" to suppress the Scud missile campaign, and the US military commanders, despite their reservations, had to follow through to ensure that Israel stayed out of the conflict.[62]

These two case studies highlight an important policy lesson.[63] What may seem like a minor military nuisance for American military planners presents itself as a severe threat for allies bombarded with rocket, missile, and drone strikes. Allies will demand diversionary counterforce efforts to suppress and defeat the bombardment. American decisionmakers may need to undertake the bulk of such diversionary efforts in future conflicts to suppress and defeat the threats.

One proposed counterforce measure to offset China's regional missile deployments is a mirror imaging approach that calls for the US and allied deployment of ground-based missiles in the Asia-Pacific region.[64] The logic is that these deployments would deter Chinese aerospace strike campaigns or, failing that, provide a potent standoff counterforce tool for targeting China's ballistic missile launchers. If the stakes of the conflict are uneven, the presence of a similar aerospace arsenal may not necessarily deter their use. Israel's superior arsenal of weapons has not deterred Hamas's or Hezbollah's use of rocket and missile warfare. The bombings by the United States and its allies did not deter Nazi Germany in World War II or Iraq in the 1991 Gulf War. Furthermore, the case studies in the book show that effective counterforce operations, under the best of circumstances, are exceedingly difficult. Despite overwhelming air superiority and strenuous efforts, the US-led Coalition in the 1991 Gulf War, Israel in the 2006 Second Lebanon War, and the Saudi-led Coalition in the Yemeni War were unable to effectively suppress rocket and missile launches. In the ongoing Yemeni War, the much superior Saudi Arabian forces with complete air superiority and aided by American intelligence has not been successful in extinguishing the ballistic missile threat from the Houthis. In the case of China, its missile forces would conceivably be mobile and practicing deception tactics. How effective would ballistic missiles be as counterforce tools? Would counterforce strikes against missile-related targets carry risks of escalation if the war is intended to be limited? Particularly in the case of nuclear powers—China and North Korea—escalation risks may be measurably higher. In the future, balancing the legitimate need to suppress aerospace bombardment while ameliorating escalation risks will be the most difficult challenge facing American policymakers.

Notes

Chapter 1

1. Ian Williams, "Putin's Missile War: Russia's Strike Campaign in Ukraine," Center for Strategic & International Studies (CSIS), May 2023, 25, https://www.csis.org/analysis/put ins-missile-war. See also Igor Kossov, "How Many Missiles Does Russia Have Left?," *The Kyiv Independent*, 13 January 2023, https://kyivindependent.com/how-many-missiles-does-russia-have-left/. This article provides a tally of 3,500 missiles, including anti-ship missiles and air/missile defense interceptors that have been repurposed by the Russians as offensive strike missiles.

2. Constant Meheut, "Russia Pounds Several Ukrainian Regions With Missiles," *The New York Times*, 8 January 2024, https://www.nytimes.com/2024/01/08/world/europe/ukraine-rus sia-missiles.html.

3. Sam Cranny-Evans and Sidharth Kaushal, "The Iskander-M and Iskander-K: A Technical Profile," Royal United Services Institute, 8 August 2022, https://rusi.org/explore-our-resea rch/publications/commentary/iskander-m-and-iskander-k-technical-profile; Mark B. Schneider, "Lessons from Russian Missile Performance in Ukraine," *Proceedings*, October 2022, https://www.usni.org/magazines/proceedings/2022/october/lessons-russian-miss ile-performance-ukraine; "Everything You Need to Know About the Kh-101 Cruise Missile Russia Uses to Terrorize Ukraine," The New Voice of Ukraine, 26 May 2023, https:// english.nv.ua/nation/everything-you-need-to-know-about-the-kh-101-cruise-missile-russia-uses-to-terrorize-ukraine-50327470.html; "Kh-55 (AS-15)," Missile Threat: CSIS Missile Defense Project, 2 August 2021, https://missilethreat.csis.org/missile/kh-55/; Brad Lendon, "Russia Used a Zircon Hypersonic Cruise Missile for the First Time in Recent Strike, Ukraine Claims," CNN, 13 February 2024, https://www.cnn.com/2024/02/13/eur ope/ukraine-russia-zircon-hypersonic-missile-intl-hnk-ml/index.html; Tanmay Kadam, "Russian Tupolev Bombers Firing New Kh-32 Anti-Ship Missiles to Attack Ground Targets in Ukraine," *The EurAsian Times*, 16 February 2024, https://www.eurasiantimes.com/russ ian-tupolev-bombers-firing-new-kh-32-anti-ship-missiles-ukraine/.

4. In February 2024, John Kirby, the White House National Security Council spokesperson, highlighted the "tough" decisions faced by Ukrainians as they wrestle with the effects of diverting and reallocating air and missile defenses to the cities, leaving frontline troops vulnerable to Russian air power. See Thibault Spirlet, "Russia Exploits Ukraine Air Defense Shortages in Attacks: White House," Business Insider, 8 February, 2024, https://www.busi nessinsider.com/russia-exploits-ukraine-air-defense-shortages-in-attacks-white-house-2024-2. For more details on the Ukrainian struggle to apportion its air and missiles defenses between the conflicting goals of protecting cities and the Ukrainian frontline troops, see Constant Meheut, "Russia Launches Large-Scale Missile Attack on Ukraine," *The New York Times*, 13 January 2024, https://www.nytimes.com/2024/01/13/world/europe/russia-ukraine-missile-attacks.html; Alistair MacDonald and Ievgeniia Sivorka, "From Patriot Missiles to a Mother and Her Vintage Rifle: Inside Ukraine's Air Defense," *The Wall Street*

126 Notes

Journal, 24 December 2023, https://www.wsj.com/world/from-patriot-missiles-to-a-mot her-and-her-vintage-rifle-inside-ukraines-air-defense-406a2ca2; "How Kyiv Fended off a Russian Missile Blitz in May," *The Economist*, 13 June 2023, https://www.economist.com/ europe/2023/06/13/how-kyiv-fended-off-a-russian-missile-blitz-in-may; Tom Balmforth, "Ukraine Builds Layered Air Defences as Russia Ramps up Strikes," Reuters, 20 June 2023, https://www.reuters.com/world/europe/ukraine-builds-layered-air-defences-russia-ramps-up-strikes-2023-06-20/.

5. "How Kyiv Fended off a Russian Missile Blitz in May." Ukraine has received American Patriot missile defense systems, Norwegian NASAMs, German Iris-T, the European SAMP/T system, the German Gepard mobile anti-aircraft guns, and the American Stinger and British Starstreak man-portable air defense systems (MANPADS). Ukraine has received also American Vampires counter-drone weapons, and Norwegian CORTEX and Typhon counter-drone systems. See MacDonald and Sivorka, "From Patriot Missiles to a Mother and Her Vintage Rifle"; Alistair MacDonald and Ievgeniia Sivorka, "The Race to Defend Against Drone Warfare Plays Out in Ukraine," *The Wall Street Journal*, 15 December 2023, https://www.wsj.com/world/the-race-to-defend-against-drone-warfare-plays-out-in-ukraine-96335409.

6. Between 10% and 20% of the rockets fired by Hamas fall inside Palestinian territory, killing many Gaza residents. See Tia Goldenberg and Joseph Krauss, "Misfired Rockets May Have Killed over a Dozen in Gaza Battle," AP News, 8 August 2022, https://apnews.com/article/ middle-east-israel-tel-aviv-403d37366347e0f2446e2f90a9b0d02f. See also Human Rights Watch, "Rockets from Gaza: Harm to Civilians from Palestinian Armed Groups' Rocket Attacks," Human Rights Watch, 2009, 18–19, https://www.hrw.org/report/2009/08/06/ rockets-gaza/harm-civilians-palestinian-armed-groups-rocket-attacks.Hu

7. The State of Israel, "The 2014 Gaza Conflict, 7 July–26 August 2014: Factual and Legal Aspects," May 2015, 33–34, https://www.gov.il/en/Departments/General/operation-pro tective-edge-full-report.

8. The State of Israel, "2014 Gaza Conflict," 10.

9. The residents of southern Israel were forced to plan their daily life "by considering how long it would take you to get to a bomb shelter from every point on your route." See Human Rights Watch, "Rockets from Gaza," 17.

10. See Uzi Rubin, "The Missile Threat from Gaza: From Nuisance to Strategic Threat," The Begin-Sadat Center for Strategic Studies, Bar-Ilan University, December 2011, 64, https:// besacenter.org/wp-content/uploads/2011/12/MSPS91.pdf.

11. Yehuda Ben Meir, "Operation Protective Edge: A Public Opinion Roller Coaster," in *The Lessons of Operation Protective Edge*, ed. Anat Kurz and Shlomo Brom (Tel Aviv, Israel: Institute for National Security Studies, 2014), 130–33, https://www.inss.org.il/ publication/the-lessons-of-operation-protective-edge/#:~:text=The%20essays%20compi led%20in%20The,demilitarization%20of%20Gaza%3B%20relations%20between.

12. For the purposes of the book, "rockets" are defined as unguided artillery bomb or projectile weapons. After they are fired from their launch tubes, there is no further propulsion added to the rocket. Rockets are fired in specific directions and angles toward a predetermined target but do not have in-flight guidance capabilities. For the purposes of the book, the term "missiles" encompasses both ballistic and cruise missiles. *Ballistic missiles* are propelled by rockets (or a series of rocket stages). Generally, but not always, they are powered for only a short boosting phase of their flight and then fly toward their target under the influence of gravitational force. However, during the boost phase of a ballistic missile, it is guided

toward the target. Modern ballistic missiles offer the ability to maneuver after the boost phase by employing a variety of mechanisms and possess much higher accuracies. While close-range ballistic missiles (CRBM) have ranges similar to rockets, they have a distinct boost phase (a period of time during which the rocket motors are propelling the missile) and are armed with homing seekers or other guidance instruments to enhance their ability to strike targets. See National Air and Space Intelligence Center (NASIC), *Ballistic and Cruise Missile Threat: 2017*, NASIC-1031-0985-17 (Wright-Patterson AFB, OH: National Air and Space Intelligence Center, 2017), 14–17, http://www.nasic.af.mil/Portals/19/images/Fact%20Sheet%20Images/2017%20Ballistic%20and%20Cruise%20Missile%20Threat_Final_small.pdf?ver=2017-07-21-083234-343. *Cruise missiles* are "unmanned, armed, aerial vehicle designed to attack a fixed or relocatable target. It spends the majority of its mission in level flight, as it follows a preprogrammed path to the predetermined target." See Ibid., 34. Ballistic and cruise missiles can be launched from silos, mobile launchers, aircraft, ships, and submarines. Ballistic and cruise missiles can deliver conventional munitions or nuclear, chemical, and biological weapons. I use the term "drones" throughout the book. However, within the scope of the book, drones and unmanned aerial vehicles (UAVs) are interchangeable terms. Borrowing the US Department of Defense's definition, drones are powered, aerial vehicles "that does not carry a human operator, uses aerodynamic forces to provide vehicle lift, can fly autonomously or be remotely piloted, can be expendable or recoverable, and can carry a lethal or non-lethal payload." However, the drones discussed in this book are variants of "loitering munitions" that perform a functional role similar to missiles. See Office of the Secretary of Defense, "Unmanned Aircraft Systems Roadmap: 2005–2030" (Washington, DC: Office of Secretary of Defense, US Department of Defense, 2005), 1, https://irp.fas.org/program/collect/uav_roadmap2005.pdf.

13. Rick Atkinson, *Crusade: The Untold Story of the Persian Gulf War* (New York: Houghton Mifflin, 1993), 173–74. In his autobiography, Schwarzkopf writes, "So, in essence what they had was a weapon that could fly 300 miles and miss the target by a couple of miles with a warhead of only 160 pounds. Militarily, that was the equivalent of a single airplane flying over, haphazardly dropping one small bomb, and flying away—terrible for anyone it happened to land on, but in the grand scheme of warfare, a mosquito." See General H. Norman Schwarzkopf and Peter Petre, *The Autobiography: It Doesn't Take a Hero* (New York: Bantam Books, 1993), 484.

14. Atkinson, *Crusade*, 177. Other American military leaders shared Schwarzkopf's views. The Joint Force Air Component Commander (JFACC), Lieutenant General Charles "Chuck" Horner, viewed the Scud as "militarily insignificant." He reasoned that the Coalition was more likely to be disrupted by terrorist attacks than Scud attacks. See Diane T. Putney, *Airpower Advantage: Planning the Gulf War Air Campaign 1989–1991* (Washington DC: Air Force History and Museums Program, United States Air Force, 2004), 266–67.

15. Thomas L Friedman, "Confrontation in the Gulf; Baker-Aziz Talks on Gulf Fail; Fears of War Rise; Bush is Firm; Diplomatic Effort to Continue," *The New York Times*, 9 January 1991. Saddam Hussein, similarly, had indicated before the beginning of the war that ' "Tel Aviv would receive the first blow in the case of a Gulf war' whether or not Israel joins any multinational strike against Iraq." See Times Wire Service, "Tel Aviv Is 1st Target, Hussein Reportedly Says," *Los Angeles Times*, 25 December 1990.

16. Speech by President Saddam Hussein on 1 April 1990, translated by FBIS-NEA, 3 April 1990, 32–33, 35 as cited in Michael Eisenstadt, *"The Sword of the Arabs": Iraq's Strategic Weapons* (Washington, DC: The Washington Institute for Near East Policy, 1990), 61–62.

128 Notes

17. George Bush and Brent Scowcroft, *A World Transformed* (New York: Alfred A. Knopf, 1998), 346–47.
18. Memcon, One-on-One Meeting with PM Shamir of Israel, December 11, 1990, OA/ID CF01584-058, Richard N. Haass Files, National Security Council, Iraq—December 1990 [4] File, George Bush Presidential Library.
19. Atkinson, *Crusade*, 144.
20. Thomas A. Keaney and Eliot A. Cohen, *Revolution in Warfare? Air Power in the Persian Gulf* (Annapolis, MD: Naval Institute Press, 1995), 14–15.
21. Atkinson, *Crusade*, 147.
22. Mark E. Kipphut, *Crossbow and Gulf War Counter-Scud Efforts: Lessons from History*. The Counterproliferation Papers (Maxwell Air Force Base, AL: Air University, February 2003).
23. Anthony H. Cordesman, and Abraham R. Wagner, *The Lessons of Modern War. Volume IV: The Gulf War* (Boulder, CO: Westview Press, 1996), 861; and Lawrence Freedman, and Efraim Karsh, *The Gulf Conflict: Diplomacy and War in the New World Order, 1990–1991* (Princeton, NJ: Princeton University Press, 1991), 330.
24. Atkinson, *Crusade*, 66, 175.
25. I define coercion as the threatened or limited use of force to persuade an adversary to stop and, in some instances, reverse or alter wartime tactics and decision. See Chapter 2 for more details on the definition of coercion.
26. Lawrence Friedman and Efraim Karsh write that "few [of the Iraqi fighter aircrafts] took to the air to greet the allied offensive; most that did turned and fled as soon as they became vulnerable." The authors offer a reason for the dismal performance of the Iraqi air force. They write: "it is questionable whether the Iraqi air force ever really expected to engage. In the period before the onset of hostilities, barely 200 sorites a day were being flown by all types of Iraqi aircraft, and on the eve of hostilities hardly any were being flown at all. This may have represented a husbanding of resources, as a result of the embargo, but it ensured that the pilots were poorly trained for such tasks as air-to-air refueling and night flying." See Lawrence Freedman and Efraim Karsh, "How Kuwait Was Won: Strategy in the Gulf War," *International Security* 16, no. 2 (Fall 1991): 25–26.
27. Ibid., 28.
28. In 1991, Iraq had an inventory of advanced fighter aircrafts provided by France, Britain, and the Soviet Union. The aircrafts could have, in theory, delivered "far larger payloads to greater distances with greater accuracy" than the Scuds. See Statement of Janne E. Nolan, Senior Fellow, Brookings Institution, "Crisis in the Persian Gulf: Sanctions, Diplomacy and War," Hearings Before the Committee on Armed Services, House of Representatives, 101st Congress, Second Session, HASC No. 101-57 (Washington DC: US Government Printing Office, 1991), 163.
29. "The Possible Effect of "CROSSBOW" on "OVERLORD", 2–3 in Operation Crossbow: daily reports and summaries of enemy activity, intelligence and damage reports, counter-measures against launching sites, effects on Allied operations etc., WO 219/699, December 1943–June 1944; History of SHAEF, WO 219/3988, February–June 1944, 94; Memo for CG AAF from AC/AS Intel., CROSSBOW, 3 January 1944 as cited in Joseph W. Angell, "Chapter 4: CROSSBOW," in *The Army Air Forces in World War II. Volume Three—Europe: Argument to V-E Day, January 1944 to May 1945*, ed. Wesley Frank Craven and James Lea Cate (Washington, DC: Office of Air Force History, 1983), 97. See also Roy Irons, *Hitler's Terror Weapons: The Price of Vengeance* (London: Harper Collins, 2002), 85.

30. Irons, *Hitler's Terror Weapons*, 85.

31. See "The Possible Effect of "CROSSBOW" on "OVERLORD," 2–3 in Operation Crossbow: daily reports and summaries of enemy activity, intelligence and damage reports, counter-measures against launching sites, effects on Allied operations etc., WO 219/699, December 1943–June 1944.

32. Long Range Rocket Development, Report by Sir Findlater Stewart's Committee, 27 June 1943, 1, attached as Annex to War Cabinet Chiefs of Staff Committee, German Long Range Rocket Development, Note by the Joint parliamentary Secretary to the Ministry of Supply, 28 June 1943, C.O.S.(43) 348(O). The Committee reasoned that, given the significant inaccuracies, a city-sized target was more likely. The Committee wrote, "we felt it was essential to decide at the outset the objective at which the enemy was most likely to direct this new weapon. We were advised that the enemy's fire would almost certainly be inaccurate, that roughly 50% of the missiles would fall within a circular area four miles in radius, centered on the point aimed at, and the most of the remaining 50% would fall in a similar circle of 15 miles radius; a margin of error of these dimensions clearly points to a larger target as the most likely objective, and we were generally of the opinion that, while there were other important targets such as Portsmouth and Southampton within the range of the rocket, it was more likely to be used against London."

33. Joseph W. Angell, "Chapter 15: CROSSBOW - Second Phase," in *The Army Air Forces in World War II. Volume Three—Europe: Argument to V-E Day, January 1944 to May 1945*, ed. Wesley Frank Craven and James Lea Cate (Washington, DC: Office of Air Force History, 1983), 528.

34. Angell, "Chapter 4: CROSSBOW," 89.

35. Ibid.; Air Chief Marshall Sir Philip Joubert De la Ferte, *Rocket* (London: Hutchinson & Co., 1957), 100.

36. Angell, "Chapter 4: CROSSBOW," 89.

37. Adolf Galland, *The First and the Last: The Rise and Fall of the German Fighter Forces, 1938–1945*, trans. Mervyn Savill (New York: Ballantine, 1954), 235.

38. Eisenstadt, "Sword of the Arabs," 17.

39. Shahram Chubin, *Iran's National Security Policy: Capabilities, Intentions, and Impact* (Washington, DC: The Carnegie Endowment for International Peace, 1994), 22; Michael T. Klare, "Arms Transfers to Iran and Iraq During the Iran–Iraq War of 1980–88 and the Origins of the Gulf War," in *The Gulf War of 1991 Reconsidered*, ed. Andrew J. Bacevich and Efraim Inbar (Portland, OR: Frank Cass, 2003), 10.

40. *Guide Atlas 1*, 5th ed. (HDRDC, 2002), 61–62 as cited in Annie Tracy Samuel, *The Unfinished History of the Iran–Iraq War: Faith, Firepower, and Iran's Revolutionary Guards* (New York: Cambridge University Press, 2021), 182. See also Anthony H. Cordesman, "Creating Weapons of Mass Destruction," *Armed Forces Journal* February 1989, 54 as cited in W. Seth Carus, *The Genie Unleashed: Iraq's Chemical and Biological Weapons Program* (Washington, DC: Washington Institute for Near East Policy, 1989), 3; Shahram Chubin, "The Last Phase of the Iran–Iraq War: From Stalemate to Ceasefire," *Third World Quarterly* 11, no. 2 (April 1989): 10.

41. Saudi Prince Mohammed Bin Salman had stated confidently at the beginning of the war, "we'll finish off the Houthis in a couple of months . . . and then we'll turn our attention to cleaning up the situation in the north," See John O. Brennan, *Undaunted: My Fight Against America's Enemies at Home and Abroad* (New York: Celadon Books, 2020), 339.

42. Ibid.

130 Notes

43. Sayyed Hassan Nasrallah, speech at Rally in solidarity and Loyalty to the Yemeni People, Al-Manar, 17 April 2015, as cited in Daniel Sobelman, "Learning to Deter: Deterrence Failure and Success in the Israel–Hezbollah Conflict, 2006–16," *International Security* 41, no. 3 (Winter 2016): 173.

44. Ian Williams and Shaan Shaikh, "The Missile War in Yemen," A Report of the CSIS Missile Defense Project (Washington, DC: Center for Strategic & International Studies (CSIS) (June 2020), 14, https://www.csis.org/analysis/missile-war-yemen-1.

45. Declan Walsh and David D. Kirkpatrick, "U.A.E. Pulls Most Forces from Yemen in Blow to Saudi War Effort," *The New York Times*, 11 July 2019, https://www.nytimes.com/2019/07/11/world/middleeast/yemen-emirates-saudi-war.html.

46. Janne E. Nolan, *Trappings of Power: Ballistic Missiles in the Third World* (Washington, DC: The Brookings Institution, 1991), 95. However, Janne Nolan qualifies her argument. She writes: "The missiles that survived the opening hours of Operation Desert Storm were conventionally armed, inaccurate, and unreliable. . . . But the political impact of the missiles was inestimable. The strikes symbolized Iraq's determination to prosecute the war no matter what the cost. By threatening to involve Israel, they created severe tensions and posed the risk that the multinational military coalition would be dissolved." See Ibid., vii. Critics of missiles note that military aircrafts can often deliver munitions with higher accuracies, in greater quantities, and can be reused. All else being equal, the criticism is valid. However, all else is rarely equal. The net assessment that aircrafts are a logically superior choice for delivery of ordnance assumes away several difficulties militaries face in efficiently operationalizing their air forces. If some of the presiding assumptions are challenged, conventionally armed high-explosive aerospace weapons start to appear appealing, especially to states that cannot obtain air superiority. Aaron Karp observes that "far from being able to go anywhere, anytime, manned aircraft must be husbanded carefully to survive against modern air defenses." Additionally, the attrition rate of fighter aircraft is often very high. Particularly so for weaker states operating against a powerful state that can mount a robust air defense operation. Furthermore, the high accuracies attributed to ordnance delivered via aircraft are ideal and not routine. Karp argues that "perfect 'milk runs' are rarely possible anywhere but on the practice range." He writes that "targets are obscured by cloud, smoke and camouflage; the aircraft is approaching at maximum release speed and manoeuvring to survive; and the air crew find their concentration affected by fatigue and by men on the ground trying to kill them." See Aaron Karp, *Ballistic Missile Proliferation: The Politics and Technics* (New York: Oxford University Press, 1996), 33–34.

47. Provocation has been previously studied exclusively as a strategy for terrorist organizations aiming to generate sympathy and recruits. I have borrowed and expanded on earlier conceptualization of provocation to explore aerospace warfare as a strategy for weak actors—state and non-state—to attempt to provoke a stronger adversary. For previous scholarship on provocation, see Martha Crenshaw, "Terrorism Research: The Record," *International Interactions* 40 (2014): 558; Andrew H. Kydd and Barbara F. Walter, "The Strategies of Terrorism," *International Security* 31, no. 1 (Summer 2006): 55; Brian Blankenship, "When Do States Take the Bait? State Capacity and the Provocation Logic of Terrorism," *Journal of Conflict Resolution* 62, no. 2 (2018): 381–85.

48. Coercion can involve the use of "just enough force of an appropriate kind" to persuade the adversary to change its preferences. The use of force in coercion serves to reinforce the adversary's fear of further escalation and the adversary's vulnerability to such force. Coercion often acts alongside other instruments of military and diplomatic power,

reinforcing each other and affecting the net calculus of the adversary. See Daniel L. Byman and Matthew C. Waxman, "Kosovo and the Great Air Power Debate," *International Security* 24, no. 4 (Spring 2000): 9; Robert A. Pape, *Bombing to Win: Air Power and Coercion in War* (Ithaca, NY: Cornell University Press, 1996), 4; Robert J. Art, "To What Ends Military Power?," *International Security* 4, no. 4 (Spring 1980): 7–8; Alexander L. George, *Forceful Persuasion: Coercive Diplomacy as an Alternative to War* (Washington, DC: United States Institute of Peace Press, 1991), 5. See Chapter 2 for a detailed discussion on coercion.

49. Fear, for the purposes of the research agenda of the book, is defined as an "aversive, activated [emotional] state" motivated by the "dread of impending disaster and an intense urge to defend oneself." See Arne Öhman, "Fear and Anxiety: Overlaps and Dissociations," in *Handbook of Emotions*, ed. Michael Lewis, Jeannette M. Haviland-Jones, and Barrett Lisa Feldman, 3rd ed. (New York: Guilford, 2008), 710. See also Robin Markwica, *Emotional Choices: How the Logic of Affect Shapes Coercive Diplomacy* (Oxford: Oxford University Press, 2018), 73. Öhman notes that fear can also be a personality trait, a clinical condition that is recurrent, persistent, disproportionate in intensity, and tends to "paralyze individuals, making them helpless and unable to cope; and . . . results in impeded psychosocial or physiological functioning." See Chapter 2 for a detailed discussion on the role of fear in international politics.

50. For many states, even those with robust air forces, missiles still offer a more reliable way to threaten and execute a chemical, biological, or nuclear strike. Ballistic missiles possess several unique characteristics that make them survivable. Whereas delivering munitions at long ranges using aircraft might require putting pilots in harm's way, missiles can be safely fired from the interior of one country to the interior of another without meeting adversary forces in combat. Reiterating this argument, the 2020 missile threat report, jointly published by the National Air and Space Intelligence Center (NASIC) and the Defense Intelligence Ballistic Missile Analysis Committee (DIBMAC), asserted that "missiles are attractive to many nations as they can be used effectively against an adversary with a formidable air defense system when an attack with manned aircraft would be impractical or too costly." The 2020 report also rightly notes that missiles require "fewer maintenance, training, and logistic requirements than manned aircraft." See National Air and Space Intelligence Center (NASIC) and Defense Intelligence Ballistic Missile Analysis Committee (DIBMAC), "2020 Ballistic and Cruise Missile Threat" (Wright-Patterson AFB, OH: NASIC Public Affairs Office, July 2020), 4. Additionally, ballistic missile transporter-erector-launchers (TELs) are hard to locate, track, and destroy, even if the side using these missiles is a weaker adversary whose airspace is not secure. Furthermore, there are very few nations with defense systems that can stop a significant number of incoming ballistic missiles, therefore making ballistic missiles practically unstoppable. For all these reasons, missiles can convincingly threaten and weaponize fear.

51. My definition borrows and builds on the terminology employed in Joshua Kertzer, *Resolve in International Politics* (Princeton, NJ: Princeton University Press, 2016), 3, 8.

52. Karp, *Ballistic Missile Proliferation*, 29–50.

53. Dinshaw Mistry, *Containing Missile Proliferation: Strategic Technology, Security Regimes, and International Cooperation in Arms Control* (Seattle, WA: University of Washington Press, 2003).

54. Nolan, *Trappings of Power*; W. Seth Carus, *Ballistic Missiles in Modern Conflict* (New York: Praeger, 1991); Thomas L. McNaugher, "Ballistic Missiles and Chemical Weapons: The Legacy of the Iran-Iraq War," *International Security* 15, no. 2 (Fall

132   Notes

1990): 5–34; Steve Fetter, "Ballistic Missiles and Weapons of Mass Destruction: What Is the Threat? What Should Be Done?," *International Security* 16, no. 1 (Summer 1991): 5–42; Lyle J. Goldstein, "Pinpricks That Bleed: The Civil-Military Relations of Aerial Terror Weapons," *Security Studies* 8, no. 1 (1998): 75–107; Eric Heginbotham et al., *The US-China Military Scorecard: Forces, Geography, and the Evolving Balance of Power 1996-2017* (Santa Monica, CA: RAND Corporation, 2015), 45–70, https://www.rand.org/content/dam/rand/pubs/research_reports/RR300/RR392/RAND_RR392.pdf.

55. Bryan Robert Early et al., "Climbing the Ladder: Explaining the Vertical Proliferation of Cruise Missiles," *Journal of Conflict Resolution* 66, no. 6 (2022): 955–82.

56. Dennis M. Gormley, *Missile Contagion: Cruise Missile Proliferation and the Threat to International Security* (Westport, CT: Praeger Security International, 2008). For a detailed study that explored technology and politics of cruise missiles when it emerged in the 1980s, see Richard Betts, ed., *Cruise Missiles: Technology, Strategy, Politics*, 1st ed. (Washington, DC: Brookings Institution Press, 1981).

57. Antonio Calcara et al., "Will the Drone Always Get Through? Offensive Myths and Defensive Realities," *Security Studies* 31, no. 5 (2022): 791–825. A debate over the arguments and methods espoused by the article can be found in Paul Lushenko and Sarah Kreps, "Tactical Myths and Perceptions of Reality: Drones and Offensive Advantage – An Exchange," *Security Studies*, 2023.

58. Michael C. Horowitz, Sarah E. Kreps, and Matthew Fuhrmann, "Separating Fact from Fiction in the Debate over Drone Proliferation," *International Security* 41, no. 2 (Fall 2016): 7–42.

59. Amy Zegart, "Cheap Fights, Credible Threats: The Future of Armed Drones and Coercion," *Journal of Strategic Studies* 43, no. 1 (2020): 6–46.

60. Most of the research effort has been directed at airpower. See Byman and Waxman, "Kosovo and the Great Air Power Debate"; Daniel R. Lake, "The Limits of Coercive Airpower: NATO's 'Victory' in Kosovo Revisited," *International Security* 34, no. 1 (2009): 83–112; Pape, *Bombing to Win*; Karl Mueller, "Strategies of Coercion: Denial, Punishment, and the Future of Air Power," *Security Studies* 7, no. 3 (Spring 1988): 182–228; Michael Horowitz and Dan Reiter, "When Does Aerial Bombing Work?," *Journal of Conflict Resolution* 45 (2001): 147–73. See also Robert J. Art and Kelly M. Greenhill, "Coercion: An Analytical Overview," in *Coercion: The Power to Hurt in International Politics*, ed. Kelly M. Greenhill and Peter Krause (New York: Oxford University Press, 2018), 16.

61. A few of the prominent works studying the role of emotions in international politics include Markwica, *Emotional Choices*; Andrew A. G. Ross, *Mixed Emotions: Beyond Fear and Hatred in International Conflict* (Chicago: University of Chicago Press, 2014); Neta C. Crawford, "The Passion of World Politics: Propositions on Emotion and Emotional Relationships," *International Security* 24, no. 4 (Spring 2000): 116–56; Robert Jervis, *Perception and Misperception in International Politics* (Princeton, NJ: Princeton University Press, 1976); Yaacov Vertzberger, *The World in Their Minds: Information Processing, Cognition, and Perception in Foreign Policy Decisionmaking* (Stanford, CA: Stanford University Press, 1990); Irving Janis and Leon Mann, *Decision Making: A Psychological Analysis of Conflict, Choice, and Commitment* (New York: Free Press, 1977); Patrick M. Morgan, "Saving Face for the Sake of Deterrence," in *Psychology and Deterrence*, ed. Robert Jervis, Richard Ned Lebow, and Janice Gross Stein (Baltimore: Johns Hopkins University Press, 1985), 125–52; Stephen Peter Rosen, *War and Human Nature* (Princeton, NJ: Princeton University Press, 2005);

Notes   133

Linda Ahall and Thomas Gregory, *Emotions, Politics and War* (New York: Routledge, 2015); Shiping Tang, "Fear in International Politics: Two Positions," *International Studies Review* 10, no. 3 (2008): 451–71; Ken Booth and Nicholas J. Wheeler, *The Security Dilemma: Fear, Cooperation, and Trust in World Politics* (New York: Palgrave Macmillan, 2008).

62. Tianran Xu, "Update on the DPRK's 600 Mm Multiple Launch Rocket System," Strategic Delivery Vehicle Developments Series (Vienna, Austria: Open Nuclear Network, February 12, 2023), https://opennuclear.org/publication/update-dprks-600-mm-multiple-launch-rocket-system; "North Korean Artillery Rockets," GlobalSecurity.org, accessed 14 July 2023, https://www.globalsecurity.org/military/world/dprk/kpa-mrl.htm.

63. US Defense Intelligence Agency, "Iran Military Power: Ensuring Regime Survival and Securing Regional Dominance" (Washington, DC: Defense Intelligence Agency, 2019), 60, https://www.dia.mil/Military-Power-Publications/.

64. Sangar Khaleel and Jane Arraf, "Rocket Attack in Iraq Kills a US Military Contractor," *The New York Times*, 15 February 2021, https://www.nytimes.com/2021/02/15/world/middlee ast/iraq-us-contractor-killed.html.

65. Jane Arraf and Helen Cooper, "Rockets Hit Iraqi Base Where US Troops Are Stationed," *The New York Times*, 3 March 2021, https://www.nytimes.com/2021/03/03/world/middlee ast/iraq-base-rocket-attack.html.

66. Ibid.

67. Jim Garamone, "U.S.US Responds to Attack That Killed US Contractor in Syria," US Department of Defense, 24 March 2023, https://www.defense.gov/News/News-Stor ies/Article/Article/3341127/us-responds-to-attack-that-killed-us-contractor-in-syria/ ; "Rocket Attack Targets US Base in Syria, No Casualties," Military.com, 10 April2023, https://www.military.com/daily-news/2023/04/10/rocket-attack-targets-us-base-syria-no-casualties.html.

68. National Air and Space Intelligence Center (NASIC) and Defense Intelligence Ballistic Missile Analysis Committee (DIBMAC), "2020 Ballistic and Cruise Missile Threat," 4. The report observed that several states will soon possess close-range and short-range ballistic missiles with increased accuracy, range, and lethality enabling "precision strike capability against high profile targets" while simultaneously developing countermeasures to defeat point and theater missile defenses. See Ibid., 15, 19.

69. US Defense Intelligence Agency, "Iran Military Power: Ensuring Regime Survival and Securing Regional Dominance," 30. See pages 43–47 for details on Iran's ballistic missile arsenal.

70. Ibid. The 2019 Iran Military Power report noting that Iran's most-capable aircrafts are those acquired from the United States in the 1960s and 1970s, points out that "Iran's combat air-craft remain significantly inferior to those of its regional adversaries equipped with modern Western systems." See Ibid., 64.

71. US Defense Intelligence Agency, "Iran Military Power: Ensuring Regime Survival and Securing Regional Dominance," 31.

72. Alissa J. Rubin et al., "Iran Fires on US Forces at 2 Bases in Iraq, Calling It 'Fierce Revenge,'" *The New York Times*, 8 January 2020, https://www.nytimes.com/2020/01/07/world/mid dleeast/iran-fires-missiles-us.html.

73. Alissa J. Rubin, "'It Was Like a Scene from an Action Movie,'" *The New York Times*, 13 January 2020, https://www.nytimes.com/2020/01/13/world/middleeast/Iran-missile-att ack-American-base.html.

74. Rubin et al., "Iran Fires on US Forces."

134 Notes

75. David Martin and Mary Walsh, "Who Would Live and Who Would Die: The Inside Story of the Iranian Attack on Al Asad Airbase," CBS News, 8 August 2021, https://www.cbsnews.com/news/iranian-attack-al-asad-air-base-60-minutes-2021-08-08/.

76. Gina Harkins, "Al Asad Missile Attack Nearly Killed 150 US Troops, Destroyed 30 Aircraft: Report," Military.com, 2 March 2021, https://www.military.com/daily-news/2021/03/01/al-asad-missile-attack-nearly-killed-150-us-troops-destroyed-30-aircraft-report.html.

77. Martin and Walsh, "Who Would Live."

78. Mihir Zaveri, "More Than 100 Troops Have Brain Injuries From Iran Missile Strike, Pentagon Says," *The New York Times*, 10 February 2020, https://www.nytimes.com/2020/02/10/world/middleeast/iraq-iran-brain-injuries.html. See also Gina Harkins, "29 Purple Hearts Approved for Soldiers Injured in Al Asad Missile Attack," Military.com, 4 May 2020, https://www.military.com/daily-news/2020/05/04/29-purple-hearts-approved-soldiers-injured-al-asad-missile-attack.html.

79. Lara Seligman, "19 US Troops Diagnosed with Traumatic Brain Injury Following Attacks in Iraq and Syria," Politico, 26 October 2023, https://www.politico.com/news/2023/10/25/several-u-s-troops-report-brain-injury-from-attacks-in-iraq-and-syria-00123485.

80. Jaganath Sankaran, "Missile Defenses and Strategic Stability in Asia: Evidence from Simulations," *Journal of East Asian Studies* 20, no. 3 (November 2020): 491.

81. Ibid.

82. Ibid.

83. National Air and Space Intelligence Center (NASIC) and Defense Intelligence Ballistic Missile Analysis Committee (DIBMAC), "2020 Ballistic and Cruise Missile Threat," 2. China's People's Liberation Army Rocket Force (PLARF) holds approximately 750–1,500 short-range ballistic missiles (300–1,000 km), 150 to 450 conventional medium-range ballistic missiles (1,000–3,000 km), and a limited number of intermediate-range ballistic missiles (3,000–5,000 km). See Jaganath Sankaran, "Missile Wars in the Asia Pacific: The Threat of Chinese Regional Missiles and US-Allied Missile Defense Response," *Asian Security* 17, no. 1 (2021): 25.

84. Sankaran, "Missile Wars in the Asia Pacific;" 25.

85. US Department of Defense, *2019 Missile Defense Review* (Washington DC: Office of the Secretary of Defense, US Department of Defense, 2019), v.

86. Ibid., iv, vi.

87. Gregory Sanders et al., "Rising Demand and Proliferating Supply of Military UAS" (Washington, DC: Center for Strategic & International Studies (CSIS), May 2023), 17–31, https://www.csis.org/analysis/rising-demand-and-proliferating-supply-military-uas; Kerry Chavez, "Learning on the Fly: Drones in the Russian-Ukrainian War," *Arms Control Today*, February 2023, https://www.armscontrol.org/act/2023-01/features/learning-fly-drones-russian-ukrainian-war; Jeffrey A. Edmonds and Samuel Bendett, "Russia's Use of Uncrewed Systems in Ukraine" (Arlington, VA: Center for Naval Analyses, March 2023), https://www.cna.org/reports/2023/05/russias-use-of-drones-in-ukraine; Jack Watling and Nick Reynolds, "Ukraine at War: Paving the Road from Survival to Victory" (London: Royal United Services Institute for Defence and Security Studies, 4 July 2022), 11, https://www.rusi.org/explore-our-research/publications/special-resources/ukraine-war-paving-road-survival-victory.

88. Particularly so when adversaries seek to actively leverage their ability to use chemical, biological, or nuclear warheads to induce fear in the target.

Notes   135

89. Dwight D. Eisenhower, *Crusade in Europe* (Garden City, NY: Doubleday, 1948), 260

90. Dennis Gormley, studying the German V-1 and V-2 missile attacks on London during World War II writes, "however ineffective ballistic missiles armed with conventional warheads would prove to be objectively, their capacity to invoke a heavy sense of defense-lessness demonstrated that they could take a significant toll psychologically and thus politi-cally, which, after all, is the prime objective of warfare." See Gormley, *Missile Contagion*, 17.

91. Ibid.

92. McNaugher, "Ballistic Missiles and Chemical Weapons," 15.

93. David Makovsky and Jeffrey White, "Lessons and Implications of the Israel-Hizballah War: A Preliminary Assessment" (Washington, DC: The Washington Institute for Near East Policy, October 2006), 20, https://www.washingtoninstitute.org/policy-analysis/less ons-and-implications-israel-hizballah-war-preliminary-assessment.

Chapter 2

1. R. V. Jones, *Most Secret War*, 6th ed. (New York: Penguin Books, 2009), 455–57.

2. Benjamin King and Timothy J. Kutta, *Impact: The History of Germany's V-Weapons in World War II* (New York: Sarpedon 1998), 211.

3. Long Range Rocket Development, 23. See also David Irving, *The Mare's Nest* (Boston, MA: Little, Brown, 1965), 127.

4. History of SHAEF, WO 219/3988, February–June 1944, 94; Angell, "Chapter 4: CROSSBOW," 96–97. See also "The Possible Effect of "CROSSBOW" on "OVERLORD," 2–3 in Operation Crossbow: daily reports and summaries of enemy activity, intelligence and damage reports, counter-measures against launching sites, effects on Allied operations etc., WO 219/699, December 1943–June 1944.

5. See footnote in Irving, *Mare's Nest*, 308.

6. *Yedinot Aharonot*, 29 April 1990, translated in *Mideast Mirror*, 30 April 1990, 7, as cited in Eisenstadt, "*Sword of the Arabs*," 51.

7. Gadi Eisenkot, "The Features of a Possible Conflict in the Northern Arena and the Home Front," lecture given at University of Haifa symposium, 30 November, 2010, Haifa, Israel, as cited in Sobelman, "Learning to Deter," 153. See also "What's Hot with Razi Barkai," IDF Radio, October 30, 2014 as cited in Ibid.

8. In Israel, two more died due to heart attack and seven died due to suffocation from misuse of gas masks. See Anthony H. Cordesman, and Abraham R. Wagner, *The Lessons of Modern War. Volume IV: The Gulf War* (Boulder, CO: Westview Press 1996), 857.

9. On dictators who have weaponized fear, Hitler would be the prime candidate. The weapon-ization of fear, hatred, and contempt toward other groups to normalize mass killing was at the core of Hitler's Nazi regime. See Neta C. Crawford, "Institutionalizing Passion in World Politics: Fear and Empathy," *International Theory* 6, no. 3 (October 2014): 536.

10. On democracies that have responded disproportionately to fear, the American debates and policies to the Sputnik scare, the missile gap, and the bomber gap are examples. A detailed history of the American reactions to the Sputnik scare can be found in Rip Bulkeley, *The Sputnik Crisis and Early United States Space Policy: A Critique of the Historiography of Space* (Bloomington: Indiana University Press, 1991). For a study on how the fear of the missile gap animated American politics see Christopher A. Preble, *John F. Kennedy and the Missile Gap* (DeKalb: Northern Illinois University Press, 2004).

136 Notes

11. Neta Crawford provides a cogent summary the centrality of emotions in realist theories. See Crawford, "Passion of World Politics," 120–23. Excellent discussions on the role of emotions in international politics and warfare can be found in Samuel Zilincik, "The Role of Emotions in Military Strategy," *Texas National Security Review* 5, no. 2 (Spring 2022): 12–25; Janice Gross Stein, "The Micro-Foundations of International Relations Theory: Psychology and Behavioral Economics," *International Organization* 71, no. Supplement 2017 (2017): S249–63; Emma Hutchinson and Roland Bleiker, "Theorizing Emotions in World Politics," *International Theory* 6, no. 3 (November 2014): 494; Crawford, "Institutionalizing Passion in World Politics"; Markwica, *Emotional Choices*; Crawford, "Passion of World Politics"; Booth and Wheeler, *Security Dilemma*; Ross, *Mixed Emotions*; Andrew A. G. Ross, "Realism, Emotion, and Dynamic Allegiances in Global Politics," *International Theory* 5, no. 2 (2013): 273–99; Ahall and Gregory, *Emotions, Politics and War*; Roger D. Petersen, *Western Intervention in the Balkans: The Strategic Use of Emotions in Conflict* (New York: Cambridge University Press, 2011); Tang, "Fear in International Politics"; Richard Ned Lebow and Janice Gross Stein, "Deterrence and the Cold War," *Political Science Quarterly* 110, no. 2 (1995): 157–81; Janis and Mann, *Decision Making*; Robert Jervis et al., eds., *Psychology and Deterrence* (Baltimore: Johns Hopkins University Press, 1989); Jervis, *Perception and Misperception*.

12. Hutchinson and Bleiker, "Theorizing Emotions in World Politics," 492. See also Stein, "Micro-Foundations of International Relations Theory," S255–57; Crawford, "Passion of World Politics."

13. Robin Markwica, for instance, has recently developed a novel methodological approach to study the role of emotions in how decisionmakers respond to coercion. See Markwica, *Emotional Choices*, 4.

14. Ohman, "Fear and Anxiety," 710. Fear can also be a personality trait, a clinical condition that is recurrent, persistent, disproportionate in intensity, and tends to "paralyze individuals, making them helpless and unable to cope; and . . . results in impeded psychosocial or physiological functioning." See Ibid. The definitions of fear employed in this book exclude this aspect. Similarly, while closely related to fear, anxiety is distinct from fear, and it emerges from unresolved fear. Anxiety is induced when the "nature and location of the threat remain more obscure and thus are difficult to cope with by active defensive maneuvers." See Ibid. See also Margaret E. Kemeny and Avgusta Shestyuk, "Emotions, the Neuroendocrine and Immune Systems, and Health," in *Handbook of Emotions*, ed. Michael Lewis, Jeannette M. Haviland-Jones, and Barrett Lisa Feldman, 3rd ed. (New York: Guilford, 2008), 663.

15. Markwica, *Emotional Choices*, 68–70.

16. Ibid., 74.

17. Paul Thagard and A. David Nussbaum, "Fear-Driven Inference: Mechanisms of Gut Overreaction," in *Model-Based Reasoning in Science and Technology: Studies in Applied Philosophy, Epistemology and Rational Ethics*, ed. L. Magnani, vol. 8 (Heidelberg: Springer, 2014), 43. The authors note that "from the perspective of conventional theories of rationality based on probability and utility theory, fear-driven inference is bizarre. Theories of rationality assume a firewall between probabilities and utilities. . . . The brain, however, does not appear to separate probabilities and utilities nearly so rigorously . . . [in studies] the neural correlates of belief included brain areas associated with emotional processing, such as the ventromedial prefrontal cortex (for belief) and the anterior insula (for disbelief). Hence it is not surprising that the brain confuses emotional arousal with believability." See Ibid., 50–51.

18. Markwica, *Emotional Choices*, 74. See also Lisa J. Carlson and Raymond Dacey, "The Use of Fear and Anger to Alter Crisis Initiation," *Conflict Management and Peace Science* 31, no. 2 (2014): 168–92; Jennifer S. Lerner and Dacher Keltner, "Fear, Anger, and Risk," *Journal of Personality and Social Psychology* 81, no. 1 (2001): 146–59; Jervis, *Perception and Misperception*, 378–79. Neta Crawford makes a similar argument, arguing that when fear is institutionalized it biases the assessment of threat, privileging information that confirms the threat while discounting disconfirming evidence. Crawford writes that fear can become institutionalized "almost independent of its initial trigger, and difficult to dislodge even in the face of evidence that the threat has diminished." See Crawford, "Institutionalizing Passion in World Politics," 548.

19. Roger Petersen and Evangelos Liaras, "Countering Fear in War: The Strategic Use of Emotion," *Journal of Military Ethics* 5, no. 4 (2006): 320. See also Cass R. Sunstein and Richard Zeckhauser, "Overreaction to Fearsome Risks," *Environ Resource Econ* 48 (2011): 435–49; Cass Sunstein, *Laws of Fear: Beyond the Precautionary Principle* (Cambridge: Cambridge University Press, 2005). Joseph Lepgold and Alan Lamborn make a similar argument. They write that "affective reactions may have durable half-lives . . . if an ambiguous signal arrives after an earlier, stronger one, there may be carryover from the earlier cue." They also note that "when an identifiably affective cue precedes a cognitive cue as an attitude is being formed, that attitude is less susceptible to cognitive than to affective counterarguments." See Joseph Lepgold and Alan C. Lamborn, "Locating Bridges: Connecting Research Agendas on Cognition and Strategic Choice," *International Studies Review* 3, no. 3 (December 2001): 7.

20. Petersen and Liaras, "Countering Fear in War," 319–20; Crawford, "Passion of World Politics," 137–40.

21. Overreaction to fearful risks occurs in a variety of policymaking arenas. See Sunstein and Zeckhauser, "Overreaction to Fearsome Risks," 437–38. In fear-induced events of any kind, people, including decisionmakers, are susceptible to probability neglect and "will give up too much" to be reassured that all is being done to ameliorate the effects of the event. See Ibid., 436.

22. Markwica, *Emotional Choices*, 69.

23. The other two action tendencies spurred by fear are flight and freeze. See Ibid., 73.

24. William L. Waugh, *International Terrorism: How Nations Respond to Terrorists* (Salisbury, NC: Documentary Publications, 1982), 27; Grant Wardlaw, *Political Terrorism: Theory, Tactics, and Counter-Measures*, 2nd ed. (New York: Cambridge University Press, 1989), 43–44.

25. David G. Hubbard, *Winning Back the Sky: A Tactical Analysis of Terrorism* (San Francisco, CA: Saybrook, 1986), xii.

26. On the political institutionalization of fear after the 9/11 terrorist attacks, see John Mueller, "Six Rather Unusual Propositions About Terrorism," *Terrorism and Political Violence* 17 (2005): 487–505; Crawford, "Institutionalizing Passion in World Politics," 549.

27. "Breaking News: With Dr. John Steinbruner," *The Washington Post*, 11 September 2001, https://www.washingtonpost.com/wp-srv/liveonline/01/nation/attack_steinbruner.htm.

28. Ibid.

29. Mueller, "Six Rather Unusual Propositions," 491–96.

30. The need to fight back and "score public relations victories" was also documented in World War II bombing campaigns conducted with bombers and fighter planes. See Daniel Byman

138　Notes

and Matthew C. Waxman, *The Dynamics of Coercion: American Foreign Policy and the Limits of Military Might* (New York: Cambridge University Press, 2020), 43–44.

31. See Byman and Waxman, "Kosovo and the Great Air Power Debate," 9. See also Pape, *Bombing to Win*, 4; Art, "To What Ends Military Power?," 7–8. This definition incorporates both deterrence and compellence, the two forms of coercion. This definition also focuses on military coercion. Other instruments of coercion include economic sanctions, diplomatic isolation and pressure, economic blockades, etc. Coercion does not always entail convincing an adversary to stop or change course. The literature on coercion, compellence, and deterrence is vast. Some of the recent and prominent works include Byman and Waxman, *Dynamics of Coercion*; Kelly M. Greenhill and Peter Krause, eds., *Coercion: The Power to Hurt in International Politics* (New York: Oxford University Press, 2018); Todd S. Sechser and Matthew Fuhrmann, *Nuclear Weapons and Coercive Diplomacy* (New York: Cambridge University Press, 2017); Todd S. Sechser, "Militarized Compellent Threats, 1918–2001," *Conflict Management and Peace Science* 28, no. 4 (2011); Robert J. Art and Patrick M. Cronin, eds., *The United States and Coercive Diplomacy* (Washington, DC: US Institute of Peace, 2003); Kelly M. Greenhill, *Weapons of Mass Migration: Forced Displacement, Coercion, and Foreign Policy* (Ithaca, NY: Cornell University Press, 2010); Lawrence Freedman, *Strategic Coercion: Concepts and Cases* (New York: Oxford University Press, 1998); Alexander L. George and William E. Simons, eds., *The Limits of Coercive Diplomacy* (Boulder, CO: Westview, 1994); Thomas C. Schelling, *Arms and Influence* (New Haven, CT: Yale University Press, 1966); Morgan, "Saving Face"; Jervis et al., *Psychology and Deterrence*; Barry M. Blechman and Stephen S. Kaplan, *Force Without War: US Armed Forces as a Political Instrument* (Washington, DC: Brookings Institution Press, 1978).

32. George, *Forceful Persuasion*, 5. See also Ibid., 539; Pape, *Bombing to Win*, 4, 13; Byman and Waxman, *Dynamics of Coercion*, 3. Deterrence, a subset of coercion, relies on threats to dissuade the initiation of a future action. See Art, "To What Ends Military Power?," 6. However, the analytical differentiation of deterrence and compellence in wartime is challenging. Thomas Schelling writes that actions taken to deter something the opponent is already doing "has some of the character of a compellent threat." See Thomas C. Schelling, *Arms and Influence*, Veritas paperback edition, 2020 (New Haven, CT: Yale University Press, 1966), 77. Similarly, Robert Powell argues that the distinction between deterrence and compellence is conceptually elusive, noting, "the difference between deterring an adversary from attacking and compelling it not to attack is unclear. . . . In each case, a state is trying to coerce its adversary into acting in certain ways and not in others." See footnote 2 in Robert Powell, *Nuclear Deterrence Theory: The Search for Credibility*, Digitally printed version (New York: Cambridge University Press, 2008), 7. In agreement with these two statements, Byman and Waxman also note that distinguishing compellence and deterrence is simplest in a nuclear context. However, in a conflict involving conventional weapons, they point out that differentiating compellence and (immediate) deterrence is much more difficult. See Byman and Waxman, *Dynamics of Coercion*, 5–9. Robert Art and Kelly Greenhill, also point out the difficulties of practically distinguishing compellence and deterrence in war. See Art and Greenhill, "Coercion," 5–6.

33. Byman and Waxman, "Kosovo and the Great Air Power Debate," 9. See also Schelling, *Arms and Influence*, 1966, 2. Schelling writes, "To be coercive, violence has to be anticipated. And it has to be avoidable by accommodation."

34. Schelling, *Arms and Influence*, 1966, 3. Schelling notes that "brute strength is usually measured relative to enemy strength, the one directly opposing the other, while the power to

35. Scholars have recently recognized and highlighted this tactical advantage in drones. See Zegart, "Cheap Fights, Credible Threats," 25.

36. The study of interstate wartime military coercion has been limited and focused on traditional airpower (i.e., the ability of a state to use fighter and bomber aircrafts to attack an adversary). See Art and Greenhill, "Coercion," 16. For research on traditional airpower and coercion, see Byman and Waxman, "Kosovo and the Great Air Power Debate"; Lake, "Limits of Coercive Airpower"; Pape, *Bombing to Win*; Mueller, "Strategies of Coercion,"; Horowitz and Reiter, "When Does Aerial Bombing Work?" In contrast, I employ empirical data on rockets, missiles, and drones to advance the state of knowledge on interstate wartime coercion.

37. Sobelman, "Learning to Deter," 151, 162. See also Ivan Arreguin-Toft, *How the Weak Win Wars: A Theory of Asymmetric Conflict* (New York: Cambridge University Press, 2005); T. V. Paul, *Asymmetric Conflict: War Initiation by Weaker Powers* (New York: Cambridge University Press, 1994).

38. See Pape, *Bombing to Win*, 13.

39. Challenging this assertion, Richard Overy writes, "There has always seemed something fundamentally implausible about the contention of bombing's critics that dropping almost 2.5 tons of bombs on tautly-stretched industrial systems and war-weary urban populations would not seriously weaken them. Germany and Japan had no special immunity. Japan's military economy was devoured in the flames; her population desperately longed for escape from bombing. German forces lost half of the weapons needed at the front . . . and the economy gradually creaked almost to a halt . . . the air offensive was one of the decisive elements in Allied victory." See Richard Overy, *Why the Allies Won* (New York: Norton, 1996), 133.

40. See Pape, *Bombing to Win*, 20. A robust discussion on relaxing the core interest assumption, is provided in Mueller, "Strategies of Coercion," 192–93.

41. However, it is worth noting that such diversionary effects are not unique to punishment campaigns. Even in strategies aiming to achieve denial of specific military capabilities, unforeseen second-order diversionary effects can prove crucial. Burton Klein, who served in the expert group assembled to survey the effects of strategic bombing in World War II, writes while the pre-invasion bombings did not lead to the anticipated reduction in the manufacture of German fighter aircrafts, it forced the Germans "to devote a very significant part of their war production efforts and also a large number of highly trained military personnel to air defense. . . . It can be seen, therefore, that where the pre-invasion attacks really paid off was not nearly so much the damage they did, but rather in the effect they had on causing the Germans to put a very significant part of their total war effort into air defense." Burton H. Klein, *Germany's Economic Preparations for War* (Cambridge, MA: Harvard University Press, 1959), 232–33 as cited in Barry D. Watts and Thomas A. Keaney, *Gulf War Air Power Survey. Volume II: Operations and Effects and Effectiveness* (Washington, DC: US Government Printing Office, 1993), 62.

42. C. G. C. Treadway, Major, USAF, "More Than Just a Nuisance: When Aerial Terror Bombing Works" (Maxwell Air Force Base, Alabama, School of Advanced Airpower Studies, Air University, 1998), 10, https://apps.dtic.mil/sti/citations/ADA338813.

43. Ibid.

44. Ibid.

140 Notes

45. David Lloyd George, *War Memoirs of David Lloyd George: 1917* (Boston, MA: Little, Brown, 1934), 116–17.

46. John Grigg, *Lloyd George: War Leader, 1916–1918* (New York: Allen Lane, The Penguin Press, 2002), 248.

47. George, *War Memoirs*, 115–17; Treadway, "More Than Just a Nuisance," 11–12.

48. Grigg, *Lloyd George*, 248; George, *War Memoirs*, 116–17.

49. Grigg, *Lloyd George*, 248.

50. Ibid., 247; Raymond H. Fredette, *The Sky on Fire: The First Battle of Britain, 1917–1918* (Tuscaloosa: The University of Alabama Press, 2006), 143. Interestingly, the citizens of London were as much perturbed by the falling anti-aircraft shells as they were by German bombs. See Treadway, "More Than Just a Nuisance," 10.

51. Fredette, *The Sky on Fire*, 145.

52. Francis K. Mason, *Battle Over Britain: A History of the German Air Assaults on Great Britain, 1917–1918 and July–December 1940, and of the Development of Britain's Air Defences between the World Wars*, 1990th ed. (Bourne Ends, UK: Aston., 1990), 23–24; Fredette, *The Sky on Fire*, 145.

53. Fredette, *The Sky on Fire*, 146–47.

54. Ibid., 147.

55. James G. Roche and Barry D. Watts, "Choosing Analytical Measures," *Journal of Strategic Studies* 14, no. 2 (1991): 185.

56. The direct first-order effects were slight. Sixteen B-25s were launched from the US aircraft carrier *USS Hornet* stationed at a distance of 700 nautical miles from Tokyo. A variety of targets in Tokyo and other Japanese cities were hit. Evaluated by criteria that privilege the estimation of direct effects on Japanese combat power or Japanese war industry, the raids were a failure. See Watts and Keaney, *Gulf War Air Power Survey*, 52–53.

57. Roche and Watts, "Choosing Analytical Measures," 186.

58. Senshi Sosho [War History Series] as cited in Edwin T. Layton, Roger Pineau, and John Costello, *"And I Was There": Pearl Harbor and Midway—Breaking the Secrets* (New York: William Morrow & Co, 1985), 387–88; Watts and Keaney, *Gulf War Air Power Survey*, 53.

59. Roche and Watts, "Choosing Analytical Measures," 186–87.

60. An official history of World War II published in the 1970s by the Japanese Defense Agency concluded that the Doolittle raid directly led to the diversion of these four fighter groups. See Senshi Sosho [War History Series] as cited in Layton, Pineau, and Costello, *"And I Was There,"* 387–88.

61. Roche and Watts, "Choosing Analytical Measures," 187.

62. Ibid.

63. Ibid.

64. Steven Rosen calls it the relative willingness to suffer. Rosen writes, "The guerilla's superiority is not in his ability to harm, but in his greater willingness to be harmed." He continues, "Castro's victory in Cuba, the Communist victory in China, and perhaps even the revolutionists' victory in the American colonies were won by sheer persistence in the face of overwhelming odds. In each case, a highly committed party exhausted a materially stronger opponent by making the costs of victory exceed the privileged party's willingness to suffer." Rosen's analysis is fundamentally about a weak actor that is clearly aware of the adversary's military superiority but has identified a potential path to victory. See Steven Rosen and Bruce M. Russett, "War Power and the Willingness to Suffer," in *Peace,*

War, and Numbers (Beverly Hills, CA: Sage, 1972), 168; Steven Rosen, "A Model of War and Alliance," in *Alliance in International Politics*, ed. Julian R. Friedman, Christopher Bladen, and Steven Rosen (Boston, MA: Allyn and Bacon, 1970), 223–30. See also Henry A. Kissinger, "The Vietnam Negotiations. Foreign Affairs January 1969," *Survival*, January 1969; Andrew Mack, "Why Big Nations Lose Small Wars: The Politics of Asymmetric Conflict," *World Politics* 27, no. 2 (January 1975): 175–200; Jeffrey Record, "Why the Strong Lose," *Parameters*, Winter 2005, 16–31; Arreguin-Toft, *How the Weak Win Wars*.

65. Stanley Karnow, "A Verdict on Vietnam," *The Washington Post*, 28 October 1984, https://www.washingtonpost.com/archive/entertainment/books/1984/10/28/a-verdict-on-vietnam/ca05dbd0-1838-4998-8be0-42c14b5ad1e5/.

66. Barton Gellman, "US and China Nearly Came to Blows in '96," *The Washington Post*, 21 June 1998, https://www.washingtonpost.com/archive/politics/1998/06/21/us-and-china-nearly-came-to-blows-in-96/926d105f-1fd8-404c-9995-90984f86a613/.

67. Ibid.

68. Patricia L. Sullivan, "War Aims and War Outcomes: Why Powerful States Lose Limited Wars," *Journal of Conflict Resolution* 51, no. 3 (June 2007): 500. A detailed and well-done treatment on how weak states can use the cost-benefit expectations to coerce and engage with stronger adversaries is Paul C. Avey, *Tempting Fate: Why Nonnuclear States Confront Nuclear Opponents* (Ithaca, NY: Cornell University Press, 2019).

69. For this aspect of coercion to work, the adversary should be reticent to pay these costs. See Mack, "Why Big Nations Lose Small Wars," 185.

70. Byman and Waxman, *Dynamics of Coercion*, 136–37. However, empirical attempts at validating these arguments have been challenging. There is very little clear and reliable data on decisionmaking during crises in which nuclear threats were made. Evidence is often circumstantial. Furthermore, in many cases, as Richard Betts notes, "the complexity and ambiguity" in the objectives of the various sides "means that the evidence can be cited or emphasized selectively to support different verdicts—that [nuclear] threats were effective, irrelevant, or counterproductive." See Richard K. Betts, *Nuclear Blackmail and Nuclear Balance* (Washington, DC: Brookings Institution Press, 1987), 216–17.

71. Byman and Waxman, *Dynamics of Coercion*, 215–16.

72. Ibid., 136–37, 225. On the other hand, if both parties have reasonable stakes, nuclear and conventional asymmetries may be crucial for successful coercion. The US threats of nuclear escalation in the 1950s during the Korean War are seen as an example. See Ibid., 103; Pape, *Bombing to Win*, 38. These scholars argued that because the United States already made a significant military commitment, it was able to credibly exercise nuclear coercion to bring the conflict to an end on terms it preferred. For a skeptical assessment of nuclear coercion, see Todd S. Sechser and Matthew Fuhrmann, *Nuclear Weapons and Coercive Diplomacy* (New York: Cambridge University Press, 2017), 72–95.

73. Byman and Waxman, *Dynamics of Coercion*, 216.

74. Ibid., 217.

75. Gregg Easterbrook, "The Meaninglessness of 'WMD': Term Limits," *The New Republic*, 7 October 2002.

76. Mueller, "Six Rather Unusual Propositions," 488–89; Easterbrook, "Meaninglessness of 'WMD,'" 22.

77. Easterbrook, "Meaninglessness of 'WMD,'" 23. A 1993 study by the Office of Technology Assessment notes that a sunny day with a light breeze would reduce the fatalities of sarin gas by an order of magnitude, from 8,000 to 700 casualties. See Office of Technology Assessment,

142 Notes

United States Congress, "Proliferation of Weapons of Mass Destruction: Assessing the Risks" (Washington, DC: Office of Technology Assessment, August 1993), 54, https://ota.fas.org/reports/9341.pdf.

78. Matthew Meselson, "The Myth of Chemical Superweapons," *Bulletin of the Atomic Scientists* 47, no. 3 (1991): 12. Meselson writes, "Most British and American mustard casualties resulted from failure to put on the gas mask or removing it too soon. . . . Relatively few were injured by passing through the contaminated area, and fewer still from direct exposure to liquid mustard from exploding munitions." See Ibid., 14.

79. Meselson, "Myth of Chemical Superweapons," 15.

80. Nazi Germany's chemical weapons commander during World War II, Herman Ochsner, made a similar argument. He argued that "there was no room for hope that if the V weapons had been given a gas charge, the effect would have been any greater than that of an explosive charge. Under existing circumstances [with the British population protected], gas casualties undoubtedly would have been less than those caused by explosive bombs." See Hearings on National Defense Authorization Act for Fiscal Years 1992 and 1993— H.R. 2100 and Oversight of Previously Authorized Programs, Readiness Subcommittee Hearings, Committee on Armed Services, US House of Representatives, 102nd Congress, 1st Session, H.A.S.C. No. 102-10, P.759.

81. Sunstein and Zeckhauser, "Overreaction to Fearsome Risks," 446.

82. Ibid.

83. Demands for withdrawal can quickly attain political significance and reverse policy choices. The Clinton administration, for instance, judged the 18 fatalities in the Battle of Mogadishu, Somalia, in 1993, as too high a price and promptly withdrew American forces. See Bryan Craig, "Presidential Transition: Somalia," UVA Miller Center, 8 December 2016, https://millercenter.org/issues-policy/foreign-policy/presidential-transition-somalia; Eric Schmitt, "Somali War Casualties May Be 10,000," *The New York Times*, 8 December 1993, https://www.nytimes.com/1993/12/08/world/somali-war-casualties-may-be-10000.html. Adversaries could hope to engineer similar withdrawals through persistent aerospace bombardment.

84. Egypt's concessions in 1970, in the Israeli—Egyptian War of Attrition and Russia's concessions in 1995, in the Chechen War are limited examples. See Byman and Waxman, *Dynamics of Coercion*, 66, 68. Such fears can exist despite empirical evidence demonstrating that even massive bombings of a population do not lead to uprisings and the overthrow of the regime. For a discussion on the empirical evidence, see Ibid., 68–72.

85. Byman and Waxman, *Dynamics of Coercion*, 37–38; Byman and Waxman, "Kosovo and the Great Air Power Debate," 9.

86. Byman and Waxman, *Dynamics of Coercion*, 30–33; Byman and Waxman, "Kosovo and the Great Air Power Debate," 15; Art and Greenhill, "Coercion," 15.

87. Alex S. Wilner, *Deterring Rational Fanatics* (Philadelphia: University of Pennsylvania Press, 2015), 184–86.

88. Sobelman, "Learning to Deter," 162–63.

89. More broadly speaking, however, a clearly communicated threat is not a necessary factor in efforts at coercion. While, for the purposes of this book, clearly articulated coercive statements have been identified throughout the empirical chapters, the focal point should be the target's decisionmaking. As Pape notes, "even if the coercer makes no threats, no demands, and does not even imagine that the target might make concessions before being

militarily defeated, if the coercer's actions cause the target to make concessions, coercion has succeeded." See Pape, *Bombing to Win*, 12.

90. Benjamin King and Timothy Kutta, *Impact: The History of Germany's V-Weapons in World War II* (Rockville Centre, NY: SARPEDON, 1998), 313.

91. Between August 1943 and March 1945, the Allied forces undertook 68,913 air strike sorties and used close to 122,000 tons of bombs to suppress the German missile launches. See footnote in Irving, *Mare's Nest*, 308.

92. Theodore A. Postol, "Lessons of the Gulf War Experience with Patriot," *International Security* 16, no. 3 (Winter 1991): 119–71.

93. Keaney and Cohen, *Revolution in Warfare?*, 14–15. US forces were unable to accurately assess a successful hit on a Scud mobile launcher throughout Operation Desert Storm. For an excellent illustration of the difficulties, see Colin L. Powell and Joseph E. Persico, *My American Journey* (New York: Random House, 1995), 510–11.

94. Michael R. Gordon and General Bernard E. Trainor, *The General's War: The Inside Story of the Conflict in the Gulf* (New York: Back Bay Books, 1995), 230.

95. There are two distinct challenges in measuring fear. First is recognizing fear. How does one recognize the true emotion of fear from the instrumental display of fear? As Neta Crawford writes, "the ways that psychologists study emotions are not likely to be replicated anytime soon in foreign policy decision settings, nor is it easy to use archives to determine how actors felt versus what they argued." See Crawford, "Passion of World Politics," 118. However, for the subject matter of this book and in the case studies involved, there is no apparent reason for the targets of aerospace bombardment to instrumentally display fear. In fact, in the case of World War II, British politicians actively took steps to suppress any display of fear. The second challenge is the move from the individual to the collective. Individuals perceive and respond to emotional cues, including fear, in different ways. An individual's emotional intelligence is unique. A framework to understand individual emotional intelligence is offered in Peter Salovey et al., "Emotional Intelligence," in *Handbook of Emotions*, ed. Michael Lewis, Jeannette M. Haviland-Jones, and Barrett Lisa Feldman, 3rd ed. (New York: Guilford, 2008), 535. Petersen and Liaras suggest that "the same individual with the same information may develop one belief under the sway of one emotion and a different belief under the influence of a different emotion." See Petersen and Liaras, "Countering Fear in War," 320. Finally, how do decisionmakers experience the fear of others? There are no easy answers. The best way forward is to use proxy variables and acknowledge the possible limitations. As an important side note, equally challenging is the measurement of cognition and perception. See Michael D. Young and Mark Schafer, "Is There Method in Our Madness? Ways of Assessing Cognition in International Relations," *Mershon International Studies Review* 42 (1998): 63–96.

96. The recent instances include the 2006 Second Lebanon War, the 2022 Armenia–Azerbaijan conflict, the ongoing Yemeni War, and the ongoing Russia–Ukraine War.

97. One instance of such efforts at nonmilitarized coercive diplomacy using aerospace weapons is the 2022 Chinese missile drills in the Straits of Taiwan after the visit of US House of Representatives Speaker Nancy Pelosi. See Yimou Lee and Sarah Wu, "Furious China Fires Missiles near Taiwan in Drills after Pelosi Visit," Reuters, 5 August 2022, https://www.reut ers.com/world/asia-pacific/suspected-drones-over-taiwan-cyber-attacks-after-pelosi-visit-2022-08-04/. China made similar use of its ballistic missiles in coercive diplomacy in 1995–1996, during the Third Taiwan Straits Crisis. See Gellman, "US and China Nearly Came to Blows."

144   Notes

Chapter 3

1. Nazi Propaganda Minister, Josef Goebbels designated the rockets *die Vergeltungswaffen* or "vengeance weapons," which later became V-1 and V-2. See David Johnson, *V-1 V-2: Hitler's Vengeance on London* (Briarcliff Manor, NY: Stein and Day, 1982), 5.
2. Irons, *Hitler's Terror Weapons*, 119.
3. See "The Possible Effect of 'CROSSBOW' on 'OVERLORD,'" 2–3, in Operation Crossbow: daily reports and summaries of enemy activity, intelligence and damage reports, counter-measures against launching sites, effects on Allied operations etc., WO 219/699, December 1943–June 1944.
4. Irving, *Mare's Nest*, 9.
5. "The Possible Effect of 'CROSSBOW' on 'OVERLORD,'" 2–3, in Operation Crossbow: daily reports and summaries of enemy activity, intelligence and damage reports, counter-measures against launching sites, effects on Allied operations etc., WO 219/699, December 1943–June 1944; History of SHAEF, WO 219/3988, February–June 1944, 94; Memo for CG AAF from AC/AS Intel., CROSSBOW, 3 January 1944, as cited in Angell, "Chapter 4: CROSSBOW," 97. See also Irons, *Hitler's Terror Weapons*, 85.
6. A word of caution is warranted while discussing the accuracies of the V-1 and V-2. At the time of World War II, inaccuracy wasn't unique to the German missiles. America's use of the Norden bombsight employed in bombing operations was not very accurate by today's standards. See King and Kutta, *Impact*, 317.
7. A Chiefs of Staff report estimated that, at the shortest range, half of German missiles would land in a zone of 7.5 miles, whereas at the longest range, half the missiles would land in a zone of 13 miles. The report notes that the German military planners might not be able to effectively target the Southampton and Portsmouth ports that served as a staging ground for the Allied troops set to land on the beaches of Normandy. The report pointed out that even if the German aimed their missiles at the ports, there was 50% chance that a missile would land anywhere in the region of the Southampton-Portsmouth town. See "The Possible Effect of 'CROSSBOW' on 'OVERLORD,'" 1, in Reports by Chiefs of Staff of effects on Operation Overlord, WO 219/292, July 1943–June 1944.
8. Memo for CG AAF from AC/AS Intel., CROSSBOW, 3 January 1944, as cited in Angell, "Chapter 4: CROSSBOW," 97.
9. Long Range Rocket Development, Report by Sir Findlater Stewart's Committee, 27 June 1943, 1, attached as Annex to War Cabinet Chiefs of Staff Committee, German Long Range Rocket Development, Note by the Joint Parliamentary Secretary to the Ministry of Supply, 28 June 1943, C.O.S.(43) 348(O). The Committee reasoned that, given the significant inaccuracies, a city-sized target was more likely. The Committee wrote, "we felt it was essential to decide at the outset the objective at which the enemy was most likely to direct this new weapon. We were advised that the enemy's fire would almost certainly be inaccurate, that roughly 50% of the missiles would fall within a circular area four miles in radius, centered on the point aimed at, and the most of the remaining 50% would fall in a similar circle of 15 miles radius; a margin of error of these dimensions clearly points to a larger target as the most likely objective, and we were generally of the opinion that, while there were other important targets such as Portsmouth and Southampton within the range of the rocket, it was more likely to be used against London."

Notes **145**

10. "Crossbow" Committee No. 7 of 1944, 18 July 1944: Cabinet papers, 98/36 as cited in Martin Gilbert, *Winston S. Churchill. Volume VII: Road to Victory, 1941–1945* (Hillsdale, MI: Hillsdale College Press, 1986), 856. In a 3 July 1944 War Cabinet meeting, Churchill had also suggested that the Cabinet consider publishing a list of 100 of the smaller towns in Germany the RAF would bomb if the German missile bombardment continued. See Ibid., 839.

11. Prime Minister's Personal Minute, D.238/4, 29 July 1944: Cabinet Papers, 120/775, as cited in Gilbert, *Winston S. Churchill*, 865. See also Ibid., 840, 841.

12. Irons, *Hitler's Terror Weapons*, 89–90.

13. Ibid.

14. Angell, "Chapter 4: CROSSBOW," 89; De la Ferte, *Rocket*, 100.

15. Angell, "Chapter 4: CROSSBOW," 89.

16. King and Kutta, *Impact*, 313.

17. Irving, *Mare's Nest*, 308–09.

18. Ibid. Additionally, seven unsuccessful attempts with pilotless B-17's loaded with high explosive were undertaken.

19. Galland, *The First and the Last*, 235.

20. Ibid.

21. Irving, *Mare's Nest*, 239. See also King and Kutta, *Impact*, 136, 317.

22. Angell, "Chapter 15: CROSSBOW – Second Phase," 528.

23. Adam L. Gruen, *Preemptive Defense: Allied Air Power Versus Hitler's V-Weapons, 1943–1945* (Maxwell Air Force Base, AL: Air Force History and Museums Program, United States Air Force, 1998), 25–26. These losses occurred between the period of December 1943 and June 1944.

24. Karp, *Ballistic Missile Proliferation*, 44. See also Irons, *Hitler's Terror Weapons*, 119.

25. Hitler granted the armistice to the French. As part of the armistice arrangement, Alsace-Lorraine, the region taken by the Germans in 1871 and returned to France in 1919, was made part of the German Reich again. The northern and western parts of France, including Paris, remained occupied German territories, and the Petain government was exiled to Vichy. See Irons, *Hitler's Terror Weapons*, 37; BBC, "History: Philippe Pétain (1856–1951)," BBC, 2014, https://www.bbc.co.uk/history/historic_figures/petain_philippe.shtml

26. Irons, *Hitler's Terror Weapons*, 36.

27. Ibid.

28. Ibid., 13, 19.

29. King and Kutta, *Impact*, 25.

30. Irons, *Hitler's Terror Weapons*, 13, 19.

31. King and Kutta, *Impact*, 25.

32. Irons, *Hitler's Terror Weapons*, 19.

33. Ibid.

34. King and Kutta, *Impact*, 25–26.

35. Ibid.

36. The military actions of France and Belgium were justified as a response to German's inability to pay war reparations as stipulated in the Versailles Treaty. See Ibid.

37. In *Mein Kampf*, Hitler writes, "And so it had all been in vain. In vain all the sacrifices and privations; in vain the hunger and thirst of months which were often endless; in vain the hours in which, with mortal fear clutching at our hearts, we nevertheless did our duty [as

146 Notes

soldiers]; and in vain the death of two millions who died. . . . Was this the meaning of the sacrifice which the German mother made to the fatherland when with sore heart she let her best-loved boys march off, never to see them again? Did all this happen only so that a gang of wretched criminals could lay hands on the fatherland? Was it for this that the German soldier had stood fast in the sun's heat and in snowstorms, hungry, thirsty, and freezing, weary from sleepless nights and endless marches? Was it for this that he had lain in the hell of the drumfire and in the fever of gas attacks without wavering, always thoughtful of his one duty to preserve the fatherland from the enemy peril?" See Adolf Hitler, *Mein Kampf* (1925), translated by Ralph Manheim. (Boston: Houghton Mifflin, 1943), 199–206.

38. Irons, *Hitler's Terror Weapons*, 15.
39. King and Kutta, *Impact*, 25, 75.
40. Gruen, *Preemptive Defense*, 2–3.
41. Ibid.
42. Ibid.
43. Christer Bergström, *The Battle of Britain: An Epic Conflict Revisited* (London: Casemate UK, 2015), 195–96.
44. King and Kutta, *Impact*, 87. Germany responded with the Baedeker raids on historic British cities.
45. Irving, *Mare's Nest*, 88.
46. Ibid., 89.
47. Ibid.
48. King and Kutta, *Impact*, 324–25.
49. Ibid.
50. Ibid., 325–26.
51. Irons, *Hitler's Terror Weapons*, 47.
52. King and Kutta, *Impact*, 75.
53. Irons, *Hitler's Terror Weapons*, 38–39.
54. Ibid., 47.
55. King and Kutta, *Impact*, 325.
56. Ibid.
57. Ibid. By mid-1944, German industry was producing hundreds of aircraft but had neither the fuel to fly nor pilots to man the aircraft. See Williamson Murray, *Strategy for Defeat: The Luftwaffe, 1933–1945* (Maxwell Air Force Base, AL: Air University Press, 1983), 275.
58. Irons, *Hitler's Terror Weapons*, 173. The British and the American Air Forces were superior in quality of aircraft and quality of pilots. The Allied Air Forces also had more aircraft. The decline in the competence of the Luftwaffe was one of the reasons the British felt comfortable reallocating 48 squadrons of fighter aircraft to missile defense operations. Ordway III and Sharpe write that "the rapid decline in the fighting strength and the will to win of the Luftwaffe, coupled with what [Air Marshall Sir Roderic] Hill calls the 'extraordinarily ineffective' navigation, target marking, and bombing of those few German planes that did continue to harass Britain, made this reduced defensive force possible." See Frederick I. Ordway III and Mitchell R. Sharpe, *The Rocket Team* (New York: Thomas Y. Crowell, 1979), 207.
59. Irons, *Hitler's Terror Weapons*, 173. Another factor that undermined pilot training was debilitating shortage of fuel. The Allied bombing of German fuel plants and the Russian occupation of Romanian oil wells necessitated the periodic grounding of fighter aircraft, which left no room for pilot training. See Ibid., 147.

Notes **147**

60. Irons, *Hitler's Terror Weapons*, 173.
61. Jeremy Stocker, *Britain and Ballistic Missile Defence: 1942–2002* (New York: Frank Cass, 2004), 33. While in principle the Germans could have repurposed the materials and efforts directed at the V-1 and V-2 program into building fighter aircrafts to mount a defense against the British and American air forces, it would not have solved the pilot and fuel shortages that grounded the Luftwaffe. See Irons, *Hitler's Terror Weapons*, 174.
62. Joseph Warner Angell, "Guided Missiles Could Have Won," in *World War II in the Air: Europe*, ed. Major James F. Sunderman, USAF (New York: Franklin Watts, 1963), 311, 313.
63. Ibid.
64. Ibid.
65. Jones, *Most Secret War*, 455.
66. Ibid., 455–57.
67. War Cabinet Chiefs of Staff Committee, German Long Range Rocket Development, Third Interim Report by the Joint Parliamentary Secretary, Ministry of Supply, 28 June 1943, C.O.S.(43) 349(O), 2.
68. As late as 2 November 1943, the Minister of Aircraft Production Sir Stafford Cripps argued it was possible to build a 60- to 70-ton rocket to operate with a 10-ton warhead at a range of 130 miles. See Irons, *Hitler's Terror Weapons*, 80. See also Angell, "Chapter 4: CROSSBOW," 97. However, it later turned out that the missile was armed with a 1-ton warhead.
69. The Findlater Stewart Committee noted "it is clear that the rocket could be loaded with poison gas or with high explosives . . . nevertheless, we feel it is on balance unlikely that the first use of gas will come in this way." See Long Range Rocket Development, Report by Sir Findlater Stewart's Committee, 27 June 1943, 4, attached as Annex to War Cabinet Chiefs of Staff Committee, German Long Range Rocket Development, Note by the Joint parliamentary Secretary to the Ministry of Supply, 28 June 1943, C.O.S.(43) 348(O). In a 21 August 1943 document submitted to the Chiefs of Staff Committee, Duncan Sandys notes that intelligence sources indicated that missiles armed with explosives based on the "atom splitting" principle were under development. See War Cabinet, Chiefs of Staff Committee, German Long-Range Rocket, Note by the Joint Parliamentary Secretary, Ministry of Supply, 21 August 1943, C.O.S. (43) 483 (O). Roy Irons points out that such speculation was not without basis. He writes that there was evidence that Heinrich Himmler had small spherical bombs containing radioactive waste. See Irons, *Hitler's Terror Weapons*, 78. In a similar vein, on 5 January 1944, Lieutenant-General Jacob Devers, commanding general, ETOUSA informed Churchill about the "possibility of the existence of a German bomb which emitted some liquid starting radioactivity over an area as a large as two miles square, causing nausea and death, and making the area unapproachable . . . the Americans had made many experiments in this direction and it seemed probable that the Germans had also achieved success." See Irving, *Mare's Nest*, 196–97.
70. The investigation also evaluated the implications of one rocket fired every 6 hours and one fire every 24 hours. See Long Range Rocket Development, Report by Sir Findlater Stewart's Committee, 27 June 1943, 1, attached as Annex to War Cabinet Chiefs of Staff Committee; Long Range Rocket Development, Report by Sir Findlater Stewart's Committee, 27 June 1943, 20, attached as "Annexe VIII: A. Appreciation of the Effect of the Rocket from the Point of View of the London Civil Defence Services" in Annex to War Cabinet Chiefs of Staff Committee, German Long Range Rocket Development, Note

148 Notes

by the Joint parliamentary Secretary to the Ministry of Supply, 28 June 1943, C.O.S.(43) 348(O). See also King and Kutta, *Impact*, 121–22.

71. The Committee extrapolated the effect of one missile based on the damage effects of a 2,500-kilogram bomb which fell at Hendon on 12 February. Roy Irons writes that the blast from the bomb that fell on Hendon leveled 19 homes and damaged 84 beyond repair. He notes that the bomb caused the death of 85, serious injuries and hospitalization of 148, and injured another 300. The civil relief operations lasted for 70 hours. See Irons, *Hitler's Terror Weapons*, 69–70. The Committee assumed that the effect of a 10-ton missile warhead would be 7–8 times worse that the 2,500-kilogram bomb. See Long Range Rocket Development, 20–21.

72. Long Range Rocket Development, 20–21.

73. Ibid.

74. The Committee noted that casualties for the Type A bomb would be more than for Type B. The Committee also suggested that the ratio of injured to killed would be higher for the Type A bomb. See Long Range Rocket Development, 21.

75. Long Range Rocket Development, 22. Reacting to this estimate by the Ministry of Home Security, Duncan Sandys observed that "even if the casualties and damage were half as great as that estimated by the Ministry of Home Security, and attack of this nature upon the capital would undoubtedly inflict very grievous loss of life and property and would gravely disorganize transport, production and the machinery of the Government." See War Cabinet Chiefs of Staff Committee, German Long Range Rocket Development, Third Interim Report by the Joint Parliamentary Secretary, Ministry of Supply, 28 June 1943, C.O.S.(43) 349(O), 5.

76. Ibid.

77. Long Range Rocket Development, 23. See also Irving, *Mare's Nest*, 127.

78. Ibid., 130. The Morrison shelters—named after Herbert Morrison, the Minister of Home Security and Home Secretary during World War II—were a type of indoor air raid shelter distributed to Londoners during the Blitz. These shelters measured 6′ 6″ × 4′ × 2′ 6″ and could accommodate two to three individuals living in a house; they offered added safety as people slept in their homes. See "Morrison 'Table' Shelter," Imperial War Museums, accessed August 4, 2022, https://www.iwm.org.uk/collecti ons/item/object/30082790.

79. Long Range Rocket Development, 6–7. A limited evacuation plan developed by the Committee suggested the evacuation of certain priority classes of London residents: (1) unaccompanied children, (2) mothers with children, and (3) expectant mothers. See Long Range Rocket Development, 17.

80. History of SHAEF, WO 219/3988, February–June 1944, 94; Irons, *Hitler's Terror Weapons*, 85. In a December 1943 memo from General Dwight Eisenhower to General Henry Arnold and General George Marshall, it was estimated that the "equivalent of at least a 2,000-ton bombing attack [could be achieved] in a period of 24 hours." See Headquarters, European Theater of Operations, G-2, memorandum to the chief of staff, United States Army, providing all known details on German V-weapon programs, 13 December 1943, 4, as cited in Mark E. Kipphut, "Crossbow and Gulf War Counter-Scud Efforts: Lessons from History," The Counterproliferation Papers (Maxwell Air Force Base, AL: Air University, February 2003), 6.

81. History of SHAEF, WO 219/3988, February–June 1944, 94; Angell, "Chapter 4: CROSSBOW," 96–97.

Notes   149

82. History of SHAEF, WO 219/3988, February–June 1944, 94. See also "The Possible Effect of 'CROSSBOW' on 'OVERLORD,' " 2–3 in Operation Crossbow: Daily reports and summaries of enemy activity, intelligence and damage reports, counter-measures against launching sites, effects on Allied operations etc., WO 219/699, December 1943–June 1944.

83. Angell, "Chapter 4: CROSSBOW," 89.

84. Ibid.

85. Ibid.

86. Ibid., 84.

87. Ibid.

88. Ibid., 90.

89. Irving, *Mare's Nest*, 8.

90. Gruen, *Preemptive Defense*, 14.

91. Angell, "Chapter 4: CROSSBOW," 90.

92. Irving, *Mare's Nest*, 115.

93. Ibid., 116; Angell, "Guided Missiles Could Have Won," 307.

94. Irving, *Mare's Nest*.

95. Colonel Walter Dornberger notes that, on observing the very limited damage, he ordered a deception operation to convince Allied forces that the damage was significant. He had roads and building blown up and fires set up to make sure aerial reconnaissance photos would mislead the British to believe that the required level of destruction was achieved. See Johnson, *V-1 V-2*, 15; Angell, "Guided Missiles Could Have Won," 307; Irving, *Mare's Nest*, 119.

96. Irving, *Mare's Nest*, 119.

97. Angell, "Chapter 4: CROSSBOW," 91; Gruen, *Preemptive Defense*, 14.

98. Ibid.

99. Angell, "Guided Missiles Could Have Won," 307. Each structure was approximately 300 meters in length. After D-Day, these sites were captured by Allied troops. In June 1944, American air commander, Lieutenant General Louis H. Brereton, inspecting the seven large sites and the ski sites on the Cherbourg peninsula, estimated several of these sites to be "more extensive than any concrete construction we have in the United States with the exception of Boulder Dam." See Ibid., 311; Angell, "Chapter 4: CROSSBOW," 90. One account suggests that 150 ski sites were initially surveyed by the Germans, with 96 eventually built. Of the 96 sites, 22 were totally completed, while 74 were more than 50% completed. See Ibid., 91.

100. Angell, "Guided Missiles Could Have Won," 309; Angell, "Chapter 4: CROSSBOW," 93.

101. Angell, "Guided Missiles Could Have Won," 309; Angell, "Chapter 4: CROSSBOW," 91.

102. Angell, "Guided Missiles Could Have Won," 309.

103. Angell, "Chapter 4: CROSSBOW," 95. Mission No. 164 emerged from Allied frustrations over previous unsuccessful bombing efforts by tactical air force units to destroy the ski sites. See Ibid.

104. "Germany's 'Secret' Weapon," *The New York Times*, December 24, 1943, 12. The editorial further argued, "whether these new weapons of which the Nazis have been boasting are as formidable as advertised cannot be known until they are used. . . . There is no justification for dismissing German threats of reprisals as mere propaganda for domestic consumption. In war, especially against so resourceful a foe as Germany, constant vigilance must be maintained against surprises. . . . But until it is known that the threatened rocket bombardment of Britain is mere idle boasting it cannot be ignored." See also "AIR ATTACK

150 Notes

SHIFTS: Bombers Concentrate on 'Secret Weapon' Strip at Pas-de-Calais BERLIN IS ATTACKED New Blow Is Reported as RAF Follows up with Night Smash," *The New York Times*, December 24, 1943, 1.

105. King and Kutta, *Impact*, 180.

106. Gruen, *Preemptive Defense*, 24–25.

107. Ibid. General Spaatz argued that he did not have enough aircraft to support Operation Overlord, let alone Operation Pointblank. American air force generals also believed that the British approach to bombing German missile sites was flawed. American military leaders after extensive field testing at the Eglin Air Base in Florida believed minimum-altitude bombing technique conducted by fighter aircrafts, rather than bombers, was the ideal approach to hit Crossbow targets. British Air Chief Marshal Leigh-Mallory, however, insisted on using heavy bombers at high altitude to avoid German anti-aircraft defenses. General Arnold was angered at British insistence on using heavy bombers. See Ibid., 24. Eisenhower, threading the delicate balance of coalition management, conceded to Leigh-Mallory and approved the continued use of heavy bombers despite the evidence emerging from the Eglin field tests. See King and Kutta, *Impact*, 172.

108. Angell, "Guided Missiles Could Have Won," p. 309; Gruen, *Preemptive Defense*, 24–25.

109. Gruen, *Preemptive Defense*, 24–25.

110. The V-1 "flying bomb" is an early variant of the modern-day cruise missile. The V-1 cruise missile was powered by a pulse jet engine to fly to its target. However, during the terminal phase, the V-1 missile would execute a free fall dive to its target akin to an air-dropped bomb. For details on the V-1 missile, see Steven J. Zaloga, *V-1 Flying Bomb 1942–52: Hitler's Infamous "Doodlebug"* (Long Island City, NY: Osprey, 2005).

111. Irving, *Mare's Nest*, 233.

112. Ibid.

113. Angell, "Chapter 4: CROSSBOW," 84.

114. Irving, *Mare's Nest*, 234. See also King and Kutta, *Impact*, 185, 191–92. A few British and American military leaders had contended that the large German sites and ski sites were a hoax to frighten and force the diversion of Allied efforts to invade the Europe. General Spaatz, US Strategic Air Force in Europe (USSTAF) Commander, for instance, was very skeptical of the purposes of the German sites and suggested it may well be an "inspired German feint." See Angell, "Chapter 4: CROSSBOW," 91–92.

115. Irving, *Mare's Nest*, 234.

116. In a message to his Commander in Chief, Hitler declared "commitment of the V-1 on the beachhead [in Normandy] does not promise success. The V-1 is intended primarily as a terror weapon against inhabited localities, whereas the beachhead contains only ground troops which artillery and aerial bombardment will have a like effect." See Ordway III and Sharpe, *Rocket Team*, 181. Some of the German military leadership, however, wanted to focus the bombardment on ports from which the Allied offensive was being launched. These ports and the cities near them had a large concentration of troops and stockpiles of munitions, presenting an enticing target to disrupt the Allied offensive. Ordway III and Sharpe write that "both the Commander in Chief, West (Field Marshal Gerd von Rundstedt) and General Heinemann wanted to hit the Allied troop embarkation ports of Southampton and Portsmouth as well as targets on the Normandy peninsula at and near Cherbourg, but Hitler was adamant." So London became the target. However, General Heinemann had fired between 60 and 80 missiles targeting Southampton ports. He was reprimanded for this decision by the German military higher headquarters. See Ibid., 181, 207.

117. Irving, *Mare's Nest*, 235.

118. Angell, "Guided Missiles Could Have Won," 310. The decision was not an easy one to politically accept. By late June, Hitler's forces had launched nearly 2,000 V-1 missiles against the British capital. At every war cabinet meeting, grim news piled up. The missiles were hitting hospitals, churches, schools, factories, bridges, and homes and killing and injuring Londoners. David Irving writes that 20,000 houses a day were damaged, and one-sixth of the war production capacity was lost. See Irving, *Mare's Nest*, 9.

119. Irons, *Hitler's Terror Weapons*, 114. See also Irving, *Mare's Nest*, 241.

120. Irons, *Hitler's Terror Weapons*, 115. However, the British fighter aircraft employed in anti-aircraft defenses against the missiles faced significant operational challenges. Churchill writes, "our fastest fighters, specially stripped and vigorously boosted, could barely overtake the speediest missiles. Many bombs did not fly as fast as their makers intended, but even so it was often difficult for our fighters to catch them in time. To make things worse, the enemy fired the bombs in salvoes, in the hope of saturating our defences. Our normal procedure of 'scrambling' was too slow, and so the fighters had to fly standing patrols, finding and chasing their quarry with the help of instructions and running commentaries from radar stations and observer corps posts on the ground." See Winston S. Churchill, *The Second World War. Volume 6: Triumph and Tragedy* (Boston, MA: Houghton Mifflin, 1953), 41.

121. The Germans retrofitted the V-1 cruise missiles with cable-cutting wing edges. As many as 600 balloons were disabled by this technique. See Johnson, *V-1 V-2*, 63.

122. Irving, *Mare's Nest*, 241.

123. Gruen, *Preemptive Defense*, 29.

124. Irving, *Mare's Nest*, 236.

125. The bombing of Crossbow targets took priority over all other targets with the exception of aerial support provided to the battle on the beaches of Normandy. German cities, aircraft factories, and oil targets were all subordinated to Crossbow targets. See Ibid. See also Angell, "Guided Missiles Could Have Won," 310; Gilbert, *Winston S. Churchill, Volume 7: Road to Victory, 1941–1945*, 809.

126. Gruen, *Preemptive Defense: Allied Air Power Versus Hitler's V-Weapons, 1943-1945*, 32. The Germans also began using a new explosive, Trialen—an aluminum explosive with double the effects of TNT—around this time. See Johnson, *V-1 V-2: Hitler's Vengeance on London*, 63.

127. Gilbert, *Winston S. Churchill. Volume 7*, 867.

128. Ibid.

129. Winston S. Churchill, *Triumph and Tragedy, Vol. 6: The Second World War* (Boston, MA: Houghton Mifflin, 1953), 39. Air Chief Marshall Sir Philip Joubert de la Ferté make a similar argument. He writes that "for those who actually experienced the V1 attack it may be said that the winter blitz of 1940 was a very mild strain on the nerves compared with that imposed by the sounds of the approaching V1. It was the wait for the moment when the motor would stop and the weapon plunge to the earth, bringing death and destruction to men and material, that racked the nerves of the population. Aircraft overhead were a fairly remote threat. A bomb fell swiftly and catastrophe was soon over. But the long-drawn-out threat of the pulsating, flaming terror that flew unrelenting across the sky was something in a quite different category." See De la Ferte, *Rocket*, 111.

130. King and Kutta, *Impact*, 211. For several residents of London, the landing of Allied troops in Normandy beaches in France signaled an end to the war and their suffering. Instead,

152 Notes

they faced German rocket bombardment, triggering disappointment and anxiety. The British government became the target of resentment. See Johnson, *V-1 V-2*, 49, 69.

131. King and Kutta, *Impact*, 211.

132. Irons, *Hitler's Terror Weapons*, 117.

133. The telegram sent by the Combined Chiefs of Staff requested that Eisenhower, in his war plans, "ensure that due weight is given to the elimination of this threat." See COS(44)254th meeting (O); PRO WO106-4394 as cited in Ibid., 99–100.

134. Gruen, *Preemptive Defense*, 32.

135. Ibid., 36.

136. Ibid., 32.

137. Angell, "Guided Missiles Could Have Won," 311.

138. Ibid.

139. Ibid., 309. The Germans were able to build these modified ski sites more and more quickly. Initially, it took the Germans a month to build these modified ski sites. By May 1944, they were doing it in 10 days. By October 1944, the Germans were able to build the modified ski sites in less than a day. See Ordway III and Sharpe, *Rocket Team*, 177, 181.

140. Angell, "Guided Missiles Could Have Won," 309.

141. See "Supplement to the London Gazette of Tuesday 19th October, 1948: Air Operations by Air Defence of Great Britain and Fighter Command in Connection with the German Flying Bomb and Rocket Offensives, 1944–1945," 5593.

142. See Ibid.

143. Irving, *Mare's Nest*, 280.

144. Ibid., 281.

145. Ibid.

146. By the end of the war, the Germans managed to fire approximately 1,100 V-2 against England from Western Holland. See Angell, "Guided Missiles Could Have Won," 314. The Allied air forces responded with bombing campaigns. Notably, in one raid on 17 September 1944, British Bomber Command flew close to 700 sorties and delivered 3,800 tons of explosives on airfields in Holland basing the He-111s involved in the launching of missiles against London. See Gruen, *Preemptive Defense*, 38.

147. King and Kutta, *Impact*, 242–43.

148. Norman Longmate, *Hitler's Rockets: The Story of the V-2s* (New York,: Skyhorse, 2009), 171. Field Marshall Montgomery writes in his memoirs, "On the 9 September I received information from London that on the previous day the first V-2 rockets had landed in England; it was suspected that they came from areas near Rotterdam and Amsterdam and I was asked when I could rope off those general areas. So far as I was concerned that settled the direction of the thrust line of my operations to secure crossing over the Meuse and Rhine; it must be towards Arnhem." See Viscount Montgomery of Alamein and Bernard Law Montgomery, *The Memoirs of Field-Marshall the Viscount Montgomery of Alamein, K. G.* (New York: World Publishing, 1958), 246.

149. King and Kutta, *Impact*, 245.

150. Viscount Montgomery of Alamein and Law Montgomery, *Memoirs*, 246.

151. King and Kutta, *Impact*, 246.

152. Ibid., 100.

153. Irons, *Hitler's Terror Weapons*, 100–101. Roy Irons, in examining Eisenhower's choices, writes, "In the always clear and irresponsible glow of hindsight, the rocket had not proved a serious danger—but this was not an error of the Supreme Commander's. Patton's advance

was not guaranteed success, nor was disaster impossible. What would have been the state of the Grand alliance, had Patton failed, and London, ignored by the American General, blasted?" See Ibid. See also Viscount Montgomery of Alamein and Law Montgomery, *Memoirs*, 246–48.

154. Steve R. Waddell, *United States Army Logistics: The Normandy Campaign 1944* (Westport, CT: Greenwood Press, 1994), 99.

155. Ordway III and Sharpe, *Rocket Team*, 198.

156. King and Kutta, *Impact*, 268. See also Irons, *Hitler's Terror Weapons*, 141.

157. Mike Dean, "The UK's First Ballistic Missile Early Warning System," *Journal of Defence Studies*, 2, no. 1, January 1997, 33; AIR 20/2647 SHAEF S-65726 Nov 061945A as cited in Stocker, *Britain and Ballistic Missile Defence*, 24.

158. King and Kutta, *Impact*, 268, 273; Waddell, *United States Army Logistics*, 99.

159. King and Kutta, *Impact*, 278, 279, 281, 282; Peter Caddick-Adams, *Snow & Steel: The Battle of the Bulge, 1944–45* (New York: Oxford University Press, 2015), 121; Patrick Delaforce, *Smashing the Atlantic Wall: The Destruction of Hitler's Coastal Fortress* (South Yorkshire, UK: Pen & Sword, 2006), 210. For details of the effect of the attack on civilians in Antwerp and the dock workers, see Irons, *Hitler's Terror Weapons*, 145; King and Kutta, *Impact*, 64–265.

160. King and Kutta, *Impact*, 278, 279, 281, 282; Caddick-Adams, *Snow & Steel*, 121; Delaforce, *Smashing the Atlantic Wall*, 210.

161. Germany had fired as much as 16,000 V-1s and 14,000 V-2s at England and at targets in Europe by the end of World War II. See Angell, "Chapter 4: CROSSBOW," 84. Approximately, 2,500 V-1 missiles and 100 V-2 missiles detonated on England. Around 10,000 British civilians were killed and 25,000 were seriously injured. As a result of the missile bombardment, as many as 200,000 buildings (principally dwellings) were totally destroyed or damaged beyond repair; 1,339,000 buildings were less seriously damaged but required repair. Finally, nearly 4,500,000 British civilians were rendered homeless or affected in a similar fashion. See Angell, "Guided Missiles Could Have Won," 314.

162. Irving, *Mare's Nest*, 302. How well the missile campaign fared depends on what is being measured to evaluate the campaign's effectiveness. R. V. Jones suggests comparing the balance between Allied expenditure in countermeasures and the damage that would have occurred if those countermeasures had not been undertaken. By the metric outlined by R. V. Jones, the V-weapons certainly seem a good investment for the Germans. Particularly if one considers the argument given the high attrition rates of the German air force. A bomber could perform five or six flights over England before being shot down, it could carry only a total of six to eight tons of bombs. The total loss of a bomber, including the cost of training the crew, was roughly three times the price of a missile. See Ordway III and Sharpe, *Rocket Team*, 185–86.

163. The costs included the loss of production, loss of aircraft and crews, extra fighter defenses, extra balloon barrage, the clearance of material damage (but not permanent repairs), and the massive "Crossbow" bombing offensive. See Irving, *Mare's Nest*, 302. Later, the Ministry of Housing estimated that permanent repairs to housing destroyed or damaged by the missiles would cost at least another £25,000,000. See Ibid., 303. For another detailed estimation of the costs involved in the German missile program, see Karp, *Ballistic Missile Proliferation*, 39–40.

164. Irving, *Mare's Nest*, 302. See also Karp, *Ballistic Missile Proliferation*, 39–40.

165. Eisenhower, *Crusade in Europe*, 260.

154 Notes

166. General Curtis LeMay and MacKinlay Kantor, *Mission with LeMay: My Story* (Garden City, NY: Doubleday, 1965), 397.

167. Karp, *Ballistic Missile Proliferation*, 44.

168. Angell, "Chapter 4: CROSSBOW," 87. Walter Dornberger, Wernher von Braun, and Willy Messerschmitt have argued that the missiles could have been brought to duty in time and in sufficient quantity if its program activities had not interrupted. See Angell, "Guided Missiles Could Have Won," 314.

169. Hitler had also slowed down other military industrial research and developmental efforts in the early 1940s. General LeMay notes, "when Hitler came to power in 1933, the Germans fired up an enormous research and development program. It paid off. They built a military machine, the most impressive that the world had ever seen. But after Hitler overran Poland and France and the Lowlands in such a comparatively short period of time, and nullified all threat from Scandinavia, he cut off his intensive program. He built himself into a real gap, right then and there. England didn't collapse as the Nazis expected; and we Americans got into the war. It looked like it was going to be a long-term affair, so Hitler had to blast off his whole program again." See LeMay and Kantor, *Mission with LeMay*, 397.

170. On 23 November 1939, Hitler halved the steel allocation for the missile development effort. After the victory in Poland, Hitler concluded that he would not be needing the missiles. See Irving, *Mare's Nest*, 18. In March 1943, Hitler had dreamed that the V-2 would never strike England and downgraded its priority again. Albert Speer, placed in charge of German war production efforts, refocused Hitler's mind to the V-2 missile and had it restored again. Later, on 7 July 1943, Hitler summoned Dornberger and von Braun to his headquarters to inform them that the V-2 missile would play a major role in the campaign against England. He then noted to them, "If only I had had faith in you earlier! In all my life I have owed apologies to two people only—General Field Marshal Von Brauchitsch who repeatedly drew my attention to the importance of the A-4 [V-2] for the future, and yourself. If we had had the A-4 earlier and in sufficient quantities, it would have had decisive importance in this War. I didn't believe in it." See Angell, "Chapter 4: CROSSBOW," 88; Angell, "Guided Missiles Could Have Won," 318. See also Walter Dornberger, "A Night at the Fuhrer's Headquarters," in *V-2*, trans. James Cleugh and Geoffrey Halliday, 3rd printing (New York: Vail-Ballou, 1958), 107.

171. De la Ferte, *Rocket*, 20.

Chapter 4

1. Klare, "Arms Transfers to Iran and Iraq," 6.

2. Kevin M. Woods et al., *Saddam's Generals: Perspectives of the Iran–Iraq War* (Alexandria, VA: Institute for Defense Analyses, 2010), 27.

3. After Iraq managed to learn to use chemical weapons effectively on the battlefield, it quickly retook all its territories from Iranian troops. A declassified 1988 CIA intelligence assessment on the Iran–Iraq war notes, "chemical agents were critical to Iraq's willingness to launch [successful] military offensives that recaptured significant pieces of territory this year. We further believe that chemical warfare played a decisive role in curbing the threat to the Iraqi Government from Iranian-backed Kurdish rebels in northern Iraq." See Central Intelligence Agency, "Iraq's National Security Goals: An Intelligence Assessment,"

December 1988, https://nsarchive2.gwu.edu/NSAEBB/NSAEBB80/. On how Iraq was able to acquire the raw materials and industrial capacity to produce chemical weapons, see Kenneth R. Timmerman, *The Death Lobby: How the West Armed Iraq* (New York: Houghton Mifflin, 1991), 133; Seymour M. Hersh, "U.S. Aides Say Iraqis Made Use of a Nerve Gas," *New York Times*, 30 March 1984; John J. Fialka, "Fighting Dirty: Western Industry Sells Third World the Means To Produce Poison Gas," *Wall Street Journal*, 16 September 1988; John J. Fialka, "Fighting Dirty: Chemical Weapons Spread in Third World, Pose Challenge to West," *Wall Street Journal*, 15 September 1988.

4. Eisenstadt, *"Sword of the Arabs,"* 17; Warren Richey, "Iranians Await Iraqi Attacks in Campgrounds and Luxury Hotels," *Christian Science Monitor*, 15 April 1988. See also Williamson Murray and Kevin M. Woods, *The Iran–Iraq War: A Military and Strategic History* (Cambridge: Cambridge University Press, 2014), 339; Chubin, *Iran's National Security Policy*, 22.

5. "Transcripts of Meetings between Saddam and Senior Iraqi Officials Discussing Military Tactics During the War with Iran, Including the Use of Napalm and Cluster Bombs, Tank Maneuvering, and Attacking Oil Refineries," conflict Records and Research Center, CRRC Record Number: SH-PDWN-D-001-021, Document Date: 6 October 1980.

6. Anthony H. Cordesman, *Weapons of Mass Destruction in the Middle East* (McLean, VA: Brassey's, 1991), 41–42. For details on the Iranian and Iraqi air and missile campaigns before 1988, see Edgar O'Ballance, *The Gulf War* (New York: Brassey's Defence Publishers, 1988), 102, 126–27, 153–54, 169–70, 182; Steven Zaloga, "Ballistic Missiles in the Third World: Scud and Beyond," *International Defense Review*, 1988; Cordesman and Abraham H. Wagner, *The Lessons of Modern War. Volume II: The Iran–Iraq War* (Boulder, CO: Westview Press, 1990), 157, 495–502; Dilip Hiro, *The Longest War: The Iran–Iraq Military Conflict* (New York: Routledge Chapman & Hall, 1991), 134–35.

7. Cordesman, *Weapons of Mass Destruction*, 41–42.

8. Hospitals in Tehran stockpiled medicine and other supplies to respond to large-scale chemical attacks. Additionally, special trucks designed to spray anti-chemical weapons agents were positioned throughout the city. See Richey, "Iranians Await Iraqi Attacks."

9. Chubin, *Iran's National Security Policy*, 22; Klare, "Arms Transfers to Iran and Iraq," 10.

10. *Guide Atlas 1*, 5th ed. (HDRDC, 2002), 61–62 as cited in Samuel, *Unfinished History*, 182. See also Anthony H. Cordesman, "Creating Weapons of Mass Destruction," *Armed Forces Journal*, February 1989, 54 as cited in Carus, "Genie Unleashed," 3; Chubin, "Last Phase of the Iran–Iraq War," 10.

11. Cordesman and Wagner, *Lessons of Modern War. Volume II*, 503.

12. Eisenstadt, *"Sword of the Arabs,"* 17.

13. Iran and Iraq also had disputes over the sovereignty of several points along their land border. See Cordesman and Wagner, *Lessons of Modern War. Volume II*, 15–16.

14. Ibid., 16–17.

15. Ibid.

16. Dilip Hiro, *The Iranian Labyrinth: Journeys Through Theocratic Iran and Its Furies* (New York: Nation Books, 2005), 214.

17. Cordesman and Wagner, *Lessons of Modern War. Volume II*, 17.

18. Rick Francona, *Ally to Adversary: An Eyewitness Account of Iraq's Fall from Grace* (Annapolis, MD: Naval Institute Press, 1999), 9–10.

156 Notes

19. Iraq laid claims to Khuzistan Province in Iran. Iraq also tried to extend its territorial sovereignty in the Gulf to 12 miles. Iraq demanded Iran cede its sheltered anchorage at Khorramshahr. See Cordesman and Wagner, *Lessons of Modern War. Volume II*, 17.
20. Hiro, *Iranian Labyrinth*, 214.
21. Ibid.
22. Cordesman and Wagner, *Lessons of Modern War. Volume II*, 19; Hiro, *Iranian Labyrinth*, 215.
23. Walid Khalidi, "Iraq vs. Kuwait: Claims and Countermeasures," in *The Gulf War Reader: History, Documents, Opinions*, ed. Micah L. Sifry and Christopher Cerf (New York: Times Books, 1991), 62; Hiro, *Iranian Labyrinth*, 215.
24. The Kurdish guerillas were at one point in time able to tie down four-fifths of Iraq's troops and half its tanks. See Hiro, *Iranian Labyrinth*, 215. See also Murray and Woods, *Iran–Iraq War*, 62.
25. See Hiro, *Iranian Labyrinth*, 216.
26. Newspapers controlled by the Iranian clergy declared that Iran would support Shiite factions in Iraq and facilitate attempts to establish "a government within a government" in Iraq to force Saddam's downfall. See William E. Smith, Raji Samghabadi, and Barry Hillenbrand, "Clouds of Desperation," *Time Magazine*, 19 March 1984. After Khomeini came to power, he supported Iraq's Shia cleric, Ayatollah Muhammad Baqir al-Sadr and publicly called for overthrowing the Baathist regime. In 1980, Shia militants linked with al-Sadr attempted to assassinate Tariq Aziz, Saddam Hussein's trusted foreign minister. Saddam Hussein immediately arrested al-Sadr, took severe action against Shia rioters, and deported tens of thousands of Shiites to Iran. See Steven A. Ward, *Immortal: A Military History of Iran and Its Armed Forces* (Washington, DC: Georgetown University Press, 2009), 243. See also Cordesman and Wagner, *Lessons of Modern War. Volume II*, 15 & 22.
27. Ward, *Immortal*, 243.
28. Cordesman and Wagner, *Lessons of Modern War. Volume II*, 13–14.
29. John Bulloch and Harvey Morris, *Saddam's War: The Origins of the Kuwait Conflict and the International Response* (Winchester, MA: Faber and Faber, 1991), 76.
30. Iranian leadership constantly referred to the war as the "imposed war" (*jang-i tahmili*). See James A. Bill, "Morale vs. Technology: The Power of Iran in the Persian Gulf War," in *The Iran–Iraq War: The Politics of Aggression*, ed. Farhang Rajaee (Gainesville: University Press of Florida, 1993), 205.
31. Chubin, "Last Phase of the Iran–Iraq War," 3.
32. Ward, *Immortal*, 258.
33. Smith, Samghabadi, and Hillenbrand, "Clouds of Desperation."
34. Bill, "Morale vs. Technology," 205.
35. Chubin, *Iran's National Security Policy*, 17. See also Bill, "Morale vs. Technology," 204.
36. Klare, "Arms Transfers to Iran and Iraq," 4.
37. Cordesman and Wagner, *Lessons of Modern War. Volume II*, 48.
38. The 1983 bombing of the US embassy in Beirut, believed by the United States to have been orchestrated by Iran, again tilted the United States away from Iran and toward Iraq. See Timmerman, *Death Lobby*, 128–30.
39. U.S. Department of State Cable, Talking Points for Amb. Rumsfeld's Meeting with Tariq Aziz and Saddam Hussein, 14 December 1983, https://nsarchive2.gwu.edu/NSAEBB/NSAEBB82/.

Notes **157**

40. George P. Shultz, *Turmoil and Triumph: My Years as Secretary of State* (New York: Charles Scribner's Sons, 1993), 235. See also Smith, Samghabadi, and Hillenbrand, "Clouds of Desperation."

41. By December 1982, the Commodity Credit Corporation of the US Department of Agriculture quietly authorized a $300 million line of credit to facilitate Iraqi purchase of American wheat and rice. The credit provided Iraq vital financial relief to continue the war without losing domestic support. Saudi Arabia and Kuwait had grown wary of providing continued loans and financial support to Iraq. Iraq was desperate for cash, and the United States became Iraq's financial lifeline. American financial support to Iraq continued to grow. By 1987, Iraq received $961 billion in agricultural commodity credits to purchase American goods. See Timmerman, *Death Lobby*, 126, 127, 131; Hiro, *Longest War*, 239.

42. The White House, National Security Decision Directive 139, "Measures of Improve US Posture and Readiness to Respond to Developments in the Iran–Iraq War," April 5, 1984, https://fas.org/irp/offdocs/nsdd/nsdd-139.pdf

43. Such intelligence-sharing materialized quickly and grew progressively as the war unfolded. The United States also provided Iraq with imagery of Iranian troop deployments and other intelligence information. The intelligence information enhanced Iraq's ability to concentrate and direct its forces with significant advantages. See Klare, "Arms Transfers to Iran and Iraq," 17. See also Timmerman, *Death Lobby*, 130–31.

44. An illustration of such overt and covert assistance can be found in Timmerman, *Death Lobby*, 127. The United States may have also traded weapons and spares supply for Soviet and North Korea military equipment that Iraq possessed or seized from the Iranians. Lieutenant Colonel Rick Francona, a Defense Intelligence Agency (DIA) officer stationed in Iraq recounts American interest in acquiring an unusual 170 mm bore artillery field gun seized by the Iraqis from Iranian forces. Francona writes that the Iraqis did not realize it, but the weapon was designed and built by North Korea. See Francona, *Ally to Adversary*, 26–27.

45. For the Soviet Union's geopolitical motivations at the beginning of the Iran–Iraq War, see Timmerman, *Death Lobby*, 120.

46. Mohiaddin Mesbahi, "The USSR and the Iran–Iraq War: From Brezhnev to Gorbachev," in *The Iran–Iraq War: The Politics of Aggression*, ed. Farhang Rajaee (Gainesville: University Press of Florida, 1993), 74. See also Murray and Woods, *Iran–Iraq War*, 155; O'Ballance, *Gulf War*, 103.

47. "Arms Agreement between Iraq and the Soviet Union Signed in 1981 and 1983," Conflict Records Research Center, CRRC Record Number: SH-PDWN-D-000-552, Document Date: 1981–1989. The Soviet Union was getting worried that Iraq was tilting toward the United States. Iran, on the other hand, was not receptive to Soviet overtures. Soviet leaders decided they needed to be invested in the region and have influence on how the war was prosecuted and would ultimately end. By November 1982, more than 1,000 Soviet military advisors had arrived in Iraq to help with the war effort. The Soviet Union supplied 400 T-55 tanks, 250 T-72 tanks, many Grad missiles, Frog 7 missiles, SAM 9 missiles, and Scud B missiles. Additionally, MiG-25 reconnaissance fighters and Mi-24 helicopter gunships were deployed in Iraq to support its war effort. See Timmerman, *Death Lobby*, 121–22.

48. Mesbahi, "USSR and the Iran–Iraq War," 88–89. The Soviet Union, like the United States, also bartered its weapons for Iraqi supply of captured American military equipment— such as the Phoenix, Sparrow, and Sidewinder air-to-air missiles—that were employed by

158 Notes

the Iranians. See Murray and Woods, *Iran–Iraq War*, 220. Major General Mizher Rashid al-Tarfa al-Ubaydi, a Iraqi military intelligence officer, has indicated that the Soviet Union offered code-breaking experts to Iraq in exchange for Iran's American-made F-4 aircraft. Woods et al., *Saddam's Generals*, 108.

49. Mesbahi, "USSR and the Iran–Iraq War," 88–89.
50. Chubin, *Iran's National Security Policy*, 18; Chubin, "Last Phase of the Iran–Iraq War," 4.
51. Chubin, *Iran's National Security Policy*, 18.
52. Ward, *Immortal*, 244.
53. The loss in manpower had a devastating effect, particularly on the Iranian air force. The purging of skilled military personnel led to improper maintenance of aircrafts and insufficient pilot training, which were attributed to the loss of several aircraft during the war. See Cordesman and Wagner, *Lessons of Modern War. Volume II*, 159.
54. Murray and Woods, *Iran–Iraq War*, 150.
55. "Transcript of a Meeting Between Saddam Hussein and Senior Officers," Conflict Records Research Center, CRRC Record Number: *SH-MISC-D-001-334, Document Date: February–March 1981 as cited in Ibid., 151.
56. "Commentary on New Lethal Weapons, 12 Apr (FBIS-MEA-83-071)," *Foreign Broadcast Information Service Daily Reports* (1983) as cited in Ibid., 222.
57. Smith, Samghabadi, and Hillenbrand, "Clouds of Desperation."
58. Ibid.
59. A declassified CIA document notes that "during the early days of the war, Iraq's use of CW agents was often ineffective.... In some cases the Iraqis would use agents under unsuitable weather conditions, such as when the wind was blowing toward their own troops. In the case of aerial CW bombs, Iraqi pilots would release chemical munitions from altitudes too high to permit accurate, concentrated strikes. [However] As the war progressed, the Iraqis became much more proficient in the use of chemical weapons." See CIA Directorate of Intelligence, "Iraq's Chemical Warfare Program: More Self-Reliant, More Deadly. A Research Paper," August 1990, Declassified 21 June 2011,25.
60. S. Taheri Shemirani, "The War of the Cities," in *The Iran–Iraq War: The Politics of Aggression*, ed. Farhang Rajaee (Gainesville: University Press of Florida, 1993), 33.
61. Ibid.
62. Ibid.
63. Ibid.
64. Joost R. Hiltermann, *A Poisonous Affair: America, Iraq, and the Gassing of Halabja* (New York: Cambridge University Press, 2007), 69.
65. Ibid.
66. Iraqis learned to make their chemical bombs reliable and better fused to explode at the appropriate altitudes. By 1988, the Iraqi Army had demonstrated its ability to use a variety of chemical weapons to smartly disable Iranian troop movements while retaining Iraqi ability to assault Iranian forces. Iraqi forces employed persistent mustard gas to limit Iran's rear area operations, while using nonpersistent nerve gas to soften up forward positions for a surprise assault. See Cordesman, *Weapons of Mass Destruction*, 90. See also Ward, *Immortal*, 293.
67. Saddam Hussein and his military advisers had been considering a chemical weapons attack on the Kurdish rebels for a number of years. In a 1985 conversation with his military advisers, Saddam Hussein is heard saying, "This meeting is about those who [are carrying] out sabotage in northern Iraq. We need [to utilize our technological advantage since] our

army is preoccupied with the major battles against the Iranian foe . . . during time of war, even the international area views the rebellion as an attempt to weaken Iraq and to exploit the war to benefit forces whether inside or outside Iraq . . . the use of a special arsenal that will be used against a specific location that harbors the leadership. We need to use the air force that is equipped with the special arsenal to attack leadership and command centers. Then we execute special forces' air drop from planes to destroy those who have managed to survive." See SH-SHTP-A-001-045, Saddam and High Ranking Officers Discussing Plans to Attack Kurdish "Saboteurs" in Northern Iraq and the Possibility of Using Special Ammunition (Weapons), Undated (Circa 1985) as cited in Murray and Woods, *Iran–Iraq War*, 254.

68. Woods et al., *Saddam's Generals*, 49.

69. Shemirani, "War of the Cities," 33.

70. Woods et al., *Saddam's Generals*, 49.

71. Abbas Abd-al Razzaq Akbar recounts in an interview, "I saw whole families—mothers with their children—that nobody had touched. One of the first survivors I met was a young woman whose father I had known, a photographer named Omar Rassam. She took me to the cellar of her house. Inside, everyone was dead. She was the only survivor. All the people I met were in shock. In another cellar a dead woman was holding her son, her arm outstretched as if to beg for help. . . . The gas had killed all natural life, animals and trees. I saw thousands of goats and sheep, all dead. Also wolves. I saw a whole dead cow whose calf was still alive, trying to suckle. I filmed hundreds of dead animals on the roads around Halabja. I couldn't hear anything. No birds. There was absolutely no sound. Everything had died. I had to leave town every so often to go to an area where I could hear birds, because the silence drove me crazy." See Hiltermann, *Poisonous Affair*, 105.

72. An Iraqi military assessment concluded that "use of special ammunition in strikes on saboteur headquarters and other places where they congregate has caused casualties among the saboteurs, has terrified and panicked them, and has weakened their morale, forcing many to return to the national ranks." See Mudiriyat al-Istikhbarat al-Askariya al-'Ameh, Baghdad, 6 April 1988, HRW ref. 880/8-A as cited in Ibid., 129. Saddam Hussein's campaign against the Kurds continued after the end of the Iran–Iraq war. His goal was to establish a *cordon sanitaire* in Iraq's northern border. By mid-1989, Iraq had destroyed 4,000 Kurdish settlements and resettled 45,000 square kilometers of Kurdish territory with Arabs immigrants. See Bulloch and Morris, *Saddam's War*, 90.

73. Al-Hamdani, Lieutenant General Ra'ad Majid. *Memoir: From Golan to the Collapse to Baghdad: Six Wars in Thirty Years* (Baghdad: Unpublished), 2003 as cited in Murray and Woods, *Iran–Iraq War*, 321. In addition to satellite imagery, there may have been extensive intelligence and military planning assistance from the United States to Iraq. While controversial and contested by several American policymakers, there is some evidence that the United States offered substantial covert assistance to the Iraqis. According to a news article by Patrick Tyler in the *New York Times*, more than 60 officers of the US DIA "were secretly providing detailed information on Iranian deployments, tactical planning for battles, plans for airstrikes and bomb-damage assessments for Iraq." In the news article, Tyler, cites retired DIA officer Colonel Walter P. Lang as suggesting that the United States was "desperate to make sure that Iraq did not lose . . . the use of gas on the battlefield by the Iraqis was not a matter of deep strategic concern . . . [while the US] would have never accepted the use of chemical weapons against civilians, but the use against military objectives was seen as inevitable in the Iraqi struggle for survival." See Patrick E. Tyler, "Officers Say US Aided Iraq

160 Notes

in War despite Use of Gas; Battle Planning on Iran; New Details of 1980's Program - Help Continued as Iraqis Used Chemical Agents," *The New York Times*, 18 August 2002. See also Hiltermann, *Poisonous Affair*, 139.

74. Saddam Hussein extensively purged the Iraqi Army after taking power in 1979. He believed that the army was the only force capable of overthrowing him. He particularly made sure that the most competent senior officers, who could also theoretically execute a successful coup, were forced to retire. He replaced them with loyalists despite a lack of military acumen and credentials. At the end of Iran–Iraq War, Saddam Hussein temporarily promoted competent officers only to reverse this act after the war ended. See Murray and Woods, *Iran–Iraq War*, 62–63, 287, 303; Caitlin Talmadge, "The Puzzle of Personalist Performance: Iraqi Battlefield Effectiveness in the Iran–Iraq War," *Security Studies* 22, no. 2 (2013): 180–221.

75. CIA Directorate of Intelligence, "Iraq's Chemical Warfare Program: More Self-Reliant, More Deadly. A Research Paper," August 1990, Declassified 21 June 2011, 25.

76. Ibid. The Iraqis used several chemical agents including mustard gas, sarin, and CS tear gas during its offensive operation in Al-Faw. See Hiltermann, *Poisonous Affair*, 140. Lieutenant Colonel Rick Francona, a DIA officer stationed in Iraq insists that Iraq employed chemical weapon, including nerve gas, in the Al-Faw campaign. He writes that on a tour of the newly liberated Al-Faw peninsula, he found used atropine injections—useful only as an antidote to nerve gas—in deserted Iranian command bunkers and field hospitals. See Francona, *Ally to Adversary*, 24. See also US Air Force Intelligence Agency, "Iran/Iraq Chemical Warfare Casualties. 6G (undated), obtained from US Central Command as cited in Hiltermann, *Poisonous Affair*, 140.

77. Murray and Woods, *Iran–Iraq War*, 87.

78. CIA Directorate of Intelligence, "Iraq's Chemical Warfare Program: More Self-Reliant, More Deadly. A Research Paper," August 1990, Declassified 21 June 2011, 25.

79. Timmerman, *Death Lobby*, 1991, 304.

80. Murray and Woods, *Iran–Iraq War*, 327.

81. Ibid.

82. Ibid.

83. CIA Directorate of Intelligence, "Iraq's Chemical Warfare Program: More Self-Reliant, More Deadly. A Research Paper," August 1990, Declassified 21 June 2011, 25. See also Woods et al., *Saddam's Generals*, 49.

84. Bill, "Morale vs. Technology," 204.

85. At one point in time, the large number of *Basij* volunteers could not be absorbed into the *Pasdaran* or the Iranian Army. Several of these volunteers were sent to eastern Iran instead to police and fight against drug smugglers. See Ward, *Immortal*, 248.

86. Murray and Woods, *Iran–Iraq War*, 79. The *Basij* volunteers were given a mere two weeks' of basic small arms training. But they were constantly exposed to revolutionary indoctrination infused with religious speeches and Quranic readings. See Ward, *Immortal*, 246.

87. Efraim Karsh, *The Iran–Iraq War 1980–1988* (Osceola, WI: Osprey, 2002), 39.

88. Hiltermann, *Poisonous Affair*, 144.

89. "Iraq, Saying It Hit Tankers, Threatens Chemical Strikes," *International Herald Tribune*, 30 March 1998.

90. "Transcript from Three Audio Files of a Meeting of the General Command of the Armed Forces," Conflict Records Research Center, CRRC Record Number: SH-AFGC-D-000-731, Document Date: 24 March 1988, 13-14.

91. See "Saddam and His Advisers Discussing the Importance of Morale, Mobilizing Popular Support, and Targeting Iranian Cities," Conflict Records Research Center, CRRC Record Number: SH-SHTP-A-001-023, Document Date: 6 March 1987.

92. Tehran was targeted with the extended-range Scud missiles, the Al-Hussein. In addition to the Al-Hussein missiles, Iraq may have also managed to launch Soviet SS-12s armed with a 2,000-kilogram warhead and air-launched Styx missile with a heavier payload into Tehran. While the Soviets insisted that they retained political control over Iraqi use of SS-12 and had not approved the use of these missiles against Tehran, the Iranians were incensed at the Soviet Union for providing Iraq with weapons to attack Iran. See Patrick E. Tyler, "Iraq Targets Bigger Missile on Tehran; More Powerful Warheads Raise the 'Terror' Factor," *The Washington Post*, March 28, 1988; Chubin, *Iran's National Security Policy*, 88, note 23. See also Rafsanjani interview on Tehran TV (18 April in ME/0130/A/ 6, 20 April 1988); Rafsanjani, Tehran home service (15 April in ME/0128/A/4, 18 April 1988) as cited in Ibid., 23.

93. Tyler, "Iraq Targets Bigger Missile on Tehran."

94. Hiltermann, *Poisonous Affair*, 145.

95. Richey, "Iranians Await Iraqi Attacks," 11 as cited in Eisenstadt, *"Sword of the Arabs,"* Some of the wealthier residents of Tehran managed to live in reinforced-concrete luxury hotels and ride out the ballistic missile bombardment.

96. Tyler, "Iraq Targets Bigger Missile on Tehran."

97. Youssef M. Ibrahim, "Iran Reports New Iraqi Gas Raids; And Says Cities May Be Hit Next," *The New York Times*, 2 April 1988.

98. Ibid.

99. Iraq struck Dezful, Abadan, Ahwaz, Susangerd, Andimeshk, Ilam, Kermanshah, and other smaller cities with its Scud missiles. The Iranians retaliated with shelling and bombing runs targeting Basra, al-Faw, al-Qurnah, Mandali, and Khanaqin. See Pierre Razoux, *The Iran–Iraq War*, trans. Nicholas Elliott (Cambridge, MA: Belknap, 2015), 302.

100. Saddam Hussein saw these missile attacks on Baghdad as a personal affront to the legitimacy of his regime. He took pride in the fact that the Iranians had not been able to strike Baghdad. While Iran was able to target Baghdad with its missiles, Saddam's forces did not have missiles that could reach Tehran. While the Ti-16 bombers in the Iraqi air force could reach Tehran, it carried significant risks. The Iraqis, however, did use their missiles to target other Iranian cities near the Iran–Iraq border. See Ibid., 324–27.

101. Woods et al., *Saddam's Generals*, 26–27; W. Seth Carus, "Missiles in the Middle East: A New Threat to Stability," Research Memorandum Number Six (Washington, DC: The Washington Institute for Near East Policy, June 1988), 5. The third and fourth War of the Cities commenced after Iran launched the Karbala-5 Operation against Basra. Iraq retaliated with missile and air strikes and left 3,053 dead and 11,150 injured. See Shemirani, "War of the Cities," 37.

102. Iran had great difficulty acquiring ballistic missiles, while Iraq was able to procure them directly from the Soviets. As a result, in the fifth War of the Cities, Iran could barely manage to retaliate with one-third the number of ballistic missiles fired at it by Iraq. Iraq, however, was confidently demonstrating its ability to acquire and replenish its arsenal with ease. See Chubin, "Last Phase," 11.

103. Razoux, *Iran–Iraq War*, 435. Earlier in the war, geography favored the Iranians. Several major Iraqi cities were very close to the Iran–Iraq border. However, Tehran was 580 kilometers away from the Iran–Iraq border and outside the range of missiles that Iraq

162 Notes

possessed. As a result, until 1988, while Iran was able to target Baghdad with missiles, Iraq was not able to target Tehran. See Timothy V. McCarthy and Jonathan B. Tucker, "Saddam's Toxic Arsenal: Chemical and Biological Weapons in the Gulf Wars," in *Planning the Unthinkable: How New Powers Will Use Nuclear, Biological, and Chemical Weapons*, ed. Peter R. Lavoy, Scott D. Sagan, and James J. Wirtz (Ithaca: Cornell University Press, 2000), 54.

104. Razoux, *Iran–Iraq War*, 436.

105. Ibid.

106. Ibid.

107. Gregory F. Giles, "The Islamic Republic of Iran and Nuclear, Biological, and Chemical Weapons," in *Planning the Unthinkable: How New Powers Will Use Nuclear, Biological, and Chemical Weapons*, ed. Peter R. Lavoy, Scott D. Sagan, and James J. Wirtz (Ithaca: Cornell University Press, 2000), 82.

108. Ibid., 81.

109. While initially opposed to employing chemical weapons, the Iranian leadership faced increasing pressure from the Iranian armed forces to respond in kind. In the last few years, Khomeini apparently gave in to the pressure from the Iranian armed forces to employ chemical weapons against Iraq. See Ibid., 83. See also Ibrahim, "Iran Reports New Iraqi Gas Raids."

110. Cordesman, *Weapons of Mass Destruction*, 87–90. Cordesman writes that, even when Iranian forces had defensive equipment, "they did not organize or train to use if effectively . . . many Iranians still died because they did not shave often enough to allow their gas masks to make a tight seal or could not stand wearing their protection gear in the heat and humidity."

111. Timmerman, *Death Lobby*, 294.

112. Elaine Sciolino, "How the US Cast Off Neutrality in Gulf War," *The New York Times*, 24 April 1988.

113. Hiltermann, *Poisonous Affair*, 128; Bulloch and Morris, *Saddam's War*, 88–89. Hiltermann provides a vivid description of American diplomatic efforts to shield Iraq from international censure. See Hiltermann, *Poisonous Affair*, 37–64, 125–29. The Reagan administration also shielded Iraq from the scrutiny of the US Congress and other actors. Lieutenant Colonel Rick Francona, a DIA officer stationed in Iraq during the Iran–Iraq War to coordinate military intelligence sharing, writes that while he was able to observe first-hand the use of chemical weapons by Iraq, there was still support with the US administration for continuing military cooperation with Iraq. He writes, "senior US Defense Department officials became concerned that cooperation with a country that had used chemical weapons on its own citizens was politically indefensible in Congressional and public forums as well as morally reprehensible. However heinous the use of chemicals on the Kurds, the US administration did not want an Iranian victory, so cooperation with Iraq—by the both the CIA and the Defense Department—continued until the Iranians accepted a United Nations Security Council resolution to take effect in August, thus ending the war." See Francona, *Ally to Adversary*, 24.

114. Iran may have also used chemical weapons in the Halabja campaign. A Pentagon study of the 1988 Halabja massacre asserted that "Iranian forces used more than 50 chemical bombs and artillery shells . . . filled with cyanide gas into Halabja when Iranian commanders mistakenly believed Iraqi forces were occupying the city." The Pentagon study was based on intercepts of battlefield communications and participant accounts. The study asserted

Notes **163**

that Iraq does not use cyanide gas, while Iran does. Given the large number of deaths from cyanide poisoning, the study concluded that Iran had used cyanide chemical arms on Halabja. See Patrick E. Tyler, "Both Iraq and Iran Gassed Kurds in War, US Analysis Finds," *The Washington Post*, 3 May 1990. See also Anthony H. Cordesman, *Iraq and the War of Sanctions: Conventional Threats and Weapons of Mass Destruction* (Westport, CT: Praeger, 1999), 534; Cordesman, *Weapons of Mass Destruction*, 91.

115. Cordesman, *Weapons of Mass Destruction*, 93. He further noted that it was "made very clear during the war that these weapons are very decisive . . . we should fully equip ourselves in the defensive and offensive use of chemical, bacteriological and radiological weapons."

116. Timmerman, *Death Lobby*, 294. See also Murray and Woods, *Iran–Iraq War*, 222.

117. At the end stages of the war, Iran had great difficulty finding recruits. Iranian men were dodging the draft. The *Basij* had to draft men for the first time and recall reservists. In 1986, Iran reportedly closed its universities to facilitate further recruitments among teachers and students. See Ward, *Immortal*, 277, 289.

118. See Ibid., 276.

119. Hiro, *Iranian Labyrinth*, 228–29.

120. Ibid.

121. Chubin, "Last Phase of the Iran–Iraq War," 13.

122. Ibid.

123. Murray and Woods, *Iran–Iraq War*, 318.

124. Chubin, "Last Phase of the Iran–Iraq War," 13.

125. Francona, *Ally to Adversary*, 28–29.

126. Ibid.

127. Ibid.

128. Saddam Hussein clearly demonstrated a willingness to use chemical weapons in the battlefield. However, it is certainly debatable if Saddam Hussein might have launched large-scale chemical warfare against Tehran. The CIA speculated that a strategic breakthrough by Iran would be the scenario most likely to trigger chemical attacks on Iran's major cities. See Director of Central Intelligence, "National Intelligence Daily, Tuesday, 5 April 1988," 9, as cited in Hiltermann, *Poisonous Affair*, 144–45. See also Cordesman, *Weapons of Mass Destruction*, 36.

Chapter 5

1. Only half of the Iraqi Scud missiles were expected to hit within a 2-mile zone around their intended target. See Atkinson, *Crusade*, 145.

2. See Ibid. The precision strike capabilities of the Coalition's bombs and missiles is best described by General Peter de la Billiere, the Commander-in-Chief of British Forces in his autobiography. He writes: "before the war began, many British service people, myself included, without direct experience of these weapons, have been faintly skeptical about the claims which the Americans made for them. Now we saw that everything they had said was justified." He continues: "I've seen delivery-aircraft pictures of a bombing run and it is incredible. They put 2000 lb bombs into air vents on the roof and, in the case of ten-storey building, the bomb went to the bottom on the lift-shaft before exploding and the whole building imploded. . . . The strikes have been extraordinarily accurate and there

164 Notes

has been minimum damage to civilian targets." See General Sir Peter de la Billiere, *Storm Command: A Personal Account of the Gulf War* (London: Harper Collins, 1992), 212.

3. Atkinson, *Crusade*, 173–74.

4. Ibid., 177.

5. If one looked only at the total number of casualties caused by the ballistic missiles at the end of the war, it would seem that these military leaders were correct. Approximately, a total of 82 missiles were fired by Iraq against targets in Israel, Saudi Arabia, and Qatar. See Gregory S. Jones, *The Iraqi Ballistic Missile Program: The Gulf War and the Future of the Missile Threat* (Marina del Rey, CA: American Institute for Strategic Cooperation 1992), 75–78; George N. Lewis, Steve Fetter, and Lisbeth Gronlund, *Casualties and Damage from Scud Attacks in the 1991 Gulf War* (Cambridge, MA: Defense and Arms Control Studies Program, Massachusetts Institute of Technology, DACS Working Paper 1993), 42–50. In total, in Israel, two Israelis were killed as direct casualties, two died due to heart attack, and seven died due to suffocation from misuse of gas masks. See Cordesman and Wagner, *Lessons of Modern War. Volume IV*, 857. In one particular instance, a missile landing on US military barracks in Dhahran, Saudi Arabia, killed 28 American soldiers. See Lewis, Fetter, and Gronlund, *Casualties and Damage from Scud Attacks*, 4. While these deaths were unfortunate, the casualty numbers were much lower than what was expected in the planning phases of the 1991 Gulf War.

6. Kipphut, "Crossbow and Gulf War Counter-Scud," 16.

7. Cordesman and Wagner, *Lessons of Modern War. Volume IV*, 861; and Freedman and Karsh, *Gulf Conflict*, 330.

8. Douglas C. Waller, *Commandos: The Making of America's Secret Soldiers, from Training to Desert Storm*, Reprint edition (Simon & Schuster, 1995), 341. The special operations forces deployed hundreds of mines on suspected Scud mobile missile launch hide sites and operating areas. See Atkinson, *Crusade*, 179. While these forces claimed more than a dozen Scud mobile launcher kills, it later became apparent that most of them were decoys. See Gordon and Trainor, *General's War*, 245–46. These special forces missions were also extremely dangerous and resulted in casualties. See Schwarzkopf and Petre, *Autobiography*, 485–86. Brent Scowcroft evaluates the special operations forces as "singularly unsuccessfully" in their Scud-hunting missions. See Brent Scowcroft, George H. W. Bush Oral History Project, Interview #2 with Brent Scowcroft, Miller Center, University of Virginia, 10 August 2000, 86, https://millercenter.org/the-presidency/presidential-oral-histories/brent-scowcroft-oral-history-part-ii.

9. Echoing this point, Colin Powell writes that while a lousy military weapon, the Scuds turned out to be an extremely useful political weapon and forced a large diversion of military efforts. See Powell and Persico, *My American Journey*, 511.

10. Schwarzkopf, in particular, was seen by American and Israelis decisionmakers as being insensitive to the political realities. Rick Atkinson writes that "the CINC seemed oddly tone deaf in his public remarks about the Scuds. After the first barrage hit Israel, he had decried the 'absolutely insignificant results' while adding, 'We were delighted to see that the Iraqis did exactly what we thought they'd do.' Such remarks hardly endeared him to the Israelis, who viewed the attack as neither insignificant or delightful, or to Pentagon civilians. 'The guy supposedly has read Clausewitz and knows wars are political, right?' Wolfowitz asked caustically." See Atkinson, *Crusader*, 119. See also Gordon and Trainor, *General's War*, 235.

11. Gordon and Trainor, *General's War*, 234.

12. Ibid. On another occasion, Colin Powell had snapped at Schwarzkopf in a phone call yelling "Goddam it, I want some fucking airplanes out there." See Atkinson, Crusade, 143.

13. Cable, From White House, Re: Letter from George Bush to Prime Minister Shamir, 23 January 1991, OA/ID CF00946-007, Robert M. Gates Files, National Security Council Office, [Persian Gulf Conflict – January 1991][1], George Bush Presidential Library.

14. Ibid.

15. Ibid.

16. Atkinson, Crusade, 144.

17. A 13 February 1990 meeting between Hussein Kamil, the head of the Iraqi Ministry of Industry and Military Industrialization (MIMI) and Richard Murphy, a consultant for the First City Bancorporation of Texas, offers a view of the Iraqi leaderships fears. Murphy recounts his meeting with Hussein Kamil: "The Iraqis were worried that Israel was planning an attack against them, and Hussein Kamil said they had solid evidence to back up their suspicions. What evidence? I asked. Never mind, he said. It's just a given. Israel is going to repeat its 1981 attack on us, and soon." See Timmerman, Death Lobby, 372.

18. Micah L. Sifry and Christopher Cerf, eds., "Kuwait: How the West Blundered," in The Gulf War Reader: History, Documents, Opinions (New York: Times Books, 1991), 104. See also: Schwarzkopf and Petre, Autobiography, 337–38.

19. James A. Baker, III and Thomas M. DeFrank, The Politics of Diplomacy: Revolution, War & Peace, 1989–1992 (New York: Putnam, 1995), 265.

20. Iraq enjoyed broad political support in the United States. By 1989, Iraq was the ninth-largest market for American agricultural products, often supported through the Department of Agriculture's Commodity Credit Corporation (CCC) loans and credit guarantees. Iraq's repayment record was believed to be stellar. Consequently, Iraq enjoyed strong political support, particularly from senators and farm-state representatives. See Ibid., 263.

21. Ibid., 266.

22. The White House, "National Security Directive – 26" (Washington, DC: The White House, 2 October 1989), 2, https://fas.org/irp/offdocs/nsd/nsd26.pdf. While NSD-26 reiterated that the United States would defend its vital interests in the region with force, if necessary, the warning was directed at the Soviet Union and Iran, not Iraq.

23. Ibid. While NSD-26 warned that use of chemical and/or biological weapons would trigger economic and political sanctions, there was no intent to impose such sanctions immediately. In fact, NSD-26 suggested that the United States actively pursue opportunities for US firms to participate in the reconstruction of the Iraqi economy.

24. Eisenstadt, "Sword of the Arab," 44.

25. McCarthy and Tucker, "Saddam's Toxic Arsenal," 66.

26. Eisenstadt, "Sword of the Arabs," 44. See also Klare, "Arms Transfers to Iran and Iraq," 73.

27. Klare, "Arms Transfers to Iran and Iraq," 73. Steinberg writes that had the Iraqi military activities near the Israeli–Jordanian border continued it could have triggered military confrontations between Israel and Iraq. Israelis warned that they would react with overwhelming military force if Iraqi troops entered into Jordan or used Jordanian airspace to launch attacks on Israel. See Gerald M. Steinberg, "Israeli Responses to the Threat of Chemical Warfare," Armed Forces & Society 20, no. 1 (Fall 1993): 87. See also Yosef Zuriel, "Arens: 'We Will React Forcefully If Iraq Enters Jordan,'" Ma'ariv, 16 August 1990; Joshua Brilliant, "Arens Again Warns Iraq Against Strike," Jerusalem Post, 16 August 1990 as cited

166 Notes

in Shai Feldman, "Israeli Deterrence and the Gulf War," in *War in the Gulf: Implications for Israel*, ed. Joseph Alpher, eBook (New York: Routledge, 2020), 197.

28. Eisenstadt, *"Sword of the Arabs,"* 44. See also Klare, "Arms Transfers to Iran and Iraq," 73.

29. Dilip Hiro, *Desert Shield to Desert Storm: The Second Gulf War* (London: Harper Collins, 1992), 66–67.

30. Ibid.

31. Ibid., 66–68. See also Bulloch and Morris, *Saddam's War*, 93–96.

32. Hiro, *Desert Shield to Desert Storm*, 72.

33. Ibid., 66–68.

34. Speech by President Saddam Hussein on 5 January 1990, marking the 69th anniversary of the establishment of the Iraqi Army, translated in FBIS-NEA, 5 January 1990, 16 as cited in Eisenstadt, *"Sword of the Arabs,"* 61.

35. Hiro, *Desert Shield to Desert Storm*, 71.

36. Ibid.

37. Ibid., 72–73.

38. Baghdad Domestic Service, translated in FBIS-NEA, 17 April 1990, 7 as cited in Eisenstadt, *"Sword of the Arabs,"* 44–45.

39. Saddam Hussein's had provocatively announced, "By God, we will burn half of Israel, if it tries to harm or attack Iraq, or any part of Iraq. We do not need a nuclear bomb. We possess the binary chemical. Whoever threatens us with nuclear weapons, we will destroy him with chemical weapons." See Richard M. Price, *The Chemical Weapons Taboo* (Ithaca, NY: Cornell University Press, 1997), 147. See also Speech by President Saddam Hussein on 1 April 1990, translated by FBIS-NEA, 3 April 1990, 32–33, 35 as cited in Eisenstadt, *"Sword of the Arabs,"* 61–62.

40. Baker and DeFrank, *Politics of Diplomacy*, 268.

41. There were apparently attempts by Israel as well to reassure Saddam Hussein. See David Makovsky, "Israel to Egypt: No Attacks Planned," *The Jerusalem Post International Edition*, 26 May 1990, 1–2 as cited in Eisenstadt, *"Sword of the Arabs,"* 45.

42. Micah L. Sifry and Christopher Cerf, eds., "US Senators Chat with Saddam (April 12, 1990)," in *The Gulf War Reader: History, Documents, Opinions* (New York Times Books, 1991), 119–20. Senator Dole had also said, in response to Saddam Hussein's complaints that the American press was unfairly accusing him, that "there are fundamental differences between our countries. We have free media in the U.S.... There is a person who did not have the authority to say anything about ... [your] government. He was a commentator for the VOA (the Voice of America, which represents the government only) and this person was removed from it." Senator Simpson, similarly, had said: "I believe that your problems lie with the Western media and not with the US government. As long as you are isolated from the media, the press—and it is a haughty and pampered press; they all consider themselves political geniuses, that is, the journalists do; they are cynical—what I advise is that you invite them to come here and see for themselves."

43. Letter from Senator Bob Dole to President Bush, 17 April 1990, OA/ID 91143-003, Brent Scowcroft Files, Desert Shield/Desert Storm [May 1990][1], George Bush Presidential Library. See also Bush and Scowcroft, *A World Transformed*, 308. In the meeting with Senator Dole, Saddam Hussein reportedly warned that "if Israel strikes, we will strike back.... If Israel uses atomic bombs, we will strike it with binary chemical weapons.... We have given instructions to the commanders of the air bases and the missile formations that once they hear Israel has hit any place in Iraq with the atomic bomb, they will load

the chemical weapon with as much as will reach Israel and direct it at its territory.".See
FBIS-NES-90-076, 17 April 1990, 7, as cited in McCarthy and Tucker, "Saddam's Toxic
Arsenal," 58.

44. Letter from Brent Scowcroft to Senator Bob Dole, 22 May 1990, OA/ID 91143-003, Brent
Scowcroft Files, Desert Shield/Desert Storm [May 1990][1], George Bush Presidential
Library. However, the letter raises concerns about Iraqi behavior. Scowcroft writes: "I think
Saddam is beginning to understand the serious problem he has created for us in trying to
sustain a 'business as usual' relationship. We continue to reiterate at every opportunity our
intense displeasure with Iraq's illegal procurement activity related to its nuclear program,
his statement on chemical weapons use, and his threatening to retaliate against an Israeli
attack." See Ibid.

45. Sifry and Cerf, "Kuwait," 104.

46. Micah L. Sifry and Christopher Cerf, eds., "The Glaspie Transcript: Saddam Meets the
US Ambassador (July 25, 1990)," in *The Gulf War Reader: History, Documents, Opinions*
(New York: Times Books, 1991), 130. During the 25 July 1990 meeting, Ambassador
Glaspie referring to Iraqi troops massed at the Kuwaiti border, said to Saddam: "We have no
opinion on the Arab-Arab conflicts like your border disagreement with Kuwait.... All that
we hope is that these issues are solved quickly."

47. Powell and Persico, *My American Journey*, 461–62.

48. Hiro, *Desert Shield to Desert Storm*, 43–43.

49. Ibid., 62.

50. Ibid. Iraq had recruited close to 60% of its adult male population to wage the eight-year
Iran–Iraq War. As a result, Iraq faced acute labor shortages. Iraq overcame these shortages
by employing close to 1 million foreign workers to service its industries and society. See
Ibid., 43. Iraqi men after they were discharged from the armed forces were unable to find
employment and vented their ire at Arab expatriates who had been employed to keep the
Iraqi economy functioning during the war against Iran. Egyptians were one the significant Arab expatriate group employed in Iraq. In 1989, violent clashes occurred between
the Egyptians employed in Iraq and the demobilized Iraqi men returning to the labor force.
Dilip Hiro writes that "the fear of attack, and a new law limiting the size of remittances (to
help Iraq save its foreign exchange), caused an outflow of thousands of Egyptians back to
their country." See Ibid., 62.

51. Baker and DeFrank, *Politics of Diplomacy*, 262.

52. Secretary Baker writes in his memoirs that Arab allies consistently argued that Saddam
was only posturing, and that confrontation by the United States would make matters
worse. See Ibid., 274. Similarly, Chairman of the Joint Chiefs of Staff, Colin Powell, writes
in his memoirs that Arab leaders kept insisting that "Arab brothers did not war against
each other." See Powell and Persico, *My American Journey*, 460. Norm Schwarzkopf, the
commander-in-chief of CENTCOM during the 1991 Gulf War, writes that the belief that
Saddam Hussein was saber-rattling to bargain for financial assistance was also evident in
the analysis of the State Department and other US governmental agencies. He writes: " the
[Kuwaiti] emir assumed Saddam could be placated with money.... American diplomats
agreed that Saddam would not attack. During the last week of July at Central command, we
received analyses from both the State Department and the international diplomatic community saying things like 'Saddam is merely saber rattling to gain leverage over Kuwait in
the oil-pricing debate' and 'No Arab nation will ever attack another.'" See Schwarzkopf and
Petre, *Autobiography*, 339.

168 Notes

53. Baker and DeFrank, *Politics of Diplomacy*, 260. Scowcroft states that President Mubarak had visited with Saddam Hussein a few days before the Kuwaiti invasion and reported back to the American administration that it was all for show. President Mubarak advised: "Don't respond, don't react—he's not going to attack. And if you respond with some belligerent moves, you may push him into an attack." See Scowcroft, George H. W. Bush Oral History Project, Interview #2 with Brent Scowcroft, Miller Center, University of Virginia, 57. Scowcroft also states that by not responding proactively or preemptively pursing military options, the United States managed to get all the other Arab states on the American side. He notes, "There was nobody who said, 'Well, you provoked him into it.' They all supported us strongly, because the evidence was absolutely unmistakable that this was deliberate, unprovoked aggression." See Ibid.

54. Baker and DeFrank, *Politics of Diplomacy*, 260. In fact, even after the Iraqi invasion into Kuwait, both Egyptian President Hosni Mubarak and King Hussein of Jordan believed Saddam Hussein would retreat quickly after securing financial concessions from the Arabs. President Bush and his National Security Advisor, Scowcroft recount a conversation between the President and King Hussein, with the King arguing: "I really implore you, sir, to keep calm. . . . We want to deal with this in an Arab context, to find a way that gives us a foundation for a better future. . . . [Saddam Hussein is] determined to pull out as soon as possible, maybe in days." See Bush and Scowcroft, *A World Transformed*, 318.

55. Hiro, *Desert Shield to Desert Storm*, 34.

56. Ibid.

57. Ibid., 35.

58. Ibid.

59. Ibid.

60. Khalidi, "Iraq vs. Kuwait," 60–61.

61. Ibid.

62. Ibid.

63. Ibid., 63.

64. Ibid.

65. Ibid., 60–61.

66. Ibid., 63.

67. Ibid. See also Memorandum of Conversation [between the US Secretary of State and Tariq Aziz, Iraqi Deputy PM and Foreign Minister], Hotel International, Geneva, Switzerland, 9 January 1991, OA/ID CF000946, Robert Gates Files, National Security Council, [Persian Gulf Conflict – January 1991] [2 of 2], George Bush Presidential Library, 21.

68. The Rumaila oil field lies on the disputed limits of the Iraq–Kuwait border. See Ibid., 64.

69. Ibid. The Iraq–Kuwait border disagreement has a long history. Iraq claimed that, in the days of the Ottoman Empire, Kuwait had been an administrative subdistrict of the Iraqi province of Basra. Iraq has argued that the British Empire carved out Kuwait as a separate state to weaken Iraq. Glenn Frankel writes that the "modern borders of Iraq, Saudi Arabia, and Kuwait were established by British imperial fiat [in 1922] at what become known as the Uqair conference. Britain had won, and all the others believed they had lost." While Saudi Arabia and Kuwait eventually came to accept the map drawn by the British Empire, Iraq did not. Iraq saw the borders as unjust, particularly the explicit plan to deny it an outlet and access to Persian Gulf waters. The British limited Iraq's ability to access the Gulf coastline to 36 miles and prevented it from possession of a deep-water harbor. A sense of injustice festered over three generations among the Iraqi political elite. Iraq repeatedly

attempted to regain Kuwaiti territory through force and diplomacy. Iraq had attempted to lease the islands of Warba and Bubiyan from Kuwait to obtain an alternative access to the Gulf. See Glenn Frankel, "Lines in the Sand," in *The Gulf War Reader: History, Documents, Opinions*, ed. Micah L. Sifry and Christopher Cerf (New York: Times Books, 1991), 16–18; Hiro, *Desert Shield to Desert Storm*, 12–13; Khalidi, "Iraq vs. Kuwait," 61–62.

70. Sifry and Cerf, "Kuwait," 104.

71. Ibid.

72. Sifry and Cerf, "The Glaspie Transcript," 124.

73. Ibid., 126.

74. Schwarzkopf and Petre, *Autobiography*, 348.

75. Minutes, Meeting of the National Security Council, Re: Minutes of NSC Meeting on Iraqi Invasion of Kuwait, 4 August 1990, OA/ID 90002-017, H-Files, NSC Meeting Files, National Security Council, NSC0050 – August 04, 1990 – Iraqi Invasion of Kuwait, Persian Gulf, George Bush Presidential Library, 2.

76. Schwarzkopf and Petre, *Autobiography*, 348.

77. Ibid.

78. Ibid.

79. Minutes, Meeting of the National Security Council, Re: Minutes of NSC Meeting on Iraqi Invasion of Kuwait, 4 August 1990, OA/ID 90002-017, H-Files, NSC Meeting Files, National Security Council, NSC0050 – August 04, 1990 – Iraqi Invasion of Kuwait, Persian Gulf, George Bush Presidential Library, 2. Other factors such as "military leaders' fear of punishment for failure, and lack of interservice cooperation" were also identified as weaknesses of the Iraqi Army. See United States Army Intelligence and Threat Analysis Center, *How They Fight: Desert Shield – Order of Battle Handbook*, AIA-DS-2-90 (Washington, DC: US Department of Defense, 1990), 43.

80. Freedman and Karsh, "How Kuwait Was Won, 25–28.

81. United States Army Intelligence and Threat Analysis Center, *How They Fight*, 43.

82. Ibid.

83. Schwarzkopf and Petre, *Autobiography*, 474.

84. Bulloch and Morris, *Saddam's War*, 11. Iraqi leadership discussed American casualty aversion and ways to exploit it in internal deliberations. In a meeting that included Saddam Hussein, Tariq Aziz states "Christmas and New Year's . . . they are times for family gathering and entertainment, and the president who brings corpses to his country at Christmas time will be skinned alive in the US. Because if a war happens, they know it would not end between November 15 and December 15. It would not end in one month and they know it, which would mean New Year's and Christmas would come with the tragic results of the war obvious to them. He will not risk it." See Kevin M. Woods, David D. Palkki, and Mark E. Stout, eds., *The Saddam Tapes: The Inner Workings of a Tyrant's Regime 1978–2001* (New York: Cambridge University Press, 2011), 37.

85. *INA*, 18 January 1991, in British Broadcasting Corporation (BBC), *Summary of World Broadcasts* (*SWB*), 18 January 1991, ME/0973/A1 as cited in Freedman and Karsh, "How Kuwait Was Won," 28–29.

86. Ibid., 29.

87. Ibid., 28.

88. Pape, *Bombing to Win*, 252. Saddam Hussein was not wrong to expect a casualty of 10,000. Furthermore, he was willing to sacrifice as many Iraqi lives as necessary to impose casualties on the American troops. In fact, President Bush was warned that the war

170 Notes

could cause 5,000 American casualties. See "The Secret History of the War," *Newsweek*, 18 March 18, 1991, 25 as cited in Freedman and Karsh, "How Kuwait Was Won," 37. In another worst-case scenario, in a classified briefing given to Cheney and Powell, they were informed by medical personnel that their planning was based on casualties of 20,000 Americans including about 7,000 killed in the war. See Bob Woodward, *The Commanders* (New York: Simon & Schuster, 1991), 348.

89. Eisenstadt, "*Sword of the Arabs*," 18–19. Iraq was also suspected of having tested a space launch vehicle in late 1989. On 8 December 1989, the US Defence Intelligence Agency (DIA) confirmed the launch of an Iraqi space launch vehicle. Later reports indicated that the supposed space launch vehicle was a failure, flying for 130 seconds before falling to the ground. See Hiro, *Desert Shield to Desert Storm*, 61.

90. Both these missiles were produced by cannibalizing Soviet Scud-B missiles, expanding their propellant tanks, and reducing the amount of explosive payload. The modification of the Al-Hussein missile had been achieved with the assistance of German and Egyptian scientists. See Eisenstadt, "*Sword of the Arabs*," 18–19.

91. Ibid. A DIA assessment gives a lower performance estimation, suggesting that while it can travel up to 600 kilometers, the CEP of the Al-Hussein is 2,000 meters or more for that range. See Report, Defense Intelligence Memorandum, Re: Iraqi Short-Range Ballistic Missile – The Missiles of October, October 1990, OA/ID CF01346-006, Daniel B. Poneman Files, National Security Council, Iraq [6], George Bush Presidential Library, 2.

92. Ibid. The DIA estimated the Al-Abbas missile has a CEP of 3,000 meters at 600-kilometer range. See Report, Defense Intelligence Memorandum, Re: Iraqi Short-Range Ballistic Missile – The Missiles of October, October 1990, OA/ID CF01346-006, Daniel B. Poneman Files, National Security Council, Iraq [6], George Bush Presidential Library, 2.

93. Ibid.

94. Ibid., 21. Iraq was a participant in an Argentine-Egyptian-Iraqi joint venture to develop the solid-fuel Condor II medium-range missile with a range of 900 kilometers, a payload of 500 kilograms, and an improved CEP of approximately 100 meters. The project was aborted after American pressure forced the Egyptians and Argentinians to back out. See Ibid.

95. Report, Re: Missile/Chemical/Intelligence Agency, 7 November 1990, OA/ID CF01449-008, William Tobey, Subject File, National Security Council, Iraq SS-22 [Missiles], George Bush Presidential Library.

96. Eisenstadt, "*Sword of the Arabs*," 23–24.

97. Ibid., 5–6; Powell and Persico, *My American Journey*, 468. Iraq's primary chemical weapons production facility was determined to be located at Samarra, at a distance of 70 kilometers from Baghdad. Iraq is believed to have commenced development of its chemical weapons production capability in 1974.

98. A comprehensive effort was undertaken to procure vaccines, antibiotics, and military gear that could enable US forces to operate in a contaminated environment. See Memo to Richard Haass from Office of the Vice Chairman Joint chiefs of Staff, Implementing a Desert Shield BW Protection Program, 21 December 1990, OA/ID CF00946, Robert Gates Files, National Security Council, [Persian Gulf Conflict - Pre-1991], George Bush Presidential Library.

99. Eisenstadt, "*Sword of the Arabs*," 8; Powell and Persico, *My American Journey*, 494. Iraq had also reportedly experimented with weaponizing anthrax, typhoid, and cholera. Eisenstadt writes that unverified reports suggest that Iraq may have intentionally contaminated

the drinking water in the Kurdish town of Al-Suleimaniyah in 1988 with cultures of laboratory-produced typhoid. See Eisenstadt, "*Sword of the Arabs*," 8.

100. There were also debates about a secret radiological weapon. However, it seems the threat was quickly dismissed. The CIA had evaluated the veracity of the publication of an article in the Iraqi Defense Ministry newspaper that suggested possession of a secret weapon that could cause tens of thousands of casualties. While dismissing the possibility of a nuclear bomb, the CIA speculated Iraq could possess a way to disperse radioactive material using a conventional explosive charge. The CIA technical staff, in a memorandum to the Director, noted that such an Iraqi explosive radiological device would not be militarily significant. The memorandum, however, pointed out that there would be substantial psychological impact on the targets and their leaders. See Memo, National Intelligence Officer for Warning and National Intelligence Officer for Science, Technology, and Proliferation, Re: Possible Iraqi Radiological Weapons, 15 January 1991, OA/ID CF01346, Daniel B. Poneman, National Security Council, George Bush Presidential Library.

101. Memo, To Director of Central Intelligence, Re: Iraqi CBW, n. d., OA/ID 90018-031, H-Files, NSC/DC Meeting Files, National Security Council, NSC/DC 252 – 29 January 1991 – NSC/DC Meeting on Gulf Crisis via SVTS, Keywords: Persian Gulf, George Bush Presidential Library. Some analysts have suggested that Iraq may have had around 30 crude nerve gas warheads in their arsenal. See Jones, *Iraqi Ballistic Missile Program*, 44; and Cordesman and Wagner, *Lessons of Modern War. Volume IV*, 851, 858. Furthermore, the Iraqis apparently also fired a few Scuds that detonated in a fashion intended to disperse chemical agents. Additionally, American spy satellites may have observed Iraqi military trucks "leaving the Samarra chemical weapons warehouse near Baghdad with suspected warheads for missiles." See Waller, *Commandos*, 335.

102. Gordon and Trainor, *General's War*, 183.

103. Martin Navias, "Non-Conventional Weaponry and Ballistic Missiles during the 1991 Gulf War," in *Non-Conventional-Weapons Proliferation in the Middle East: Tackling the Spread of Nuclear, Chemical, and Biological Capabilities*, ed. Efraim Karsh, Martin S. Navias, and Philip Sabin (New York: Oxford University Press, 1993), 54.

104. Thomas L Friedman, "Confrontation in the Gulf; Baker-Aziz Talks on Gulf Fail; Fears of War Rise; Bush Is Firm; Diplomatic Effort to Continue," *The New York Times*, 9 January 1991.

105. Times Wire Service, "Tel Aviv Is 1st Target, Hussein Reportedly Says," *Los Angeles Times*, 25 December 1990.

106. For instance, see Memo to Richard Haass from Office of the Vice Chairman Joint chiefs of Staff, Implementing a Desert Shield BW Protection Program, 21 December 1990, OA/ID CF00946, Robert Gates Files, National Security Council, [Persian Gulf Conflict - Pre-1991], George Bush Presidential Library.

107. Schwarzkopf and Petre, *Autobiography*, 509.

108. Ibid. Colin Powell, however, offers a sanguine view of the ability of American forces to operate under chemical attack. He speculates that an Iraqi chemical attack would have been manageable. He reasons that since American forces would be moving fast and operating in a open desert environment, the effects of chemical weapons would be limited. See Powell and Persico, *My American Journey*, 468. Similarly Scowcroft states in a 2000 Oral History interview that American forces were well prepared to fight in a chemical warfare environment. However, he points out that it may have made military operations complicated. See Scowcroft, George H. W. Bush Oral History Project, Interview #2 with

172 Notes

Brent Scowcroft, Miller Center, University of Virginia, 84. Finally, General Peter de la Billiere, the Commander-in-Chief of the British Forces during the 1991 Gulf War writes in his autobiography that an effective chemical weapons strike "with weapons exploding upwind of their target, and gas dispersing in the right direction, would be exceedingly difficult to bring off and in any case we British had the best chemical protection in the world. I was confident, therefore, that if Saddam did try anything with chemicals, our equipment would keep casualties relatively light." See Billiere, *Storm Command*, 98.

109. Moshe Arens, *Broken Covenant: American Foreign Policy and the Crisis Between the US and Israel* (New York: Simon & Schuster, 1995), 172.

110. *Yedinot Aharonot*, 29 April 1990, translated in *Mideast Mirror*, 30 April 1990, 7, as cited in Eisenstadt, "*Sword of the Arabs*," 51.

111. *Yedinot Aharonot*, 29 April 1990, translated in *Mideast Mirror*, 30 April 1990, 7, as cited in Ibid.

112. Feldman, "Israeli Deterrence and the Gulf War," 197.

113. Zuriel, "Arens,"; Brilliant, "Arens Again Warns Iraq Against Strike," as cited in Ibid.

114. David Makovsky, "Levy: 'Those Who Attack Israel Won't Live to Remember,' " *Jerusalem Post*, 27 September 1990 as cited in Ibid., 198.

115. Shlomo Shamir, "Levy at UN: 'If Israel Is Attacked by Iraq-It Will Operate Immediately and Independently,'" *Ha'aretz*, 2 October 1990 as cited in Ibid.

116. Bush and Scowcroft, *World Transformed*, 346–47.

117. Ibid.

118. Powell and Persico, *My American Journey*, 488.

119. Ibid. See also Deptula notes, 2 September 1990/2115 and 2245 as cited in Putney, *Airpower Advantage*, 181–182.

120. It is unclear how enthusiastic Iran would have been to come to the defense of Iraq. Iran had just emerged, arguably defeated, from a grueling conflict with Iraq. Additionally, Iran was cooperating silently with the United States. Scowcroft states in an Oral History conversation that the United States "had a reasonable dialogue, much of it indirect, with Iran. We were fairly comfortable with Iran's role. . . . When Saddam sent his air force over to Iran for safety, we had a momentary flurry, because we scoped out a possibility of a massive one-strike from Iran by his forces that could do a great deal of damage to the ports of Saudi Arabia. But they made it quite clear to us that there would be no flights of Iraqi aircraft out of Iran." See Scowcroft, George H. W. Bush Oral History Project, Interview #2 with Brent Scowcroft, Miller Center, University of Virginia, 73.

121. Hiro, *Desert Shield to Desert Storm*, 325.

122. Bush and Scowcroft, *World Transformed*, 424–25.

123. Memcon, One-on-One Meeting with PM Shamir of Israel, 11 December 1990, OA/ID CF01584-058, Richard N. Haass Files, National Security Council, Iraq – December 1990 [4] File, George Bush Presidential Library.

124. Bush and Scowcroft, *World Transformed*, 424–25. See also Memorandum from C. David Welch to Brent Scowcroft, Re: For one-on-one meeting with PM Shamir, OA/ID CF01405-001, Richard N. Haass Files, Presidential Visit with [Israeli] Prime Minister [Yitzhak] Shamir – 15 November 1989, George Bush Presidential Library.

125. Yitzhak Shamir, the Israeli President, writes in his autobiography that it was evident to him that Arab states had conveyed to President Bush that "they would not remain in the coalition if Israel joined in." He further writes that President Bush was insistent that the coalition remain intact and "nothing was to be allowed to threaten its viability or unity."

See Yitzhak Shamir, *Summing Up: An Autobiography* (London: Weidenfeld and Nicolson, 1994), 221. See also Arens, *Broken Covenant*, 154; Moshe ##Arens, *In Defense of Israel: A Memoir of a Political Life* (Washington, DC: Brookings Institution Press, 2018), 166.

126. Bush and Scowcroft, *A World Transformed*, 424–25. President Sharmir, in his autobiography, recalls that he had responded that Israel would act in its national interest but would consult with the American administration. He suggests that President Bush understood that consult meant Israel would not seek permission. Shamir also writes that he asked for a secure line of communication between Israel and the United States and airspace deconfliction in case of Israeli strike. See Shamir, *Summing Up: An Autobiography*, 221–22.

127. Michal Yudelman, "Israel will Certainly Retaliate if Saddam Attacks, Levy Says," *Jerusalem Post*, January 9, 1991 as cited in Feldman, "Israeli Deterrence and the Gulf War," 198.

128. "Arens: 'We are Ready and Prepared, and if Attacked we will Respond Without Hesitation,'" *Yediot Aharnot*, January 11, 1991 as cited as Ibid. Defense Minister Aren's warning was reiterated by Chief of Staff Shomron. Shomron warned of "a very forceful response by Israel in case of an Iraqi attack or an attempted Iraqi attack." See "The CoS: 'We are Ready for any Contingency,'" *Maàriv*, January 13, 1991; David Ridge, "Arens: 'If attacked, Israel will Respond,'" *Jerusalem Post*, January 14, 1991 as cited in Ibid.

129. Bush and Scowcroft, *A World Transformed*, 452–53.

130. Ibid.

131. Ibid.

132. Ibid.

133. Scowcroft writes any Israeli air strike would have required overflying Syrian, Jordanian or Saudi Arabian airspace. None of these Arab states would acquiesce to such an operation and any action without their approval would provoke military responses. Any Arab-Israeli conflict resulting from Israeli violation or Arab airspace was feared to undo the broad coalition of states assembled against Saddam Hussein. See Ibid.

134. Ibid.

135. Ibid. Eagleburger reportedly also remarked, "if they've been hit with chemicals, Katie bar the door because they're going to do something. I know these people. They're going to retaliate. If it's nerve gas, we'll never stop them." See Atkinson, *Crusade: The Untold Story of the Persian Gulf War*, 82.

136. General Schwarzkopf writes that several Israeli jets were airborne in the immediate aftermath of the Scud attack and waiting political clearance to breach Jordanian or Saudi Arabian airspace and mount a strike on Israel. However, Washington had persuaded Israel to hold back. See Schwarzkopf and Petre, *The Autobiography: It Doesn't Take a Hero*, 484. One of the alternative discussed was to let Israel strike back at Iraq with its Jericho missiles instead of an air strike. See Bush and Scowcroft, *A World Transformed*, 452–53; Atkinson, *Crusade: The Untold Story of the Persian Gulf War*, 85. Scowcroft suggests that in at least one instance Israeli forces rolled out their Jericho missiles indicating an impending retaliatory strike against Iraq. See Scowcroft, George H. W. Bush Oral History Project, Interview #2 with Brent Scowcroft, Miller Center, University of Virginia, 87.

137. Gordon and Trainor, *The General's War: The Inside Story of the Conflict in the Gulf*, 232. Secretary Baker may have persuaded the leaders of Egypt, Saudi Arabia, Kuwait, and Syria to remain committed to the Coalition's mission even if Israel struck Iraq. However, Secretary Baker was not completely reassured these leaders would be able to keep their word if and when the event transpired. See Atkinson, *Crusade: The Untold Story of the Persian Gulf War*, 83.

174 Notes

138. Gordon and Trainor, *The General's War: The Inside Story of the Conflict in the Gulf*, 232.

139. Bush and Scowcroft, *A World Transformed*, 452–53.

140. Atkinson, *Crusade: The Untold Story of the Persian Gulf War*, 83.

141. Bush and Scowcroft, *A World Transformed*, 452–53.

142. Ibid., 454–55.

143. Ibid.

144. Ibid.

145. Ibid. Other Israeli leaders had also made the same argument. Minister, Yitzhak Rabin, in an interview in July 1988, had stated: "one of our fears is that the Arab world and its leaders might be deluded to believe that the lack of international reaction to the use of missiles and gases [in the Iran–Iraq War] gives them some kind of legitimization to use them. They know they should not be deluded to believe that, because it is a whole different ball game when it comes to us. If they are, God forbid, they should know we will hit them back 100 times harder." See Jerusalem Domestic Service, translated in FBIS-NEA, 12 July 1988, 28–29 as cited in Eisenstadt, " 'The *Sword of the Arabs*:' Iraq's Strategic Weapons," 54. Israeli chief of Staff Lieutenant Dan Shomron had similarly argued: "I find it inconceivable that [Iraq] would freely use missiles or chemical weapons against Israel as they did against Iran and are doing against the Kurds, because they know that we have a powerful response capability." See *Yediot Aharnot*, September 23, 1988, 6–7, translated in JPRS-NEA, December 6, 1988, 36 as cited in Ibid.

146. Steinberg, "Israeli Responses to the Threat of Chemical Warfare," 94.

147. Klare, "Arms Transfers to Iran and Iraq during the Iran–Iraq War of 1980–88 and the Origins of the Gulf War," 77; Bush and Scowcroft, *A World Transformed*, 456.

148. Memcon, Minutes of Meeting with Israeli Defense Minister Moshe Arens on February 11, 1991, 11:37 a.m.–12:05 p.m., OA/ID CF01584-005, Richard N. Haass Files, National Security Council, Iraq – February 1991 [3], George Bush Presidential Library. See also Arens, *Broken Covenant: American Foreign Policy and the Crisis Between the US and Israel*, 188; Atkinson, *Crusade: The Untold Story of the Persian Gulf War*, 210.

149. Ibid.

150. Ibid.

151. Ibid. A description of Israeli Defense Forces plan to intervene in Western Iraqi theater to suppress Scud launches during the 1991 Gulf War is detailed in Arens, *In Defense of Israel*, 178.

152. Ibid.

153. Bush and Scowcroft, *World Transformed*, 468. Richard Haass sums up the meeting by observing that Defense Minister Arens had "crapped all over us." See also Atkinson, *Crusade*, 280.

154. Bush and Scowcroft, *World Transformed*, 455.

155. Ibid. General Schwarzkopf, in his autobiography, reiterates the Saudi leadership's insistence against any Israeli action against Iraq. Schwarzkopf writes that the Israelis were contemplating a massive counterstrike employing "one hundred planes the following morning, one hundred more planes the following afternoon, attacks by Apache helicopters the following night, and commando raids—all to enter Iraq through Saudi Arabian airspace." Schwarzkopf recounts that he had called Colin Powell and pointed out that "the Saudis will never buy this, and you can't sneak it by them. They have people up in our AWACS and they're gonna know." Schwarzkopf writes that the Saudi King "swiftly replied with the Arabic equivalent of 'no way' " when asked about the possibility of an

Israeli overflight. See Schwarzkopf and Petre, *Autobiography*, 484–85. For a contradicting viewpoint see Putney, *Airpower Advantage*, 269.

156. The Israelis, while acknowledging these concerns, were apparently not as worried as the Americans. Israeli Prime Minister Shamir writes in his autobiography that the diplomatic fallout could have been managed. See Shamir, *Summing Up*, 223–24. It seems that Richard Armitage was dispatched by President George H. W. Bush to obtain Jordanian acquiescence to Israeli overflight of their airspace. The Jordanians may have begrudgingly agreed. During the meeting, Armitage and King Hussein agreed that "if Israel pilots flew certain attack routes over Jordan there would be little that Jordan could do about it. The understanding was never publicized." See Gordon and Trainor, *General's War*, 236. See also Atkinson, *Crusade*, 133–34.

157. Bush and Scowcroft, *World Transformed*, 455.

158. The Israelis certainly understood that Saddam was trying to divide the coalition by peeling off the Arab states. In a letter to the US Secretary of Defense Cheney, Israeli Defense Minister Arens writes that Iraq had falsely accused Israel of preparing to participate "with the US forces in hostilities against Iraq." He continues: "These allegations help Iraq create a plausible casus belli—hoping to regain Arab unity and solidarity with Iraq." See Letter [Letter from the Embassy of Israel], 9 August 1990, OA/ID CF01478-028, Richard N. Haass Files, National Security Council, George Bush Presidential Library.

159. Bush and Scowcroft, *World Transformed*, 455.

160. President Bush seems to have suggested an Israeli counterstrike with its Jericho missiles as a way to hit back at Iraq. See Ibid.

161. Eagleburger was instructed to politely deny any Israeli demands for deconflicting the airspace to facilitate an Israeli strike. See Ibid., 456. In a message to Eagleburger sent through the White House situation room channels, Scowcroft states: "In dealing with this threat to Israel, American lives will be lost. Enhanced cooperation must be based upon Israeli willingness to take US interests equally into account. Therefore, we are asking Israel not to respond to these Iraqi provocations with military force. Last, I am instructed to say that under present conditions the United States will not 'deconflict' should the Government of Israel seek to retaliate for conventional Scud attacks. We realize the above points are tough. Feel free to translate the tone into 'Eagleburgerese,' but the message must remain clear." See Cable, From White House, Re: Message for Eagleburger, 24 January 1991, OA/ID CF00946-007, Robert M. Gates Files, [Persian Gulf Conflict – January 1991][1], George Bush Presidential Library. Unfortunately, the Israelis saw the message as an unfriendly ultimatum. Prime Minister Sharmir apparently retorted to Eagleburger: "So if we don't do what you want us to do, you'll let people here get killed? This is not the way to speak to a friend. It leads to questions about what kind of relationship we will have in the future." See Atkinson, *Crusade*, 132.

162. The Israeli requests were routed to CENTCOM via the Pentagon. They proposed culverts, railroad trestles, bridges, and the Iraqi phosphate mines located at Al Qaim as targets. See Gordon and Trainor, *General's War*, 236.

163. Deptula notes, 2 September 1990/2115 and 2245 as cited in Putney, *Airpower Advantage*, 181–82.

164. Deptula notes, 2 September 1990/2115 and 2245 as cited in Ibid.

165. Ibid., 182.

166. Ibid., 340.

167. Gordon and Trainor, *General's War*, 220.

176 Notes

168. Putney, *Airpower Advantage*, 341.

169. Ibid.

170. Ibid.

171. Ibid., 343.

172. Keaney and Cohen, *Revolution in Warfare?*, 14–15.

173. Schwarzkopf and Petre, *Autobiography*, 485–86.

174. Ibid.

175. Atkinson, *Crusade*, 66, 175.

176. Ibid., 175.

177. Schwarzkopf and Petre, *Autobiography*, 485–86; Powell and Persico, *My American Journey*, 511–12; Atkinson, *Crusade*, 175.

178. Atkinson, *Crusade*, 147.

179. Schwarzkopf and Petre, *Autobiography*, 485–86.

180. Atkinson, *Crusade*, 147.

181. In frustration, a plan was explored to flatten most of Western Iraq by mounting three days of a continuous carpet bombing-like operation using nearly all allied aircraft. Additionally, it was explored if bombers could drop mines on all the roads in Western Iraq and destroy "more than sixty underpasses" on the Amman-Baghdad highway suspected to be the favored hiding spot for Scud mobile missile launchers. The plan was rejected. See Ibid., 147–48.

182. Keaney and Cohen, *Revolution in Warfare?*, 14–15. The US forces were unable to accurately assess a successful hit on a Scud mobile launcher throughout Operation Desert Storm. For an excellent illustration of the difficulties, see Powell and Persico, *My American Journey*, 510–11.

183. Gordon and Trainor, *General's War*, 230.

184. "Iraqi Short-Range Ballistic Missiles in the Persian Gulf War: Lessons and Prospects," Defense Intelligence Agency Memorandum, March 1991 as cited in Ibid., 227, 496–97. The memorandum pointed out that the Iraqis had effectively adopted "denial and deception techniques, including launching under the cover of darkness or clouds and excellent communications security, which was largely successful in hiding SRBM mobile launchers from Coalition discovery and air attacks. The use of decoy equipment figured prominently in this effort . . . [and] contributed significantly to Iraq's ability to continue launching till the end of the war."

185. The Israelis challenged American claims of Patriot missile defense system effectiveness throughout the war. In a 4 February 1991 conversation, Major General Avihu Ben-Nun, commander of the Israeli Air Force bluntly told Colonel Lew Goldberg, head of the Pentagon's Patriot Management cell "the Patriot doesn't work. You ought to stop producing the Patriot until you fix it." See Atkinson, *Crusade*, 278. Similarly, in a 11 February 1991 meeting at the Oval Office, Israeli Defense Minister Arens told President Bush that he estimated the Patriot missile defense system had only a 20% success rate at best. See Ibid., 280.

186. The Scud ballistic missile attacks may have done much more damage than detailed above. Freedman and Karsh suggest that the Scud-hunting efforts "delayed the suppression of the Iraqi air defence system in the Kuwaiti theatre, disrupted the coalition's operational plans and contributed to the postponement of the ground offensive." See Freedman and Karsh, *Gulf Conflict*, 309. However, the author could not find any other evidence to confirm this assertion.

187. Gordon and Trainor, *General's War*, 247.

188. Baker and DeFrank, *Politics of Diplomacy*, 387.

189. Serge Schmemann, "Soviets Say Iraq Accepts Kuwait Pullout Linked to Truce and an End to Snctions; Bush Rejects Conditions: War to Go On," *The New York Times*, 22 February 1991, https://www.nytimes.com/1991/02/22/world/war-gulf-diplomacy-soviets-say-iraq-acce pts-kuwait-pullout-linked-truce-end.html; John-Thor Dahlburg and Mark Fineman, "US Cool to Gulf Peace Plan: Bush Has 'Serious Concerns' Over Soviet-Iraqi Bid," *Los Angeles Times*, 22 February 1991, https://www.latimes.com/archives/la-xpm-1991-02-22-mn-1513- story.html.

190. "Bush Rejects Soviet Peace Proposal Pentagon Predicts Quick Ground War," *The Oklahoman*, 20 February 1991, https://www.oklahoman.com/story/news/1991/02/ 20/bush-rejects-soviet-peace-proposal-pentagon-predicts-quick-ground-war/6253 6349007/.

191. Atkinson, *Crusade*, 132. For an excellent discussion of how the domestic politics played among Israeli hardline and moderate decisionmakers, see Freedman and Karsh, *Gulf Conflict*, 333–34.

192. However, why Saddam Hussein chose to do so remains unclear. American threat of a strong retaliation, including an attempt to remove him from power, may have deterred Saddam Hussein. American political and military leadership explored several ways to dissuade Saddam Hussein from using chemical or biological weapons. Secretary of State Baker directly conveyed to Iraqi Foreign Minister Tariq Aziz a warning that the United States would dramatically escalate the aims of the conflict if chemical or biological weapons were used. In a 9 January 1991 meeting, Secretary Baker tells Foreign Minister Aziz that "if conflict ensues, and you use chemical or biological weapons against US forces, American people will demand vengeance. And we have the means to exact it. Let me say with regard to this part of my presentation, this is not a threat, it is a promise. If there is any use of weapons like that, our objective won't be the liberation of Kuwait, but the elimination of the Iraqi regime, and anyone responsible for using those weapons would be held account-able." See Memorandum of Conversation [between the US Secretary of State and Tariq Aziz, Iraqi Deputy PM and Foreign Minister], Hotel International, Geneva, Switzerland, 9 January 1991, OA/ID CF000946, Robert Gates Files, National Security Council, [Persian Gulf Conflict – January 1991] [2 of 2], George Bush Presidential Library, 7. The warnings were officially restated in the National Security Directive 54. See The White House, "National Security Directive (NSD) 54: Responding to Iraqi Aggression in the Gulf," Federation of American Scientists, 15 January 1991, https://irp.fas.org/offdocs/nsd/nsd_ 54.htm.NSD. For excellent discussions on how and why Saddam was deterred from using chemical or biological weapons in the 1991 Gulf War, see Byman and Waxman, *Dynamics of Coercion*, 104–05; Richard L. Russell, "Iraq's Chemical Weapons Legacy: What Others Might Learn From Saddam," *The Middle East Journal* 59, no. 2 (Spring 2005): 199–204; Scott D. Sagan, "Deterring Rogue Regimes: Rethinking Deterrence Theory and Practice," PASCC Final Report (Stanford, CA: Center for International Security and Cooperation (CISAC), Stanford University, 8 July 2013), https://apps.dtic.mil/sti/pdfs/ADA586065. pdf; Paul C. Avey, *Tempting Fate: Why Nonnuclear States Confront Nuclear Opponents* (Ithaca, NY: Cornell University Press, 2019), 58–62.

193. Other potential counterfactuals, in addition to a chemically armed Scud missile attack on Israel, may have also altered the conduct of the battle. Saddam Hussein was not successful in targeting the assembled Coalition troops with Scud missiles. With the exception of a

178   Notes

Scud strike on Al Khobar, a suburb of Dhahran, on 25 February 1991, that killed 28 troops and wounded 98 others, Scuds did not directly cause any other casualties among military personnel. See Gordon and Trainor, *General's War*, 239. However, Gordon and Trainor write that "according to an internal Army report, the risk of even more substantial casualties was greater than generally realized. With the VII Corps deployments from Germany to Saudi Arabia behind schedule, huge number of Americans waited for their equipment in crowded camps near the ports at Ad Dammam and Al Jubail. It was not for nothing that the 1st Armored Division dubbed the camps at Al Jubail 'the Scud Bowl.'" See Ibid., 240. If Saddam had used his missile arsenal to strike the assembled Coalition troops, it may have precipitated an earlier attack on Iraqi forces, which may have led to many more casualties. For instance, in one incident, "a Scud missile hit the water 130 yards off the port side of the *USS Tarawa* as it docked in Al Jubail to unload its AV-8 Harrier planes. But the missile warhead did not detonate." See Ibid., 239. If the warhead had struck and sunk the ship, American decisionmakers may have been forced to escalate.

194. Shamir, *Summing Up*, 217.

Chapter 6

1. Shai Feldman, "The Hezbollah-Israel War: A Preliminary Assessment" (Waltham, MA: Crown Center for Middle East Studies, Brandeis University, September 2006), 5, 7.

2. Augustus Richard Norton, *Hezbollah: A Short History* (Princeton, NJ: Princeton University Press, 2007), 84; Jean-Loup Samaan, "Missile Warfare and Violent Non-State Actors: The Case of Hezbollah," *Defence Studies* 17, no. 2 (2017): 159; Nicholas Blanford, *Warriors of God: Inside Hezbollah's Thirty-Year Struggle Against Israel* (New York: Random House, 2011), 147.

3. Blanford, *Warriors of God*, 174, 175.

4. Matt M. Matthews, "We Were Caught Unprepared: The 2006 Hezbollah-Israeli War" (Fort Leavenworth, KS: US Army Combined Arms Center, Combat Studies Institute Press, 2008), 35–36.

5. Amos Harel and Avi Issacharoff, *34 Days: Israel, Hezbollah, and the War in Lebanon* (New York: Palgrave Macmillan, 2008), 75–76. Pedersen, upset at Hezbollah's cavalier response, replied, "do you know what you've just done? You've started a war. We warned you. You've made a stupid mistake and the cost will be exorbitant."

6. Ibid., 92.

7. Matthews, "We Were Caught Unprepared," 35–36.

8. Blanford, *Warriors of God*, 378. After the war, in a television interview on 27 August 2006, Hassan Nasrallah observed, "we did not think, even 1 percent that the capture would lead to a war at this time and of this magnitude. You ask me, if I had known on July 11 . . . that the operation would lead to such a war, would I do it? I say no, absolutely not." See Hassan Nasrallah, interview on NTV, 27 August 2006, as cited in Makovsky and White, "Lessons and Implications of the Israel–Hizballah War: A Preliminary Assessment," 19.

9. Raphael Cohen-Almagor and Sharon Haleva-Amir, "The Israel–Hezbollah War and the Winograd Committee," *Journal of Parliamentary and Political Law* 2, no. 1 (2008): 27.

10. Blanford, *Warriors of God*, 381.

11. Andrew Exum, "Hizballah at War: A Military Assessment" (Washington, DC: The Washington Institute for Near East Policy, December 2006), 4, https://www.washingtoninstitute.org/policy-analysis/hizballah-war-military-assessment.

Notes   **179**

12. Makovsky and White, "Lessons and Implications of the Israel–Hizballah War," 20.

13. Uzi Rubin, "The Rocket Campaign Against Israel During the 2006 Lebanon War" (Ramat Gan, Israel: The Begin-Sadat Center for Strategic Studies, Bar-Ilan University, June 2007), 3, https://besacenter.org/the-rocket-campaign-against-israel-during-the-2006-lebanon-war-2-2/.

14. Efraim Inbar, "How Israel Bungled the Second Lebanon War," *Middle East Quarterly*, Summer 2007, 59–60.

15. Makovsky and White, "Lessons and Implications of the Israel–Hizballah War," 7.

16. Rubin, "Rocket Campaign," 14.

17. Israel's major seaport in Haifa was closed. Haifa's oil refinery, a major facility in the country, was shutdown. The Israeli naval detachment at Haifa's harbor was relocated. See Ibid.

18. Daniel Byman, "The Lebanese Hizballah and Israeli Counterterrorism," *Studies in Conflict & Terrorism* 34, no. 12 (2011): 918.

19. Massaab Al-Aloosy, "Deterrence by Insurgents: Hezbollah's Military Doctrine and Capability Vis-a-Vis Israel," *Small Wars & Insurgencies* 33, no. 6 (2022): 1000.

20. Ibid., 1000–1001.

21. Ibid., 1001.

22. Matthews, "We Were Caught Unprepared," 6.

23. Itai Brun, "Chapter 13: The Second Lebanon War, 2006," in *A History of Air Warfare*, ed. John Andreas Olsen (Washington, DC: Potomac Books, 2010), 299; Al-Aloosy, "Deterrence by Insurgents," 1001.

24. The security zone occupied 850 kilometers (~10%) of Lebanese territory. See Byman, "Lebanese Hizballah and Israeli Counterterrorism," 921.

25. Matthews, "We Were Caught Unprepared," 7.

26. An excellent review of the role of Iran and Syria in the emergence and dominance of Hezbollah can be found in Byman, "Lebanese Hizballah and Israeli Counterterrorism," 920–21. In 2005, for a short period, Israel hoped that Syrian influence in Lebanon would recede. The assassination of Lebanese Prime Minister Rafik Hariri in February 2005 led to the Cedar Revolution forcing Syrian forces out of Lebanon. On 5 March 2005, the Syrian President declared that the troops would be coming home and all Syrian forces had been evacuated within seven weeks. The revolution led to the resignation of the pro-Syrian Lebanese government. The revolution brought Fouad Siniora to power in Lebanon. While initially the Syrian expulsion was expected to generate positive dividends for Israel, ultimately Syria continued to supply weapons and rockets to Hezbollah. A vast majority of rockets used by Hezbollah in the 2006 Second Lebanon War were of Syrian origin. See Harel and Issacharoff, *34 Days*, 54; Brun, "Chapter 13: The Second Lebanon War, 2006," 301.

27. Israel's withdrawal was precipitated by declining public approval for continued military presence in the security zone. By 1999, 74% of Israelis came to believe that the security zone was not worth the lives of Israeli soldiers being harmed in the effort. See Iver Gabrielsen, "The Evolution of Hezbollah's Strategy and Military Performance, 1982–2006," *Small Wars & Insurgencies* 25, no. 2 (2014): 262.

28. Harel and Issacharoff, *34 Days*, 38.

29. Daniel Sobelman, "New Rules of the Game: Israel and Hizbollah After the Withdrawal from Lebanon" (Tel Aviv, Israel: Jaffe Center for Strategic Studies, Tel Aviv University,

180 Notes

January 2004), 68, https://www.inss.org.il/publication/new-rules-of-the-game-israel-and-hizbollah-after-the-withdrawal-from-lebanon/; Harel and Issacharoff, *34 Days* 38.

30. Harel and Issacharoff, *34 Days*, 38.

31. Exum, "Hizballah at War," 4.

32. Ze'ev Schiff, "Kidnap of Soldiers in July Was Hezbollah's Fifth Attempt," *Haaretz*, 19 September 2006, https://www.haaretz.com/2006-09-19/ty-article/kidnap-of-soldiers-in-july-was-hezbollahs-fifth-attempt/0000017f-e09a-d9aa-afff-f9da2e180000. Previously, in October 2000, Hezbollah kidnapped three IDF soldiers. In January 2004, Hezbollah kidnapped three IDF soldiers. The bodies of these soldiers were swapped for Lebanese and Palestine prisoners. In November 2005, Hezbollah launched a failed attempt to kidnap IDF soldiers. The fourth attempt was made two months before the events leading to the 2006 war. See Nicholas Blanford, "Terrorism and Insurgency: Deconstructing Hizbullah's Surprise Military Prowess," *Janes Intelligence Review* 18, no. 11 (November 2006): 21.

33. Schiff, "Kidnap of Soldiers in July."

34. Ibid. Similarly, in mid-2005, a senior IDF officer had told UNIFIL commander that if Hezbollah attempted another kidnapping "we will burn Beirut." See Blanford, "Terrorism and Insurgency," 21.

35. A listing of Israel's miliary capabilities and those of other Arab states in 2006 can be found in Anthony H. Cordesman, George Sullivan, and William D. Sullivan, *Lessons of the 2006 Israeli–Hezbollah War* (Washington, DC: Center for Strategic and International Studies (CSIS), 2007), 158–60.

36. Edward Cody and Molly Moore, "'The Best Guerrilla Force in the World' Analysts Attribute Hezbollah's Resilience to Zeal, Secrecy and Iranian Funding," *The Washington Post*, 14 August 2006, https://www.washingtonpost.com/archive/politics/2006/08/14/the-best-guerrilla-force-in-the-world-span-classbankheadanalysts-attribute-hezbollahs-resilience-to-zeal-secrecy-and-iranian-fundingspan/1107737d-a7c1-451a-b3ca-049c9320005c/.

37. Hezbollah's command and control was also modular. No single member of any unit of Hezbollah had knowledge of the entire bunker structure, preventing any massive leak in intelligence. See Alastair Crooke and Mark Perry, "How Hezbollah Defeated Israel. Part 1: Winning the Intelligence War," *Asia Times Online*, 2006, https://www.scoop.co.nz/stories/HL0610/S00206.htm. See also Exum, "Hizballah at War," 12.

38. Ibid., 3; Blanford, *Warriors of God*, 331.

39. Blanford, *Warriors of God*, 331. Hezbollah seems to have expended a great deal of effort to avoid Israeli detection of the bunker networks before the war. Some of the bunkers were extremely close to UNIFIL observation posts and the Israeli border. Nicholas Blanford writes, "How was it possible for Hezbollah to construct such a large facility with neither UNIFIL nor the Israelis having any idea of its existence? 'We never saw them build anything,' a UNIFIL officer told me. 'They must have brought the cement in by the spoonful.'" See Ibid., 332. A massive deception campaign was employed by the Hezbollah to evade Israeli detection of the construction efforts. Some bunkers were built under the surveillance of Israeli drone vehicles or in a manner that Lebanese citizens with close ties to the Israelis would be to observe and report back. These bunkers served as decoys intended to attract Israeli strikes during a conflict. On the other hand, the actual bunkers were constructed in extreme secrecy. See Alastair Crooke and Mark Perry, "How Hezbollah Defeated Israel. Part 1: Winning the Intelligence War," *Asia Times Online*, 2006, https://www.scoop.co.nz/stories/HL0610/S00206.htm

Notes **181**

40. Blanford, *Warriors of God*, 331.
41. Crooke and Perry, "How Hezbollah Defeated Israel. Part 1."
42. Uzi Mahnaimi, "Humbling of the Supertroops Shatters Israeli Army Morale," *The Sunday Times*, 27 August 2006; Matthews, "We Were Caught Unprepared," 44.
43. Brun, "Chapter 13: The Second Lebanon War, 2006," 302.
44. Ibid., 317.
45. Blanford, *Warriors of God*, 123.
46. Ibid.
47. Brigadier General Itai Brun, "'While You're Busy Making Other Plans': The 'Other RMA,'" *Journal of Strategic Studies* 33, no. 4 (2010): 558–59.
48. The Concept of Operations document was reportedly drafted by Hezbollah's then director of operations Haj Hallil. The 13 principles laid out in the document include: (1) avoid the strong, attack the weak—attack and withdraw; (2) protecting our fighters is more important than causing enemy casualties; (3) strike only when success is assured; (4) surprise is essential to success—if you are spotted, you've failed; (5) don't get into a set-piece battle—slip away like smoke, before the enemy can drive home his advantage; (6) attaining the goal demands patience, in order to discover the enemy's weak points; (7) keep moving, avoid formation of a front line; (8) keep the enemy on constant alert, at the front and in the rear; (9) the road to the great victory passes through thousands of small victories; (10) keep up the morale of the fighters, avoid notions of the enemy's superiority; (11) the media has innumerable guns whose hits are like bullets—use them in the battle; (12) the population is a treasure—nurture it; and (13) hurt the enemy, and then stop before he abandons restraint. See Ehud Ya'ari, "Hizballah: 13 Principles of Warfare," *Jerusalem Report*, 21 March 1996 as cited in Daniel Isaac Helmer, "Flipside of the Coin: Israel's Lebanese Incursion Between 1982–2000" (Fort Leavenworth, KS: Combat Studies Institute Press, 2007), 53–54. See also Blanford, *Warriors of God*, 123.
49. See Naim Qassem, trans. by Dalia Khalil, *Hizbullah: The Story from Within* (London: SAQI, 2005), 71.
50. See Naim Qassem, *Hizbullah*, 71. Qassem identifies four distinct effects Hezbollah's Concept of Operations will have on Israeli forces: (1) confusing the enemy and obliging its command to call for a constant state of alert, eventually leading to the exhaustion and decline in power; (2) spreading panic among enemy troops; the fear of death persisted after every successful or possible resistance attack. This served to shake enemy morale and subsequently affected troop performance; (3) forbidding further expansionist goals from being realized, given the pressure exerted in already occupied areas; and (4) liberating the land as a final and ultimate objective; this occurred in stages, and through many confrontations. Examples include Israeli withdrawal from Toumat Niha and other Western Bekaa areas, retreat from many areas surrounding Jezzine in the south and then from Jezzine itself, and the final wide-range and first-time victory in five decades represented by the liberation of the larger part of South Lebanon and the Western Bekaa on May 24, 2000.
51. Brun, "'While You're Busy,'" 547–51. On pain tolerance and willingness to suffer, see Sullivan, "War Aims and War Outcomes," 500.
52. Makovsky and White, "Lessons and Implications of the Israel–Hizballah War," 9.
53. In a TV interview a few months before the 2006 conflict, Hassan Nasrallah stated that Hezbollah operatives are integrated with Lebanese civilians "in their houses, in their schools, in their churches, in their fields, in their farms and in their factories. [Therefore] you can't destroy them in the same way you would destroy an army." See "Whose War

182 Notes

Crimes?," *Wall Street Journal*, 11 December 2006, https://www.wsj.com/articles/SB116580099231046067.

54. Stephen Biddle and Jeffrey A. Friedman, "The 2006 Lebanon Campaign and the Future of Warfare: Implications for Army and Defense Policy" (Carlisle, PA: Strategic Studies Institute, US Army War College, 2008), 50–51, https://press.armywarcollege.edu/monographs/641/.

55. Blanford, *Warriors of God*, 98–99.

56. Nicholas Noe (ed.), *Voice of Hezbollah: The Statements of Sayyed Hassan Nasrallah* (New York: Verso Books, 2007), 62 as cited in Samaan, "Missile Warfare and Violent Non-State Actors," 163. See also Blanford, *Warriors of God*, 99. Ten years later, Hassan Nasrallah confidently declared that Hezbollah had "created a balance of terror with the help of the Katyusha, a weapon which is likened in military science to a water pistol." See Harel and Issacharoff, *34 Days*, 32.

57. Blanford, *Warriors of God*, 146.

58. Helmer, "Flipside of the Coin," 55–56.

59. Hezbollah's Deputy Secretary-General, Sheik Naim Qassem refers to the oral agreement as the July Accord. He writes, "it was thus decided that Israel would halt its assault in return for the ceasing of Katyusha bombardment. And so on the evening of July 31, 1993, precisely at 6:00 PM, the agreement which later became known as the 'July Accord,' was put into force, an expression of oral concord achieved through mediators without any formally written blueprint." See Qassem, *Hizbullah*, 111.

60. Feldman, "Hezbollah–Israel War," 5, 7.

61. Norton, *Hezbollah*, 84; Samaan, "Missile Warfare and Violent Non-State Actors," 159; Blanford, *Warriors of God*, 147.

62. Nicholas Noe, ed., *Voice of Hezbollah: The Statements of Sayyed Hassan Nasrallah*, trans. Ellen Khouri (New York: Verso Books, 2007), 107. Nasrallah further noted in his interview: "This formula was imposed by the Katyusha, and not the operations of the resistance in the border belt. . . . If the settlements are bombarded again, then Rabin will be forced to stand in front of all his people and all [Israel's] political forces to answer the question: What did the seven-day operation achieve? This is why Rabin understands that there is a new formula. . . . The rule of the game used to be that we got bombarded while the settlements remained safe. The enemy destroys Maydun, Yatir, and Kafra while we were only allowed to move in the security zone. But the resistance imposed a new formula through the Katyusha. . . . We stopped the bombardment with the missiles."

63. Blanford, *Warriors of God*, 147, 154–55.

64. Ibid., 133. The March 1995 rocket strikes were justified by Hezbollah as retribution for the death of 16 Lebanese civilians, the injury of 60, the bombing of 75 villages, and the destruction of 212 homes.

65. Human Rights Watch, "Israel/Lebanon: 'Operation Grapes of Wrath': The Civilian Victims," 1 September1997, https://www.refworld.org/docid/3ae6a7e60.html.

66. Blanford, *Warriors of God*, 158, 175.

67. Ibid., 159, 175.

68. Ibid.

69. Ibid., 160; Matthews, "We Were Caught Unprepared," 9.

70. Hala Jaber, *Hezbollah: Born With a Vengeance* (New York: Columbia University Press, 1997), 178.

71. Blanford, *Warriors of God*, 174, 175.

Notes   **183**

72. Ibid., 175.
73. Human Rights Watch, "Israel/Lebanon."
74. The rockets were stationed in southern Lebanon and ready to be fired into Israel. However, Hezbollah choose to withhold the rocket bombardment. See Blanford, *Warriors of God*, 247–48.
75. Ibid., 452.
76. Ibid., 248.
77. Ibid.
78. Harel and Issacharoff, *34 Days*, 91. Nicholas Blanford writes that the success of Operation Specific Weight may be exaggerated. Hezbollah had installed several decoy missile launchers with fake heat signatures to attract Israeli strikes while the real launchers remain hidden. See Blanford, "Terrorism and Insurgency," 22. Similarly, Uzi Rubin suggests that while most of the long-range rockets may have been destroyed, some probably remained. He argues that Iran did not grant permission to Hezbollah to use the long-range rockets it had supplied. He attributes Iranian attitude to its need to avoid drawing any attention to itself and its nuclear program. See Rubin, "Rocket Campaign Against Israel," 7; Steven Erlanger and Richard A. Oppel Jr., "A Disciplined Hezbollah Surprises Israel with Its Training, Tactics and Weapons," *The New York Times*, 7 August 2006, https://www.nytimes.com/2006/08/07/world/middleeast/07hezbollah.html.
79. Mahnaimi, "Humbling of the Supertroops"; "Halutz: 'Mr. PM, We Won the War,'" Ynet news, 27 August 2006, https://www.ynetnews.com/articles/0,7340,L-3296031,00.html. Similarly, on 17 July 2006, General Halutz reportedly argued to the Knesset Foreign Affairs and Defense Committee that Israel was achieving its goals with airpower and artillery alone, without the need for a ground operation. See Avi Kober, "The Israel Defense Forces in the Second Lebanon War: Why the Poor Performance?," *Journal of Strategic Studies* 31, no. 1 (February 2008): 23.
80. Harel and Issacharoff, *34 Days*, 92.
81. Ibid.
82. On 13 July, Hezbollah shot off nearly 125 Katyushas. See Ibid.
83. Blanford, *Warriors of God*, 379.
84. Chris McGreal, "Capture of Soldiers Was 'Act of War' Says Israel," *The Guardian*, 12 July 2006, https://www.theguardian.com/world/2006/jul/13/israelandthepalestinians.lebanon1.
85. Inbar, "How Israel Bungled the Second Lebanon War," 62.
86. Ibid.
87. Dan Halutz, the Israeli chief of Staff, in particular, believed strongly that air power would be sufficient to force Hezbollah to surrender. Halutz had previously argued, "air operations were generally implemented without a land force, based on a worldview of Western society's sensitivity to losses . . . this obliges us to part with a number of anachronistic assumptions. First of all, that victory equals territory. Victory means achieving the strategic goal and not necessarily territory. I maintain that we also have to part with the concept of a land battle. We have to talk about the integrated battle and about the appropriate force activating it. Victory is a matter of consciousness. Air power affects the adversary's consciousness significantly." See Ze'ev Schiff, "The Foresight Saga," *Haaretz*, 11 August 2006, https://www.haaretz.com/2006-08-11/ty-article/the-foresight-saga/0000017f-db8f-df62-a9ff-dfdf53230000. See Kober, "Israel Defense Forces in the Second Lebanon War," 22; Harel and Issacharoff, *34 Days*, 92.

184 Notes

88. Harel and Issacharoff, *34 Days*, 101. Hezbollah had anticipated and prepared for strikes on the al-Manar station. The al-Manar station continued transmitting from a secret location where it was linked to three Arab satellites. Throughout the war, the station managed to continue broadcasting despite several aerial strikes on relay towers and antennas. See Cody and Moore, "'The Best Guerrilla Force in the World.'"
89. Harel and Issacharoff, *34 Days*, 102.
90. Blanford, "Terrorism and Insurgency," 23; Ze'ev Schiff, "Analysis: How IDF Blew Chance to Destroy Short-Range Rockets," *Haaretz*, 3 September 2006, https://www.haaretz.com/2006-09-03/ty-article/analysis-how-idf-blew-chance-to-destroy-short-range-rockets/0000017f-da76-d432-a77f-df7f30be0000.
91. Blanford, "Terrorism and Insurgency," 23.
92. Matthews, "We Were Caught Unprepared," 17; Exum, "Hizballah at War," 4.
93. Exum, "Hizballah at War," 4.
94. William M. Arkin, "Divine Victory for Whom? Airpower in the 2006 Israel–Hezbollah War," *Strategic Studies Quarterly*, Winter 2007, 103. In fact, as early as 13 July 2006, Israeli Prime Minister Ehud Olmert declared that the "events are not a terror attack, but the act of a sovereign state that attacked Israel for no reason and without provocation . . . the Lebanese government, of which Hezbollah is a part, is trying to undermine regional stability. Lebanon is responsible, and Lebanon will bear the consequences of its actions." See Amos Harel, Aluf Benn, and Gideon Alon, "Gov't Okays Massive Strikes on Lebanon," *Haaretz*, 13 July 2006. However, the Israeli notion that the government of Lebanon when pressured would, in turn, be able to pressure and contain Hezbollah was flawed. See Harel and Issacharoff, *34 Days*, 192; Cordesman, Sullivan, and Sullivan, *Lessons of the 2006 Israeli-Hezbollah War*, 20.
95. Byman, "Lebanese Hizballah and Israeli Counterterrorism," 928; Brun, "Chapter 13: The Second Lebanon War, 2006," 320.
96. Brun, "Chapter 13: The Second Lebanon War, 2006," 312. The event was similar to an incident in 1996. During the 1996 Operation Grapes of Wrath, Israel had similarly hit by mistake a United Nations Interim Force in Lebanon (UNIFIL) building. Israeli artillery units intended to target Hezbollah mortar fire originating in the vicinity of the UNIFIL building. The incident led to the lead to the death of about 100 Lebanese civilians and 4 UNIFIL soldiers. The incident forced Israel to terminate the operation. See Ibid.
97. Marvin Kalb and Carol Saivetz, "The Israeli–Hezbollah War of 2006: The Media as a Weapon in Asymmetrical Conflict," *Press/Politics* 12, no. 3 (2007): 48–49.
98. Ibid.; Harel and Issacharoff, *34 Days*, 162.
99. Brun, "Chapter 13: The Second Lebanon War, 2006," 312; Byman, "Lebanese Hizballah and Israeli Counterterrorism," 929.
100. Byman, "Lebanese Hizballah and Israeli Counterterrorism," 935. Israeli media and the international news networks had access to and were to able report on the errors of the Israeli Air Force and the political debates within the leadership. However, the news networks had little to no ability to report on how Hezbollah was faring in combat. The discrepancy in access made it possible for a skewed understanding of the relative successes and failures of Hezbollah and the Israeli forces to emerge. See Makovsky and White, "Lessons and Implications of the Israel–Hizballah War," 48.
101. Ibid.
102. Harel and Issacharoff, *34 Days*, 171.
103. Ibid., 188.

104. Ibid.
105. Brun, "Chapter 13: The Second Lebanon War, 2006," 313.
106. Ibid.
107. Ibid., 298; Makovsky and White, "Lessons and Implications of the Israel–Hizballah War," 51; Cordesman, Sullivan, and Sullivan, *Lessons of the 2006 Israeli-Hezbollah War*, 123.
108. Brun, "Chapter 13: The Second Lebanon War, 2006," 320. Additionally, 900,000 Lebanese fled their homes, and 30,000 homes were destroyed or damaged.
109. "English Summary of the Winograd Commission Report," *The New York Times*, 30 January 2008, https://www.nytimes.com/2008/01/30/world/middleeast/31winograd-web.html.
110. While the major commitment of ground troops occurred on 7 August, some deployment had occurred previously. On 18 July, Israel committed a few brigades against Hezbollah troops. On 22 July, significant fighting occurred in Maroun al-Ras, Bint Jbeil, and Ayta al-Shaab in Lebanon, close to the border. The deployment of ground forces was increased again on 29 July. See Kober, "Israel Defense Forces in the Second Lebanon War," 4–5.
111. In one instance during the Second Lebanon War, Israelis terminated a combat operation because of one casualty. See Ibid., 11. A postwar investigation noted that commanders "sense of responsibility for the lives of their troops overshadowed their commitment to fulfill their missions." See Yossi Yehoshua, "Declining Values," *Yehidot Aharonot Weekend Supplement*, 13 July 2007 as cited in Ibid.
112. Feldman, "Hezbollah-Israel War," 4.
113. Gabrielsen, "Evolution of Hezbollah's Strategy and Military Performance," 276.
114. Cordesman, Sullivan, and Sullivan, *Lessons of the 2006 Israeli-Hezbollah War*, 85.
115. On 17 July 2006, in a speech to the Israeli Knesset, Prime Minister Olmert identified Israel's political objectives as (1) the return of the kidnapped soldiers, (2) a comprehensive ceasefire, (3) deployment of the Lebanese army in southern Lebanon, and (4) the expulsion of Hezbollah from southern Lebanon in accordance with UN resolution 1159. See "Prime Minister Olmert Speech to Knesset on Violence in Lebanon and Gaza Strip (July 2006)," Jewish Virtual Library, 17 July 2006, https://www.jewishvirtuallibrary.org/prime-minister-olmert-speech-to-knesset-on-violence-in-lebanon-and-gaza-strip-july-2006.
116. "Israel Warns Hizbullah War Would Invite Destruction," *Yedioth Ahronoth*, 3 October 2008, https://www.ynetnews.com/articles/0,7340,L-3604893,00.html.
117. Ibid.
118. Sayyad Hassan Nasrallah, speech at rally marking the fourth anniversary of 2006 Lebanon War, Al-Manar, 3 August 2010 as cited in Sobelman, "Learning to Deter: Deterrence Failure and Success in the Israel–Hezbollah Conflict, 2006–16," 186. See also Blanford, *Warriors of God*, 437. Hassan Nasrallah also warned that, in a tit-for-tat strike, Israel had much more to lose. He argued, "we have half an airport. They have several. They have seaports. We have one power plant, but they have large ones. We have half a refinery, which I'm not even sure works. They on the other hand have been blessed with many refineries. We have several factories; they have huge industrial zones, of all types and all kinds. The infrastructure in Israel is bigger and more significant than we have here." See Sayyad Hassan Nasrallah, annual speech in honor of Martyred Commanders, Al-Manar, 16 February 2010. Recognizing the disparity in vulnerabilities between Israel and Hezbollah, Brigadier General Itai Brun writes, "Israel needed a clear-cut victory in a quick war, and all the Hezbollah needed was to survive and demonstrate its survivability." See Brun, "'While You're Busy,'" 559.

186 Notes

119. See Gadi Eisenkot, "The Features of a Possible Conflict in the Northern Arena and the Home Front," lecture given at University of Haifa symposium, 30 November 2010, Haifa, Israel as cited in Sobelman, "Learning to Deter," 153.

120. See "What's Hot with Razi Barkai," IDF Radio, 30 October 2014 as cited in Ibid.

121. Ehud Eilam, *Israeli Strategies in the Middle East: The Case of Iran* (Cham, Switzerland: Palgrave Macmillan, 2022), 80; Judah Ari Gross, "IDF: In Future War, Hezbollah Could Fire up to 3,000 Rockets a Day for a Week," *The Times of Israel*, 14 July 2021, https://www.timesofisrael.com/liveblog_entry/idf-in-future-war-hezbollah-could-fire-up-to-3000-rockets-a-day-for-a-week/.

122. Yiftah S. Shapir, "Hezbollah as an Army," *Strategic Assessment*, January 2017, 71.

123. Ibid., 71–72.

124. Mark Landler, "US Speaks to Syrian Envoy of Arms Worries," *The New York Times*, 19 April 2010, https://www.nytimes.com/2010/04/20/world/middleeast/20syria.html. See also Blanford, *Warriors of God*, 436. See also "Nasrallah Warns: Hezbollah's Missiles Can Hit Israel's Nuclear Reactor," *The Jerusalem Post*, 16 February 2017, https://www.jpost.com/Arab-Israeli-Conflict/Nasrallah-warns-Hezbollahs-missiles-can-hit-Israels-nuclear-reactor-481789.

125. Gross, "IDF."

126. Gabrielsen, "Evolution of Hezbollah's Strategy and Military Performance," 266, 277.

127. Judah Ari Gross, "Learning from May War, IDF Simulates Hezbollah Battle Alongside Domestic Strife," *The Times of Israel*, 31 October 2021, https://www.timesofisrael.com/learning-from-may-war-idf-simulates-battle-with-hezbollah-amid-domestic-strife/. The exercise was modeled using the 11-day Guardians of the Wall conflict in May 2011 that witnessed a large barrage of rockets fired from the Gaza Strip targeting Israel while rioting simultaneously unfolded in mixed Arab-Jewish cities and neighborhoods throughout Israel.

128. Yaakov Lappin, "The IDF in the Shadow of the Pandemic" (Ramat Gan, Israel: The Begin-Sadat Center for Strategic Studies, Bar-Ilan University, 22 October 2020), https://besacenter.org/israel-pandemic-idf/.

129. Kenneth S. Brower, "Israel Versus Anyone: A Military Net Assessment of the Middle East" (Ramat Gan, Israel: The Begin-Sadat Center for Strategic Studies, Bar-Ilan University, August 2020), 8, https://besacenter.org/israel-versus-anyone/.

130. Shapir, "Hezbollah as an Army," 72; Isabel Kershner and Michael E. Gordon, "Israeli Airstrike in Syria Targets Arms Convoy, US Says," *The New York Times*, 8 October 2022, https://www.nytimes.com/2013/01/31/world/middleeast/syria-says-it-was-hit-by-strikes-from-israeli-planes.html. See also Nicholas Blanford, "Collision Course: Israel and Hizbullah Maintain Readiness for War," *IHS Jane's Intelligence Review* 25, no. 7 (2013): 8–13.

131. Eilam, *Israeli Strategies in the Middle East*, 81.

132. Barbara Opall-Rome, "Israel Sweeps Anti-Missile Sensors, Shooters into One Command," SpaceNews, 1 August 2011, https://spacenews.com/israel-sweeps-anti-missile-sensors-shooters-one-command/.

133. For instance, each Iron Dome interceptor costs between $40,000 and $100,000. Hezbollah's rockets cost a fraction of these interceptors. See Robert Farley, "Cost of Iron Dome," Daily Beast, 14 July 2017, https://www.thedailybeast.com/the-cost-of-iron-dome.

134. Eilam, *Israeli Strategies in the Middle East*, 80.

135. Blanford, *Warriors of God*, 453.

Chapter 7

1. Brennan, *Undaunted*, 339.
2. United Nations Security Council, "Final Report of the Panel of Experts on Yemen" (New York: United Nations Security Council, 31 January 2017), 2, https://digitallibrary.un.org/record/1478791?ln=en. See also Michael Knights and Alex Almeida, "The Saudi-UAE War Effort in Yemen (Part 2): The Air Campaign," The Washington Institute for Near East Policy, 11 August 2015, https://www.washingtoninstitute.org/policy-analysis/saudi-uae-war-effort-yemen-part-2-air-campaign.
3. Annelle Sheline, "The Yemen War in Numbers: Saudi Escalation and US Complicity" (New York: Quincy Institute for Responsible Statecraft, March 2022), 8–9, https://quincyinst.org/report/the-yemen-war-in-numbers-saudi-escalation-and-u-s-complicity/.
4. Dion Nissenbaum, "In a Saudi War Room, Generals Grapple with Ways to Protect Civilians in Yemen," *The Wall Street Journal*, 18 March 2018.
5. Vongai Murugani et al., "Food Systems in Conflict and Peacebuilding Settings: Case Studies of Venezuela and Yemen" (Stockholm: Stockholm International Peace Research Institute [SIPRI], December 2021), 18, https://www.sipri.org/publications/2021/other-publications/food-systems-conflict-and-peacebuilding-settings-pathways-and-interconnections. The main seaports of Aden, Hodeidah, Mukalla, and Saleef are critical points of disembarkation for Yemen's food imports—with almost 80% entering into the country through these ports. These ports were also vital for oil imports, which is essential for the Yemen's domestic agricultural production. See Ibid., 16.
6. Murugani et al., "Food Systems," 14.
7. Ibid.; Ben Hubbard and Nick Cumming-Bruce, "Rebels in Yemen Fire Second Ballistic Missile at Saudi Capital," *The New York Times*, 19 December 2017.
8. Bruce Riedel, "The Houthis Have Won in Yemen: What Next?," Brookings, 1 February 2022, https://www.brookings.edu/blog/order-from-chaos/2022/02/01/the-houthis-have-won-in-yemen-what-next/.
9. United Nations Security Council, "Final Report," 31 January 2017, 2.
10. United Nations Security Council, "Final Report of the Panel of Experts on Yemen" (New York: United Nations Security Council, 26 January 2018), 2, https://digitallibrary.un.org/record/1639536?ln=en.
11. Patrick Wintour, "Houthis Claim to Have Killed 500 Saudi Soldiers in Major Attack," *The Guardian*, 29 September 2019, https://www.theguardian.com/world/2019/sep/29/houthis-claim-killed-hundreds-saudi-soldiers-captured-thousands; Sudarsan Raghavan, "Houthis Say They Killed or Wounded 500 Saudi-Led Coalition Fighters and Captured 2,000, Showing Footage of Soldiers, Corpses," *The Washington Post*, 29 September 2019.
12. Wintour, "Houthis Claim."
13. United Nations Security Council, "Final Report of the Panel of Experts on Yemen" (New York: United Nations Security Council, 10 February 2020), 2, https://reliefweb.int/report/yemen/letter-dated-27-january-2020-panel-experts-yemen-addressed-president-security-council.
14. O'Grady Siobhán and Ali Al-Mujahed, "Battle for the Badlands," *The Washington Post*, 2 October 2021.
15. Ali al-Sakani, "Fighting Rages in Marib despite UN Truce," Al Jazeera, 18 April 2022, https://www.aljazeera.com/news/2022/4/18/fighting-rages-in-marib-despite-un-truce. The Saudi-led Coalition made significant efforts to prevent the fall of Marib to the Houthis.

The Giants Brigade, a Southern Yemeni militia funded and trained by the United Arab Emirates (UAE) was pressed into action to counter Houthi advance toward the center of Marib. The Giants Brigade, with Saudi air support, severely damaged the Houthi force and halted its advance. See Saeed Al-Batati, "Yemeni Troops Recapture District in Shabwa from Houthis," Arab News, 2 January 2022, https://www.arabnews.com/node/1996901/middle-east; "Yemen: UAE-Backed Giants Brigades Begin Withdrawing from Shabwah," Middle East Eye, 28 January 2022, https://www.middleeasteye.net/news/yemen-uae-backed-tro ops-begin-withdrawing-shabwah; al-Sakani, "Fighting Rages in Maribe."

16. al-Sakani, "Fighting Rages in Marib."

17. "US Policy in Yemen" (Washington, DC, 17 April 2018), 17, https://www.foreign.senate. gov/hearings/us-policy-in-yemen-041718.

18. Ibid.

19. Sheline, "Yemen War in Numbers," 8–9. See also "The Joint Forces Command of the Coalition to Restore Legitimacy in Yemen: Interception and Destruction of a Ballistic Missile Launched by the Terrorist Iran-Backed Houthi Militia Toward the Kingdom," The Official Saudi Press Agency, 16 June 2020, https://www.spa.gov.sa/2098542; Bruce Riedel, "Yemen War Turns Seven," Brookings, 24 March 2022, https://www.brookings.edu/blog/ order-from-chaos/2022/03/24/yemen-war-turns-seven/.

20. Williams and Shaikh, "Missile War in Yemen," 13.

21. Kate Lyons, "Saudi Arabia Oil Attack: Trump Hints at Action as US Points Finger at Iran," The Guardian, 16 September 2019, https://www.theguardian.com/world/2019/sep/16/ trump-says-us-locked-and-loaded-after-saudi-arabia-oil-attack-as-crude-prices-soar-iran-aramco; Natasha Turak, "How Saudi Arabia Failed to Protect Itself from Drones, Missile Attacks Despite Billions Spent on Defense Systems," CNBC, 19 September 2019, https://www.cnbc.com/2019/09/19/how-saudi-arabia-failed-to-protect-itself-from-dro nes-missile-attacks.html; Natasha Turak, "Drone and Missile Debris Proves Iranian Role in Attack, Saudi Defense Ministry Claims," CNBC, 18 September 2019, https://www.cnbc. com/2019/09/18/saudi-arabia-drone-and-missile-debris-proves-iranian-role-in-attack. html.

22. "Houthi Drone Attacks on 2 Saudi Aramco Oil Facilities Spark Fires," Al Jazeera, 14 September 2019, https://www.aljazeera.com/economy/2019/9/14/houthi-drone-attacks-on-2-saudi-aramco-oil-facilities-spark-fires.

23. Meg Wagner et al., "Trump Orders New Iran Sanctions after Saudi Attack," CNN, 18 September 2019, https://www.cnn.com/middleeast/live-news/trump-iran-sanctions-saudi-oil-attack/h_1c5f6b900fad932e5318dac5979b753b.

24. Williams and Shaikh, "Missile War in Yemen," 14.

25. Ibid. Seth Jones characterizes the political embarrassment as having "reputational consequences for the Saudi government." See Seth G. Jones et al., "The Iranian and Houthi War Against Saudi Arabia," CSIS Brief (Washington, DC: Center for Strategic & International Studies [CSIS], 21 December 2021), 11, https://www.csis.org/analysis/iran ian-and-houthi-war-against-saudi-arabia. See also Annelle Sheline, "Cautious Optimism Hovers over New Ceasefire in Yemen," Responsible Statecraft, 1 April 2022, https://respon siblestatecraft.org/2022/04/01/cautious-optimism-hovers-over-new-ceasefire-in-yemen/; Bruce Riedel, "Yemen: Peace at Last?," Brookings, 6 April 2022, https://www.brookings. edu/blog/order-from-chaos/2022/04/06/yemen-peace-at-last/.

26. IISS Strategic Dossier, Iran's Networks of Influence in the Middle East (London: International Institute for Strategic Studies [IISS], 2019), 160.

Notes **189**

27. The religious challenge to the Zaydi Shiite order came from Saudi Arabia, which pumped money and Wahhabi missionaries into the Sa'dah region with the implicit support of the Yemeni government. See Ibid., 17; Murugani et al., "Food Systems," 17.
28. Riedel, "Houthis Have Won in Yemen"
29. Helen Lackner, *Yemen in Crisis: Autocracy, Neo-Liberalism and the Disintegration of State*, e-book (London: Saqi Books, 2017), 131.
30. Jean-Loup C. Samaan, "Missiles, Drones, and the Houthis in Yemen," *Parameters* 50, no. 1 (Spring 2020): 51–64. At the same time, the Houthis also embraced an anti-American rhetoric. The group called itself Ansar Allah, or Supporters of God and adopted the slogan: "God is great, death to the US, death to Israel, curse the Jews, and victory for Islam." See Riedel, "Houthis Have Won in Yemen." These ideological postures may have attracted Iranian support and Yemeni recruits to the Houthi cause.
31. A detailed review of the six wars of insurgency and its geopolitical effect on Yemen, see Barak A. Salmoni, Bryce Loidolt, and Madeleine Wells, *Regime and Periphery in Northern Yemen: The Huthi Phenomenon* (Santa Monica, CA: Rand, 2010), 131–58.
32. Lackner, *Yemen in Crisis*, 133–34.
33. Samaan, "Missiles, Drones, and the Houthis in Yemen," 53.
34. Riedel, "Houthis Have Won in Yemen" Abdul-Malik al-Houthi, the half-brother of Hussein al-Houthi took over and remains the group's leader. See Peter Salisbury and Alexander Weissenburger, "The Surprising Success of the Truce in Yemen," Foreign Affairs, 28 June 2002, https://www.foreignaffairs.com/articles/yemen/2022-06-28/surprising-succ ess-truce-yemen.
35. Lackner, *Yemen in Crisis*, 133–34.
36. Ibid.
37. Samaan, "Missiles, Drones, and the Houthis in Yemen," 53.
38. Lackner, *Yemen in Crisis*, 133–34. However, the Qatari intervention did not last. The Ali Abdallah Saleh government was preventing Qatar from its reconstruction efforts in the Sa'dah region. Lackner notes that the "Saudi regime's resentment at a successful and popular intervention by its Wahhabi rivals from Qatar" may have also contributed to the failure of the Qatari effort.
39. Ibid.
40. Ibid.
41. Michael Knights, "The Houthi War Machine: From Guerilla War to State Capture," *CTC Sentinel*, September 2018, 15.
42. Williams and Shaikh, "Missile War in Yemen," 3.
43. Marieke Brandt, *Tribes and Politics in Yemen: A History of the Houthi Conflict* (New York: Oxford University Press, 2017), 338. The GCC-mediated power transfer agreement put Vice-President Abdrabuh Mansour Hadi temporarily in charge. A UN-sponsored process laid out three steps to transition to political normalcy: (1) a national dialogue to develop a new constitution, followed by elections in 2014; (2) addressing issues of transitional justice; and (3) reforming the Yemeni armed forces. See Ibid.
44. IISS Strategic Dossier, *Iran's Networks of Influence*, 163.
45. Ibid.
46. Brandt, *Tribes and Politics in Yemen*, 339, 342; Williams and Shaikh, "Missile War in Yemen," 3; Samaan, "Missiles, Drones, and the Houthis in Yemen," 54; IISS Strategic Dossier, *Iran's Networks of Influence*, 163. However, President Saleh was assassinated in 2017. See Murugani et al., "Food Systems," 18.

190 Notes

47. IISS Strategic Dossier, *Iran's Networks of Influence*, 163.
48. Williams and Shaikh, "Missile War in Yemen," 3; IISS Strategic Dossier, *Iran's Networks of Influence*, 163.
49. IISS Strategic Dossier, *Iran's Networks of Influence*, 163.
50. Ibid. Operation Decisive Storm began with a massive shelling and aerial bombardment campaign targeting vital transportation nodes, airports, bridges, military bases, ammunition depots, and Houthi strongholds. See Brandt, *Tribes and Politics in Yemen*, 1.
51. For an excellent review of the ground campaign and air campaign by the Saudi-led Coalition in 2015, see Michael Knights and Alex Almeida, "The Saudi-UAE War Effort in Yemen (Part 1): Operation Golden Arrow in Aden," Washington Institute for Near East Policy, 10 August 2015, https://www.washingtoninstitute.org/policy-analysis/saudi-uae-war-effort-yemen-part-1-operation-golden-arrow-aden; Knights and Almeida, "Saudi-UAE War Effort in Yemen (Part 2)."
52. Daniel Byman, "Yemen's Disastrous War," *Survival* 60, no. 5 (2018): 141–58.
53. Brandt, *Tribes and Politics in Yemen*, 341.
54. Yara Bayoumy and Phil Stewart, "Exclusive: Iran Steps up Weapons Supply to Yemen's Houthis via Oman," Reuters, 26 October 2016, https://www.reuters.com/article/us-yemen-security-iran/exclusive-iran-steps-up-weapons-supply-to-yemens-houthis-via-oman-officials-idUSKCN12K0CX; Jared Szuba, "Iran Sending More Weapons to Yemen's Houthis Amid Cease-Fire Effort: Pentagon," Al-Monitor, 11 August 2021, https://www.al-monitor.com/originals/2021/08/iran-sending-more-weapons-yemens-houthis-amid-cease-fire-effort-pentagon; Isabel Debre, "UK Warship Seizes Advanced Iranian Missiles Bound for Yemen," *The Washington Post*, 7 July 2022, https://www.washingtonpost.com/world/uk-warship-seizes-advanced-iranian-missiles-bound-for-yemen/2022/07/07/087f4086-fde3-11ec-b39d-71309168014b_story.html.
55. Williams and Shaikh, "Missile War in Yemen," 16.
56. A UN Experts Panel report details allegations that "arms and other equipment from the stores of the Government of Yemen military have been diverted to Houthi forces by individuals associated with senior Government of Yemen commanders." See United Nations Security Council, "Final Report of the Panel of Experts on Yemen" (New York: United Nations Security Council, 22 January 2021), 27, https://www.securitycouncilreport.org/un-documents/document/s-2021-79.php.
57. Brandt, *Tribes and Politics in Yemen*, 337.
58. Ibid.; United Nations Security Council, "Final Report of the Panel of Experts on Yemen," 10 February 2020, 2.
59. Karen DeYoung, "Officials: Saudi-Led Action Relied on US Intelligence," *The Washington Post*, 26 March 2015, https://www.washingtonpost.com/world/national-security/officials-saudi-led-action-in-yemen-relied-heavily-on-us-intelligence/2015/03/26/6d15302c-d3da-11e4-8fce-3941fc548f1c_story.html?postshare=4381427462812748.
60. Ibid.
61. Michael Stephens, "Mixed Success for Saudi Military Operation in Yemen," BBC News, 12 May 2015, https://www.bbc.com/news/world-middle-east-32593749.
62. Helen Cooper, Thomas Gibbons-Neff, and Eric Schmitt, "Army Special Forces Secretly Help Saudis Combat Threat from Yemen Rebels," *The New York Times*, 3 May 2018; " 'Decisive Storm' Destroys Houthi Missile Stockpile," Al Arabiya News, 28 March 2015, https://english.alarabiya.net/News/middle-east/2015/03/28/-Decisive-Storm-destroys-Houthi-missile-stockpile-.

63. "Asiri: We Destroyed 80% of Houthi Weapons Stores," *Sky News*, 19 April 2015, https://www.skynewsarabia.com/middle-east/739335. See also Knights and Almeida, "The Saudi-UAE War Effort in Yemen (Part 2): The Air Campaign"; "Arab Coalition 'Has Destroyed Most of Yemen Rebels' Missiles'," *The Times of Israel*, 28 March 2015, http://www.timesofisrael.com/arab-coalition-has-destroyed-most-of-yemen-rebels-missiles/.

64. "Asiri."

65. "Yemenis Repair Soviet Missiles to Counter Saudi Coalition Attacks," SPUTNIK International, 30 March 2017, https://sputniknews.com/20170330/yeminis-repair-soviet-missiles-1052137016.html.

66. Samaan, "Missiles, Drones, and the Houthis in Yemen." The Houthis also took precautions to ensure that the missile forces remained under their control. A Yemeni military informant, in an interview with Michael Knights, notes, "[the Houthis] didn't trust us. The missiles were moved from Sana'a to Sa'ada early on. [The Houthis] were quickly self-sufficient and didn't need the Republican Guard or missile forces." See Knights, "Houthi War Machine," 20.

67. Samaan, "Missiles, Drones, and the Houthis in Yemen," 58. During the administration of President Ali Abdallah Saleh, the Yemeni Republican Guards controlled the 89th Artillery Brigade, which was believed to operate Yemen's missile arsenal. After the ouster of President Saleh, the administration of President Abdrabbuh Mansur Hadi disbanded the Yemeni Republican Guard, and the missile brigades were placed under the command of Muhammad Nasser Ahmed al-Atifi. Major-General Muhammad Nasser Ahmed al-Atifi defected from the Hadi government and now serves as the Houthis Defense Minister. See Tom Cooper, "How Did the Houthis Manage to Lob a Ballistic Missile at Mecca?," War Is Boring, 28 October 2016, https://warisboring.com/how-did-the-houthis-manage-to-lob-a-ballistic-missile-at-mecca/.

68. Noah Browning, "Houthi Missile Arsenal Holds a Key to Future Yemen Peace," Reuters, 22 November 2016, https://www.reuters.com/article/us-yemen-security-missiles-analysis/houthi-missile-arsenal-holds-a-key-to-future-yemen-peace-idUSKBN13H1UU; Cooper, "How Did the Houthis Manage?" Yemeni government forces had procured these missiles over the course of several years from the Soviet Union and North Korea. Yemen may have possessed at least 18 Scud-B missiles and procured 90 Hwasong-6 (Scud-C missile) from North Korea. See United Nations Security Council, "Final Report of the Panel of Experts on Yemen," 26 January 2018, 26. In December 2002, the US Navy had interdicted a Yemen-bound North Korean ship with 15 Scud missiles. However, President Bush released the ship after Yemen's President protested. See David E. Sanger and Thom Shanker, "Threats and Responses: War Matériel; Reluctant US Gives Assent for Missiles to Go to Yemen," *The New York Times*, 12 December 2002, https://www-nytimes-com.ezproxy.lib.utexas.edu/2002/12/12/world/threats-responses-war-materiel-reluctant-us-gives-assent-for-missiles-go-yemen.html.

69. It should be noted that the Houthis drone technological capabilities have quickly evolved from small, propeller-powered to larger aerodynamic variants. See Dion Nissenbaum and Warren P. Strobel, "Mideast Insurgents Enter the Age of Drone Warfare," *The Wall Street Journal*, 2 May 2019, https://www.wsj.com/articles/mideast-insurgents-enter-the-age-of-drone-warfare-11556814441?shareToken=stb4d012f88e2d444f8a056823ae80ffca.

70. IISS Strategic Dossier, *Iran's Networks of Influence*, 167.

71. Samaan, "Missiles, Drones, and the Houthis in Yemen," 58.

72. United Nations Security Council, "Final Report of the Panel of Experts on Yemen" (New York: United Nations Security Council, 26 June 2019), 32, https://reliefweb.int/rep

192   Notes

ort/yemen/letter-dated-25-january-2019-panel-experts-yemen-addressed-president-security-council. The United Nations report highlights that "whereas in 2015 and 2016, complete or partially assembled weapons systems such as extended-range short-range ballistic missiles were supplied to the Houthis forces from abroad, they are now increasingly relying on the import of high-value components, which are then integrated into locally assembled systems." See Ibid., 26–27. Iranians reiterate the same argument. An Iranian Armed Forces spokesperson, Abu al-Fadl Shikaraji, indicated recently that Yemen has developed a capacity to indigenously assemble and manufacture missiles and drones. He stated, "it is not like we give them missiles from Iran. We have passed on our experience and knowledge to the Yemeni people. We transferred the technological experience in the field of defense to them and they have learned to produce missiles, UAVs and weapons in Yemen themselves." See "Iran Reveals Their Transfer of Missile, Drone Information to Yemen," Al-Masdar News, 22 September 2020, https://www.almasdarnews.com/article/iran-reveals-their-transfer-of-missile-drone-information-to-yemen.

73. United Nations Security Council, "Final Report of the Panel of Experts on Yemen," 31 January 2017, 35.

74. Ibid.

75. Lubold Gordon, "Saudi Arabia Pleads for Missile-Defense Resupply as Its Arsenal Runs Low," *The Wall Street Journal*, 7 December 2021. See also Ben Hubbard, Palko Karasz, and Stanley Reed, "Two Major Saudi Oil Installations Hit by Drone Strike, and US Blames Iran," *The New York Times*, 14 September 2019, https://www.nytimes.com/2019/09/14/world/middleeast/saudi-arabia-refineries-drone-attack.html.

76. Samaan, "Missiles, Drones, and the Houthis in Yemen," 58.

77. Williams and Shaikh, "Missile War in Yemen," 10; Samaan, "Missiles, Drones, and the Houthis in Yemen," 59.

78. Ammar al-Ashwal, "Houthis Taking Battle to Saudis with Upgraded Weapons Cache," Al-Monitor, 5 July 2019, https://www.al-monitor.com/originals/2019/07/yemen-houthis-drone-attacks-saudi-arabia-uae-iran.html.

79. Ibid.

80. Sayyad Hassan Nasrallah, speech at rally marking the fourth anniversary of 2006 Lebanon War, Al-Manar, 3 August 2010 as cited in Sobelman, "Learning to Deter," 186. See also Samaan, "Missiles, Drones, and the Houthis in Yemen," 59.

81. "Yemen's Houthis Announce Three-Day Ceasefire after Saudi Attacks," Al Jazeera, 16 March 2022, https://www.aljazeera.com/news/2022/3/26/yemens-houthis-announce-three-day-ceasefire-after-saudi-attacks. The attacks struck the Aramco oil facilities located very near a Formula One racing track hosting the Jeddah Grand Prix. The attacks almost jeopardized the Jeddah Grand Prix, a major tourist attraction.

82. Ibid.

83. "Saudi-Led Coalition Announces Yemen Ceasefire from Wednesday," Al-Monitor, 29 March 2022, https://www.al-monitor.com/originals/2022/03/saudi-led-coalition-announces-yemen-ceasefire-wednesday.

84. Lisa Barrington, "Yemen's Houthis Say Saudi, UAE in Missile Range If Hodeidah Truce Cracks," Reuters, 22 April 2019, https://www.reuters.com/article/us-yemen-security/yemens-houthis-say-saudi-uae-in-missile-range-if-hodeidah-truce-cracks-idUSKCN1RY1FE.

85. Browning, "Houthi Missile Arsenal." See also "UAE Servicemen Die in Yemen," [N]UAE, 3 September 2015, https://www.thenationalnews.com/uae/government/uae-service

men-die-in-yemen-1.123498; "UAE in Three-Day Mourning After 45 Soldiers Killed in Yemen," Middle East Eye, 5 September 2015, https://www.middleeasteye.net/fr/news/uae-three-day-mourning-after-45-soldiers-killed-yemen-465722699; Uzi Rubin, "Hezbollah and the Yemeni Missiles" (Begin-Sadat Center for Strategic Studies, 2017), http://www.jstor.org/stable/resrep16867.

86. "UAE in Three-Day Mourning."

87. "UAE Servicemen Die in Yemen."

88. Ibid.

89. Ibid.

90. For instance, in 2018, Yemeni troops supported and trained by United Arab Emirates unsuccessfully tried to dislodge the Houthis from controlling Hodeidah and its port. A commander of the Giant Brigades, Brigadier General, Sheik Abdel Rahman al-Laji, conceded that their assault was stalled. The Houthis deployed "land mines—many of them encased in fiberglass and painted to look like rocks" and other weaponry that made it impractical for the Giant Brigades forces to make quick progress. See Asa Fitch, "With Much at Stake in Yemen Port, Coalition Puts Advance on Hold," *The Wall Street Journal*, 8 July 2018.

91. Williams and Shaikh, "Missile War in Yemen," 5.

92. Elana DeLozier, "Houthis Kill Top UAE-Backed Separatist Yemeni Commander," Washington Institute for Near East Policy, 1 August 2019, https://www.washingtoninstitute.org/policy-analysis/houthis-kill-top-uae-backed-separatist-yemeni-commander.

93. Walsh and Kirkpatrick, "U.A.E. Pulls Most Forces from Yemen."

94. Ibid.

95. "Houthi Rebels Will Have Role in Yemen's Future, Says UAE," Al Jazeera, 10 November 2019, https://www.aljazeera.com/news/2019/11/10/houthi-rebels-will-have-role-in-yemens-future-says-uae.

96. For example, in October 2021, the Giants Brigade, a militia group supported by the United Arab Emirates, was pressed into action and succeeded in halting the Houthis advance on Marib. See Al-Batati, "Yemeni Troops Recapture District in Shabwas"; "Yemen: UAE-Backed Giants Brigades Begin Withdrawing from Shabwah." See also Ibrahim Jalal, "The UAE May Have Withdrawn from Yemen, but Its Influence Remains Strong," Middle East Institute, 25 February 2020, https://www.mei.edu/publications/uae-may-have-withdrawn-yemen-its-influence-remains-strong. In reaction to the involvement of the Giants Brigade, the Houthis responded with renewed ballistic missiles, cruise missiles, and drone strikes targeting the United Arab Emirates. A January 2022 strike targeted the Al-Dhafra air base hosting American and French troops. Yousef Al Otaiba, the UAE ambassador to the United States, indicated that "several attacks, a combination of cruise missiles, ballistic missiles and drones, targeted civilian sites . . . several were intercepted, a few of them [weren't], and three innocent civilians unfortunately lost their lives." See Jesn Judson and Joe Gould, "THAAD, in First Operational Use, Destroys Midrange Ballistic Missile in Houthi Attack," Defense News, 21 January 2022, https://www.defensenews.com/land/2022/01/21/thaad-in-first-operational-use-destroys-midrange-ballistic-missile-in-houthi-attack/. The Houthi attack also led to the first known use in a military operation of the terminal high altitude area defense (THAAD) missile defense system. See Ibid. The Houthis quickly followed up with a coercive message declaring, "we warn foreign companies, citizens and citizens residing in the UAE to stay away from sensitive sites and facilities in order to save their lives. We declare that the UAE will be an insecure country if the attacks on Yemen continue." See Seth J. Frantzman, "Iran Reveals Key Details of Yemen

194 Notes

Houthi Attack on UAE – Analysis," *The Jerusalem Post*, 19 January2022, https://www.jpost.com/middle-east/iran-news/article-693957.

97. Jon Gambrell, "Mysterious Air Base Being Built on Volcanic Island off Yemen," AP News, 25 May 2021, https://apnews.com/article/mysterious-air-base-volcanic-island-yemen-c8cb2018c07bb5b63e1a43ff706b007b; "UAE Building a 'Mysterious' Air Base on Mayun Island near Yemen," Middle East Monitor, 26 May 2021, https://www.middleeastmonitor.com/20210526-uae-building-a-mysterious-air-base-on-mayun-island-near-yemen/.

98. al-Ashwal, "Houthis Taking Battle to Saudis."

99. "Houthi Military Expert Lieutenant-General Abed Al-Thour: UAE Like a Cave Full of Bats; We Can Destroy It; UAE Soldiers Will Have No Place to Return to," Middle East Media Research Institute TV Monitor Project, clip no. 7524 as cited in Samaan, "Missiles, Drones, and the Houthis in Yemen," 59.

100. Mahmoud Mourad and Alexander Cornwell, "UAE Blocks Missile Strike as Israeli President Visits," Reuters, 31 January 2022, https://www.reuters.com/world/middle-east/yemens-houthis-say-disclose-details-new-military-operation-against-uae-tweet-2022-01-30/.

101. Michael Knights details other supporting techniques and technologies used by the Houthis to execute their sea denial strategy. He writes that the Houthis have developed "around 30 coast-watcher stations, spy dhows, drones, and the maritime radar of docked ships to create targeting solutions for attacks. See Knights, "Houthi War Machine," 20.

102. Williams and Shaikh, "Missile War in Yemen," 6.

103. Rania El Gamal, "Saudi Arabia Halts Oil Exports in Red Sea Lane after Houthi Attacks," Reuters, 25 July 2018, https://www.reuters.com/article/us-yemen-security/saudi-arabia-halts-oil-exports-in-red-sea-lane-after-houthi-attacks-idUSKBN1KF0XN.

104. "Yemen: Houthis Claim Attack on UAE Military Vessel," Al Jazeera, 2 Octobe 2016, https://www.aljazeera.com/news/2016/10/2/yemen-houthis-claim-attack-on-uae-military-vessel.

105. Ibid.

106. Sam LaGrone, "Officials: 3 US Warships Off Yemen Following Attack on UAE Ship," USNI News, 4 October 2016, https://news.usni.org/2016/10/04/official-3-u-s-warships-off-yemen-following-attack-uae-ship.

107. Ibid.

108. Williams and Shaikh, "Missile War in Yemen," 6.

109. Courtney Kube and Corky Siemaszko, "Pentagon Vows to Retaliate for Missile Attack on USS Mason Near Yemen," NBC News, 11 October 2016, https://www.nbcnews.com/news/world/pentagon-vows-retaliate-missile-attack-uss-mason-near-yemen-n664591.

110. Courtney Kube, "DoD: Second Missile Attack on USS Mason Near Yemen," CNBC, 12 October 2016, https://www.cnbc.com/2016/10/12/dod-second-missile-attack-on-uss-mason-near-yemen.html.

111. Courtney Kube and Phil Helsel, "US Launches Strikes in Yemen After Missiles Aimed at American Ships," NBC News, 12 October 2016, https://www.nbcnews.com/news/world/u-s-launches-strikes-yemen-after-missiles-aimed-american-ships-n665506.

112. Courtney Kube, "USS Mason Fired on Again Off Coast of Yemen: Officials," NBC News, 15 October 2016, https://www.nbcnews.com/news/world/uss-mason-fired-again-coast-yemen-officials-n666971.

113. Williams and Shaikh, "Missile War in Yemen," 6.

114. Aziz El Yaakoubi, "Yemen's Houthis Threaten to Block Red Sea Shipping Lane," Reuters, 9 January 2018, https://www.reuters.com/article/us-yemen-security/yemens-houthis-threaten-to-block-red-sea-shipping-lane-idUSKBN1EY2AP.

115. Williams and Shaikh, "Missile War in Yemen," 6.

116. El Gamal, "Saudi Arabia Halts Oil Exports."

117. Ibid. However, by 4 August 2018, the Saudis were able to resume oil shipments through Bab al-Mandeb straits after taking "necessary measures" to ensure the safety of oil shipments. See "Saudi Arabia Resumes Oil Shipments Through Red Sea Strait," AP News, 4 August 2018, https://apnews.com/article/ba03e90a24d942468c85eab608a3b990.

118. Mohamed Saied, "Egypt Fears for Red Sea Security as Yemen Cease-Fire Teeters," Al-Monitor, 16 June 2022, https://www.al-monitor.com/originals/2022/06/egypt-fears-red-sea-security-yemen-cease-fire-teeters.

119. Al Arabiya English, "Houthi Militia Hijacks UAE-Flagged Cargo Ship Carrying Medical Supplies: Report," Al Arabiya News, 3 January 2022, https://english.alarabiya.net/News/gulf/2022/01/03/Houthi-militia-hijacks-UAE-flagged-cargo-ship-carrying-medical-supplies-Report.

120. Lyons, "Saudi Arabia Oil Attack"; Turak, "How Saudi Arabia Failed to Protect Itself"; Turak, "Drone and Missile Debris."

121. Hubbard, Karasz, and Reed, "Two Major Saudi Oil Installations Hit."

122. Turak, "Drone and Missile Debris"; "Houthi Drone Attacks."

123. Turak, "Drone and Missile Debris."

124. Lyons, "Saudi Arabia Oil Attack."

125. Turak, "Houthi Drone Attacks." American leaders have argued that while the Houthis have taken credit for the strike, Iran launched it. American President Donald Trump wrote in a tweet, "[we] are locked and loaded depending on verification but are waiting to hear from the Kingdom [of Saudi Arabia] as to who they believe was the cause of this attack and under what terms we could proceed." Mike Pompeo, the American Secretary of State, alleged that there no forensic evidence to indicate the attack was launched from Yemen and argued that Iran had conducted "an unprecedented attack on the world's energy supply." Iran denied these allegations. See Lyons, "Saudi Arabia Oil Attack." An investigation by the United Nations Panel of Experts on Yemen has provided some credence to the American assertion that the Houthi may not have executed the operation. The report by the United Nations Panel of Experts notes that their investigation "finds that, despite claims to the contrary, the Houthi forces are unlikely to be responsible for the attack, as the estimated range of the weapon systems used does not allow for a launch from Houthi-controlled territory." See United Nations Security Council, "Final Report of the Panel of Experts on Yemen," 10 February 2020, 2.

126. Isabel Debre, "Yemen Rebels Launch Barrage of Strikes on Saudi Sites," AP News, 20 March 2022, https://apnews.com/article/business-iran-dubai-united-arab-emirates-middle-east-7b9c303fc9ca485f70ba7aee3bb36a58; "Houthis Launch Multiple Strikes on Saudi Sites," Al Jazeera, 20 March 2022, https://www.aljazeera.com/news/2022/3/20/houthis-launch-attacks-on-saudi-energy-desalination-facilities.

127. Debre, "Yemen Rebels Launch Barrage of Strikes." The Saudis may have had limited success in building a narrative that the fire at the Yanbu refinery was the result of high temperatures in the desert and not a Houthi attack. See Dan Tsubouchi, "Oil Markets Must Believe the Saudi Aramco Yanbu Refinery Fire Was Caused by Hot Weather and Not a Houthi Missile," SAF Group, 25 July 2017, https://safgroup.ca/oil-markets-must-beli

196 Notes

eve-the-saudi-aramco-yanbu-refinery-fire-was-caused-by-hot-weather-and-not-a-houthi-missile/.

128. David S. Cloud, "US Sends Patriot Missiles to Saudi Arabia, Fulfilling Urgent Request," *The Wall Street Journal*, 21 March 2022, https://www.wsj.com/articles/u-s-sends-patriot-missiles-to-saudi-arabia-filling-an-urgent-request-11647822871.

129. Hassan Ammar, Jerome Pugmire, and Jon Gambrell, "Yemen Rebels Strike Oil Depot in Saudi City Hosting F1 Race," ABC News, 25 March 2022, https://abcnews.go.com/International/wireStory/fire-saudi-city-ahead-f1-race-yemen-rebels-83671349; "Yemen's Houthis Announce Three-Day Ceasefire after Saudi Attacks." In addition to the Aramco oil facility in Jeddah, the Houthis also targeted Riyadh and an electrical substation near the Yemini border located in southwestern Saudi Arabia. See Ammar, Pugmire, and Gambrell, "Yemen Rebels Strike Oil Depot."

130. Ammar, Pugmire, and Gambrell, "Yemen Rebels Strike Oil Depot."

131. "Yemen's Houthis Announce Three-Day Ceasefire."

132. Mustafa Awad, "152 Feared Dead in Yemen Ballistic Missile Strike," Defense News, 14 December 2015, https://www.defensenews.com/home/2015/12/14/152-feared-dead-in-yemen-ballistic-missle-strike/.

133. Stephen Kalin and Sarah Dadouch, "Saudi Arabia Intercepts Missile Over Riyadh, Loud Explosions Heard," Business Insider, 11 April 2018, https://www.businessinsider.com/saudi-arabia-intercepts-missile-riyadh-2018-4.

134. Bethan McKernan, "Yemen: Death Toll Rises to 116 from Suspected Houthi Missile Attack," *The Guardian*, 21 January 2020, https://www.theguardian.com/world/2020/jan/21/yemen-death-toll-rises-houthi-missile-attack-government-forces.

135. Jeremy Binnie, "Houthis Claim Cruise Missile Attack on Saudi Arabia," Janes, 24 June 2020, https://www.janes.com/defence-news/news-detail/houthis-claim-cruise-missile-attack-on-saudi-arabia.

136. "Yemen's Houthis Fire Missiles, Drones Towards Saudi Arabia," Al Jazeera, 23 June 2020, https://www.aljazeera.com/news/2020/6/23/yemens-houthis-fire-missiles-drones-towards-saudi-arabia.

137. "Yemen's Houthis Say Saudi Oil Facility Hit in Overnight Attack," Al Jazeera, 13 July 2020, https://www.aljazeera.com/news/2020/7/13/yemens-houthis-say-saudi-oil-facility-hit-in-overnight-attack.

138. Ibid.

139. "Yemeni Houthis Say They Hit Saudi Oil Facility in Drone, Missile Attack," Reuters, 12 July 2020, https://www.reuters.com/article/us-saudi-security-yemen/yemeni-houthis-say-they-hit-saudi-oil-facility-in-drone-missile-attack-idUSKCN24D0U6.

140. Rubin, "Hezbollah and the Yemeni Missiles."

141. Cooper, "How Did the Houthis Manage?" Saudi forces claimed that their missile defenses intercepted the incoming missiles 40 miles away from the holy site. See Ibid.

142. Shuaib Almosawa and Anne Barnard, "Saudis Intercept Missile Fired from Yemen That Came Close to Riyadh," *The New York Times*, 4 November 2017. The Houthis were retaliating against an air strike conducted on the night of 31 October 2017, targeting a building in the center of a market located in Saada. According to publicly available reports, the strike led to the death of 25 civilians, including children. See Ibid.

143. Almosawa and Barnard, "Saudis Intercept Missile."

144. Saudi Arabia's foreign minister, Adel Jubair, declared that "we see this as an act of war. Iran cannot lob missiles at Saudi cities and towns and expect us not to take steps." See David

D. Kirkpatrick, "Saudi Arabia Charges Iran with 'Act of War,' Raising Threat of Military Clash," *The New York Times*, 6 November 2017, https://www.nytimes.com/2017/11/06/world/middleeast/yemen-saudi-iran-missile.html. Iran denied the accusation. Iranian foreign minister, Mohammad Javad Zarif countered that Saudi Arabia bombs "Yemen to smithereens, killing 1000's of innocents including babies, spreads cholera and famine, but of course blames, Iran." See Ibid. Nikki Haley, the US representation at the United Nations, has offered support to the Saudi claims. See John Ismay and Helen Cooper, "US Accuses Iran of UN Violation, but Evidence Falls Short," *The New York Times*, 14 December 2017, https://www-nytimes-com.ezproxy.lib.utexas.edu/2017/12/14/world/middleeast/nikki-haley-iran-weapons-yemen.html. Independent investigation by the United Nations Panel of Experts does strongly indicate Iranian assistance and help in the Houthi ballistic missile program. For instance, the report by the Panel of Experts notes that the internal features of the ballistic missiles used by the Houthis such as "the reversal of the position of the fuel and oxidizer tanks in the missile body" have only been observed "on the obsolete Scud-A and the Iranian Qiam-1 missiles." See footnote 110 in United Nations Security Council, "Final Report of the Panel of Experts on Yemen," 26 January 2018, 28.

145. Hubbard and Cumming-Bruce, "Rebels in Yemen."

146. Ibid.

147. "Houthis 'Fire 10 Ballistic Missiles' at Saudi Airport," Al Jazeera, 25 August 2019, https://www.aljazeera.com/news/2019/8/25/houthis-fire-10-ballistic-missiles-at-saudi-airport. The Saudi-led Coalition claimed that it had successfully intercepted six of these ballistic missiles.

148. Aziz El Yaakoubi, "Saudi Arabia Says It Intercepts Yemen Missiles Ahead of G20 Meeting," Reuters, 20 February 2020, https://www.reuters.com/article/us-saudi-yemen-missiles/saudi-arabia-says-it-intercepts-yemen-missiles-ahead-of-g20-meeting-idUSKBN20F01N. These missile strikes derailed non-official talks between the Saudis and the Houthis. Aziz El Yaakoubi writes that "factions in Yemen's Saudi-backed government had provoked the unrest to try to undermine the talks, fearful that a deal may weaken their own position in any wider negotiations." See Ibid.

149. "The Joint Forces Command of the Coalition to Restore Legitimacy in Yemen: Interception and Destruction of a Ballistic Missile Launched by the Terrorist, Iran-Backed Houthi Militia from (Sana'a) Toward the Kingdom," The official Saudi Press Agency, June 23, 2020, https://www.spa.gov.sa/2101064.

150. Ibid.

151. "Houthis Say Drone Attacks Target Several Saudi Cities," Al Jazeera, 20 November 2021, https://www.aljazeera.com/news/2021/11/20/yemens-houthis-say-they-attacked-saudi-cities-aramco-facilities; "Yemen's Houthis Say They Attacked Saudi Cities, Aramco Facilities," Reuters, 20 November 2021, https://www.reuters.com/world/middle-east/yemens-houthis-say-they-attacked-saudi-cities-aramco-facilities-2021-11-20/.

152. "Houthis Say Drone Attacks Target Several Saudi Cities."

153. United Nations Security Council, "Final Report of the Panel of Experts on Yemen," 26 January 2018, 25.

154. Bruce Riedel, "In Yemen, Iran Outsmarts Saudi Arabia Again," Brookings, 6 December 2017, https://www.brookings.edu/blog/markaz/2017/12/06/in-yemen-iran-outsmarts-saudi-arabia-again/.

155. Gordon, "Saudi Arabia Pleads for Missile-Defense Resupply." See also Hubbard, Karasz, and Reed, "Two Major Saudi Oil Installations Hit." In addition to the cost differential,

Saudi Arabian claims of successful intercepts have been challenged. For example, investigating claims of a successful Patriot missile defense intercept of a short-range ballistic missile on 4 November 2017, a United Nations Panel of Experts wrote that there was no clear evidence of fragmentation from an interceptor missile. Furthermore, an impact crater was observed at the target site—the King Khalid International Airport. These observations raise serious doubts on the argument that a successful intercept had occurred. See footnote 98 in United Nations Security Council, "Final Report of the Panel of Experts on Yemen," 26 January 2018, 26. For a more encouraging assessment of the performance of the Patriot missile defense systems in Yemen, see Barbara Opall-Rome, "Raytheon: Arab-Operated Patriots Intercepted over 100 Tactical Ballistic Missiles since 2015," Defense News, 14 November 2017, https://www.defensenews.com/digital-show-dailies/dubai-air-show/2017/11/14/raytheon-saudi-based-patriots-intercepted-over-100-tbms-since-2015/. For a skeptical assessment of the performance of the Patriot missile defense system in protecting Saudi Arabia critical military and civilian infrastructure, see Max Fisher et al., "Did American Missile Defense Fail in Saudi Arabia?," The New York Times, 4 December 2017, https://www-nytimes-com.ezproxy.lib.utexas.edu/interactive/2017/12/04/world/middleeast/saudi-missile-defense.html.

156. The Saudis, in December 2021, pleaded for urgent replenishment of their Patriot missile defense interceptors from the US, Europeans, and other Gulf allies. See Gordon, "Saudi Arabia Pleads for Missile-Defense Resupply"; Andrew England, Samer Al-Atrush, and James Politi, "Saudi Arabia Turns to Gulf States to Replenish Depleted Air Defences," Financial Times, 8 January 2022, https://www.ft.com/content/4d0fc8a0-ca28-436f-9e1d-dd1e6afb17a6. The United States ultimately provided these replenishments in March 2022, by approving the transfer of the interceptors from the stockpiles of other Persian Gulf countries. See Cloud, "US Sends Patriot Missiles to Saudi Arabia."

157. See Gordon, "Saudi Arabia Pleads for Missile-Defense Resupply."

158. See Conflict Armament Research, "Iranian Technology Transfers to Yemen: 'Kamikaze' Drones Used by Houthi Forces to Attack Coalition Missile Defence Systems" (London: Conflict Armament Research, March 2017), 2, https://www.conflictarm.com/perspectives/iranian-technology-transfers-to-yemen/. See also Aziz El Yaakoubi, Maher Chmaytelli, and Tuqa Khalid, "Yemen's Houthis Threaten to Attack United Arab Emirates Targets," Reuters, 18 September 2019, https://www.reuters.com/article/us-saudi-aramco-houthis-emirates/yemens-houthis-threaten-to-attack-united-arab-emirates-targets-idUSKBN1W3282.

159. Cooper, Gibbons-Neff, and Schmitt, "Army Special Forces Secretly Help Saudis." The presence of Green Beret commandos near the Yemeni border was perceived to be in contradiction to Pentagon's assertion that the United States was only providing limited aerial refueling, logistics, and general intelligence-sharing to the Coalition. For instance, in his 17 April 2018 testimony, Robert Karem, the Assistant Secretary of Defense for Policy, did not offer any clues to American involvement in missile-hunting missions. Instead, he testified that the "US military advisors are focused on helping Coalition forces implement best practices and procedures to reduce civilian casualties and collateral damage. Aerial refueling allows Coalition aircraft to spend more time in the air, thus giving our partners time to validate targets, practice tactical patience, and reduce the risk of civilian casualties." See "US Policy in Yemen," 18.

160. Cooper, Gibbons-Neff, and Schmitt, "Army Special Forces Secretly Help Saudis."

Notes **199**

161. Williams and Shaikh, "Missile War in Yemen," ix; United Nations Security Council, "Final Report of the Panel of Experts on Yemen," 26 January 2018, 3.

162. See Almosawa and Barnard, "Saudis Intercept Missile Fired from Yemen"; Kirkpatrick, "Saudi Arabia Charges Iran with 'Act of War.'"

163. Gordon, "Saudi Arabia Pleads for Missile-Defense Resupply."

164. See Sheline, "Cautious Optimism"; Riedel, "Yemen."

165. "Press Statement by the UN Special Envoy for Yemen Hans Grundberg on a Two-Month Truce," OSESGY: Office of the Special Envoy of the Secretary-General for Yemen, 1 April 2022, https://osesgy.unmissions.org/press-statement-un-special-envoy-for-yemen-hans-grundberg-two-month-truce.

166. Riedel, "Yemen."

167. Browning, "Houthi Missile Arsenal."

168. Ali al-Sakani, "Yemen Inaugurates New Presidential Council," Al Jazeera, 19 April 2022, https://www.aljazeera.com/news/2022/4/19/yemen-inaugurates-new-presidential-coun cil; Khalid Al-Karimi, "Two Months in, Yemen Presidential Council Still Faces Uphill Task," Al Jazeera, 3 June 2022, https://www.aljazeera.com/news/2022/6/3/yemens-new-leadershiperadicating-divisions-in-anti-houthi-force.

169. Salisbury and Weissenburger, "Surprising Success of the Truce in Yemen."

170. "Yemen: Warring Parties Lay down Weapons in First Nationwide Truce since 2016," *The Guardian*, 2 April 2022, https://www.theguardian.com/world/2022/apr/03/yemen-warr ing-parties-lay-down-weapons-in-first-nationwide-truce-since-2016.

171. Salisbury and Weissenburger, "Surprising Success of the Truce in Yemen"; Bruce Riedel, "Biden's Trip to Saudi Arabia Is a Chance to End the War in Yemen," Brookings, 28 June 2022, https://www.brookings.edu/blog/order-from-chaos/2022/06/28/bidens-trip-to-saudi-arabia-is-a-chance-to-end-the-war-in-yemen/.

172. Peter Baker, "Chinese-Brokered Deal Upends Mideast Diplomacy and Challenges US," *The New York Times*, 11 March 2023, https://www.nytimes.com/2023/03/11/us/politics/saudi-arabia-iran-china-biden.html.

173. Aziz El Yaakoubi and Mohammed Alghobari, "Houthis Leave Riyadh after Talks with Saudis, Some Progress Reported," Reuters, 19 September 2023, https://www.reuters.com/world/middle-east/houthi-negotiators-leave-riyadh-after-talks-with-saudi-officials-sour ces-2023-09-19/.

174. Michael Knights and Farzin Nadimi, "Yemen's 'Southern Hezbollah' Celebrates Coup Anniversary in Deadly Fashion," The Washington Institute, 28 September 2023, https://www.washingtoninstitute.org/policy-analysis/yemens-southern-hezbollah-celebrates-coup-anniversary-deadly-fashion.

175. Abdulrahman Al-Ansi, "Yemen Houthis Flex Military Muscle in Parade as Riyadh Seeks Ceasefire," Reuters, 21 September 2023, https://www.reuters.com/world/middle-east/yemen-houthis-flex-military-muscle-parade-riyadh-seeks-ceasefire-2023-09-21/.

176. Ibid.

Chapter 8

1. Matti Golan, *Shimon Peres: A Biography*, trans. Ina Friedman (New York: St. Martin's Press, 1982), 118.

200 Notes

2. Ibid. The conversation between President Kennedy and Israel's Deputy Defense Minister Shimon Peres occurred in the context of Egypt's attempt to acquire an indigenous ballistic missile capability. In his book, *David's Sling*, Shimon Peres describes a similar conversation two years later, during the Johnson administration. The American delegation in a Pentagon meeting argued that "Israel should thank heaven . . . that Nasser is investing considerable sums on something as foolish as primitive ground-to-ground missiles. This is a waste of resources on a grand scale, for this weapon is of little practical value . . . even if they possessed 900 missiles . . . the lethal weight they could pour into Israel would be no more than 200 to 300 tons, bursting at random targets scattered over a wide area. What kind of results were these, they asked, for so great a cost?" Shimon Peres responds by noting that "Egyptian missile development, however primitive, has been unexpected, and we might again be taken by surprise, perhaps too late, by their sophisticated improvement . . . they are likely to serve as a hallucinating political drug inducing illusions of invincibility in the minds of their owners and prompting them to irresponsible military adventures." See Shimon Peres, *David's Sling* (London: Willmer Brothers Limited, 1970), 99–105. For an excellent historical study on Egypt's ballistic missile program, see Owen L. Sirrs, *Nasser and the Missile Age in the Middle East* (New York: Routledge, 2006).

3. Tyler, "Iraq Targets Bigger Missile on Tehran."

4. Hiltermann, *Poisonous Affair*, 145.

5. Thomas L Friedman, "Confrontation in the Gulf; Baker-Aziz Talks on Gulf Fail; Fears of War Rise; Bush is Firm; Diplomatic Effort to Continue," *The New York Times*, 9 January 1991; Times Wire Service, "Tel Aviv Is 1st Target, Hussein Reportedly Says," *Los Angeles Times*, 25 December 1990.

6. Tyler, "Iraq Targets Bigger Missile on Tehran."

7. King and Kutta, *Impact*, 313.

8. Judah Ari Gross, "Gas Masks, Missiles and Irony: Defense Ministry Releases Photos of 1991 Gulf War," *The Times of Israel*, 6 January 2021, https://www.timesofisrael.com/gas-masks-missiles-and-irony-defense-ministry-releases-photos-of-1991-gulf-war/; Postol, "Lessons of the Gulf War Experience."

9. Schwarzkopf and Petre, *Autobiography*, 485–86; Powell and Persico, *My American Journey*, 511–12; Atkinson, *Crusade*, 175.

10. Atkinson, *Crusade*, 147.

11. Makovsky and White, "Lessons and Implications of the Israel-Hizballah War," 20.

12. Arkin, "Divine Victory for Whom?," 103.

13. Brun, "Chapter 13: The Second Lebanon War, 2006," 298; Makovsky and White, "Lessons and Implications of the Israel–Hizballah War," 51; Cordesman, Sullivan, and Sullivan, *Lessons of the 2006 Israeli–Hezbollah War*, 123.

14. While the Saudis claim a high rate of interception against Houthi missiles, independent sources have not validated the assertion. A United Nations Panel of Experts investigation, examining claims of a successful Patriot missile defense intercept of a short-range Houthi ballistic missile, noted, " from the evidence inspected, the Panel can only comment that the rocket motor assembly may have been intercepted. The propellant tank, which is designed to separate, had no traces of fragmentation from an interceptor missile warhead. There was also a crater at the point of impact (King Khalid International Airport)." See footnote 98 in United Nations Security Council, "Final Report of the Panel of Experts on Yemen," 26 January 2018, 26. For an encouraging assessment of the performance of the Patriot missile defense systems in Yemen, see Opall-Rome, "Raytheon." For a skeptical assessment of the

performance of Patriot missile defense system in protecting Saudi Arabia critical military and civilian infrastructure, see Fisher et al., "Did American Missile Defense Fail?"

15. The Houthis have used drones to strike and damage Patriot missile defenses and then launched missiles before the missile defense systems can be fixed. See Gordon, "Saudi Arabia Pleads for Missile-Defense Resupply." UAE forces have experience similar Houthi tactics. Using open-source GPS coordinates of the Patriot systems, the Houthis had programmed their Qasef-1 drone to attack UAE Patriot missile defense systems radars. Once the radars were disabled, the Houthis targeted other sites with missiles unhindered. See Conflict Armament Research, "Iranian Technology Transfers to Yemen," 2. See also El Yaakoubi, Chmaytelli, and Khalid, "Yemen's Houthis Threaten to Attack United Arab Emirates Targets."

16. Wagner et al., "Trump Orders New Iran Sanctions After Saudi Attack."

17. Sheline, "The Yemen War in Numbers," 8–9.

18. On 17 July 2006, in a speech to the Israeli Knesset, Prime Minister Olmert identified Israel's political objectives as (1) the return of the kidnapped soldiers, (2) a comprehensive ceasefire, (3) deployment of the Lebanese army in southern Lebanon, and (4) the expulsion of Hezbollah from southern Lebanon in accordance with UN resolution 1159. See "Prime Minister Olmert Speech to Knesset on Violence in Lebanon and Gaza Strip (July 2006)."

19. The Saudi defensive and offensive military countermeasures against the Houthi missiles are exceedingly costly. The Saudi-led Coalition forces may be spending approximately $5–6 billion monthly on various military countermeasures. See Riedel, "In Yemen."

20. Karp, *Ballistic Missile Proliferation*, 45.

21. Harry Howard, "France DID Lie to Britain about Exocet Missile 'Kill Switch,'" *Daily Mail*, 6 May 2022, https://www.dailymail.co.uk/news/article-10788731/France-DID-lie-Britain-Exocet-missile-kill-switch-Falklands-War.html.

22. Two books that could be a good starting point to study the coercive effect of the Argentine Exocet missile campaign are Admiral Sandy Woodward, *One Hundred Days: The Memoirs of the Falklands Battle Group Commander*, 8th ed. (Annapolis, MD: Naval Institute Press, 1997); and Ewen Southby-Tailyour, *Exocet Falklands: The Untold Story of Special Forces Operations* (South Yorkshire, UK: Pen & Sword Books, 2014).

23. Gregory Sanders et al., "Rising Demand and Proliferating Supply of Military UAS" (Washington, DC: Center for Strategic & International Studies [CSIS], May 2023), 20.

24. "Russia Pounds Ukraine's Two Biggest Cities in New Wave of Attacks | Reuters," accessed 16 February 2024, https://www.reuters.com/world/europe/russia-launches-drone-attack-kyiv-ukraine-says-2024-01-02/; Constant Meheut, "How a Russian Barrage Evaded Ukraine's Defenses to Wreak Deadly Chaos," *The New York Times*, 30 December 2023, https://www.nytimes.com/2023/12/30/world/europe/russia-ukraine-missiles-kyiv.html; Williams, "Putin's Missile War," 23.

25. Williams, "Putin's Missile War," 23; Meheut, "How a Russian Barrage Evaded Ukraine's Defenses."

26. Roman Olearchyk, Ben Hall, and Felicia Schwartz, "Military Briefing: Escalating Air War Depletes Ukraine's Weapons Stockpile," Financial Times, 13 December 2022, https://www.ft.com/content/fbd6dc6e-4a41-4bfa-977b-8c3ef4482dcc.

27. Gibbons-Neff, Barnes, and Yermak, "Russia"; Hall and Olearchyk, "Military Briefing."

28. Josef Federman and Issam Adwan, "Hamas Surprise Attack out of Gaza Stuns Israel and Leaves Hundreds Dead in Fighting, Retaliation," AP News, 7 October 2023, https://apnews.

202 Notes

com/article/israel-palestinians-gaza-hamas-rockets-airstrikes-tel-aviv-11fb98655c256 d54ecb5329284fc37d2.

29. Marianne Guenot, "Why Israel's Iron Dome Couldn't Stop Every Rocket Strike From Hamas," Business Insider, 11 October 2023, https://www.businessinsider.com/how-effect ive-is-israel-iron-dome-against-rockets-hamas-gaza-2023-10.

30. "Rocket & Mortar Attacks Against Israel by Date (2001 - Present)," Jewish Virtual Library: A Project of AICE, accessed 4 November 2023, https://www.jewishvirtuallibrary. org/palestinian-rocket-and-mortar-attacks-against-israel#2023. See also Becky Sullivan and Bill Chappell, "Medical Team, Supplies, Allowed into Gaza; Tel Aviv Hit by Rare Rocket Strike," NPR, 27 October 2023, https://www.npr.org/2023/10/27/1208947303/israel-gaza- palestinian-death-toll.

31. Michael Evans, "Arsenal Made in Gaza with Iranian Know-How," *The Times*, 11 October 2023.

32. Ido Efrati, "Direct Rocket Hits, Partial Protection: How a Hospital Operates in Israel's Most Bombarded City," *Haaretz*, 1 November 2023, https://www.haaretz.com/israel-news/2023- 11-01/ty-article/.premium/hospital-serving-israels-most-bombarded-city-operating-at- 30-percent-capacity/0000018b-8887-dd28-a7df-9897d1dd0000.

33. David K. Li, "Israel's 'Iron Dome' Has Never Been More Important as It Fends off Hamas Attacks," ABC News, 10 October 2023, https://www.nbcnews.com/news/world/israels- iron-dome-never-important-fends-hamas-attacks-rcna119782. Israelis have claimed the Iron Dome defense system is highly effective (90%). But other experts have cast doubt on its performance, suggesting that the intercept probability of the system may be 40% or less. See William J. Broad, "Weapons Experts Raise Doubts About Israel's Antimissile System," *The New York Times*, 21 March 2013, sec. World, https://www.nytimes.com/2013/03/21/world/ middleeast/israels-iron-dome-system-is-at-center-of-debate.html; David Talbot, "Israeli Rocket Defense System Is Failing at Crucial Task, Expert Analysts Say," MIT Technology Review, 10 July 2014, https://www.technologyreview.com/2014/07/10/172100/israeli-roc ket-defense-system-is-failing-at-crucial-task-expert-analysts-say/.

34. Jon Gambrell, "Yemen's Houthi Rebels Claim Attacks on Israel, Raising Risk of Widened Conflict," *Time*, 31 October 2023, https://time.com/6330338/yemen-houthi-rebels-attack- israel-iran/; Maha El Dahan, "Yemen's Houthis Enter Mideast Fray, Hardening Spillover Fears," Reuters, 31 October 2023, https://www.reuters.com/world/middle-east/yemens- houthis-enter-mideast-fray-hardening-spillover-fears-2023-10-31/??oref=newsletter_ dbrief.

35. For details see Nathan Strout, "Exclusive: How the Space Force Foiled an Iranian Missile Attack with a Critical Early Warning," C4ISRNET, 7 January 2021, https://www.c4isrnet. com/battlefield-tech/space/2021/01/07/exclusive-how-the-space-force-foiled-an-iran ian-missile-attack-with-a-critical-early-warning/; Nathan Strout, "Report: Iran Used Commercial Satellite Images to Monitor US Forces Before Attack," 1 March 2021, https:// www.armytimes.com/intel-geoint/2021/03/01/report-iran-used-commercial-satell ite-images-to-monitor-us-forces-before-attack/; "Denmark Had Six Hours' Warning of Iranian Attack on Iraqi Bases," Reuters, 10 January 2010, https://www.reuters.com/article/ uk-iraq-security-denmark/denmark-had-six-hours-warning-of-iranian-attack-on-iraqi- bases-tv-idUKKBN1Z91NY; David Martin, "Inside the Attack That Almost Sent the US to War with Iran," CBS News, 8 August 2021, https://www.cbsnews.com/news/iran-missle-str ike-al-asad-airbase-60-minutes-2021-08-08/; Joseph Trevithick, "Everything New We Just Learned About the 2020 Iranian Missile Attack on US Forces in Iraq," The Drive, 3 March

2021, https://www.thedrive.com/the-war-zone/39527/everything-new-we-just-learned-about-the-iranian-missile-attack-on-al-asad-air-base.

36. National Air and Space Intelligence Center (NASIC) and Defense Intelligence Ballistic Missile Analysis Committee (DIBMAC), "2020 Ballistic and Cruise Missile Threat," 4.

37. Ibid.

38. US Defense Intelligence Agency, "Iran Military Power: Ensuring Regime Survival and Securing Regional Dominance," 30. See pages 43–47, 67–69 for details on Iran's aerospace weapons arsenal. See also National Air and Space Intelligence Center (NASIC) and Defense Intelligence Ballistic Missile Analysis Committee (DIBMAC), "2020 Ballistic and Cruise Missile Threat"; National Research Council of the National Academies, *Making Sense of Ballistic Missile Defense: An Assessment of Concepts and Systems for US Boost-Phase Missile Defense in Comparison to Other Alternatives* (Washington DC: The National Academies Press, 2012).

39. US Defense Intelligence Agency, "Iran Military Power," 30.

40. Ibid.

41. Ibid., 58–63.

42. Ibid., 31.

43. Michael R. Gordon and David S. Cloud, "US Held Secret Meeting With Israeli, Arab Military Chiefs to Counter Iran Air Threat," *The Wall Street Journal*, 26 June 2022, https://www.wsj.com/articles/u-s-held-secret-meeting-with-israeli-arab-military-chiefs-to-counter-iran-air-threat-11656235802.

44. Defense Intelligence Agency, "North Korea Military Power: A Growing Regional and Global Threat" (Washington, DC: Defense Intelligence Agency, 2021), 30, https://www.dia.mil/Portals/110/Documents/News/NKMP.pdf.

45. See Jaganath Sankaran, "Missile Defenses and Strategic Stability in Asia: Evidence from Simulations," *Journal of East Asian Studies*, 27 May 2020, https://www-cambridge-org.ezproxy.lib.utexas.edu/core/journals/journal-of-east-asian-studies/article/missile-defenses-and-strategic-stability-in-asia-evidence-from-simulations/2FC19D4EEAD358DD7C5BEB50784DC0A6; National Air and Space Intelligence Center (NASIC) and Defense Intelligence Ballistic Missile Analysis Committee (DIBMAC), "2020 Ballistic and Cruise Missile Threat"; National Air and Space Intelligence Center (NASIC), *Ballistic and Cruise Missile Threat: 2017.*

46. Sankaran, "Missile Defenses and Strategic Stability in Asia: Evidence from Simulations," November 2020, 491.

47. Ibid.

48. Ibid.

49. Ibid.

50. US Department of Defense, *2019 Missile Defense Review*, v. See also Jaganath Sankaran, "Missile Wars in the Asia Pacific: The Threat of Chinese Regional Missiles and US-Allied Missile Defense Response," *Asian Security*, June 2020, https://doi.org/10.1080/14799855.2020.1769069; National Air and Space Intelligence Center (NASIC) and Defense Intelligence Ballistic Missile Analysis Committee (DIBMAC), "2020 Ballistic and Cruise Missile Threat."

51. Sankaran, "Missile Wars in the Asia Pacific: The Threat of Chinese Regional Missiles and US-Allied Missile Defense Response," 2021, 25.

52. Frank A. Rose, "Not in My Backyard: Land-Based Missiles, Democratic States, and Asia's Conventional Military Balance," Brookings, 10 September 2020, https://www.brookings.

edu/blog/order-from-chaos/2020/09/10/not-in-my-backyard-land-based-missiles-democratic-states-and-asias-conventional-military-balance/. As of May 2022, Frank Rose is the current Principal Deputy Administrator of the National Nuclear Security Administration and former Assistant Secretary of State for Arms Control, Verification, and Compliance from 2014–2017.

53. Andrew Roth, "US Confirms Withdrawal from Nuclear Arms Treaty with Russia," *The Guardian*, 23 October 2018, https://www.theguardian.com/world/2018/oct/23/bolton-inf-treaty-russia-putin-moscow-meeting.

54. Ibid.

55. Gruen, *Preemptive Defense*, 24–25.

56. Ibid., 24.

57. Ibid.

58. King and Kutta, *Impact*, 172.

59. Angell, "Guided Missiles Could Have Won," 309; Gruen, *Preemptive Defense*, 24–25.

60. Gordon and Trainor, *General's War*, 234.

61. Atkinson, *Crusade*, 143.

62. Ibid., 144.

63. The ongoing Yemeni War presents a similar lesson. The Saudis have repeatedly turned to the United States for operational assistance and material support to defend against the Houthi missile strikes. In 2015, a joint Saudi–US cell to share real-time surveillance and targeting information was established in Riyadh. See DeYoung, "Officials: Saudi-Led Action Relied on US Intelligence." In 2018, American Green Beret Army special forces were secretly deployed to aid the Saudi-led Coalition missile-hunting operations. A *New York Times* piece describing the deployment notes that "a team of about a dozen Green Berets arrived on Saudi Arabia's border with Yemen, in a continuing escalation of America's secret wars." The special forces were "helping locate and destroy caches of ballistic missiles" and target launch sites used by the Houthis to attack Riyadh and other Saudi Arabian cities. See Cooper, Gibbons-Neff, and Schmitt, "Army Special Forces Secretly Help Saudis."

64. In 2019, Mark Esper, then Secretary of Defense, days after the US withdrawal from the INF Treaty suggested that he favored the quick deployment of INF-range missiles to Asia. See Thomas Gibbons-Neff, "Pentagon Chief in Favor of Deploying US Missiles to Asia," *The New York Times*, 3 August 2019, https://www.nytimes.com/2019/08/03/world/asia/us-missiles-asia-esper.html; Jesse Johnson, "US Looks to Deploy New Missiles to Asia, Defense Chief Says amid Tensions with China," *The Japan Times*, 4 August 2019, https://www.japantimes.co.jp/news/2019/08/04/asia-pacific/u-s-looks-deploy-new-missiles-asia-defense-chief-says-amid-tensions-china/. For a good starting point to understand the various strategic facets involved in the decision to deploy INF-range missiles to Asia, see Jacob L. Heim, "Missiles for Asia? The Need for Operational Analysis of US Theater Ballistic Missiles in the Pacific" (Santa Monica, CA: RAND Corporation, 2016); Jeffrey W. Hornung, "Ground-Based Intermediate-Range Missiles in the Indo-Pacific: Assessing the Positions of US Allies" (Santa Monica, CA: RAND Corporation, 2022).

Index

For the benefit of digital users, indexed terms that span two pages (e.g., 52–53) may, on occasion, appear on only one of those pages.

9/11 attacks, 19

Abdul-Ghafur, Abdul-Ghani, 56–57
action tendencies. *See* international relations: action tendencies
aerospace weapons
  accuracy of, 30
  defense against, 20, 26, 27–28, 119–23
  effectiveness (general), 5, 7–8, 10, 20, 23–25, 28–30, 113–23, 130n.46
  history of, 2, 3–4, 7, 29
airpower (general), 20. *See also* Germany: air force; Great Britain: air force; Iran: air force; Iraq: air force; Israel: air force; North Korea: air force; Saudi Arabia: air force; United Arab Emirates: air force; United States: air force
airpower theory, 10, 21
Al Qaeda, 19
al-Ahmar, Ali Mohsen, 101–2
al-Atifi, Nasser Ahmed, 103, 112
al-Fakhri, Sabah, 53–54
al-Hamdani, Ra'ad Majid Rashid, 54, 55
al-Houthi, Hussein Badr al-Din, 100–1
  death of, 100–1
al Maliki, Turki, 99, 116
al-Mashali, Munir Mahmoud Ahmad, 105
al-Mashat, Mahdi, 104–5
al-Rashid, Maher Abed, 53–54
al-Sadr, Muhammad Baqir, 156n.26
al-Saeidy, Abd al-Wahhab, 57
al Sahyan, Abdullah, 108–9
al-Samad, Saleh, 107
al-Thour, Abed, 106
al-Yafai, Abu Yamamah. *See* al-Mashali, Munir Mahmoud Ahmad
al-Zubeidi, Abdul Ghani, 104, 106
Algiers Agreement, 49–50

Amal, 83
Angell, Joseph, 40
appraisal tendencies. *See* international relations: appraisal tendencies
Arab League, 69, 102
Arab Spring (2011), 101
Arab states (general), 64, 66–69, 73, 74, 75–76, 84, 91, 120, 167n.52, 172–73n.125, 173n.133, 173n.137, 174n.145
Arens, Moshe, 72–74, 75, 78, 175n.158
Armenia-Azerbaijan conflict, 13, 118
Armitage, Richard, 175n.156
Arnold, Henry "Hap," 41, 121–22, 150n.107
Atkinson, Rick, 115–16, 164n.10
Aziz, Tariq, 4, 52, 64–65, 69, 72, 114, 156n.26, 169n.84, 177n.192

Baker, James, 64, 66, 72, 74, 78, 167n.52, 173n.137, 177n.192
balance of power (military), 27–28, 48–49, 51–52, 69, 84, 86, 87–89, 93–95, 96, 102, 110, 113, 122–23
Balkans, 36
Basij volunteers, 53, 54, 56, 160nn.85–86, 163n.117, *See also* Iran: military
Bazargan, Mehdi, 60
Bazoft, Farzad Rabati, 65
Becker, Karl Emil, 34–35
Beidetz, Yossi, 90
Belgium, 34, 44–45
Bin Salman, Mohammed, 97
bin Sultan, Bandar, 74
biological weapons, 8, 24, 53, 71–72
  and anthrax, 24
Blanford, Nicholas, 183n.78
Blitzkrieg
  and shelters, 148n.78
  See also Germany; World War II: Battle of Britain

206 Index

bombing to provoke theory
definition of, 2–3, 8
Bosnia, 119
Brennan, John, 97
Bull, Gerald, 65–66
Bush, George H. W., 4–5, 63, 64–65, 66, 67,
69–70, 73–77, 78, 122, 172–73nn.125–
26, 175n.156. *See also* Gulf War (1991)

Cairo Agreement (1969), 82
Calcara, Antonio, 9–10
Central Intelligence Agency (CIA), 55, 71–
72, 97, 163n.128, 171n.100
Chechen War, 142n.84
chemical weapons
and Gulf War, 14, 16–17, 62–63, 66, 71–72,
74, 78–79, 165n.21, 170n.97, 171–
72n.108, 177–78nn.192–93
and international response, 58–59, 60–61,
72–73, 165n.23, 174n.145
and Iran-Iran War, 4, 5, 6, 8, 16–17, 24,
30, 47, 48, 52, 53–59, 60–61, 114,
154–55n.3, 158n.59, 158–59nn.66–
67, 159n.71, 160n.76, 162n.109,
162–63nn.113–14
and World War II, 32, 37, 142n.78,
142n.80, 147n.69
Cheney, Dick, 63, 74, 122
Cherwell, Lord Frederick Lindemann, 41
China
attacks on United States, 11, 12, 119–21
and Iran, 53
and missile arsenal, 12, 120–21, 122–23,
134n.83
and Saudi Arabia, 112
and Taiwan, 23, 143n.97
Churchill, Winston, 31–32, 35, 42–43, 151n.120
civilian targets, 21, 22
and Gulf War, 62–63, 72–74, 75, 78–79
and international rebuke, 91
and Iran-Iraq War, 47, 53, 56–58, 59,
159n.71, 161–62n.103
and Saudi Arabia, 99, 104, 108–10
and Second Lebanon War, 80, 81, 86–88,
89, 91, 92, 92t, 93, 94, 95
and United Arab Emirates, 104
and Yemen, 97–98, 107
Clinton, Bill, 142n.83
coercion, 142–43n.89
definition of, 20, 21, 23, 25–26, 130–
31n.48, 138n.31

and denial, 21
and punishment, 21, 139n.41

Defense Intelligence Ballistic Missile
Analysis Committee (DIBMAC),
11, 119–20
de la Billiere, Peter, 163–64n.2, 171–72n.108
democracy/democracies, 29–30, 115,
135n.10
deterrence, 138nn.31–32
dictators (general), 25
Dole, Bob, 66, 166n.42, 167n.44
Dornberger, Walter, 34–35, 39–40, 149n.95
Downing, Wayne, 3–4
drones, 9–10, 13, 30, 77, 88–89, 98–99, 102–
3, 107–8, 110, 118
accuracy of, 7

Eagleburger, Lawrence, 74, 76, 173n.135,
175n.161
Eagleton, William, 52
Early, Bryan Robert, 9–10
Eglin Air Base, FL, 121–22, 150n.107
Egypt, 67, 167n.50, 200n.2, *See also* Hosni
Mubarak
Eisenhower, Dwight D., 14, 41, 42–43, 44, 45,
121–22, 150n.107, 152–53n.153
Eisenkot, Gadi, 94–95
emotions. *See* international relations:
emotion of fear

Falklands War (1982), 117–18
fear, definition of, 18
measure of, 143n.95, *See also* international
relations: emotion of fear
First Lebanon War, 82–83
France, 21–22, 23, 33–34, 36, 40, 43,
51–52, 83, 89, 145n.25. *See also*
World War II: Operation Overlord
Francona, Rick, 157n.44, 162n.113
Freeman, Charles "Chas," 23

Galland, Adolf, 32
Gargash, Anwar, 105–6
Gaza War (2014), 2. *See also* Israel-
Hamas War
George, David Lloyd, 21–22
Germany
and air force, 32, 34, 35–37, 42, 146n.59,
147n.61
and Allied bombings, 139n.39, 139n.41

and army, 34–35, 45
and missile types, 14, 16, 31, 33, 34–35, 36–38, 39, 41, 42–43, 45–46, 114, 121–22, 150n.110, 150n.116
and navy, 34
and Weimar Republic, 34–35
and WWI bombing effectiveness, 16–18, 37
and WWII bombing effectiveness, 5, 14, 16, 26, 31–34, 37–39, 40, 41, 43, 45–46, 115, 121–22, 129n.32, 135n.90, 144nn.6–9, 149–50n.104, 151n.118, 151n.129, 153nn.161–62
Glaspie, April, 66, 69, 70, 167n.46
Glosson, Buster C., 76
Goering, Herman, 35–36
Golan, Yair, 94–95
Goldwasser, Ehud, 80, 83
Gordon, Michael, 63
Gormley, Dennis, 9–10
Great Britain
and air force, 22, 32–33, 35–37, 39–40, 42–43, 45, 46–33, 121–22, 146n.58, 151n.120, 152n.146
and Argentina, 117–18
and Germany, 5–6, 21–22, 31–32, 35–45, 121–22
and Iran, 49–50
and Iraq, 64, 65–66, 168–69n.69
and Israel, 64
and missile defense system, 22, 32, 38, 39–40, 42–43
and navy, 117–18
Grundberg, Hans, 111–12
guerilla fighting (general), 140–41n.64
Gulf Cooperation Council (GCC), 101
Gulf War (1991), 3–5, 16–17, 115–16, 119, 122, 165n.17
and casualties, 70–71, 164n.5, 164n.8, 169–70n.88, 177–78n.193
and military capabilities, 66–67, 68t, 69–70, 71–72, 176n.184
and pretext for, 62–69
and US operations, 69–79, 115–16

Hadi, Abdrabuh Mansour, 97, 101–2, 111–12, 189n.43
Haig, Douglas, 22
Hallil, Haj, 181n.48
Halutz, Dan, 90, 183n.87
Hamas, 1–2, 118–19, 122–23
and bombing effectiveness, 2, 118–19

Harel, Amos, 92
Harris, Arthur, 35
Hass, Richard, 74
Hezbollah, 5, 6, 122–23
and air defense, 96
and bombing effect on Israel, 6, 11, 16–17, 25–26, 80–82, 84–87, 89–92, 92t, 93–94, 95, 116, 117, 182n.59, 182n.62
and bunkers, 84, 86–87, 91, 180n.39
and Concept of Operations, 181nn.48–50
and fighting style, 84, 86–87, 93–94
formation of, 82–83, 179n.26
and Houthis, 100–1, 103, 104
and Iran, 82–83
and kidnappings, 80–81, 83, 180n.32
and military strength, 84, 86, 93
and missile types, 14–15, 80, 83, 84, 85, 85t, 87, 88–89, 95, 182n.56
mission of, 83, 86, 104–5
and Syria, 83, 95. *See also* Second Lebanon War
Hill, Roderic, 43
historiography, 8–10, 18, 28–29
Hitler, Adolf, 5–6, 16, 31–42, 45, 145–46n.37
and fear, 135n.9
and France, 145n.25
and missile program, 33–37, 40, 41–42, 43–46, 148n.71, 150n.116, 154nn.169–70, *See also* Germany
World War II
Horner, Charles "Chuck," 76, 77, 127n.14
Horowitz, Michael C., 9–10
Houthis, 5, 6
and allies, 103
and bombing effect on Saudi coalition, 6–7, 15, 16–17, 98–99, 102–4, 105–6, 107–12, 116, 117, 193n.90
and fighting style, 100–1, 102–3, 104–5, 106–7
and Hezbollah, 100–1, 103, 104–5
insurgency of, 100–2
and Israel, 118–19
marginalization of, 100
and missile costs, 110
and missile types, 102–3, 106–10, 112
and northern Yemen, 98
origins of, 100–1
and propaganda, 104, 107–10, 112
and raids, 98
and religious affiliation, 100
resistance of, 97–99, 102–3, 112

208 Index

Houthis (*cont.*)
  and United Arab Emirates, 102, 103–8, 110
  and United States, 189n.30
  and Yemeni military, 191n.66, 193–94n.96
Hussein, King (Jordan), 67, 168n.54,
    175n.156, *See also* Jordan
Hussein, Saddam, 4, 14, 16–17
  and Arab states, 64, 66–69, 175n.158
  and army, 160n.74
  and Great Britain, 64, 65–66
  and Iran, 47–48, 50, 53, 54–57, 59, 60, 64,
    161n.100, 163n.128
  and Israel, 62–66, 67, 71, 72–79, 114,
    166n.39, 166–67n.43, 175n.158
  and Kurds, 158–59n.67, 159n.72
  and Kuwait, 27, 52, 64, 66–69, 73, 78–79
  and oil, 68–69
  paranoia of, 64–66, 69
  and United States, 52, 60–61, 62–67, 70–79,
    122, 166–67nn.42–44, 167n.52, 177n.192
  See also chemical weapons; Gulf War;
    Iran-Iraq War

innovation (weapons strategies), 29
Intermediate-Range Nuclear Forces (INF)
    Treaty, 120–21
international relations
  and action tendencies, 19–20
  and appraisal tendencies, 18–20
  and emotion of fear, 10, 18–20, 113–15,
    136n.14, 136–37nn.17–23
Iran, 6, 119, 172n.120
  and air force, 158n.53
  and attacks on United States, 11–12, 120
  and Hamas, 118–19
  and Hezbollah, 82–83, 179n.26, 183n.78
  and Houthis, 100–1, 103, 109, 112,
    195n.125
  and Iranian Revolution (1979), 50, 52, 56, 67
  and Iranian Revolutionary Guards, 53, 54
  and Karnak Dam, 47–48
  and military, 47, 50–52, 53, 54, 55–56,
    58–60, 120
  and missile arsenal, 120
  and Quds Forces, 12
  and Saudi Arabia, 112, 196–97n.144
  and United States, 11–12, 49–50, 51–53,
    55, 59, 60, 119–20, 195n.125
  and Yemen, 191–92n.72
  See also chemical weapons: Iran-Iraq War;
    Iran-Iraq War

Iran Hostage Crisis, 52
Iran-Iraq Frontier Treaty, 49
Iran-Iraq War, 5, 6, 16–17, 47–58, 115
  aftermath of, 64–65, 66–69
  and Arab states, 67
  and border disputes, 49–50, 55
  and casualties, 47, 161n.101
  and civilians, 47, 53, 56–58, 59
  and religious disputes, 50
  and Shatt al-Arab waterway, 49, 60
  and War of the Cities, 58, 71,
    161nn.101–2
  and weapons capabilities, 51–53, 58–59
  See also chemical weapons: Iraq
Iranian Revolution (1979). *See* Iran: Iranian
    Revolution
Iraq, 4–5, 11
  and air force, 5, 49–50, 54, 65, 69–70, 78,
    128nn.26–28
  and bombing effect, 5, 6, 14, 16–17, 27
  and bombing effect on Iran, 47, 48–49, 55,
    56, 57, 58–61, 114
  and bombing effect on Israel, 62–63, 71–
    73, 74–79, 114
  debts of, 66–69
  economy of, 66–67, 69, 167n.50
  invasion of Kuwait, 64, 66–67, 69, 70, 73,
    78, 168–69n.69
  and military, 53–57, 66–67, 68t, 69–
    70, 71–72
  and military spending, 66–67
  and missile types, 65, 69–70, 71–72,
    170n.90, 170n.94
  and United States, 4–5, 16–17, 51–54, 55,
    59, 60–61, 62–79, 68t, 114, 157n.41,
    157n.44, 159–60n.73, 162n.113,
    165n.20, 169n.84
  See also chemical weapons: Iraq; Iran-Iraq
    War; Scud missiles
Iron Dome, 96, 118–19. *See also* Israel:
    missile defense
Irons, Roy, 42–43, 152–53n.153
Islam, 50
Ismay, Hastings, 41
Israel
  and air force, 75–76, 80–81, 84–86, 88–89,
    90–92, 95–96, 116, 183n.79, 183n.87,
    184n.100
  and casualties, 1–2, 17, 80, 86–88, 92,
    92t, 93–94
  and Hamas, 1–2, 118–19

Index **209**

and Hezbollah, 6, 11, 16–17, 25–26, 80–96, 116, 118–19, 183n.79, 183n.87, 184n.94, 184n.96, 184n.100
and Houthis, 118–19
and Iraq, 4–5, 17, 62–66, 67, 72–79, 165n.17, 165–66n.27, 166n.39, 175n.161
and Israeli Defense Forces (IDF), 80–81, 82–84, 86, 88–89, 90, 93, 94–95, 96, 118–19
and kidnapped nationals, 80–81, 83
and Kurds, 49–50, 156n.24
and missile defense, 1–2, 72, 74–76, 78, 81, 87–89, 90–91, 92, 95–96, 113, 118–19
and Palestine Liberation Organization (PLO), 82–83
and Zionism, 78–79, 88
Israel-Egyptian War, 142n.84
Israel-Hamas War (2023), 118–19. *See also* Gaza War (2014)
Issacharoff, Avi, 92
Ivri, David, 16–17, 72–73

Japan, 12, 120, 139n.39
and Doolittle raids, 22–23, 140n.56
and navy, 22–23
Jones, R. V., 16, 37, 41
Jordan, 52, 65, 67, 75–76, 165–66n.27, 175n.156, *See also* Hussein, King
Joubert de la Ferté, Philip, 46, 151n.129

Kamil, Hussein, 56, 155n.17
Karem, Robert, 98–99
Karp, Aaron, 9, 33
Kennedy, John F., 113
Khomeini, Ayatollah Ruhollah, 47, 50, 53, 56–57, 58–61, 114, 156n.26, 162n.109
Kirby, John, 125–26n.4
Knight, Michael, 191n.66, 194n.101
Kurds, 6, 48, 49–50, 54, 65, 156n.24, 158–59n.67, 159n.72
Kuwait, 27, 52, 54, 60
and border history, 168–69n.69
and Gulf War, 64, 66–69, 73, 78–79
and Iran-Iraq War, 67–69

Lakman, Sharaf, 103
Lebanon
and demographics, 82
history of, 82
and Israeli settlement, 82–83, 84, 86–87, 88, 89, 94

and military, 82, 83
and Southern Lebanon Army (SLA), 83
terrain of, 93–94
See also Second Lebanon War
Leigh-Mallory, Trafford, 121–22, 150n.107
LeMay, Curtis, 45–46
Levy, David, 72–74
Libya, 53, 58, 119
Livni, Tzipi, 90

Marshall, George, 44
Mehdi, Sadi, 72
military balance of power. *See* balance of power (military)
Minh, Ho Chi, 23
missiles
definition of, 126–27n.12
use of, 131n.50, *See also* aerospace weapons; biological weapons; chemical weapons; drones; nuclear weapons; weapons of mass destruction (WMD)
Missile Technology Control Regime (MTCR), 9
Mistry, Dinshaw, 9
Montgomery, Bernard Law, 43–44, 152n.148
Morrison, Herbert, 43
Mubarak, Hosni, 67, 168nn.53–54, *See also* Egypt
Murphy, Richard, 165n.17
Mussawi, Sayyed Abbas, 87

Nagorno-Karabakh War (2020), 118
Nasrallah, Hassan, 6–7, 81, 83, 84, 86, 87, 88, 90, 94–95, 104, 178n.8, 181–82n.53, 182n.56, 182n.62, 185n.118
National Air and Space Intelligence Center (NASIC), 11, 119–20
National Security Decision Directive (NSSD), 52
Nazis. *See* Germany; Adolf Hitler; World War II
Netanyahu, Benjamin, 2
Nolan, Janne, 7, 130n.46
non-state actors
strategy of, 5, 26, 28
Normandy invasion. *See* World War II: Operation Overlord
North Africa, 36
North Atlantic Treaty Organization (NATO), 119

210 Index

North Korea
  and air force, 12
  attacks on United States, 11, 12, 119–20
  and Iran, 53
  and missile arsenal, 11, 12, 120, 122–23
nuclear weapons, 8, 23–24, 30, 65–66, 113,
    122–23, 141n.70, 141n.72

oil, 6–7, 50, 60, 68–69, 98, 99, 107–8,
    197–98n.155
Olmert, Ehud, 81, 90, 92, 184n.94, 185n.115
Organization of Petroleum Exporting
    Countries (OPEC), 68–69

Pahlavi, Mohammad Reza Shah, 49–50,
    51–52, 53
Palestine Liberation Organization (PLO), 82
Pape, Robert, 21
Patton, George, 44, 152–53n.153
Pedersen, Geir, 80–81
Peres, Shimon, 113
Persian Gulf, 49–50, 52, 54, 60
Pétain, Philippe, 33–34
Poland, 34, 36
Pompeo, Mike, 195n.125
Powell, Colin, 63, 73, 122, 165n.12, 167n.52,
    171–72n.108
provocation, 2–3, 8, 10, 17, 19–20, 113
  and Al Qaeda, 19
  and Germany, 32–33
  and Hamas, 1–2, 118–9
  and Hezbollah, 80–81, 84
  and Houthis, 98–99
  and Iraq, 17, 47–48, 58–59, 71–74
  and Russia, 2

Qassem, Sheik Naim, 86, 181n.50,
    182n.59

Rabin, Yitzhak, 88, 174n.145
Rafsanjani, Akbar Hashemi, 50, 57, 59, 115
Reagan, Ronald, 52, 59
Red Sea, 107, 108
Regev, Eldad, 80, 83
resolve, 2–3, 8, 17, 23–24, 26, 27, 113–14, 117
  and China, 23
  and Hamas, 118–19
  and Hezbollah, 86–87, 93–94, 117
  and Houthis, 99–100, 105, 110–11
  and Iran, 48–49, 56, 57, 59, 60–61, 117
  and Israel, 81–82, 90, 93–94, 117, 118–19

and Saudi Arabia, 99–100, 110–11, 117
and Ukraine, 1, 118
and United Arab Emirates, 105
and United States, 26–27, 33, 70, 78, 116
and Vietnam, 23
and World War II, 26, 33
Riedel, Bruce, 111–12
rockets
  definition of, 126–27n.12
  See also aerospace weapons; biological
    weapons; chemical weapons; drones;
    nuclear weapons; weapons of mass
    destruction (WMD)
Rubin, Uzi, 2, 81, 183n.78
Rumsfeld, Donald, 52
Russia
  and bombing effectiveness, 1, 2
  and drones, 1
  and missile arsenal, 1, 12–13
  and missile types, 1
  See also Russia-Ukraine War; Soviet Union
Russia-Ukraine War (2022), 1, 2, 13, 30, 118, 121
  and bombing statistics, 1

Salam, Mohammed Abdul, 98
Saleh, Ali Abdallah, 100–2
Sandys, Duncan, 39, 42, 43
Saree, Yahya, 107–9
Saudi Arabia, 5, 6–7, 16–17, 52, 54, 74, 75–76
  and air force, 97–98, 99, 102–3, 110, 116
  and allies/coalition, 97, 102–3
  and Gulf War, 75–76, 174–75n.155
  and Houthi rebels, 97–112
  and internal political debates, 115
  and Iran, 112, 196–97n.144
  and Iran-Iraq War, 67
  and military strength, 97–98, 102, 110–11
  and missile defense, 102–3, 104, 110, 111,
    116, 198n.156, 200–1nn.14–15, 204n.63
  and United States, 102–3, 107, 110,
    204n.63
  and Yemen government, 97, 101–2,
    110–12
Schwarzkopf, Norman, 3–4, 62, 63, 69–70,
    72, 77, 115–16, 122, 127n.13, 164n.10,
    167n.52, 173n.136, 174–75n.155
Sciolino, Elaine, 59
Scowcroft, Brent, 66, 74, 167n.44, 168nn.53–
    54, 173n.133, 175n.161
Scud missiles, 3–5, 6, 16–17, 27, 56, 57–58
  accuracy of, 62, 71

defense against, 4–5, 62–63, 75, 76–77, 122, 164n.8, 176n.185
effectiveness of, 4–5, 57, 62–63, 71–72, 77–79, 176n.184, 176n.186, 177–78n.193
and Hezbollah, 95
and Iran, 161n.92, 161nn.99–100
against Israel, 4–5, 62–66, 70–79, 122, 173n.136
and Soviet-Afghan War, 117–18
See also chemical weapons
Second Lebanon War, 5, 6, 16–17, 114, 116
background of, 82–84, 87
casualties of, 80, 86–87, 91–92, 92*t*, 93–94
end of, 94–96
pretext for, 80–81, 83
rules of engagement, 80, 83, 87–89, 90, 94–95
Shah of Iran. *See* Pahlavi, Mohammad Reza Shah
Shalal, Moshe, 88–89
Shamir, Yitzhak, 4, 63, 72–76, 78–79, 172–73nn.125–26, 175n.156
Shatt al-Arab waterway, 49, 60
Shultz, George, 52
Soleimani, Qassem, 119
Somalia, 142n.83
South Korea, 12, 120
Soviet Union, 27, 35–36, 78, 117–18
and Iran-Iraq War, 51–52, 58, 71, 157–58nn.47–48, 161n.92, 161n.102
See also Russia; Russia-Ukraine War; Soviet-Afghan War
Soviet-Afghan War (1979–1989), 117–18
Spaatz, Carl, 41, 121–22
Speer, Albert, 154n.170
spies, 65, 171n.101, *See also* Central Intelligence Agency (CIA); United States: intelligence
Sputnik, 135n.10
Steinbruner, John, 19
Stewart, Findlater, 37–38
Suleimani, Qassim, 12
Sununu, John, 74
Syria, 11
and Hezbollah, 83, 89, 95, 179n.26
and Iran, 53

Taiwan, 23
technology changes, 29
terrorism, 19, 87–88

Trainor, Bernard, 63
Turkey, 107

Ukraine
and missile defense, 126n.5
survival of, 1
See also Russia-Ukraine War (2022)
United Arab Emirates (UAE), 6–7, 66, 97, 98–99, 102, 103–8, 110, 111
and air force, 105
and missile defense, 110
and naval forces, 106–7
United Nations, 47, 58–59, 71–73, 80–81, 94, 98, 102, 110, 111–12, 120, 189n.43, 191–92n.72, 197–98n.155
United States
and air force, 32–33, 35–36, 39–41, 42–43, 45–33, 62–63, 76–77, 121–22, 139n.39, 146n.58, 150n.107
and bombing missions, 22–23, 32–33, 40, 41, 76–77, 122–23
and defense of Israel, 62–64, 71–79, 83, 89, 95, 122, 175n.161
and defense of Kuwait, 27, 60, 63, 78
and defense of Taiwan, 23
and defense of Ukraine, 1
and defense of Yemen, 107, 195n.125
and drones, 12, 77
and intelligence, 70, 71, 119–20, 157n.43, 159–60n.73
and Iran, 49–50, 51–53, 55, 59, 60
and Iraq, 51–54, 55, 59, 60–61, 62–72, 115–16, 122–23, 157n.41, 157n.44, 159–60n.73, 162n.113, 165n.20, 175n.156
and military base bombings, 11, 12, 98–99, 156n.38, 164n.5
and military personnel, 12, 68*t*, 110
and missile defense (general), 13, 15, 119–23
and navy, 107
and North Korea, 120
and Saudi Arabia, 102–3, 107, 110, 204n.63
and terrorism, 19, 119–20, 127n.14
See also World War II: Allied defense
unmanned aerial vehicles (UAVs), 109–10
unmanned combat aerial vehicles (UCAVs), 30. *See also* drones
US Army Intelligence and Threat Analysis Center (USAITAC), 70
US Department of Agriculture, 157n.41, 165n.20

212 Index

US Department of Defense, 11, 107, 122
  reports of, 11
US Missile Defense Review (MDR), 12, 120–21
US Navy, 60

Vietnam, 23
von Braun, Wernher, 34–35

war costs, 17, 19, 45, 110, 153n.163
weapons. *See* aerospace weapons; biological
  weapons; chemical weapons; drones;
  nuclear weapons
weapons of mass destruction (WMD),
  23, 30, 71
Winograd Commission, 93
Wolfowitz, Paul, 76
World War I, 21–22, 72
  and bombing casualties, 21, 24
  and Versailles Treaty, 33–35
World War II, 2
  and Allied defense, 5–6, 16, 26, 31–33, 35–
    33, 115, 121–23
  and Battle of Britain, 5, 16, 36, 42–43,
    151n.129
  and Battle of Midway, 22–23
  and bombing casualties, 35, 37–38, 39–40,
    42–43, 75, 153n.161
  and Doolittle raids, 22–23, 140n.56,
    140n.60
  and Operation Crossbow, 5–6, 31–33, 33*t*,
    39, 40, 41, 42–43, 115, 121–22

and Operation Hydra, 39–40
and Operation Market Garden, 44
and Operation Overlord, 5–6, 14, 16, 31–
  32, 36, 38–39, 40–42, 44, 45–46, 121–22,
  149n.99
and Operation Pointblank, 41, 121–22
and Pearl Harbor attack, 22
and reconnaissance missions, 5–6,
  32, 39

Xiong Guangkai, 23

Yemen
  and food insecurity, 97–98, 187n.5
  and Giant's Brigade, 187–88n.15, 193n.90,
    193–94n.96
  and government, 100–2
  history of, 100
  and Houthi insurgency, 100–2
  and missile arsenal, 191n.68, 191–92n.72
  and Republican guards, 191n.67
  unification of, 100
  and United States, 107, 121
Yemeni War, 5, 6–7, 13, 16–17, 97–112;
  114, 121
  casualties of, 105
  and ceasefire negotiations, 111–12
  See also Houthis; Saudi Arabia

Zegart, Amy, 9–10
zeppelins, 21